THE JAPANESE ECONOMIC SYSTEM
AND ITS HISTORICAL ORIGINS

JAPAN BUSINESS AND ECONOMICS SERIES

This series provides a forum for books on the workings of Japan's economy, its business enterprises, its management practices, and its macroeconomic structure. Japan has achieved the status of a major economic world power and much can be learned from an understanding of how this has been accomplished and how it is being sustained.

The series aims to balance empirical and theoretical work. It also implicitly takes for granted that both the significant differences between Japan and other countries and the similarities between them are worth knowing about. The series will present a broad range of work on economics, politics, and systems of management, in analysing the performance of one of the major players in what may well be the largest economic region in the twenty-first century.

Series Board

The Japanese Economic System and Its Historical Origins

Edited by

TETSUJI OKAZAKI

and

MASAHIRO OKUNO-FUJIWARA

Translated by

SUSAN HERBERT

OXFORD
UNIVERSITY PRESS

This book has been printed digitally and produced in a standard specification
in order to ensure its continuing availability

OXFORD
UNIVERSITY PRESS

Great Clarendon Street, Oxford OX2 6DP

Oxford University Press is a department of the University of Oxford.
It furthers the University's objective of excellence in research, scholarship,
and education by publishing worldwide in

Oxford New York

Auckland Bangkok Buenos Aires Cape Town Chennai
Dar es Salaam Delhi Hong Kong Istanbul Karachi Kolkata
Kuala Lumpur Madrid Melbourne Mexico City Mumbai Nairobi
São Paulo Shanghai Singapore Taipei Tokyo Toronto

Oxford is a registered trade mark of Oxford University Press
in the UK and in certain other countries

Published in the United States
by Oxford University Press Inc., New York

English language edition © Oxford University Press 1999

This English edition has been translated from the original
Japanese language publication © 1993 by Tetsuji Okazaki
and Masahiro Okuno-Fujiwara

The moral rights of the author have been asserted
Database right Oxford University Press (maker)
Reprinted 2002

ISBN 0-19-828901-4

CONTENTS

PREFACE TO THE
ENGLISH EDITION

The Japanese economy and the customs and practices it encompasses have many distinctive features: Japanese-style relations between labour and management as exemplified in lifelong employment, seniority pay, and company unions; Japanese-style corporate governance that places more importance on employees than shareholders; a financial system centred on main banks; a method of supplying parts based mainly on subcontracting; the practice of 'administrative guidance' that intervenes in even the most detailed aspects of corporate management without any clear rules. If we call the sum of all these practices and institutions the present-day Japanese economic system and then compare the system with those of other countries (particularly the Anglo-Saxon and other Western countries), differences will be apparent, and these differences are attracting mounting interest both from within Japan and overseas.

The Japanese economy's special features have been analysed from many different stances. On the one hand there is the view, seen in theories that stress Japan's 'uniqueness', that cultural factors and individual circumstances have produced the present economic system. This view would suggest that the system symbolizes the pre-modern aspects of Japanese society and is therefore in need of urgent reform to become a more open and transparent system on the Western model. But there is also a well-established school of thought that maintains there is nothing unique about the Japanese system. It works rationally, and any criticism that it is closed or that it endorses social inequities either indicates a distorted perception of reality, or else is politically motivated. To determine which of these viewpoints is closer to the truth, or whether indeed there might not be a further explanation, a study of when and how the basic institutions that constitute the Japanese economy came into being will surely be useful.

However, regardless of whether one sees the Japanese system as a one-off or demonstrating universal truths, the use of Western economies as the standard against which to measure its rationality is in itself a one-sided approach based on the progressive view of history and the Anglo-Saxon viewpoint. We believe that what is now needed is a reasoned analysis of the economic system based on multiple approaches and including comparative institutional analysis, which makes a theoretical analysis of economic systems through a comparison of their individual features, such as incentive systems, and so on. For that purpose a historical perspective is vital so that we might clarify the mechanisms by which past or differing systems have come about. We can perhaps say that study of the 'new' economic history (cliometrics), which began some decades ago with the introduction of econometric analysis, is now being replaced by an even newer economic history and the study of the history of management. Elucidation of the process through which the present-day economic system came into being is thus also important from the standpoint of comparative institutional analysis.

Never before has there been a time of greater questioning the world over as to how to proceed with economic reform. Other countries decry the closed nature of the Japanese economy and its lack of transparency, and complaints are heard within Japan that society places greater priority on the interests of the corporate sector than on those of individuals. In the face of these criticisms a powerful body of opinion calls for reform of the Japanese system to create a society more transparent, more open, and more oriented to the needs of consumers. Meanwhile, opinions range widely as to how to proceed with reforms that will effectively promote market economies in the former socialist countries, and there is a strong belief that Japan's experience of turning wartime defeat into a startling economic recovery might be relevant here. Moreover, developing countries are very keen to study the possibility of switching to Japanese- or East Asian-model economic policy as a strategy for their own economic development. Nevertheless, the subject of economic reform, the 'dynamic economic issue of the future', remains beset with many obscurities and uncertainties. That being so, a study of the past—of how and when the present-day economic system came about—must surely be a useful first step in any consideration of system reform for the future.

This book is the product of two years' joint research into the origins of Japan's present-day economic system, in particular the financial and corporate systems, labour relations, and the relations between the government and the corporate sector. It was undertaken by scholars researching the fields of economics, economic history, and the history of management who all share an awareness of the issues outlined above.

What we attempt to show in this book is that many of the major constituent elements of the Japanese system were deliberately created during the war period that lasted through the 1930s to 1945, and that prior to this Japan had in effect a classical market economy based on the Anglo-Saxon model. Before the war it was common for employees to move from one enterprise to another, most industrial funding was secured through issues of stocks and bonds, and shareholders were granted high status in corporate governance. Frequent bankruptcies brought down businesses of all types, including banks, and the government introduced no economic planning or detailed regulations. Transformation of this classical market economy into what we now refer to as the Japanese-style economic system began during the war period. More precisely, to mobilize limited resources for the 'total war' effort, resources were allocated through plans such as the Materials Mobilization Plan drawn up by the Cabinet Planning Board and implemented by the corporate sector. The system specifically created to accomplish this was the prototype for the present-day economic system.

In the preface to the Japanese edition, we neglected to mention that the idea of examining the war period to determine the origins of the post-war economic system is not particularly new. Clearly, one of the earliest publications pioneering this approach was a paper by Hidetoshi Sakakibara and Yukio Noguchi entitled 'Ōkura-shō Nichigin Ōchō no Bunseki—Sōryokusen Keizai Taisei no Shuen' (Analysis of the Ministry of Finance/Bank of Japan Dynasty: The End of the Total War Economic System), published in the journal *Chūō Kōron* in August 1977. Takafusa Nakamura's book *Nihon Keizai* (The Japanese Economy, University of Tokyo Press, 1977) also made similar assertions. The most fundamental points of difference between these earlier publications and the present research is that for this study we had the advantage of being able to refer to earlier studies, and also, through new theoretical developments explained in detail in Chapter Nine, we have sought to investigate the mechanism by which economic systems evolve. We have pursued a more thorough understanding of phenomena that hitherto have received only superficial explanation in such terms as 'cultural practices', or the outcome of 'irreversible historical events'. From here derives the second point of difference, which is the emphasis this study places on the broader institutional framework such as the financial system, corporate governance, the employment system, the subcontracting system, relations between government and private-sector enterprise, and so on, as against the more narrowly defined, legally established institutions on which earlier publications focus. This has come about because it is only on the basis of these new theoretical advances in economics that we are able to understand the significance of the wartime economy in the appearance and development of this wider range of institutions and practices.

The following point needs to be appended: upon publication of the Japanese edition, this study was well received, mostly by those critical of Japan's present-day economic system; those holding affirmative views of the system were in many cases disapproving. But on both sides, views were based on a fundamental misrepresentation of this study's position as described above. Based on the theoretical framework set out in this book, our conclusion that the prototype of the present-day economic system was formed during the war period does not imply that the present-day system is identical to that of the war period. This is self-evident from the fact that whereas the wartime system was planned and controlled, the present-day system is fundamentally a market economy. The shift from the wartime planned, controlled system to a market economy was brought about, as explained in Chapter One, by the economic policy measures known as the Dodge Plan. But other factors, too, spurred big changes in the system: rampant inflation in the immediate post-war period, the various reforms instituted by the Occupation authorities, labour conflict, the introduction of new technology and organizational structures from overseas, massive shifts in the labour force, measures introduced from the 1960s onward to liberalize and deregulate various sectors of the economy, and so on. None the less, it is important to remember that despite these changes, the effects of the system-wide 'shock' that the wartime economy represented can still be recognized today. The present-day Japanese economic system, differing as it does from the Anglo-Saxon type of market economy, was based on various institutions and practices introduced during the war period, and has been shaped through the impact of many different events that occurred in the post-war period. In this sense the present-day system is seen as 'path-dependent'.

Finally, let us summarize the contents of this book. Chapter One (Tetsuji Okazaki, Masahiro Okuno-Fujiwara) first sets out the characteristic features of the present-day economic system seen from a historical and also an international perspective, and then provides an overview from the standpoint of comparative institutional analysis of the processes whereby various features were introduced during wartime and took root during the post-war recovery period. Chapter Two (Kazuo Ueda) links the features of the present-day Japanese financial system to the formation of a system to supply long-term funds through the mutually complementary behaviour of various types of financial institutions including government institutions, as well as to the important role played by discretionary control. It shows how the system's origins lie in various regulations introduced in the inter-war period and in the wartime controls. Chapter Three (Juro Teranishi) describes the process by which the main bank system, a major systemic characteristic of Japan's financial system, came about in relation to changes in corporate governance structure, tracing its origins to the voluntary joint financing of the wartime period. It stresses the role the main bank system played after the war in encouraging growth in corporate enterprises, aided by financial regulations. Chapter Four (Tetsuji Okazaki) explains the characteristics of the pre-war shareholder-dominated corporate governance structure, focusing on managements' monitoring and incentive mechanisms. It shows how the wartime economy forced concurrent changes on the various institutions sustaining corporate governance, and how Japan's present system of corporate governance took hold during the post-war economic recovery, supported by newly formed and mutually complementary institutions. Chapter Five (Konosuke Odaka) shows how some of the various elements making up what is known as Japanese-style labour relations can be traced back to the start of mass production during the 1920s, and how the present-day system was formed with the addition of further elements in the war years and during the post-war recovery and high-growth periods. Chapter Six (Seiichiro Yoneyama) identifies the exchange of information between government and the corporate sector through industrial associations as an institutional device that has boosted the effectiveness of Japan's post-war economic policies, and traces its origin to the control associations of the war period. Chapter Seven (Naohiko Jinno) defines Japan's tax and fiscal system as a centralized, deconcentrated system and explains how it took shape, tracing it back to the 'full mobilization' tax and fiscal system of the wartime era. Chapter Eight (Toshihiko Kawagoe) focuses on the food-control system and the association of agricultural co-operatives, Nōkyō, as the main institutional features of present-day agriculture in Japan. It explains the process by which the food-control system was introduced during the war, and the related process that has enabled agricultural co-operatives to grow to massive size. Chapter Nine (Masahiro Okuno-Fujiwara) uses comparative institutional analysis to give a theoretical explanation of the mutual complementarity of the various institutions and practices that make up the present-day economic system, and explains how this complementarity has brought about stability.

This book draws on the individual research work of each of the participants of this joint study, and was compiled in its final form after much lively discussion at a series of conference sessions held in spring and autumn 1992, and spring 1993. We are most grateful for all the useful criticism and valuable advice received from those attending the sessions, including Takafusa Nakamura (Ochanomizu Women's University), Masahiko Aoki (Stanford University), Kazumasa Iwata (Tokyo University), and Yoshio Higuchi (Keio University). This joint research was undertaken as part of a project by the Tokyo Economic Research Centre 'Kigyō, Keizai, Gyōsei Shisutemu no Hikaku Seido Ron-teki Kenkyū—Nichibei no Hikaku to Yūgō no tame no Kokusai Rūru no Waku-gumi o Motomete' (Comparative Institutional Analysis of Corporate, Economic, and Administrative Systems—US–Japan Comparison in Search of an Institutional Framework for International Coordination). It was carried out with financial assistance provided by the Japan Foundation for Global Partnership. We would like to express our deep appreciation to the Tokyo Economic Research Centre and the Japan Foundation for Global Partnership for their warm co-operation and generosity. We are also grateful to Hiromi Tojima for handling the complicated secretarial duties necessary to support the joint research work, and to Tsuneo Taguchi and Osamu Masuyama of Nihon Keizai Shimbun-sha publishing division for their patience and enthusiasm in bringing the Japanese edition to print. Finally we would like to thank our translator, Susan Herbert, and the Daido Life Foundation for financial support for the English translation.

Tetsuji Okazaki and Masahiro Okuno-Fujiwara

1

Japan's Present-Day Economic System and Its Historical Origins

Tetsuji Okazaki and Masahiro Okuno-Fujiwara

1. Introduction

A number of characteristic features serve to differentiate Japan's present-day socio-economic system from its counterparts in the West, particularly those of the Anglo-Saxon countries. One is the relationship between corporate owner-ship and its management: Japanese management is directed to benefit em-ployees rather than shareholders. Another feature is the long-term nature of relationships within firms, as demonstrated in the lifetime-employment system, pay based on seniority, enterprise-based labour unions, and so on. Long-term relations between different firms are also important, as seen in the main bank system, the subcontracting system, or in relations among affiliated firms in *keiretsu* groupings. For the provision of capital, indirect financing centred on bank lending predominates over the floating of shares and bonds on the open market. A further feature is the close-knit relationship between government and private-sector firms, seen in official control through administrative guidance or via industrial associations or similar business organizations.

Endowed with such features, the Japanese economic system has generated considerable interest, both within the country and, even more, overseas. First, it has been held to be the source of Japan's international competitive strength, and attempts have been made to unlock its 'secrets'. This line of thinking, however, has been undergoing some modification recently. In the West the Japanese system has come in for severe criticism on the grounds that it is closed and unfair, while within Japan there is strong discontent that present-day society is excessively business-oriented, and the interests of consumers and wage- and salary-earners do not receive sufficient attention. Both viewpoints have brought about calls for the reform of the current system into something more desirable.

A second reason for such interest springs from a sense that much can be learned from Japan's experience to help in the reform of other economic systems. With the collapse of the former socialist planned economies of the Soviet Union and East European countries, it may be that something of

Japan's experience in recovering from defeat in 1945 and the ensuing chaos to current economic prosperity could provide useful lessons for these countries in their switch to market economies. Many developing countries, too, have displayed great interest in Japan's post-war economic policies and methodology, as pointers to help direct their own economic development.

Whichever way we look at it, whether from the need to reform Japan's current economic system, or from the viewpoint of other countries using the Japanese experience to build systems for their own economic development, an examination of the historical circumstances out of which this system has grown will no doubt be extremely beneficial.

From the historical viewpoint, the most significant feature of Japan's economic system lies in the fact that many of its important components came into being during the 1930s and the first half of the 1940s, in the process of building up the heavy and chemical industries and adapting the economy for war. Prior to this Japan had an orthodox capitalist, market-oriented system which, though backward in some respects, differed little from those of the USA and European countries. It was common for workers to change jobs, moving from one firm to another, and wages fluctuated up and down. Banks proliferated to more than 2,000 in number, and many collapsed during periods of recession. Corporate investment capital and business funds were in large part raised through open markets in the form of shares and bonds, rather than through bank lending, and only small numbers of shares were held by financial institutions. This gave financial institutions little say over corporate activities. The *zaibatsu* groups set up organizational monitoring systems for their subsidiaries, and in many non-*zaibatsu* firms influential large shareholders held positions as directors (see Chapter Four). Furthermore, in many cases annual shareholders' meetings produced tangible results, and the wishes of shareholders were widely reflected in corporate management. Hostile buyouts were not at all rare.

This market-based economic system saw gradual change from the 1920s onwards, change that was greatly accelerated when the government embarked on building a wartime economic system during the 1930s. Already during the 1920s some large firms were taking steps to keep hold of their skilled workers, setting up labour–management consultative forums called 'factory committees'. During the war period, however, the government restricted the free movement of workers between companies, and firms of all types were forced to set up industrial patriotic societies (*sangyō hōkoku kai*) that had representatives from management and labour. The switch of wages to a system of 'livelihood pay' (*seikatsukyū*) and the spread of the bonus system both occurred during the war years. In the financial system, the official encouragement of bank mergers that followed the financial crisis of 1927 was intensified during the war period, and by the end of the war the policy of one regional bank for each prefecture had been accomplished. The Great Depression prompted the organization of a system of syndicated loans facilitated by the National

Finance Control Association (*Zenkoku Kin'yū Tōseikai*). This was based on experiments in joint lending known as 'financing leagues' (*yūshi renmei*) and revolved largely around the Industrial Bank of Japan. The syndicate loan system of the war period was the prototype of the main bank system. Meanwhile in the corporate world, plans for a 'New Economic System' called for restrictions on shareholders' rights, based on the principle of separation of ownership and control, and these demands were carried through into legislation in the 1943 Munitions Corporations Law.

Thus, Japan's present-day economic system is, historically speaking, relatively new. Much of it grew out of the system of control put in place by the Planning Board (*Kikakuin*) specifically to mobilize resources for the war effort during the Sino-Japanese and Pacific Wars. In the end, however, these wars cost more than three million lives and consumed over a quarter of Japan's national wealth. The system for total war was itself modelled on the German wartime economic system formulated under the Nazi dictatorship, and the socialist planned economy of the Soviet Union that was seeking by means of central planning and issuing directives to build up its heavy and chemical industries and gain military super-power status.

Certain circumstances of those times need to be mentioned as the ideological backdrop to these sweeping changes. The Depression that began after the First World War with the crisis of 1920, and persisted after the Great Kantō Earthquake of 1923 and the financial crisis towards the end of the decade, ultimately turned into the Shōwa Crisis that followed the 1930 lifting of the gold embargo. This period saw the collapse of international commodity prices such as that of raw silk, which cut farming incomes by more than half and brought rural communities to the brink of destitution. At the same time, manufacturing industry was hit by a contraction of world trade brought on by the Great Depression and deflationary policies that followed the lifting of the gold embargo. Unemployment became so serious that in 1929 only 30 per cent of new graduates from the prestigious Imperial universities could find jobs. Disillusionment with the market economy and widespread discontent with the capitalists of the *zaibatsu* found outlets in two directions, boosting the labour movement just then in ascendancy as a result of the Russian Revolution, and adding to nationalist fervour demanding relief for rural communities and the overthrow of the *zaibatsu*. During this period, the numbers participating in labour disputes rose from 8,000 in 1915 to more than 120,000 in 1931, and there were frequent military and right-wing terrorist attacks that led up to the two *coups d'état* attempts known as the 5.15 and 2.26 incidents. Thus the abandoning of the free-market system and transformation of the Japanese economy into a command economic system under bureaucratic control matched the needs of a time in which political and social instability were leading to war.

Needless to say, the wartime systems have not survived untouched in Japan's present-day economic and social systems. The introduction of democracy under the Occupation and the rapid change to a market economy prompted by the Dodge Plan forced changes to the 'direct control' and 'command economy' aspects of the system, and more recently, internationalization of the economy and trade friction with other countries are accelerating attempts to bring Japan closer to the more transparent socio-economic systems of the West. That said, it should not be forgotten that Japan's present-day economic system has evolved out of the system created during the war years—one in which bureaucratic officials implemented their economic plans by using individual firms and corporate groupings as executing agencies.

2. The present-day economic system: international and historical comparisons

Economic development in Japan since the Meiji Restoration in 1868 has not followed a straight and steady course. During the Meiji (1868–1912) and Taisho (1912–26) periods, economic development was based in terms of both production and exports on primary industries and light industries centred on textiles. The build-up of heavy industry began with the economic boom during the First World War, and after a pause during the subsequent Depression, continued to grow rapidly all the way through to the Second World War. At the beginning of the century, primary and secondary industry accounted for 39.4 per cent and 21.2 per cent respectively of net domestic product, but by 1940 the positions had been reversed, with primary industry's share falling to 18.8 per cent, while that of secondary industry rose to 47.4 per cent. Over the same period, the heavy and chemical industries gained in importance, rising from 16.2 per cent to 58.8 per cent of all manufacturing, while the textile industry fell from 36.3 per cent to 16.8 per cent. The industrial structure also indicates how changes that began in the 1920s accelerated during the war years. During the post-war period a succession of industrial sectors—shipbuilding, iron and steel, synthetic textiles, domestic appliances, cars, and semiconductors—have taken off in turn to become major export industries, and the relative weight of light industry has fallen below 20 per cent in terms of both production and exports. The fact that heavy industries only became serious export industries after the war suggests that the institutional and physical conditions that influenced the international competitiveness of these industries changed significantly during the war years (see Figures 1.1, 1.2).

So what exactly was the nature of these changes that took place during the war years? To find out, we can use data to examine differences between the pre-war period and the present day seen in a number of aspects that are regarded as having been significant in shaping the present-day economic system. The assertion of this book is that the foundations of the present-day system were

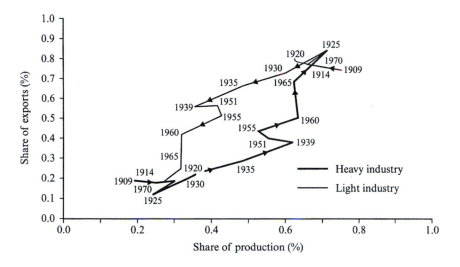

Figure 1.1. Production and exports in light and heavy industry

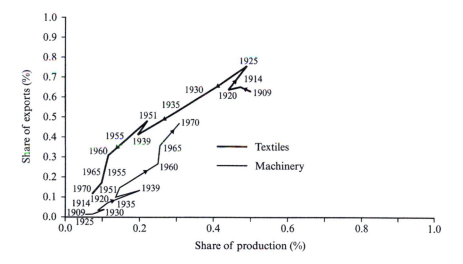

Figure 1.2. Production and exports of textiles and machinery

formed during the Sino-Japanese and Pacific Wars, and for readers to be able
to judge whether or not this is so, we have not only to re-trace the history of the
period, but to show that the preceding system was dismantled, while the new
system that replaced it had features that are still evident today.

2.1. Long-term fixed employment

The most significant characteristic of Japan's present-day economic system is that long-term fixed employment is seen as an ideal and strong incentives exist to promote it. All round the world, older employees tend to be paid more than their younger colleagues, but pay levels in Japan reflect more strongly than elsewhere an employee's number of years of continuous employment (Hashimoto and Rasian 1985; Mincer and Higuchi 1988). Forced retirement some time between the ages of 55 and 60, large lump-sum retirement payments, and twice-yearly bonuses based on a fixed proportion of salary, are all systems unique to Japan.[1] Furthermore, under the Japanese internal promotion system, in which junior staff within the organization are promoted in preference to bringing in staff from outside, it is only when the firm grows in size that the number of senior staff positions rises, and the potential for promotion increases. So if the firm does well, not only will employees benefit in terms of increases to their regular pay, bonuses, and retirement payments, but the number of senior staff positions and therefore the possibilities for promotion and the higher pay it brings will also increase, bringing further rewards to employees. This, then, creates a powerful incentive for employees to devote their working lives to a single firm. If, on the other hand, a worker leaves his job, he wipes out his years of service. Even though he may join another firm, his pay and retirement payment will be lower. All this means that employees have a strong incentive to stay over the long term with one employer. In practice, the number of organizations for which Japanese employees aged between 50 and

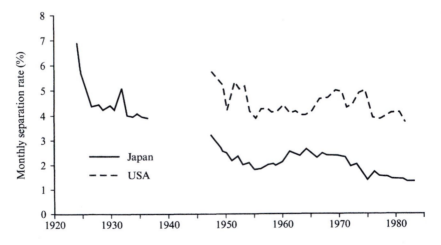

Figure 1.3. Comparison of separation rates
Source: Mincer and Higuchi (1988).

54 years had worked in their lifetime averaged 2.26 in 1977 (compared with 6.90 in the USA) (OECD *Employment Outlook*, September 1984; Aoki 1988), and the separation rate in the post-war period was only half that of the pre-war period and also only half the American post-war rate (Figure 1.3). Another factor behind long-term employment is the difference in the way firms adjust supply to meet fluctuations in demand. It is well known that Japanese firms deal with falls in demand first by running down stocks, second by reducing working hours, and third by cutting back employment of part-timers or temporary staff. Only after all these measures have been exhausted will employment of regular staff be adjusted (Shinozuka and Ishihara 1977; Hashimoto 1990; Akiyama *et al.* 1984). In other countries, and particularly the USA, the system of laying off workers means that fluctuations in demand are met with a larger degree of employment adjustment.

It is widely known that the 'Japanese' way of regulating employment was first adopted in the Depression of the 1920s in order not to lose skilled workers (Hyodo 1970; Nakamura 1980: 119). However, rates of employment adjustment continued as before to be relatively high until the first half of the 1930s. What finally brought about change was the worsening shortage of skilled workers during the war years (Table 1.1).

If we look at the internal promotion of senior executives, the number of internally promoted directors in 1900 was a mere 5.5 per cent of the total, and that percentage did not grow significantly until the war years (Table 1.2). Again, compared with pre-war figures, fluctuations in labour distribution have stabilized (Table 1.3) and this is thought to reflect greater employment stability, as well as the adoption of methods like the bonus system that enable staff to benefit directly from a rise in the company's fortunes.

Table 1.1. Rates of employment adjustment

	Rate of employment adjustment	Elasticity of substitution	Rate of technical advance
Japan (*a*) (Feb. 1927–June 1937)	0.52	0.50	—
Japan (*b*) (1960–1973)	0.35	0.92	—
Japan (*c*) (1974–1985)	0.17	0.81	—
United States (1960–1985)	0.66	0.22	3.8
West Germany (1960–1985)	0.46	0.57	3.8

Notes: All figures except for Japan (*a*) are taken from Kurosaka (1988). Figures for Japan (*a*) are calculated by correcting the monthly rate of employment adjustment to the annual figure:

$$\log (L/L_{-12}) = -0.199 - 0.00277T + 0.524 \log (X/L_{-12}) - 0.278 \log (W/P).$$
$$(-17.0) \quad (-11.5) \quad (18.4) \quad (-10.7)$$
$$R^2 = 0.897, \text{D.W.} = 0.935$$

Table 1.2. Breakdown of senior executives by background (%)

	1900	1928	1962
Proprietors	62.5	22.1	11.8
Appointed executives internally promoted from lifelong employees	5.5	22.9	47.8
Appointed executives transferred from outside firm	31.8	55.0	40.4

Source: Based on estimates in Aonuma (1965). Excludes executives whose backgrounds are unclear.

Table 1.3. Comparison of pre-war and post-war coefficients of variation (cotton-spinning industry)

Period	Wages	Profit	Value added	Rate of labour distribution
1896–1920	1.203	1.583	1.446	0.750
1921–1935	0.286	0.384	0.286	0.288
1961–1975	0.397	0.502	0.387	0.228
1976–1985	0.064	0.322	0.140	0.140

Sources: *Chōki Keizai Tōkei* (Long-Term Economic Statistics), 11; *Kōgyō Tōkei Hyō* (Tables of Manufacturing Statistics).

2.2. *Control of corporate management*

Another feature of present-day Japanese corporate organizations is the very little influence shareholders have in corporate management. This is typically demonstrated in two areas—the composition of the board of directors and crossholdings of shares (*kabushiki mochiai*). As stipulated in the Commercial Code, the role of the board of directors in joint-stock corporations was originally to oversee the running of the firm, ensuring that it reflected shareholders' intentions and interests, but boards in present-day Japan are made up almost exclusively of internally promoted directors, and very few firms, apart from foreign-capital firms, have one or more directors representing 'external' views, particularly those of shareholders. As for crossholdings of shares, about 30 per cent of the total shares of firms in the so-called *keiretsu* groupings centred on a bank are held within the *keiretsu*. Clearly, the proportion of shares in the hands of stable shareholders must be very high, for there have been virtually no hostile takeovers in Japan since the war.

The weakness of shareholders' power also reflects the means of capital provision. In present-day Japan, the primary flow in the circulation of funds takes the form of so-called indirect financing, which means that firms requiring capital are supplied with funds that capital suppliers have on deposit, as lending from financial institutions, largely banks (see Tables 1.4, 1.5). Under

Table 1.4. Composition of private-sector savings[a]

	Cash	Deposits	Insurance	Securities	Total	Private savings rate
1901–05	4.0	17.7	0.6	77.6	100	14.7
1906–10	7.5	36.2	1.7	54.6	100	10.3
1911–15	0.5	46.7	2.9	49.9	100	6.9
1916–20	8.9	53.0	1.7	36.4	100	19.8
1921–25	1.6	35.5	5.5	57.4	100	9.9
1926–30	−7.2	54.7	12.3	40.2	100	8.3
1931–35	7.7	48.1	17.9	26.4	100	8.7
1936–40	6.0	64.0	7.4	22.6	100	31.0
1941–44	12.7	72.6	7.4	7.3	100	54.8
1946–50	18.6	49.5	2.8	29.1	100	15.4
1951–55	3.8	68.0	5.6	22.6	100	16.5
1956–60	3.9	70.5	7.9	17.7	100	18.3
1961–65	3.2	74.1	6.0	16.8	100	22.4
1966–70	4.6	72.9	7.6	14.9	100	21.1

[a] Private savings as a percentage of nominal GNP (pre-1940 figures derived from Ohkawa's estimates; post-1940 figures derived from former SNA).

Sources: Chōki Keizai Tōkei (Long-Term Economic Statistics), 1, 5; *Kokumin Shotoku Hakusho* (National Incomes White Paper), 1962.

Table 1.5. Supply of industrial funds (%)

	Stocks	Bonds	Private financial institutions	Others	Total
1931–35	119.0	3.1	−25.8	3.8	100
1936–40	43.1	6.7	49.7	0.5	100
1941–45	16.7	6.4	74.9	2.0	100
1946–50	13.0	3.5	72.4	11.0	100
1951–55	14.1	3.8	71.9	10.2	100
1956–60	14.2	4.7	73.0	8.1	100
1961–65	16.2	4.4	73.0	6.5	100
1966–70	6.8	3.1	81.2	9.0	100

Source: Ministry of Finance (1978), *Shōwa Zaisei Shi*, 19.

this system of indirect financing, firms' managements are disciplined through monitoring by the lending institutions. Monitoring by banks prevents the sort of loose management that may damage capital suppliers' interests through bankruptcy or bad debts, and there has been little necessity for shareholders to use their power directly.

However, maintaining corporate management discipline through monitoring requires certain devices. Currently in Japan, discipline is maintained through financial institutions' high monitoring capability and also the efficient monitoring mechanism of the main bank system. As Dr Ueda points out in Chapter Two, the high monitoring capability of banks these days owes much to an improvement of the monitoring practices established pre-war mostly by the Industrial Bank of Japan (IBJ), and the spread of these techniques from IBJ to other banks (mainly government lending institutions) since the war. Under the main bank system, the main bank bears the burden of responsibility for credit analysis and so other institutions lending to the firm can save on their monitoring costs.[2] The main bank system thus spreads the risk attached to lending to individual firms over a number of institutions, while providing for suitable monitoring at low social cost.

In contrast to this practice, until about 1925 more than 50 per cent of capital provision was made through the stock market, and only from around 1936 did firms' capital requirements commonly take the form of borrowing from financial institutions. So before the war years the usual method of funding was direct financing—that is, raising capital by issuing shares and bonds on the open market—and although of course the *zaibatsu* holding companies held considerable quantities of shares, there was very little of the crossholding of shares, intended to limit the power of shareholders, that exists today. Because of this, supervision by shareholders was the main mechanism for scrutiny of day-to-day management, and in fact a high proportion of directors on company boards were proprietors (Table 1.2).

Unlike shareholders who can dispose of their shares at any time, indirect financing involves a long-term lending commitment, and the growth of the firm offers the lender potential for increasing deposits and more profitable investment opportunities in the future. The indirect financing system thus creates an incentive for lending institutions to make a commitment to the long-term growth and stability of the firms they lend to. In this sense, the present-day Japanese corporate financing system, which provides capital through loans from lending institutions and also imposes discipline on corporate management through monitoring by the lending institutions, is indirectly supporting the long-term employment and seniority systems, through which employees also make a long-term investment. The same sort of function is at work in relations between manufacturers and their subcontractors in the manufacturing *keiretsu* groups, as seen typically in the motor and electrical-appliance industries, and in relations between manufacturers and distributors in retailing *keiretsu* groups, or else between Japan's large corporations and their many subsidiaries. By acting as buffers to protect the parent company in times of recession, or by accepting temporary transfers of staff, subsidiaries and sub-contractors help to support the long-term employment system.[3] The subcontracting system, discussed in the next section, grew out of a system introduced to increase production and upgrade quality standards among parts manufacturers, whose development had been retarded under the wartime production system.

2.3. *Relations between government and business*

The last component making up the present-day Japanese economic system is the relationship between business and government. The long-term nature of relations between employers and employees, and between individual firms, means that, should these relations once break down, business collapse and mass unemployment could result, and the systemic risk could cause chronic problems. Through the process of post-war economic growth the Japanese government has sought to control private-sector economic activity in a variety of ways to minimize this danger. Each industry is supervised independently from above by a single administrative authority. These authorities use administrative guidance and other discretionary measures to achieve 'development' and establish 'order' in the industry. A typical model for the active control of 'development' in manufacturing industry (or the whole Japanese economy, for that matter) is the Ministry of International Trade and Industry's 'industrial policy',[4] while 'order' is maintained through the Ministry of Finance's so-called 'convoy' policy directed towards financial institutions.

Industrial policy consists of a three-stage process. First comes the 'discovery' of an industry for development, using forecasts of future trends in technology or demand. For the purposes of forecasting, various forums are used to gather information and encourage its exchange, such as government councils, unofficial research groups and informal networks. At the second stage, industries selected for development and sectors earmarked for growth have to be nurtured and given support. Various means are used for this including controls such as licences and permits, financial means such as subsidies, tax incentives, and low-interest loans, and indirect means such as information exchange through councils, extending to the role played by industrial associations to provide information and balance interests within the business sectors concerned, and the use of long-term plans to make necessary adjustments within the affected industries and sectors. The third stage requires co-ordination of the allocation of funds and other resources between industries through inducive means. The allocation of the necessary facilities, and the selection and co-ordination of firms is carried out through discretionary administrative guidance against a backdrop of regulatory and financial measures.

The result of this is that all the firms in the sector have access to the same information on new business opportunities, and have a strong incentive to get ahead of others and quickly establish a foothold in the new business. This leads to excess competition, circumstances where investment and facilities are expanded beyond the individual firm's means, and to business plans that target market share rather than profits. If the business were to fail and mass lay-offs became likely, the authorities responsible for promoting the policy would have to shoulder some of the blame, and the government would be obliged to provide assistance. In reality, the government has held these systemic risks in check with a variety of means, including recession cartels and legislation such as the Emergency Measures to Stabilize Selected Depressed Industries Act (*Tokutei Fukyō Sangyō Antei Rinji Sochi Hō*), enacted in May 1978, and the Special Measures to Upgrade Selected Industrial Sectors Act (*Tokutei Sangyō Kōzō Kaizen Rinji Sochi Hō*), enacted in May 1983. But as private-sector firms are conscious of the existence of this government safety net, excess competition has simply continued to increase.

It is precisely this 'managed competition' and 'planned allocation of resources' on the part of the government that can be traced back to the wartime planned, controlled economic system. The only points of difference between the wartime system and post-war industrial policy are that the objectives are now economic independence and growth rather than mobilization for war, and post-war objectives are achieved not through a command system of controls, but through a decentralized and less direct system using softer and more diversified policy measures, that has resulted in the appearance of excess competition.

It is helpful to deal with the 'convoy' policy in two parts: the administration of the financial industry as a whole, and the handling of individual financial institutions facing bankruptcy. The collapse of banks or other financial institutions can prompt a chain of other bankruptcies, causing great financial uncertainty. Because of the long-term, inflexible nature of employment and business, financial instability could lead to such high levels of unemployment and loss of business that the whole economy would run into crisis. On the pretext of avoiding these systemic risks, the Ministry of Finance has come up with a range of regulations to limit competition throughout the financial industry, covering eligibility, areas of business, deposit rates, opening new branches, etc. Furthermore, in banking business for example, even lending interest rates and account charges are controlled through the 'self-regulation' imposed by the National Federation of Bank Associations, and excessive profits have been secured by what in effect is a cartel. The Ministry of Finance and the Bank of Japan use discretionary measures, however, to rescue banks in financial difficulties. The circumstances facing individual banks found through inspections or audits to be in difficulties are concealed from the public, but the banks are forced into mergers or tie-ups with other secure institutions. In some cases, government intervention and support has prevented bankruptcies and financial instability.

This system functions because of the exclusive relations that exist between the Ministry of Finance/Bank of Japan and the commercial financial institutions. With the authority to regulate the industry and the ability to rescue institutions in difficulties, the Ministry of Finance fulfils its 'responsibility to supervise' by controlling competition through administrative guidance. By complying with government guidance, the financial institutions have secured assistance at times of crisis and made excessive profits. The other leading players in implementing the 'convoy' policy are business organizations such as the National Federation of Banking Associations. While co-operating in the implementation of government policy by encouraging self-regulation among member institutions and providing industry information to government, these organizations are also of benefit to the government by offering positions to re-tiring bureaucrats from supervising ministries in a system known as *amakudari*, or 'descent from heaven'.

As a result of this 'convoy' method of administration there has not been a single bankruptcy in the post-war period. Besides maintaining 'order' in this sense, it has covered the systemic risks created by financial instability. However, pre-war government–business relations were quite different in nature from those that exist now. Before the war, bankruptcies were common: for example, in the eighteen years between 1902 and 1919 there were on average 24.6 bank collapses per year, in each of the thirteen years between 1920 and 1932 there were 43.5, and in the thirteen years from 1933 to 1945 there were 7.8 (Teranishi 1982: 299, Table 5.4). The role of financial business organizations was also greatly modified through the formation of the Finance Control Association in the war years. This is evident from the fact that the proportion of retiring Ministry of Finance bureaucrats (head-office, overseas-office, or regional-office chiefs) who took up private-sector posts (including posts in business organizations) was three times as great in the period 1956–70 as in the period 1912–35 (Table 1.6).[5]

So how did the present-day economic system come about, so different as it is from its pre-war predecessor? We would like to devote the rest of this chapter to an outline of the relevant processes.

Table 1.6. Post-retirement employment of Ministry of Finance officials

	Government-related institutions	Private sector	None
Pre-war (1912–35)	31 (49.2%)	7 (11.1%)	25 (39.7%)
Post-war (1956–70)	115 (45.5%)	89 (35.2%)	49 (19.4%)

Source: Ministry of Finance (1973), *Hyakunen Shi Henshū Shitsu.*

3. The wartime planned economic system

Despite undergoing a certain degree of gradual change, the Japanese economic system remained close to a classical market economy in the pre-war period. But over the course of the eight years from the start of the Sino-Japanese War in July 1937 until the end of the Pacific War in August 1945, it was completely transformed. Demands for the mobilization of economic resources for the war effort were met by switching to a planned economic system, but attempts to run a planned economy imposed on a range of existing institutions generated considerable friction. It was through the process of dealing with this friction that the various systems within the economy came to be redesigned.

3.1. Outline of the planned economic system

Let us first examine the scale of the war mobilization from statistical data. Between 1937 and 1944 GNP in real terms remained almost constant. Directing the maximum possible level of resources to munitions industries from this fixed output was the primary concern for the government authorities running the wartime economy. Looking at a breakdown of real GNP in terms of expenditure, we find that personal consumption declined about 40 per cent over the eight-year period, while government current expenditure increased 70 per cent and fixed capital formation increased 40 per cent. The enormous squeeze on personal consumption diverted resources into military expenditure and investment in munitions-industry facilities. In terms of the investment/savings balance, there was enormous investment in the government sector as well as in the corporate sector, particularly the munitions industries, and the demand was met through the surplus savings of private individuals. During this period international trade declined drastically. The pre-war economy was heavily dependent on trade, even by contemporary standards, with exports and imports in 1937 accounting for 13.6 per cent and 16.1 per cent of GNP respectively. But by the end of the war these figures had fallen to a level of around 2–3 per cent, due largely to a blockade imposed by the Allies, and the economy had been totally transformed to a state of near-self-sufficiency (Table 1.7).

Major changes in expenditure and the degree of dependence on trade went hand in hand with changes to the industrial structure. Production indices show a clear separation between expanding and shrinking industries (Table 1.8). The largest growth industry during the war period was machinery, which included the bulk of military production of aircraft, ships, and so on, and by 1944 had recorded a 350 per cent increase in production over its 1936 level. This was followed by the iron and steel, and non-ferrous metal industries, which supplied raw materials for machinery production. On the other hand,

Table 1.7. Major macroeconomic indicators

	GNP (¥m.)	Personal consumption (¥m.)	Government current expenditure (¥m.)	Fixed capital formation (¥m.)	Ratio of exports (%)	Ratio of imports (%)
1936	17,157	11,003	2,618	3,405	15.1	15.5
1937	21,220	11,540	4,247	4,572	13.6	16.1
1938	21,935	11,382	5,491	4,745	10.0	9.9
1939	22,117	10,839	4,688	6,007	10.8	8.8
1940	20,796	9,723	4,896	5,967	9.3	8.8
1941	21,130	9,410	6,134	6,145	5.9	6.5
1942	21,405	8,956	6,460	6,557	3.3	3.2
1943	21,351	8,469	7,445	5,857	2.5	3.0
1944	20,634	7,006	7,301	6,462	1.7	2.6
1946	11,594	6,826	1,123	4,077	0.5	0.9
1947	12,573	7,410	828	4,845	1.0	2.0
1948	14,211	8,391	1,360	4,987	2.0	2.3
1949	14,524	9,297	1,619	4,041	5.0	8.4
1950	16,115	10,077	1,838	3,893	7.6	8.8

Notes: All data except ratios are real figures (1934–6 prices). Ratio of exports (imports) = nominal value of exports (imports)/nominal GNP.

Source: Management and Co-ordination Agency Statistics Bureau (1987), *Nihon Chōki Tōkei Yōran* (General Review of Long-Term Statistics for Japan), 4.

production levels in consumer-goods industries, particularly textiles and food-stuffs, responded to the fall in consumption and quickly began to decline. The textile industry had been an important export industry, and the collapse of international trade prompted a particularly large drop in production. Activity in the commercial and service sectors, typical consumption-related sectors, also declined. However, wartime was the period of rapid industrialization in the heavy and chemical industries.

Changes in expenditure and production brought about changes in the allocation of the various factors of production. The number of personnel mobilized to serve with the army and navy rose from about 1 million in 1937 to about 5 million, or 15 per cent of the male population, in 1944 (Table 1.9). As a result, the number of personnel in other forms of employment during this period declined, the contraction being particularly great in the commercial and light-industry sectors. Heavy industry, meanwhile, absorbed large numbers of new workers. There was thus a massive re-allocation of labour resources from the commercial and light-industry sectors to the military and munitions-related industries.

Table 1.8. Production indices (1936 = 100)

	1937	1938	1939	1940	1941	1942	1943	1944	1945
Mining and manufacturing	117	122	135	141	146	141	143	146	63
Mining	109	116	121	130	131	128	129	117	62
Manufacturing	102	102	94	88	77	72	72	71	65
Iron and steel	115	133	145	148	153	160	180	168	60
Non-ferrous metals	118	124	140	138	130	148	180	200	74
Machinery	136	155	191	227	264	273	300	355	145
Chemicals	114	131	140	138	138	114	100	90	38
Textiles	114	94	94	85	69	54	36	19	7
Foodstuffs	109	110	113	100	88	79	68	55	36
Agriculture	106	102	111	102	88	97	92	74	57
Commerce and services	104	104	100	96	99	89	75	61	n.a.

Note: For the commerce and services sector, net production of individual industries was converted into real terms using the GNP deflator.

Source: Management and Co-ordination Agency Statistics Bureau (1987), *Nihon Chōki Tōkei Yōran* (General Review of Long-Term Statistics for Japan), 4.

Table 1.9. Variations in employment ('000 people)

	1937	1940	1944
Total	33,234	34,679	36,734
Total for industrial sector	32,156	32,996	31,695
Primary industry	14,779	14,401	14,028
Secondary industry	7,437	8,604	10,105
Mining	412	598	787
Manufacturing	5,905	6,873	8,089
Heavy industries	2,102	3,194	5,735
Light industries	3,802	3,678	2,354
Tertiary industry	9,940	9,991	7,563
Commerce	3,882	3,845	1,556
Army and navy	1,078	1,683	5,039

Sources: Nakamura (1989), Hara (1977).

The mobilization of resources to munitions began at the end of 1936, pre-dating the Sino-Japanese War. After the assassination of Korekiyo Takahashi, the Finance Minister who had tried to hold the military in check, Eiichi Baba was appointed Finance Minister in the Hirota cabinet. He complied with the demands of the military and drew up a budget for FY1937 that incorporated a massive increase in military expenditure. There was a marked trend towards military expansion world-wide, and with the international market for munitions and raw materials getting ever tighter, the announcement of a massive budget unleashed enormous speculative demand, and from the end of 1936 prices of goods rose swiftly and a large current account deficit was created (Hara 1977). In 1937 inflation was running at 21 per cent and the current account deficit reached 2.5 per cent of GNP. Under inflationary conditions real wages declined, and between 1936 and 1937 the number of labour disputes increased fourfold. All this forced the government to acknowledge the enormous difficulties of military mobilization within a market economy. Concentrating purchasing power in the hands of the government through increased taxes and the effects of inflation and mobilizing resources to munitions by market means may have been considered as a theoretical option. However, it became clear that the distortion of incomes caused by inflation would destroy the social stability that was vital during wartime. Taxpayers were also strongly opposed to tax increases.

To resolve the issue, the government on the one hand implemented virtual price controls on commodities subject to rapid price increases (Okazaki 1987), and to deal with the current account deficit, revised the 1933 Foreign Exchange Control Law and implemented from January 1937 what amounted to trade controls, including regulations on import exchange transactions (Hara 1977). This was the start of trade controls through the regulation of foreign exchange, which were to continue until the trade liberalization of the 1960s. Next, the Hayashi cabinet that took office in February 1937 approved the implementation of a large-scale long-term expansion plan for munitions industries that the army had had under consideration. A new Planning Board (*Kikakuin*) was established as the official agency responsible for the formulation of such plans (Yamazaki 1987). While work on long-term production plans progressed, largely at the Planning Board, in May 1937 the Ministers of Finance and of Commerce and Industry announced 'Three Principles of Public Finance and Economics': 'equilibrium in the international balance of payments', 'expansion of production capacity', and 'control over the supply and demand of goods'. These principles can be interpreted as a formula for running the economy, using planning measures that sought to maximize production capacity while maintaining equilibrium in the international balance of payments, and in the demand for and supply of goods (Okazaki 1987). As foreign exchange controls were already in force, clearly what was meant by 'equilibrium' here was not autonomous market equilibrium, but an artificial equilibrium through the controlled allocation of resources.

Measures to impose economic controls were rapidly put in place after the outbreak of the Sino-Japanese War in 1937. Three laws comprised the legislative basis for these controls. The first, the Emergency Measures on Imports and Exports Act (*Yushutsunyūhintō Rinji Sochi Hō*) of September 1937, imposed controls on imports and exports, and gave the government wide-ranging authority to control the production, distribution, prices, and consumption of imported goods or products made from imported raw materials. This law gave the government an almost complete hold over the control of the material aspects of the economy. The string of directives on consumption, distribution, and price controls that were enacted during the Sino-Japanese War were almost all based on this Act (MITI 1964; Nakamura and Hara 1970).

The other two laws provided the legal basis for controls on the allocation of factors of production. Under the Emergency Funds Adjustment Law (*Rinji Shikin Chōsei Hō*) of September 1937, government approval was required for any transaction that involved more than ¥100,000 in the areas of bank lending for investment, capital increase, corporate bond issues, or starting up new firms, a measure that was tightened to ¥50,000 in August 1938 (Hara 1966; Bank of Japan 1984*a*). The State General Mobilization Act (*Kokka Sōdōin Hō*) of March 1938 conferred complete authority over economic controls, and during the Sino-Japanese War was primarily applied in such areas as labour or prices of factors of production not covered by other acts or directives.

Overlaying the economy with a web of legally based controls was in effect hampering the resource-allocation function of the market. To replace it, a range of economic plans were drawn up by the government that provided criteria for running the controls. Once the Materials Mobilization Plan (*Busshi Dōin Keikaku*) of January 1938 had started to come into effect it was followed from 1939 with a Foreign Trade Plan (*Bōeki Keikaku*), a Funds Control Plan

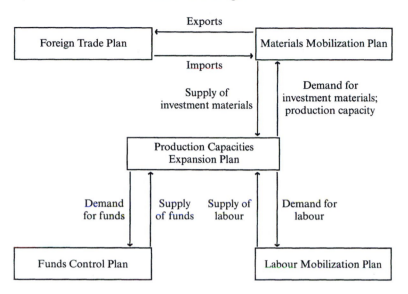

Figure 1.4

(*Shikin Tōsei Keikaku*), a Labour Mobilization Plan (*Rōmu Dōin Keikaku*), a Transportation and Electric Power Mobilization Plan (*Kōtsū Denryoku Dōin Keikaku*), and a Production Capacities Expansion Plan (*Seisanryoku Kakujū Keikaku*) (Figure 1.4).

Under the Materials Mobilization Plan, the supply of commodities was calculated on the basis of volumes of imported goods decided under the Foreign Trade Plan, production facilities decided under the Production Capacities Expansion Plan, and the supply of labour according to the Labour Mobilization Plan, and allocations were made to various purposes. In most cases supply fell short of expected demand, and so assessments of demand were made for different intended uses, in accordance with the relative importance of that use as seen by the Planning Board or the military authorities who manipulated it. The basic function of the Materials Mobilization Plan was almost identical to the Soviet system of 'material balance'. The categories of use were: A: the army, B: the navy, C2: expansion of production capacity, C3: government agencies, C4a: exports to the yen block, C4b: exports to foreign countries, and C5: general civilian demand (MITI 1964). Allocation of materials to C4b involved the Foreign Trade Plan, and allocation to C2 affected production through production facilities. Thus, all the plans were interrelated in a complex and mutually dependent way. The Planning Board tried to coordinate the plans by making iterative corrective calculations, exactly as was done under the Gosplan in the Soviet Union.

The Production Capacities Expansion Plan was successor to the army's long-term production plan referred to earlier, and took the form of a four-year plan running from FY1938 to FY1941 (MITI 1964; Nakamura and Hara 1970; Yamazaki 1987). Production estimates were made for each fiscal year for iron and steel, coal, light metals, non-ferrous metals, petroleum and substitute fuels, and fourteen other items, together with estimates of the capital, foreign currency, engineers, and so on that would be required in each. This long-term plan for production expansion was broken down by fiscal year. In the Production Capacities Expansion Implementation Plan (*Seisanryoku Kakujū Jisshi Keikaku*), plans for production and the allocation of goods and materials were broken down by firm or manufacturing plant.

The Labour Mobilization Plan calculated demand for additional labour for each industrial sector, and the plan to fulfil this demand was broken down by source of labour, such as new elementary-school graduates, those unemployed due to the Materials Mobilization Plan (workers who lost their jobs in civilian industries when allocation of raw materials to those industries was cut), those outside farming communities not gainfully occupied, agricultural workers and those not gainfully occupied in farming communities, women without employment, and so on (Saguchi 1988). Thus the demand for labour in munitions and other industries expanding production was met using workers from civilian industries, agricultural workers, and people outside the labour force.

The Funds Control Plan estimated funds requirements for national bonds, for industry, and for purposes in China and Manchuria, and matched them to various types of savings plans, such as bank deposits, financial trusts, life insurance, non-life insurance, individual investments in securities, and so on (Hara 1966). It is interesting to note that the plan was drawn up on the basis of I/S balance in each sector, replenishing the shortfall of funds in the government, corporate, and overseas sectors with the surplus savings from individual households. In short, long-term and short-term, macro and micro resource allocation all became subject to planning.

It fell to the various ministries, such as the Ministries of Finance and of Commerce and Industry, to implement the Planning Board's plans by imposing controls based on legislation. Let us now examine how the Funds Control and Materials Mobilization Plans were actually implemented. The Emergency Funds Adjustment Law mentioned earlier provided the main legal basis for implementation of the Funds Control Plan. It specified that every proposal for lending, capital increase, bond issue, and so on was to be screened by an Emergency Funds Examination Committee (*Rinji Shikin Shinsa Iinkai*), consisting of representatives of the Ministries of Finance, Commerce and Industry, and Agriculture, and from the Bank of Japan. Only those proposals compatible with Plan objectives were to be granted Ministry of Finance approval. In reality, groups of institutions each representing a different area of financial business (banking, trust banking, insurance, securities) operated their own 'autonomous' regulation, based on 'Industrial Funds Adjustment Standards' (*Jigyō Shikin Chōsei Hyōjun*), and only where very large sums of money were involved did they confer with the Bank of Japan. The Bank of

Japan, in turn, referred only the most important cases to the Emergency Funds Examination Committee. The Industrial Funds Adjustment Standards ranked industries in three classes, A, B, and C, according to their relevance to (1) the Production Capacities Expansion Plan, (2) munitions, (3) the international balance of payments, and (4) existing production capacity, supply of raw materials, etc. (Sakomizu 1941; Bank of Japan 1984*a*). Generally speaking, the system classified industries in accordance with policy objectives and long-term capital was allocated very selectively. Together with the previously mentioned foreign-currency allocation, this system continued to function well into the post-war period as an instrument of industrial policy.

Allocation of goods and materials under the Materials Mobilization Plan was the responsibility of those officials under whose jurisdiction the industries making use of those commodities fell. The Ministry of Commerce and Industry played the biggest role, allocating materials to industrial associations in different sectors in accordance with the prescriptions of the Plan. The industrial associations then distributed quota tickets to the firms they represented, on the basis of allocation-control legislation. With the distribution of raw materials channelled through this allocation system, any firm that did not belong to an industrial association was unable to obtain raw materials, so the distribution of quota tickets in effect functioned as a means of apportioning production among the various firms in that industrial sector.

It can be regarded as an essential condition for the smooth running of this system of planned allocation of capital and materials that allocations signified the granting of economic rent to the enterprises concerned. Under the system of price controls during the early part of the Sino-Japanese War, industries across the board had shown relatively high profit rates (Table 1.10), indicating that allocation meant the distribution of opportunity to secure economic rent. All industries showed high achievement rates for production plans under the Materials Mobilization Plan of 1938, but only because this form of incentive had been functioning (Table 1.11).

3.2. *Launch of the control associations*

Matters did not, however, continue in this way for long. The soaring of international commodity prices following the outbreak of war in Europe in September 1939 had a devastating effect. Fearing accelerated inflation, the government froze prices of all domestic goods at their levels of 18 September 1939 through the Price Control Directive (*Kakakutō Tōseirei*), but prices of imported raw materials rose in line with their international prices. As a result the prices of manufactured goods relative to costs declined and profit rates fell (Table 1.10; Okazaki 1987), indicating that the incentive system no longer functioned effectively. In practice, achievement rates for production plans, which had been satisfactory in FY1938, fell sharply in FY1939 (Table 1.11).

Tetsuji Okazaki and Masahiro Okuno-Fujiwara

Table 1.10. Ratios of profits to total capital (%)

	1938 1st half	1938 2nd half	1939 1st half	1939 2nd half	1940 1st half	1940 2nd half	1941 1st half	1941 2nd half	1942 1st half	1942 2nd half	1943 1st half	1943 2nd half
Mining	**9.1**	8.3	7.7	7.2	6.3	**7.3**	6.6	4.0	**4.2**	4.0	3.0	**3.6**
Metals	8.6	7.7	7.0	6.5	5.9	**6.5**	6.0	3.3	**3.9**	3.6	2.3	**3.0**
Coal	**11.2**	10.1	9.1	8.8	6.7	**7.1**	5.6	4.5	4.4	3.6	**3.8**	**4.2**
Oil	**8.7**	8.6	8.4	8.0	7.8	**11.2**	10.9	6.8	4.7	**6.0**	5.5	**5.7**
Manufacturing	7.8	7.6	**7.7**	7.1	6.9	6.6	6.0	5.1	4.9	4.5	4.1	3.9
Iron and steel	**11.5**	10.2	9.0	8.1	6.3	5.6	5.6	4.0	**4.5**	3.9	3.7	**3.9**
Non-ferrous metals	5.9	**6.8**	6.5	6.3	5.8	4.7	4.7	4.1	3.4	**3.7**	1.7	**3.4**
Shipbuilding	4.0	3.8	**3.9**	3.3	**3.7**	**4.7**	**5.0**	3.4	3.3	**3.4**	**3.5**	3.3
Machinery	8.1	7.7	7.3	**7.4**	**8.0**	7.1	6.4	5.2	4.7	**5.0**	4.3	4.2
Fertilizer	6.0	5.7	**5.8**	5.1	**5.2**	**5.4**	4.8	4.3	**4.5**	4.0	3.2	2.9
Soda	7.4	**7.7**	**8.2**	7.3	5.8	5.4	**13.6**	2.6	2.6	**3.0**	**3.3**	**4.2**
Textiles	7.2	6.9	**7.8**	7.8	**8.9**	7.9	**9.2**	6.6	6.6	5.6	5.3	4.6
Foodstuffs	8.4	8.3	**9.1**	8.9	7.8	**8.4**	8.0	7.1	6.5	6.0	5.6	5.1
Others	6.0	6.0	**6.2**	5.8	5.6	5.2	4.9	4.3	3.9	3.8	3.4	3.3

Note: Bold figures represent increases over previous period.
Source: Okazaki (1987).

Table 1.11. Ratios of real to planned production (%)

	1938	1939	1940	1941	1942	1943	1944
Ordinary iron and steel products	**106.0**	81.4	87.7	91.4	83.0	**101.8**	89.6
Ordinary pig iron	88.2	88.7	93.0	95.1	91.5	**105.4**	93.3
Special iron and steel products	**114.7**	**130.7**	**145.5**	**116.7**	**128.4**	**185.5**	80.0
Iron ore	76.3	75.1	86.3	82.3	92.3	82.6	90.6
Coal	98.6	96.8	97.7	95.5	92.9	**100.0**	80.2
Aluminium	**116.4**	92.2	89.4	97.1	83.1	92.9	87.1
Magnesium	**120.7**	73.2	88.6	69.0	46.6	69.0	77.0
Copper	**104.9**	82.9	76.3	**109.1**	91.8	89.7	**101.0**
Lead	93.4	93.6	76.0	99.3	**100.1**	**118.2**	**115.9**
Zinc	**101.4**	82.8	77.4	98.4	99.6	**102.9**	90.6
Crude oil	95.0	82.3	80.2	90.8	95.4	**102.3**	—
Synthetic oil	60.7	43.1	45.3	78.5	47.5	67.2	—
Refined oil	90.6	90.0	70.5	88.6	—	—	—
Absolute alcohol	**162.5**	71.4	83.7	84.8	71.4	70.4	**109.9**
Soda ash	91.4	88.7	93.5	**109.9**	77.3	95.9	41.3
Caustic soda	**113.1**	88.6	**101.1**	**104.0**	75.0	92.4	77.2
Ammonium sulphate	**101.5**	87.7	93.2	95.2	81.1	84.7	73.3
No. of categories where surplus production achieved	9	1	2	4	2	7	3

Notes: Except for the 1938 figures, ratios represent (real production/planned production) × 100; 1938 ratios represent (real production/expected production according to Materials Mobilization Plan) × 100. Bold figures indicate that real production exceeded the planned figure.

Source: Okazaki (1987).

The use of price controls to dampen inflation was hampering the expansion of production, also a highly important policy target, and this problem prompted intense debate at that time on the issue of the 'incompatibility of policy measures to hold down prices with policy measures to expand production'.

The two separate viewpoints that arose out of this debate involved a conflict of principles surrounding the choice of an economic system (Okazaki 1987). Working from the assumption that the fall in profit rates reduced production incentives, the view that official price ceilings should be raised to stimulate the profit motive in firms was pitted against the view that the profit motive itself should be eliminated. The conflict could alternatively be summed up in terms of whether profit-making should remain the *raison d'être* of the corporate firms, which constituted the basic units of the economic system, or whether a radical revision of the economic system should be attempted. The Planning

Board, the voice of the government, chose the latter position. At the beginning of 1940, the Planning Board took the view that 'all areas of the economy must be subjected to planning by the state in order to establish a wartime economic system, and rigid controls for the execution of those plans are absolutely essential'. For this, first, 'industrial sectors should be organized for them to function as substitute agencies of the state to implement production controls' and second, the principle governing the behaviour of corporate firms 'should be changed from one allowing the unlimited pursuit of profit as advocated by Western scholars, to one that gives production the highest priority' (Okazaki 1987). The Planning Board drew up a basic design for a planned economy that was organized in three levels, with firms at the lowest level pursuing not profit but production, industrial associations acting as government agencies at the middle level, and the government itself at the top. The economy was to be driven not by prices, but by commands given in quantitative terms and directed from the top down to the bottom.

This structure took shape through a series of 'new system' (*shin taisei*) proposals for each of the economic sectors that were drafted during 1940 and 1941. The crux of the New Economic System as a whole was corporate reform and the strengthening of the industrial associations. Corporate reform, as explained in detail in Chapter Four, sought to eliminate profit as a corporate objective by modifying corporate governance structure so that shareholders' authority was restricted while the status of managers and employees was raised (Okazaki 1993*a*). Industrial associations were strengthened through the setting up of control associations for each industrial sector, based on the Major Industrial Association Directive (*Jūyō Sangyō Dantai Rei*) of September 1941. The Iron and Steel Control Association was the first of a string of such organizations that were established one after another through to the end of 1942 (Table 1.12 on pp. 26–7; Nakamura and Hara 1971).

The Major Industrial Association Directive defined the objectives of control associations in the following terms: 'co-operation with the government in the running of a comprehensive system of controls over the relevant industry, and in the formulation and execution of national policy as it relates to that industry, in order to harness the strength of the national economy in the most effective way'. In terms of actual activities this was to include participation in formulating government plans on production, allocation, materials, capital, and labour, the control of production and allocation among member firms, and inspection of member firms (Hoashi 1941). Thus the function of the control associations can be summarized in terms of two roles. One was to assemble information from the various firms to be incorporated in government planning, and the other was to break down government plans as they applied to individual firms and monitor their implementation (Okazaki 1988). The first of these roles had the important implication of improving the process by which plans were formulated, which up to that time had lacked any way of incorporating information derived from individual firms. As explained later, the formulation process for economic and industrial policy after the war drew largely on this overall framework (Okazaki 1993*b*).

Let us examine the structure and functions of the control associations in greater detail, with reference to the Iron and Steel Control Association (Okazaki 1988). Right from the start, this association boasted a large organization with 7 divisions, 25 sections, and more than 300 full-time staff. As its predecessors, the Japan Iron and Steel Federation (*Nihon Tekkō Rengō Kai*) and the Iron and Steel League (*Nihon Tekkō Renmei*), had only about 30 staff between them, this indicates a significant step up in terms of size and capability, and corresponds to the expanded role of industrial associations that we have described. The staff consisted largely of retired employees from member firms, in particular several of manager and divisional manager status from the largest firms, Japan Iron and Steel Manufacturing (*Nippon Seitetsu*) and Showa Steel Works (*Shōwa Seikōsho*).

On the basis of the wide-ranging authority conferred by the Major Industrial Association Directive, the Iron and Steel Control Association required member firms to provide detailed prior and *ex post facto* reports on equipment, production, and materials, and with this information in hand, from FY1941 onwards it participated in formulating the Materials Mobilization and Production Capacities Expansion Plans. The way this worked, in simplified terms, is as follows. First the Planning Board notified the Association of the shipping tonnage, a highly limited resource for all industrial sectors, that could be utilized for the iron and steel industry. The control association worked out how to use this tonnage most effectively within the sector, and based on this drew up a production plan for iron and steel and submitted it to the Planning Board. The Planning Board then made a revised allocation of tonnage for the industry, taking into account production plans from other industrial sectors and changes to the shipping situation, and the process was repeated. The mechanism of formulating plans through ongoing exchange of information between the Planning Board and the control associations can be likened to the mechanism of iterative corrections used in the Soviet Union and known as the 'materials balance' method (Aoki 1971). What is important in terms of its relevance to the post-war period is that under this system the industrial association for each industry assembled information from its member firms, and co-ordinated activities within the industry, and the government co-ordinated between the different industries, in a pattern of action at two levels.

3.3. Creation of the new system and its revision

Together with the New Economic System came the drafting and implementation of a New Financial System (*Kin'yū Shintaisei*) and New Labour System (*Kinrō Shintaisei*). The most significant of the various aspects of the New Financial System concerned the stock market, which had long been the major

Table 1.12. Control associations and their successor organizations

Control association (CA)	Date established	Successor organization in post-war period	Date established
Iron and Steel CA (*Tekkō Tōseikai*)	Nov. 1941	Japan Iron and Steel Council (*Nihon Tekkō Kyōgikai*)	Dec. 1945
Coal CA (*Sekitan Tōseikai*)	Nov. 1941	Japan Coal Mining Association (*Nihon Sekitan Kōgyōkai*)	May 1946
Mining CA (*Kōzan Tōseikai*)	Dec. 1941	Japan Mining Association (*Zenkoku Kōzankai*)	Mar. 1946
Cement CA (*Yōkai Tōseikai*)	Dec. 1941	Cement Manufacturing Association (*Semento Kōgyōkai*)	
Rolling Stock CA (*Sharyō Tōseikai*)	Dec. 1941	Railway Rolling Stock Association (*Tetsudō Sharyō Kōgyō Kyōkai*)	Nov. 1945
Automobile CA (*Jidōsha Tōseikai*)	Dec. 1941	Consultative Association on Cars (*Jidōsha Kyōgikai*)	Nov. 1945
Precision Machinery CA (*Seimitsu Kikai Tōseikai*)	Jan. 1942	Japan Machine Tool Association (*Nihon Kōsaku Kikai Kyōkai*)	Jan. 1946
Electrical Machinery CA (*Denki Kikai Tōseikai*)	Jan. 1942	Japan Electrical Machinery Manufacturing Association (*Nihon Denki Kikai Seizōkai*)	Feb. 1946
Industrial Machinery CA (*Sangyō Kikai Tōseikai*)	Jan. 1942	Industrial Machinery Manufacturing Association (*Sangyō Kikai Kōgyōkai*)	Mar. 1943
Metal Manufacturing CA (*Kinzoku Kōgyō Tōseikai*)	Jan. 1942	Japan Electric Wire Association, others (*Nihon Densen Kyōkai*)	Nov. 1945

Trade CA (*Bōeki Tōseikai*)	Jan. 1942	Japan Trade Association (*Nihon Bōeki Kai*)	Oct. 1945
Shipbuilding CA (*Zōsen Tōseikai*)	Jan. 1942	Confederation of Shipbuilding Co-operatives (*Zōsen Kumiai Rengōkai*)	Dec. 1945
Railways CA (*Tekki Toseikai*)	May 1942	Japan Railways Association (*Nihon Tetsudōkai*)	Oct. 1946
Light Metals CA (*Keikinzoku Tōseikai*)	Sept. 1942	Light Metals Council (*Keikinzoku Kyōgikai*)	Oct. 1946
Wool CA (*Yōmō Tōseikai*)	Sept. 1942	Japan Textiles Association (*Nihon Sen'i Kyōkai*)	Dec. 1945
Leather and Hides CA (*Hikaku Tōseikai*)	Sept. 1942	Leather and Hides Control Co-operative (*Hikaku Tōsei Kumiai*)	Dec. 1945
Hemp CA (*Asa Tōseikai*)	Sept. 1942	Japan Textiles Association (*Nihon Sen'i Kyōkai*)	Dec. 1945
Silk and Rayon CA (*Kinu Jinken Tōseikai*)	Oct. 1942	Japan Textiles Association (*Nihon Sen'i Kyōkai*)	Dec. 1945
Cotton CA (*Mensufu Tōseikai*)	Oct. 1942	Japan Textiles Association (*Nihon Sen'i Kyōkai*)	Dec. 1945
Oils and Fats CA (*Yushi Tōseikai*)	Oct. 1942	Oils and Fats Processing Control Association, others (*Yushi Kakō Tōsei Kumiai*)	Jan. 1946
Chemical Engineering CA (*Kagaku Kōgyō Tōseikai*)	Oct. 1942	Chemical Engineering Federation (*Kagaku Kōgyō Renmei*)	Mar. 1946
Rubber CA (*Gomu Tōseikai*)	Jan. 1943	Rubber Control Co-operative (*Gomu Tōsei Kumiai*)	Dec. 1945

Sources: Nakamura and Hara (1972), Yamazaki (1991), Okazaki (1992).

source of industrial financing in Japan, and the expansion of the system of indirect financing to replace direct financing. As discussed in Chapter Four, the
stock market stagnated after 1940, due to the lower profits that resulted from
policies dating from the start of the Sino-Japanese War to limit shareholders'
power and hold down prices. The difficulties in boosting capitalization resulted in a fall in the proportion of own-capital, which in turn heightened
lending risk for the banks, and so banks took a more prudent attitude towards
lending. Thus, even for the essential industries with the highest ranking in the
Industrial Funds Adjustment Standards it became increasingly difficult to
raise funds. The failure of the allocation system to function smoothly due to
the loss of incentives we can explain as a fundamentally identical problem to
that mentioned earlier: the 'incompatibility of policy measures to hold down
prices with policy measures to expand production', which had now appeared
in the financial sector. The system introduced to resolve this problem was the
delegated monitoring or main bank system, which was designed to lower the
risks attached to lending through the systematic delegation of monitoring. A
National Finance Control Association (*Zenkoku Kin'yū Tōseikai*) was set up
in 1942, which began facilitation of joint financing. Of importance in terms of
its relevance to the post-war period is the fact that the posts of Chairman and
Vice-Chairman of the National Finance Control Association were taken by
the Governor and Vice-Governor of the Bank of Japan, and the Bank's Audit
Bureau Chief, Naoto Ichimada, 'as secretary-general of the association, was
in effect responsible for supervision and guidance of its daily affairs' (Bank of
Japan 1984*a*). Needless to say, as Governor of the Bank of Japan after the war,
Ichimada had enormous influence on financial policy-making overall, including industrial finance. And as discussed later, the Bank of Japan's facilitation
of joint financing played a major role in the recovery process of the post-war
economy.

Among the policies formulated at virtually the same time as the New Systems, those relating to the start of the subcontracting system are particularly
important. When the 'Outline for the Establishment of a New Economic
System' was passed by Cabinet in December 1940, the government issued a
circular 'Outline for Adjustment of Machinery and Steel Product Manufacturing' (*Kikai Tekkō Seihin Kōgyō Seibi Yōkō*). The best of the small
and medium-sized companies were designated exclusive subcontractors to
specific large corporations. The long-term agreement between the two parties
obligated the parent firm to provide the subcontractor with guidance and
assistance, a steady flow of orders, and raw materials. As the private sector
strongly opposed the exclusive nature of these arrangements and the enormous obligations placed on the parent organizations, designation is said not to
have proceeded smoothly. However, the starting-point of long-term subcontracting relations can be traced to this institutional reform in the 'New System'
period (Minato 1987; Ueda 1987).

Systematically planned, the New System that was put in place during the period FY1941–2 was thus, quite literally, an entirely new economic system. The turn-round in FY1941 production-plan achievement rates across the industrial spectrum (Table 1.11) may be largely attributed to this system. None the less, the New System did not resolve the most fundamental issue, and the one that had led to its creation in the first place, namely the dampening of economic activity caused by disregard for the profit motive. In FY1942 achievement rates fell further, forcing the government back into further internal debate on the merits of using profit-making as an incentive (Okazaki 1987).

In July 1942, the Planning Board was still pursuing policies to suppress the profit motive and hold down prices, but the Ministry of Commerce and Industry, with its closer contacts with the corporate world, was critical of Planning Board policy. The Ministry claimed that in reality firms continued as before to be driven by the profit motive, despite the New Economic System's principles of 'putting the public interest first' and 'production the top priority', and in view of this, the Planning Board's policies were misdirected, tending to discourage production by persisting in holding down prices. It suggested that the government would do better to guarantee corporate profits through appropriate application of price controls. With production falling and management of the wartime economy in crisis, and the control associations joining in demands for rises in official prices to deal with the situation, the government was obliged to switch policy direction and allow profits greater priority. In its 'Outline on Emergency Price Measures' (*Kinkyū Bukka Taisaku Yōkō*), approved by the Cabinet in February 1943, the government resolved to act promptly to raise producers' prices with subsidies in order to stimulate corporate efforts to expand production. In this way profit-guided factors were incorporated into the command-type planned economic system designed under the title of 'New Economic System'.

The command-type system was simultaneously undergoing modification on another flank. This was the dispatch of government officials to plants in priority industries. This procedure may appear at first glance to be a means of strengthening government control, but in reality had the effect of modifying the centralized system. These officials were not sent to inspect, but to offer on-site 'guidance, assistance, and advice'. In reality they were expected to deal with the shortages of raw materials and labour that were holding back production at individual plants, and find swift solutions. The system worked from the premise that planning and administration from central government and control associations could not deal effectively with individual problems arising at different plants, and sought to resolve those problems in a decentralized way, similar to a procedure used in the Soviet system (Okazaki 1988). Thus, the experiment with an all-out command-type planned economic system, the New Economic System, and the shortcomings that surfaced resulted in a series of modifications implemented from the second half of 1942 and through 1943 that turned it into a planned economic system incorporating the profit motive and a decentralized approach to individual problems. These reforms had some measure of success. In 1943, corporate profits that had declined steadily from the start of the Sino-Japanese War saw a turn-round, and production-plan achievement rates were second only to those of 1938.

But from the start of 1944, the deteriorating war situation accelerated the decline in the volume of shipped cargo, on which Materials Mobilization Plans were based (Nakamura 1977). This decline in tonnage, due to increasing losses of ships, failed again and again to meet expectations during the implementation period of each plan, and achievement rates fell dramatically. Despite the circumstances, however, efforts continued right up to the end to modify the system in various ways, in order to sustain the output of munitions, and particularly to boost the production of aircraft. As Chapter Four explains, the Munitions Corporations Law (*Gunju Gaisha Hō*) brought about further corporate reform by restricting the authority of shareholders as stipulated in the Commercial Code, and widening the discretionary powers of managers (Okazaki 1993*a*). In this connection, a system was introduced in which one financial institution was, in principle, designated to each munitions firm, to take on the responsibility of supplying funds. The 1940 plan relating to subcontracting, which had invoked strong resistance from the private sector, was revised. Policies that encouraged 'enterprise alignment' (into *keiretsu* groupings) and 'enterprise groupings' of 'co-operating plants' (subcontracting companies) around the major corporations were implemented. It has been shown that a considerable number of the small and medium-sized firms that were organized at this time into co-operating associations remained as subcontractors in post-war *keiretsu* groups (Ueda 1987).

Thus, we have seen how Japan's wartime economy was run basically as a planned economy, and a variety of bold institutional reforms deemed necessary for this purpose were implemented against a background of powerful government authority under the special circumstances of wartime. The post-war economic recovery was to develop out of this wartime experience.

4. Mechanisms for post-war economic recovery

Immediately after the war, the Japanese economy faced even more severe supply-side restrictions than during wartime. The General Headquarters of the Occupation authorities (GHQ) slapped controls on all imports, which were limited, in principle, to the essentials for daily life. As a result, the real value of imports fell in 1946 to one-eighth of the pre-war level, and by 1950 had still only recovered to one-third of that level. Thus one might say that in the early years after the war Japan was compelled to rely on domestic resources to rebuild the economy. At the macro level, capital stock was almost at pre-war levels, as efforts to expand production during the war virtually offset the damage caused by the war. However, capital stock was biased towards munitions industries, and was far removed from post-war demand in which munitions hardly figured (Yoshikawa and Okazaki 1993). The central issue for the wartime economy had been the switch from civilian to military demand under circumstances in which imports were heavily restricted, and now, immediately after the war, the main concern was how to switch back from military to civilian demand under very similar restrictions.

It was the system that had taken shape during the war years that was used to resolve this new issue. Initially, anticipating demands from GHQ for greater democratization, the Japanese government contrived to slim down government control and have the control associations or whatever groups succeeded them exercise 'autonomous control'. The Commerce and Industry Ministry in September and October 1945 replaced the State General Mobilization Law with a Law for the Stabilization and Improvement of the Economy (*Keizai no Antei Kōjō ni kansuru Hōritsu*), and turned the control associations into organizations that accorded with this. GHQ, however, confounded these expectations, asserting that economic recovery was the government's responsibility, and that the 'autonomous control' that the Japanese government had seen as more democratic would in fact be monopolistic and should be dismantled (Okazaki 1992).

So from the beginning of 1946, the government switched policy, reinforcing economic controls and pursuing recovery by means of a planned economic system much like the one they had installed during the war years. Through the Price Control Directive (*Bukka Tōsei Rei*) of March 1946, and the Emergency Materials Supply and Demand Adjustment Act (*Rinji Busshi Jukyū Chōsei Hō*) of October 1946, control was asserted once again over both prices and volumes. Instead of the wartime Materials Mobilization Plans, each quarter Materials Supply and Demand Plans were drawn up, which were in essence much the same as their predecessors. They were implemented through distribution controls based on the Emergency Materials Supply and Demand Adjustment Act. The celebrated Priority Production System (*Keisha Seisan Hōshiki*) launched in the fourth quarter of FY1946 was a measure to allow priority allocation of raw materials to such strategic industries as coal and steel, within the framework of these Materials Supply and Demand Plans.

Wartime methods were also utilized in the drafting and implementation of the Materials Supply and Demand Plans and the Priority Production System. First, let us look at the role of the industrial associations. In 1946 GHQ ordered the control associations disbanded and they promptly broke up. However, those precursors of the control associations, the industrial associations, reappeared through this process of breaking up and regrouping (Table 1.12), and came to play a complementary role to that of government, though subject to a range of GHQ restrictions. From its anti-monopolistic standpoint GHQ was particularly strongly opposed to their involvement in the allocation of raw materials, but because it was difficult for the government to put in place an alternative mechanism for direct control, in many industrial sectors the industrial associations took on the task of materials allocation up to the beginning of 1948, based on the Emergency Materials Supply and Demand Adjustment Act. After the abolition of this Act, to all appearances the government took direct control. However, a high proportion of the many 'Materials Regulation Officers' (*Busshi Chōsei Kan*) appointed by the Commerce and Industry Ministry for this purpose were in fact the same people who had organized allocation on the part of the industrial associations (Okazaki 1992).

To return briefly to the case of the iron and steel industry, after the war the Iron and Steel Control Association continued to be involved both in drafting Materials Supply and Demand Plans and in materials allocation until ordered to disband by GHQ in February 1946. Subsequently an autonomous organization, the Japan Iron and Steel Council (*Nihon Tekkō Kyōgikai*), was set up, which carried out 'production quota allocation, arrangements for the supply of primary and secondary materials, liaison between producers and users, preparation of statistical data and research surveys' until it was dissolved in May 1947 with the revision of the Emergency Materials Supply and Demand Act (Japan Iron and Steel Association 1959). Thus, in the early years of economic recovery, the control associations or the industrial associations that took over from them co-operated with the government in virtually the same way as they had during the war in both drafting plans and implementing them. It was the same sort of system as the co-ordination at two levels mentioned earlier.

The 'priority production' based on this system played a substantial role in economic recovery. It is well known that what prompted priority production was an assumption that the fall in coal production was hindering production of steel, while the fall in steel production was hindering the production of coal. Whether or not this assumption was correct requires separate study, but assuming it to be correct, it indicates some sort of co-ordination failure between steel and coal production. Priority production played the role of shifting the economy from a stagnant state to one of autonomous expansion of production, through government co-ordination of the two relevant industrial associations.

Priority production was backed by a system to provide finance. At the time priority production began in January 1947, the Reconstruction Finance Bank (*Fukkō Kin'yū Kinko*) was set up to provide preferential funding to strategic industries, and in February of that year Regulations on the Provision of Funds by Financial Institutions (*Kin'yū Kikan Shikin Yūzū Junsoku*) were drawn up to regulate the lending of the private-sector institutions. Limits were set on the lending each institution could offer, in order to provide strategic industries with the funds needed for recovery while holding down inflation, and priority financing based on the 'priority listing for lending industrial funds' was arranged within these limits (Ministry of Finance 1976*a*). This priority listing ranked both equipment and operating funds for 460 types of business in four categories of A1, A2, B, and C, in almost exactly the same way as the financing arrangements based on the wartime Emergency Funds Adjustment Law.

A further system introduced during the war years was used to direct funds specifically to those priority industries ranking high on the list. As described in Chapter Four, to coincide with the launch of the priority production system, in January 1947 the Bank of Japan initiated the mediation of loan consortia (*yūshi assen*), forming a Loan Mediation Committee and setting up a Loan Mediation Division in the head office (Bank of Japan 1984*b*). Under the system, the Bank of Japan would arrange loan consortia upon the request of a firm's main bank, and the main bank would undertake appropriate screening and monitoring. Thus, under the leadership of its governor, Naoto Ichimada, the Bank of Japan cultivated a main bank system that monitored firms in the priority industries and provided them with funds.

As we have seen, economic recovery in Japan in the early years after the war exploited systems for planning and control that had been created during the war years. One measure that had great impact on these systems was the Dodge Plan. Under Joseph Dodge's leadership, the situation that had existed since the war, of widespread, excessive demand brought about by extreme financial retrenchment, was corrected, and economic controls were rapidly lifted. In other words the economy was transformed back from a controlled to a market economy. During the Dodge Plan period, however, several systems were introduced which kept the allocation system functioning for a lengthy period of time. First, to end state control of international trade and return to Japan the responsibility for supervising foreign exchange, the Foreign Currency and Overseas Trade Control Act (*Gaikoku Kawase Oyobi Gaikoku Bōeki Kanri Hō*) was enacted in 1949 (Ministry of Finance 1976*b*: 47–66). This gave the government centralized control of foreign exchange, which continued until the trade liberalization of the 1960s, and allocation of foreign exchange was used as a tool to implement industrial policy. Second, viewed with respect to inflation, the Dodge Plan caused stagnation in the capital markets, which had been recovering satisfactorily. As stock and bond prices plummeted, regulation of capital expansion and bonds issues was started, which subsequently functioned as a system of long-term funds allocation (Ministry of Finance 1979: 409, 435–44). Thus, in the midst of a general abolition of economic controls in the Dodge Plan period, allocation systems for foreign currency and long-term funds survived and became the means for priority distribution of resources to priority industries, in other words, for the implementation of a strategic industrial policy.

The institutions that supported this policy also derived from the wartime or early post-war periods. The industrial associations that took over from the control associations were recognized in the 1948 Business Organizations Act (*Jigyōsha Dantai Hō*), and broad-based networks of business associations were formed. Already, delegates from some of these organizations had taken the private-sector positions on the Economic Recovery Planning Committee (*Keizai Fukkō Keikaku Iinkai*). Furthermore, many of their representatives took part in the Industrial Rationalization Council (*Sangyō Gōrika Shingikai*) set up within the Ministry of International Trade and Industry to deal with the new issue of 'industrial rationalization' advocated under the Dodge Plan strategy (Okazaki 1993*b*). One of the most important features of post-war industrial policy was the co-ordination that took place for the concurrent development of complementary industrial sectors. This was a contributing factor to the powerful international competitiveness that Japan exhibited in industries that were complementary and could exploit economies of scale. The objective of industrial rationalization in the early 1950s was the strategic nurturing of export industries. This required a co-ordinated rationalization in complementary industries such as steel and machinery, or steel and shipbuilding, using such institutions as deliberative councils and industrial associations. Needless to say, the success of these policies required the identification of strategic industries and detailed information for co-ordination between them. Councils and industrial associations compiled information drawn extensively from sources at the level of individual firms, as well as passing government information on to the firms, and by these means those conditions were systematically fulfilled.

While this sort of procedure was used to screen strategic industries, the main bank system continued to play a vital role in monitoring the individual firms within these industries. To make up the shortfall in funds brought about by the termination of reconstruction financing in 1949, the Bank of Japan increased the scope of its loan-mediation activities. Then from May 1950, the bank switched policy and withdrew from involvement in loan facilitation, judging that 'the restoration of a free economic system and the setting up of autonomous operations in the financial institutions is now well advanced, so the time has come for the provision of business funds to be undertaken through the proper method of direct negotiation between the parties concerned'. Main-bank-led loan consortia, which the Bank of Japan had sponsored and supported since the war period, were henceforth to function independently of the bank's guiding hand.

Notes

1. Bonuses in the West are related to employees' performance and may be different for each individual. South Korea has a similar bonus system to Japan.
2. For an analysis of the functions of the main bank system, see Chapter Nine, Section 4, and Chapter Three.
3. See Chapter Nine, Section 4, for more detail on this point.
4. For more on the connection between the wartime economy and post-war industrial policy, see Komiya *et al.* (1984) and Ito *et al.* (1988).

5. Retiring Ministry of Finance (central government in the pre-war period) officials who took up employment in regional government or the Manchurian administration, or became members of parliament or university professors, are excluded from this calculation.

References

Akiyama, Taro, Masahiro Okuno-Fujiwara, and Kiminori Matsuyama (1984), 'Zaiko Hendō to Koyō Chōsei (A Study on Changes in Inventories and Employment Adjustment)', *Kin'yū Kenkyū*, 3(2).

Aoki, Masahiko (1971), *Soshiki to Keikaku no Keizai Riron* (Economic Theory of Organization and Planning), Iwanami Shoten.

——(1988), *Information, Incentives and Bargaining in the Japanese Economy*, Cambridge University Press.

Aonuma, Yoshimatsu (1965), *Nihon no Keiei Sō* (Managers of Japanese Firms), Nihon Keizai Shimbun-sha.

Bank of Japan (1984*a*, *b*), *Nihon Ginko 100nen Shi* (A 100-Year History of the Bank of Japan), vols. 4, 5, Bank of Japan.

Gordon, Robert J. (1982), 'Why US Wage and Employment Behaviour Differs from That in Britain and Japan', *Economic Journal*, 92.

Hara, Akira (1966), 'Shikin Tōsei to Sangyō Kin'yū (Funds Control and Industrial Financing)', *Tochi Seido Shigaku*, 34.

——(1977), 'Senji Keizai Tōsei no Kaishi (The Introduction of Wartime Economic Controls)', *Iwanami Kōza Nihon Rekishi* (Iwanami Lectures on Japanese History), Modern Era, vol. 7, Tokyo, Iwanami Shoten.

Hashimoto, M. (1990), *The Japanese Labour Market in a Comparative Perspective with the United States*, Kalamazoo, Upjohn Institute for Employment Research.

——and J. Rasian (1985), 'Employment Tenure and Earnings Profiles in Japan', *American Economic Review*, 75.

Hoashi, Kei (1941), *Tōseikai no Riron to Jissai* (Theory and Practice in Control Associations), Tōhō-sha.

Hyodo, Tsutomu (1970), *Nihon ni okeru Rōshi Kankei no Tenkai* (Evolution of Industrial Relations in Japan), University of Tokyo Press.

Ito, Motoshige, Kazuharu Kiyono, Masahiro Okuno-Fujiwara, and Kotaro Suzumura (1988), *Sangyō Seisaku no Keizai Bunseki* (Economic Analysis of Industrial Policy), University of Tokyo Press.

Japan Iron and Steel Association (1959), *Sengo Tekkō Shi* (History of the Iron and Steel Industry in Post-war Japan), Japan Iron and Steel Association.

Komiya, Ryutaro, Masahiro Okuno-Fujiwara, and Kotaro Suzumura (1984), *Nihon no Sangyō Seisaku* (Industrial Policy in Japan), University of Tokyo Press.

Kurosaka, Yoshio (1988), *Makuro Keizaigaku to Nihon no Rōdō Shijō* (Macroeconomic Analysis of the Japanese Labour Market), Tōyō Keizai Shinpō-sha.

Minato, Tetsuo (1987), 'Ryōtaisenkan ni okeru Nihongata Shitauke Seisan Shisutemu no Hensei Katei (Formation Process of the Japanese Subcontracting Production System between the Two World Wars)', *Aoyama Kokusai Seikei Ronshū*, 7.

Mincer, Jacob and Yoshio Higuchi (1988), 'Wage Structure and Labour Turnover in the United States and Japan', *Journal of Japanese and International Economies*, 2.

Ministry of Finance, Financial History Section (1976*a*, *b*, 1979), *Shōwa Zaisei Shi: Shūsen kara Kōwa made* (Financial History of the Shōwa Era: From the End of the War to the Peace), vols. 12, 14, 15, Tōyō Keizai Shinpō-sha.

Ministry of International Trade and Industry (1964), *Shōkō Seisaku Shi* (A History of Industrial Policy), vol. 11, Shōkō Seisakushi Kankōkai.

Nakamura, Takafusa (1977), 'Sensō Keizai to sono Hōkai (The Japanese War Economy and its Collapse)', *Iwanami Kōza Nihon Rekishi* (Iwanami Lectures on Japanese History), Modern Era, vol. 8, Iwanami Shoten.

——(1980), *Nihon Keizai: Seichō to Kōzō* (The Japanese Economy: Its Growth and Structure), 2nd edn., University of Tokyo Press.

——(1989), 'Gaisetsu: 1937–54 (An Overview: 1937–54)', in Takafusa Nakamura (ed.), *'Keikakuka' to 'Minshuka'* ('Planning' and 'Democratization'), Iwanami Shoten.

——and Akira Hara (1970), 'Kaidai (Bibliographical Notes)', in Takafusa Nakamura and Akira Hara (eds.), *Gendai Shi Shiryō* (Materials on Modern History), vol. 43, Misuzu Shobō.

————(1972), 'Keizai Shintaisei (The New Economic System)', in Nihon Seiji Gakkai (ed.), *Konoe Shintaisei no Kenkyū* (Studies on the Konoe New System), Iwanami Shoten.

Ohkawa, Kazushi and Henry Rosovsky (1973), *Japanese Economic Growth*, Stanford University Press.

Okazaki, Tetsuji (1987), 'Senji Keikaku Keizai to Kakaku Tōsei (The Wartime Planned Economy and the Price-Control System)', in Kindai Nihon Kenkyūkai (ed.), *Senji Keizai* (The Japanese War Economy), Yamakawa Shuppan-sha.

——(1988), 'Dainiji Sekai Taisenki ni okeru Senji Keikaku Keizai no Kōzō to Unkō (The Structure and Working of the Wartime Planned Economy in Japan)', in University of Tokyo Institute of Social Science (ed.), *Shakai Kagaku Kenkyū*, vol. 40(4).

——(1992), 'Jukagaku Kogyō no Saiken (Reconstruction of the Heavy and Chemical Industry)', in Ministry of International Trade and Industry and International Trade and Industry Research Institute (eds.), *Tsusho Sangyō Seisakushi* (History of International Trade and Industry Policy), vol. 3, International Trade and Industry Research Institute.

——(1993*a*), 'The Japanese Firm under the Wartime Planned Economy', *Journal of the Japanese and International Economies*, 7.

——(1993*b*), 'Nihon no Seifu Kigyōkan Kankei (Government–Firm Relations in Japan: Historical Evolution of the System of Trade Associations and Deliberative Councils)', *Soshiki Kagaku*, 26(4).

Saguchi, Kazuro (1988), *Nihon ni okeru Sangyō Minshushugi no Zentei* (Preconditions for Industrial Democracy in Japan), University of Tokyo Press.

Sakomizu, Hisatsune (1941), *Rinji Shikin Chōseihō Kaisetsu* (A Commentary on the Temporary Funds Adjustment Law).

Shinozuka, Eiko and Emiko Ishihara (1977), 'Oiru Shokku Ikō no Koyō Chōsei: Yonkakoku Hikaku to Nihon no Kibokan Hikaku (Employment Adjustment during and after the Oil Shock: Cross-Country and Cross-Scale Comparisons)', *Nihon Keizai Kenkyū*, 16.

Teranishi, Juro (1982), *Nihon no Keizai Hatten to Kin'yū* (Japanese Economic Development and the Financial System), Iwanami Shoten.

Ueda, Hiroshi (1987), 'Senji Keizai Tōsei to Shitaukesei no Tenkai (Wartime Economic Controls and the Evolution of the Subcontracting System)', in Kindai Nihon Kenkyūkai (ed.), *Senji Keizai* (The Japanese War Economy), Yamakawa Shuppan-sha.

Yamazaki, H. (1991), 'Nihon Keizai no Saiken to Shōkō Tsusho Sangyō Seisaku no Kicho (Reconstruction of the Japanese Economy and Outline of Industry and Trade Policy)', in Ministry of International Trade and Industry and International Trade and Industry Research Institute (eds.), *Tsusho Sangyō Seisakushi* (History of International Trade and Industry Policy), vol. 2, International Trade and Industry Research Institute.

Yamazaki, Shiro (1987), 'Seisanryoku Kakujū Keikaku no Tenkai Katei (Development of the Production Capacities Expansion Policy)', in Kindai Nihon Kenkyūkai (ed.), *Senji Keizai* (The Japanese War Economy), Yamakawa Shuppan-sha.

Yoshikawa, Hiroshi and Tetsuji Okazaki (1993), 'Postwar Hyper-Inflation and the Dodge Plan, 1945–1950: An Overview', in Juro Teranishi and Yutaka Kosai (eds.), *The Japanese Experience of Economic Reform*, London, Macmillan.

2

The Financial System and
Its Regulations

Kazuo Ueda

1. Introduction

It is well known that much of Japan's financial system and methods of financial administration took shape in the inter-war period or during the Second
World War. The aims of this chapter are to review the various existing analyses
on this subject, and to offer a number of viewpoints for a better and more
consistent understanding of the system as a whole.

One central theme of this chapter is an analysis of the mechanism for the
provision of long-term capital. A system of long-term capital provision has
been built up during the post-war period on a framework of funding from
long-term credit banks and government financial institutions, with capital
provision made to these institutions from the Trust Fund Bureau and other
commercial banks. This system took shape during the war, when the Industrial
Bank of Japan (IBJ) played a central role in wartime financing and a mechanism was set up to supply the IBJ's capital needs from other financial institutions, including the Trust Fund Bureau. After the war, capital was directed to
different ends—the funding of economic recovery and high-speed growth—
but the system used was almost exactly the same. This chapter will explain the
advantages of this arrangement, such as the spread of risk and the efficient
deployment of monitoring capability. However, the discussion will also show
how much the system's smooth functioning owes to the existence of an enormous reservoir of postal savings, and examine its drawback of dampening price
mechanisms.

A comprehensive overview of financial controls and regulations reveals that
some have survived the fifty or so years of the post-war period and are still in
force today, while others fell out of use at certain points in time after the war.
Thus the Banking Act (*Ginkō Hō*) of 1927, for example, although revised in
the early 1980s, continues to this day as the overall framework for banking
administration, whereas regulations on interest rates introduced during the
war have largely been abolished or relaxed. This chapter will consider to what
extent these regulatory measures can be analysed on the basis of theoretical

economic criteria, and whether economic factors that may have influenced their adoption can be identified through such an analysis.

Looking in more detail, we find that financial controls can be divided into those that take the form of clearly specified laws or rules, and those in which policy-makers are left with considerable discretionary scope, such as in administrative guidance. A characteristic feature of Japanese financial controls is that in comparison with other countries, those of the second type play a far more important role.[1] I would like to consider where this feature may have sprung from.

Section 2 gives a historical breakdown of the introduction of financial regulations and changes in the financial structure during the inter-war period and the Second World War. The Banking Act and Foreign Exchange Control Law (*Gaikoku Kawase Kanri Hō*), and the creation of a wartime financial system are seen as significant events of the period. Section 3 discusses how a considerable part of the financial system that existed prior to 1945, including regulations, remained in place after the war. Section 4 offers the conclusions of this analysis and some theoretical considerations, as well as a discussion of whether a system of this sort might be applicable to developing countries.

2. Regulations introduced during the inter-war and Second World War periods

It is widely known that Japan's post-war financial and capital markets are tightly regulated and price mechanisms do not work effectively. Many of these regulations, however, do not date back to the very beginnings of the system but have been introduced gradually at specific points in time. The dates of the most important regulations are listed in Table 2.1.

2.1. The Banking Act

A significant event prompting tighter regulation of the financial system was the financial crisis of the late 1920s. Much has been written elsewhere on the process that led up to this crisis so I will focus here on its effects.

The most serious outcome of the crisis was that large numbers of banks were forced to suspend business, generating widespread mistrust of the financial system. Thirty-two banks suspended business during this period, and the Bank of Japan extended assistance to a further 315 (Shikano 1992). The Ministry of Finance's response to this financial instability was the Banking Act, which was promulgated on 30 March 1927 and came into force on 1 January 1928. Briefly, the Act introduced a bank licensing system (Clause 2),[2]

Table 2.1. Dates of introduction of main financial regulations

Year	Regulation	Details
1927	Banking Act	Promoted mergers between banks
		Strengthened authority behind administrative guidance
1932	Capital Flight Prevention Law	Control over foreign exchange and trade transactions
1933	Foreign Exchange Control Law	Legislative style in which much is left to 'delegated instructions'
1937	Emergency Funds Adjustment Law	Regulation of equipment capital
1940	Bank Funds Operating Directive	Control over operating capital
1942	Financial Control Directive	Direct financial control
	Joint financing provided by IBJ and other banks	
	System of Designated Financial Institutions	
1947	Bank of Japan loan facilitation	Arranged operating capital for large corporations
1947	Bond Flotation Adjustment Council	Arranged bond flotations and standardized issue terms
1948	Temporary Interest Rates Adjustment Law	Control over lending and deposit rates
1949	Foreign Exchange Control Law	Separation of domestic and overseas financing

it imposed a minimum capital requirement (Clauses 3, 41), which led to reorganization and mergers among the weaker banks, and it gave the Ministry of Finance considerable authority to supervise banks, audit, issue instructions, discipline, and so on (Clauses 20–3). A post-war partial revision came into effect in 1982, but the Banking Act has continued right up to the present as the legal basis for the ministry's banking administration.

A further important development deriving from the Banking Act was the increasing use of administrative guidance *vis-à-vis* the banks, or rather, preparation of the ground that would allow this to take place. The Banking Act did not set out any specific regulations on such aspects as size of net worth, maintenance of cash reserves, large-scale lending, and limits on real estate holdings. Instead 'administrative guidance' was used as a discretionary way of ensuring that banks maintained sound management practices. The Banking Act's detailed rules for implementation (published on 17 November 1927)[3] stipulated that banks submit business reports, and guidance was based on information supplied in these reports. This, then, was the origin of an important feature of bank administration that continues to this day.

The intention behind the Banking Act was somewhat different from the reasons for the tightening of various regulations that will be mentioned later. During the war years, regulations were imposed to channel capital either directly or indirectly to the munitions industries. The main objective of the Banking Act, however, was to shore up the stability of the financial system.

2.2. The Foreign Exchange Control Law

The next measure that tightened financial controls was the introduction in 1932 and 1933 of regulations on foreign exchange dealing.

In December 1931 the re-export of gold was prohibited. This caused a speculative drain on capital and the yen fell sharply in value. With an increasing number of foreign countries also implementing exchange controls at that time, Japan introduced a Capital Flight Prevention Law (*Shihon Tōhi Bōshi Hō*) in June 1932. This enabled the government to restrict the movement of capital as and when necessary, and it was intended to prevent excessive falls in the yen's value in the foreign exchange markets. The law was promulgated in July of the following year, but from August the yen began a further fall, and it became increasingly clear that the law was powerless to control capital flight through non-exchange exports (exporting without repatriating funds), or by containing leads and lags.[4] Consequently in May 1933 the Foreign Exchange Control Law came into force to authorize complete control over currency exchange. It gave the government authority to implement controls not just on exchange transactions but on all foreign trade. In this sense it symbolized a big step in moving towards a controlled economy.

At this time, as I have said, many advanced countries were introducing exchange controls. However, there was considerable variation in the nature of the controls they imposed. As Masanao Itoh (1989) has reported, policies implemented in Britain and America, basically, were careful not to obstruct the working of price mechanisms in foreign-currency markets. In Britain, a foreign exchange equalization account, set up independently of the Bank of England and based on Treasury securities, brought influence to bear on the markets through the trading of sterling as well as gold or foreign currencies.[5] In Germany, on the other hand, strict exchange and foreign-trade controls were imposed through legislation in a way that completely stifled market mechanisms. Japan's exchange controls resembled those of Germany.

An entirely separate characteristic can be identified in Japanese exchange controls, however. Kazuo Aoki comments that the Foreign Exchange Control Law was probably the first step towards a systematically controlled economy in Japan. 'It was ground-breaking legislation without any legal precedent . . . Subsequent control legislation was almost all modelled on this law. And it was highly innovative in its legislative form, in the sense that so much was left to delegated instructions.'[6]

In other words, the legislation set out only basic principles, and their application was left to the instructions or to the discretion of the official responsible at the time. Aoki suggests in his remarks that the Foreign Exchange Control Law was the origin of this style of banking administration, but as we have seen, it may well have been used previously, after the Banking Act became law.

This style of administration, as Aoki claims, had considerable influence on the way subsequent administration and legislation were designed. Hisatsune Sakomizu has the following comments on this point.

I have experienced two different types of control regulations. At the time we worked on the Foreign Exchange Control Law, the concept of reliance on administrative guidance was accepted without any hesitation. But at the time of the Emergency Funds Adjustment Law, this approval system was re-examined for its suitability as a method of control. When matters are prohibited by law, then those matters are prohibited without question and all other matters are unaffected. There were two possible methods for control, one by law and one by administrative guidance, and after the relative merits of the two had been compared, the system using administrative guidance was adopted for the Emergency Funds Adjustment Law . . . The Foreign Exchange Control Law is therefore the ancestor in this sense of all other control legislation passed during the war.[7]

The origins of this discretionary method of administration can therefore be traced to this period in which the Banking Act and the Foreign Exchange Control Law were passed.

It is perhaps not sufficient to mention only the international circumstances that prompted the enactment of the Foreign Exchange Control Law. Tsuneo Amano, then of the Ministry of Finance's Foreign Exchange Bureau, reportedly made the following comments:

The administration of Manchuria has become an immutable national policy, and running this administration has had considerable influence on the national budget, and the financial and industrial sectors. It has also had great impact on foreign trade and other transactions with countries overseas. Therefore to be ready to deal with all contingencies, it was thought essential for the government to retain much broader authority to control foreign exchange than that granted under the Capital Flight Prevention Law.[8]

Foreign exchange controls were thus one of the mechanisms needed as Japan became increasingly involved in military activity after the Manchurian Incident.

2.3. *Financial controls during wartime*

The decisive factors in stamping controls on the economy were the Sino-Japanese War of 1937 and the subsequent outbreak of the Pacific War. The controls of this period had two objectives: the smoother allocation of funds to munitions industries, and the promotion of government bond issues, which were the government's direct means of raising capital.

These objectives were achieved in the following way. The Industrial Bank of Japan (IBJ) and certain other financial institutions were utilized to finance the munitions industries. This left some smaller regional banks with idle funds, and these were directed to the purchase of government bonds, and to supplying capital to the munitions-funding institutions. In this way the capital supply route to munitions industries was made more roundabout, while the lending risks involved were concentrated on the IBJ and a limited number of other institutions.

The government also arranged for postal savings to be used to purchase government bonds and supply capital to munitions-funding institutions through the Deposits Bureau. This limited the Bank of Japan's underwriting of government bonds to some extent, and meant that some, at least, of the risk of funding munitions industries fell on the government.

It is important to note that this roundabout munitions-funding system was made possible, and worked efficiently, due to the IBJ's expertise in long-term financing, and the existence of a vast reservoir of postal savings.

2.3.1. *Control of banks' activities*

Various mechanisms were used to direct capital to munitions industries and government bonds, and here I would like to analyse the nature of government intervention in influencing the behaviour of the private-sector financial institutions, including the special banks such as the IBJ. Subsequently I will discuss the role played by public-sector financing for this purpose.

Intervention in bank lending was essential to ensure a supply of funds to munitions. The two most representative pieces of legislation were the Emergency Funds Adjustment Law (*Rinji Shikin Chōsei Hō*) of 1937, covering the provision of equipment funds, and the Bank Funds Operating Directive (*Ginkōtō Shikin Un'yō Rei*) of 1940, which authorized intervention affecting operating capital. In practice, the Emergency Funds Adjustment Law regulated business capital by making it necessary, for example, to obtain ministerial approval to lend equipment capital of ¥100,000 or more. To draw up criteria on which to base approval, an Emergency Funds Adjustment Committee was formed and a ranking of priorities for the proposed use of funds was decided. Roughly speaking, the rankings correlated to the degree of involvement with munitions industries. In the case of the Bank Funds Operating Directive, ministerial approval was required, for instance, for loans for operating capital of more than ¥50,000, if the loan amount exceeded the previous year's lending to the borrower.

Priority financing for munitions industries excluded small and medium-sized firms in all parts of the country from access to funds, and the regional financial institutions that had always financed these firms generated surplus funds as a result. These funds, too, were directed to 'wartime capital mobilization' in the form of government bond holdings and capital provision to the institutions funding munitions industries.

Strict controls were imposed on bond flotations as well as bank lending. The bond market, which had in effect closed down with the start of the Sino-Japanese War, was reopened in 1938, but the terms, periods, and sizes of flotations came under the control of the Bank of Japan, the Ministry of Finance, and the IBJ. In addition to these three, a Bond Flotation Planning Committee was formed by the Planning Board and the Postal Insurance Bureau in December of that year, to take charge of overall planning of bond flotations.

The organization responsible for the finer points of financial control was the National Finance Control Association, set up in May 1942. This Association was senior in status to other business organizations, but in reality, it was responsible solely for control activities, and it acted on the authority of the Bank of Japan and the Ministry of Finance. It imposed wide-ranging control over financial institutions' collection of funds and banking operations, but since absorption of government bonds was one of the main thrusts of financial control, as I have said, its first task was to allocate government bonds for absorption by these institutions. The Control Association also studied various means to collect funds, and in banking operations it checked financial institutions' plans for the use of funds, participated in planning bond issues, arranged and supervised joint financing, and regulated interest rates.

These controls were not implemented in total disregard of profit incentives for private-sector institutions. To encourage the absorption of government bonds, the interest rate on bonds had to exceed the cost of funds for these institutions. The devices by which this was achieved were a system of advantageous lending rates for borrowers with government bonds as collateral (see next section) and a campaign to equalize interest rates. Interest rates were reduced on deposits in regional banks, where rates tended to be higher than in Tokyo or Osaka banks. This lowered the regional banks' funding costs, enabling them to purchase government bonds.

To reduce the risk associated with funding munitions industries, funds were provided through a circuitous route. To this end, large numbers of specialized financial institutions were set up during the war period, typified by the Wartime Finance Bank, while among existing financial institutions, munitions financing was concentrated specifically on the IBJ and large city banks.

The status of the IBJ rose dramatically under the wartime system. Under the Corporate Profits, Dividends, and Capital Accommodation Directive

Table 2.2. Industrial Bank of Japan's funds procurement, 1937–1945 (%)

Sources	1937	1938	1939	1940	1941	1942	1943	1944	1945
IBJ capital–liability formation									
Bonds outstanding	58.9	64.4	50.0	61.8	61.7	63.8	58.4	49.0	39.6
Deposits	22.9	18.9	22.1	8.7	6.6	8.8	8.9	9.6	18.0
Borrowings		2.4	9.5	15.1	12.9	13.0	21.6	33.7	37.1
Total for capital and liabilities (¥m.)	1,087	1,653	1,734	2,304	3,743	5,141	7,485	13,706	19,471
IBJ bond issues, by underwriters									
Public issues	2.2	22.6	60.0	31.4	23.0	35.3	34.9	38.4	29.2
Deposits Bureau	1.4	6.8	5.5	20.1	3.6	5.7	1.9	9.5	20.7
Special gold account	92.0	62.4	2.5						
Postal Insurance Bureau	3.9	5.1	26.3	7.4	5.9	4.5			
Co-operative societies/Central Bank for Agriculture and Forestry		2.3		3.0	13.3	17.0	20.4	21.9	12.8
Regional banks			0.8	30.3	38.4	17.0	24.4	15.2	22.0
Savings banks				1.5	5.9	16.4	16.6	9.6	4.7
Total issues (¥m.)	410	642	121	676	1,016	1,337	1,326	2,098	2,656
IBJ borrowing, by lenders									
Deposits Bureau	100	75.4	59.4	6.6	18.3	8.6	13.5	3.0	7.4
Bank of Japan		24.6	39.8	89.1	69.7	66.6	43.6	24.7	9.6
Regional banks					7.6	21.3	20.6	19.2	28.4
Savings banks							17.2	9.0	9.6
Co-operative groups							37.2	43.6	42.2
Extraordinary financing							1.1	2.2	16.2
Outstanding (¥m.)	155	134	358	251	420	633	1,571	4,407	4,183

Source: Imuta (1991*b*).

(*Kaisha Rieki Haitō Oyobi Shikin Yūzū Rei*) of 1939, the Minister of Finance could instruct the IBJ to supply funds as necessary (command funding). Moreover, a syndicated loan system, in which several institutions grouped together to lend to a single borrower, came to be widely used, and in more than six cases out of ten, these lending groups were headed by the IBJ.[9] The syndicated loan system is said to have been adopted because the size of loans had increased, risks could be spread widely, and financial controls operated more smoothly. In 1944, a system of designating financial institutions for munitions-industry funding was introduced, under which the Ministry of Finance selected specific institutions to take over funding to individual munitions firms. The IBJ was selected for 146 out of a total of 831 cases, so here too the IBJ played a prominent role.[10] At the end of the war, munitions-industry funding accounted for some 76 per cent of the IBJ's outstanding loans (IBJ 1982),[11] indicating that the IBJ had become a key institution in the government policy of directing funds to munitions industries.

About 60 per cent by value of the debentures issued by the IBJ in the five years from the start of the Pacific War were absorbed by financial institutions, according to Imuta (1991*b*), and Table 2.2 indicates the rapid growth in this trend from around 1940. Regional banks and savings banks figured particularly highly in this, as some part of the spare capital that financial controls generated in these institutions was directed, as I have said, to the purchase of IBJ debentures. The IBJ also borrowed funds, almost exclusively from other financial institutions, to a total of about ¥4.2 billion by the end of the war.

In summing up this situation overall, Imuta offers the following interpretation: 'The IBJ played the role of sharing the risk of munitions funding that fell on the ordinary banks. In return for buying debentures, the ordinary banks could shift the risk onto the IBJ.'

2.3.2. The role of public finance

The wartime financial system was not achieved simply through control of private-sector finance. The Deposits Bureau of the Ministry of Finance, with its access to postal savings, and the resources of the Bank of Japan were decisively important, first in purchasing government bonds, and second in directing funds to the institutions, such as the IBJ, responsible for funding munitions industries.

Figure 2.1 shows a breakdown of government debt (bonds + bank borrowing) by underwriting institutions for five-year periods between 1925 and 1945. I mentioned earlier how vital it was to the wartime financial system to have private-sector institutions underwrite government bonds. However, as this figure shows, the use of public-sector capital from the Bank of Japan and Deposits Bureau for this purpose was just as important, and the Deposits Bureau played by far the more important role of the two. Table 2.3 gives a breakdown of the various purposes for which Deposits Bureau funds were

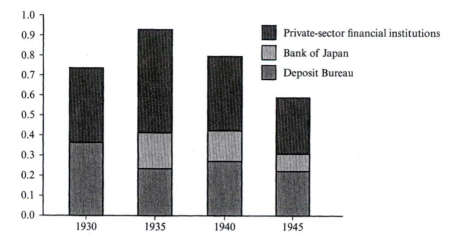

Figure 2.1. Underwriting shares of government debt (five-yearly changes)
Source: Bank of Japan (1966).

used, and shows that from 1937 more than half were directed to absorbing government bonds.[12]

Supporting this massive underwriting of government bonds by the Deposits Bureau was the growth in postal savings. Figure 2.2 uses Bank of Japan data to chart postal savings as a proportion of total bank deposits nation-wide, and it indicates the significant growth in postal savings after the financial crisis of the 1920s. After the China Incident of 1937, campaigns encouraged ordinary people to save, and some part of the growth in postal savings was compulsory savings. This accounts for the rapid growth in postal savings' share of deposits up to the end of 1945. In this way large volumes of government bonds could be issued without the risk of increased inflation.[13]

The Deposits Bureau, with its postal-savings resources, was not only responsible for absorbing government bonds in quantitative terms: after 1936 the bureau frequently bought up bonds from the market as a price-support measure. For regional and savings banks in difficulties, too, the bureau allocated other high-yield securities in quantities relative to their holdings of government bonds. It intervened frequently in the short-term money market: for instance, when strains in the call market in 1936 began to affect government bond prices negatively, the bureau made a loan of ¥125 million to the IBJ to support the short-term money markets. Again and again the Deposits Bureau behaved much like a central bank in regulating short-term credit.[14]

As mentioned earlier, to persuade private-sector financial institutions to invest in government bonds, the interest on such bonds had to exceed interest on deposits. To this end, deposit rates were regulated, and in 1932 postal savings interest rates were lowered in an attempt to bring down market deposit rates.[15]

Table 2.3. Deposits Bureau funding

FY	Government bonds (%)	Lending to general and special accounts (%)	Local government funding (%)	Business funds of special banks, firms, etc. (%)	Total (¥m.)
1932	32	11	44	0.005	3,595
1933	39	3	45	2	3,956
1934	41	2	45	1	4,166
1935	41	2	45	1	4,356
1936	44	2	42	4	4,789
1937	51	1	37	3	5,492
1938	58	1	31	4	6,391
1939	64	1	25	8	8,486
1940	65	1	20	9	11,326
1941	69	1	17	10	13,965
1942	71	1	13	13	18,125
1943	72	1	7	14	27,941
1944	73	1	6	15	36,113
1945 (end of June)	71	1	6	16	43,947

Source: Nakajima (1982).

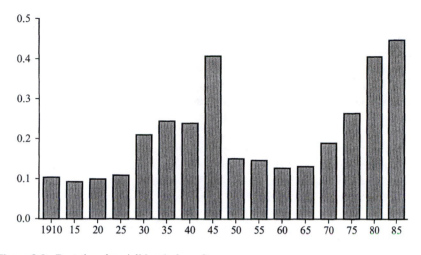

Figure 2.2. Postal savings/all bank deposits
Source: Based on data from Bank of Japan (1966).

As another measure to encourage financial institutions to hold government bonds, the Bank of Japan in 1937 introduced a system of preferential lending on government bond security. The interest rate on Bank of Japan lending based on government bond collateral was reduced to the same level as the discount rate on commercial bills.[16] It was as if financial institutions were subsidized to hold government bonds through the Bank of Japan's low-interest lending.

The second role of public finance was to support the provision of funds to institutions, such as the IBJ and the Wartime Finance Bank, financing the munitions industries. Table 2.3 shows that during the war years, Deposits Bureau resources were an important source of funds for these special banks and corporations. Ministry of Finance statistics (Ministry of Finance 1962) reveal that the Deposits Bureau's capital provision to IBJ and the Wartime Finance Bank, in the form of loans and the purchase of bonds, had exceeded ¥3 billion by FY1945, accounting for 30 per cent of its funding to the special banks. In growth terms, the Deposits Bureau's funds provision to the IBJ ballooned by a multiple of 27 between 1932 and 1945, vastly exceeding the expansion in its total operating funds, which grew by a multiple of 12.

How important was this public financing to the IBJ? Table 2.2 gives a breakdown of IBJ's capital and liabilities, borrowing, and debenture underwriting. During the war the IBJ raised capital mostly through debenture flotations and borrowing. The importance of government funds from the Deposits Bureau, the special gold account and postal insurance to absorb debentures, and public funds from the Deposits Bureau and Bank of Japan for the IBJ's borrowing is clear.[17] Using these figures and Ministry of Finance data (Ministry of

Finance 1962), the proportion of the IBJ's total funds derived from the Deposits Bureau and the Bank of Japan, on the basis of funds outstanding, is
calculated to average about 17 per cent between 1940 and 1945.[18] If we then
add postal insurance funds and in 1937 and 1938 funds of the special gold account directed to debenture underwriting, as well as the existence of separate
deposits from the Deposits Bureau, we can appreciate the great importance to
the IBJ of public-sector funds. Furthermore, under the 1942 revision of the
Emergency Funds Adjustment Law, all IBJ debentures became subject to
government guarantee. As for the Wartime Finance Bank, public-sector funds
were of even greater importance, with Deposits Bureau funds accounting for
29.6 per cent of its debenture issues, and Deposits Bureau and Bank of Japan
funds between them accounting for 86.2 per cent of its borrowing in 1945.

We have seen the extremely important role played by public-sector funds
both in underwriting government bonds and in financing munitions industries
through the IBJ and the Wartime Finance Bank. Much of the risk accom-
panying loans to munitions industries was concentrated on these two institutions, but because they depended in part on public funds, and their debentures
were government-guaranteed, the risk was ultimately shouldered by the government. This created a system that made it easy for them to raise funds from
the private sector as well.[19]

2.4. Financial controls and price mechanisms

The long-term influence of Japan's wartime financial system has persisted
through the post-war period and is felt in a number of different ways. Here I
would like to look at some examples of this and examine how they relate to
price mechanisms.

2.4.1. Increasing inflexibility of interest rates

Tightening financial controls had the predictable effect of hampering the working of price mechanisms. This is not easy to examine because of the limitations
of the available data, but a certain amount of corroborative evidence can be
given. Table 2.4, based on Bank of Japan data, shows the degree of disparity
in deposit and lending rates between different banks. Differences between the
highest and lowest rates were trimmed considerably over the period from 1937
to 1943. It was 'as if a world of finance had materialized in which interest rates
were irrelevant. In other words, government control of funds allocation and
credit rationing had become widespread throughout the economy.'[20]

However, closer examination reveals that one reason for the convergence of
rates was related to the enormous volumes of government bonds that financial
institutions were obliged to underwrite. Figure 2.3 compares government
bond yields at flotation, and interest rates for time deposits. Up to about 1930

Table 2.4. Standardization of interest rates

	Deposit rates			Lending rates		
	Highest	Lowest	Disparity	Highest	Lowest	Disparity
1937	3.8	3.5	0.3	8.39	5.69	2.70
1938	3.7	3.4	0.3	8.21	5.58	2.63
1939	3.5	3.4	0.1	7.70	5.40	2.30
1940	3.5	3.3	0.2	7.11	5.51	1.60
1941	3.4	3.3	0.1	6.90	5.30	1.60
1942	3.4	3.3	0.1	6.30	5.20	1.10
1943	3.3	3.2	0.1	6.20	4.90	1.30

Note: Deposit rates are for time deposits; lending rates are for ordinary loans.
Source: Bank of Japan, *A Hundred-Year History of the Bank of Japan*, vol. 4.

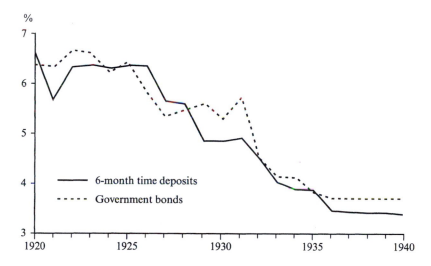

Figure 2.3. Interest rates of government bond issues and time deposits
Source: Bank of Japan (1966).

they bore no obvious relation to each other, but after the mid-1930s the government bond rate is consistently higher than the deposit rate. This assured those institutions underwriting government bonds a fixed margin of profit.[21]

Figure 2.4 indicates the disparity in yields between various bond and debenture issues. After 1930 the disparity shrank, and particularly in the second half of the decade, disparities in the issue terms of various bonds remained virtually constant, suggesting that rates had ceased to reflect variations in risk. This small disparity in yields is a feature that has persisted through the post-war period, and I would like to return to this later.

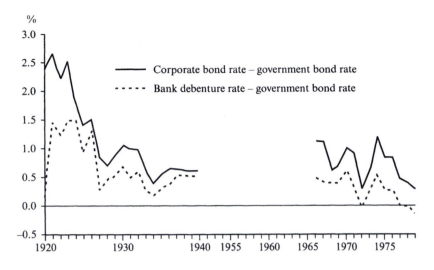

Figure 2.4. Disparity in interest rates on debenture issues
Source: Bond Underwriters Association (1980).

2.4.2. *Lack of responsibility in financial institutions*

I have already discussed this point in some detail with respect to the IBJ. During the war, financial institutions supplied funds on the basis of government instructions, and their behaviour therefore lacked a proper consideration of responsibility and risk. The situation was described as one in which 'the credibility of the banks was tied to the credibility of the state'.[22] A similar tendency has persisted all through the post-war period, and may be regarded as a characteristic feature of Japan's financial system.

Moreover, in 1944 the government announced an Outline on Wartime Emergency Financial Policy (*Senji Hijō Kin'yū Taisaku Seibi Yōryō*) under which all private-sector deposits were covered by government guarantee. Together with the control of deposit interest rates, this had the effect of eliminating almost all differences between individual financial institutions from the depositor's viewpoint. This too is a point of great interest for its similarities to the situation that developed after the war.

2.4.3. *Capital flows channelled through banks*

The expansion of equipment investment that started in the mid-1930s, spurred by the boom in munitions, increased corporate dependence on external credit. And with tightening financial controls, external credit was drawn increasingly from bank lending rather than stocks and shares. Figure 2.5 shows changes in the ratio of corporate net worth. The ratio began to fall from the mid-1930s, and despite a brief rise after the war until 1955, it continued falling during the

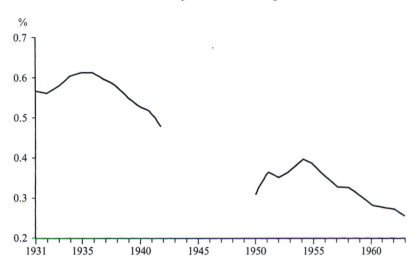

Figure 2.5. Ratio of net worth to total capital (for all industries)

Source: Based on data from Mitsubishi Economic Research Institute, *Honpō Jigyō Gaisha Keiei Bunseki* (Analysis of Management of Firms in Mainland Japan).

post-war period.[23] Again, Figure 2.6, drawn from Bank of Japan data, shows how the proportion of bank lending directed to external capital provision increased rapidly in the second half of the 1930s, and more noticeably in the first half of the 1940s. This trend persisted in the post-war period, and here we can see the origins of the post-war 'over-borrowing' phenomenon.

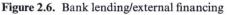

Figure 2.6. Bank lending/external financing

Source: Bank of Japan (1966), *Sangyō Shikin Kyōkyū Jōkyō (Zōgen)* (Changes in Supply and Demand of Industrial Capital).

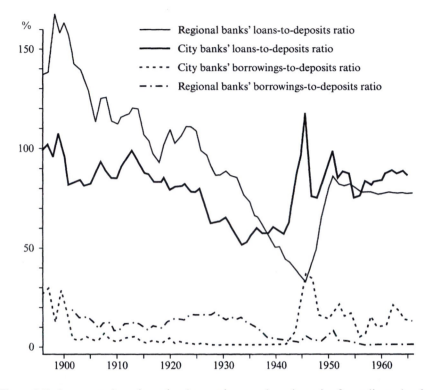

Figure 2.7. Loans-to-deposits ratios, borrowings-to-deposits ratios for ordinary banks
Source: O. Itoh (1986).

As munitions financing was undertaken mostly by the large city banks, the loans-to-deposits ratio for these banks rose sharply. The Bank of Japan started lending to these banks, the regional banks' loans-to-deposits ratio fell, and funds distribution became unbalanced. This is a pattern also seen in the post-war period, but it originated during the war. The changes in loans-to-deposits ratios are clearly shown in Figure 2.7.

The main bank system also took shape at this time and is a further feature that has persisted through the post-war period, but this subject is beyond the scope of this chapter.

3. The establishment of post-war financial policy

The process by which the post-war financial system came about was greatly influenced by the actions of GHQ, the Occupation authorities. GHQ initially planned to introduce an American-style financial system based on market

mechanisms. A characteristic example of GHQ's thinking, described in Takasugi's 'The Industrial Bank of Japan', was that long-term financial institutions
were unnecessary, and American-style long-term capital allocation through
the bond market should be adopted instead. Policies such as setting up a
'finance board' independent of the Ministry of Finance, and the separation of
banking and securities, were also worked out.

GHQ's policies changed significantly with the start of the Cold War, however, when priority was shifted to regaining economic stability rather than
installing American-style business practices. The proposed reforms were
mostly shelved, with the exception of the separation of banking and securities,
and the IBJ was permitted to continue in its role as a long-term credit bank.[24]

The Ministry of Finance's resistance to relinquishing its discretionary style
of policy implementation is an interesting point. GHQ advocated revising
the Banking Act and setting clear standards for banking operations and
accounting, in order to guarantee sound financial institutions. In response, the
Ministry of Finance acknowledged the importance of a strategy to maintain
sound institutions, but wanted to use its procedures of notification and administrative guidance. In the end, the Ministry got its way and the matter was
settled without revision of the Banking Act.[25]

In circumstances such as these, the Japanese financial system formed before
and during the Second World War was in many respects reinstated, and the
wartime system of heavy regulation persisted into the post-war period.[26] However, the objectives of these controls changed from financing the war effort to
economic recovery and high-speed growth. Let us look now at a few examples.

3.1. Long-term finance

After the war, long-term credit was advanced mainly by the long-term credit
banks and the Japan Development Bank. At the start of the 1950s, the IBJ
alone was responsible for 20–30 per cent of the equipment capital supplied by
all financial institutions. Including public-sector financial institutions' funding
for the same purpose, the figure reached 60 per cent in the first half of the
decade, and remained at 30–40 per cent towards its end. It is well known that
these funds were largely directed to the key industries of steel, coalmining,
shipbuilding, and electric power, particularly in the early post-war years. During the period 1951 to 1955, the IBJ supplied 23.5 per cent of the equipment
capital advanced by financial institutions to these four industries, and at the
close of FY1955 they accounted for 58.3 per cent of the IBJ's outstanding
loans for equipment capital.[27]

To raise funds, the long-term credit banks relied on issuing bank debentures.
Table 2.5 shows how IBJ debentures were absorbed between 1951 and 1955,
demonstrating the overwhelming importance of the Trust Fund Bureau at the
start of the decade, and the rapid increase of the financial institutions' role

Table 2.5. Purchasers of IBJ debentures (%)

	1951	1952	1953	1954	1955
City banks	16.6	20.3	24.1	25.5	34.6
Regional banks	7.7	7.2	6.9	7.3	21.6
Other financial institutions	2.9	2.8	6.7	6.3	22.4
Trust Fund Bureau	59.4	57.9	42.4	38.0	9.6
Others	13.5	11.9	19.6	22.9	11.8

Source: Industrial Bank of Japan (1982).

during its middle years. This is a remarkably similar arrangement to the underwriting of IBJ debentures during the war.

A major objective of this arrangement during the war was to concentrate the risk associated with munitions funding on the IBJ. The same type of arrangement can be seen working in the post-war period to concentrate the risk associated with economic recovery and high-speed growth on long-term institutions.[28]

The preconditions that opened the way for this arrangement were virtually identical to those of the wartime period. One was the IBJ's capability in credit analysis for long-term financing. This expertise was not only used within the IBJ, but was transferred to the Japan Development Bank and many other government financial institutions, and became fundamental to their credit activities. A further precondition was the existence of postal savings and the Trust Fund Bureau, which funded the underwriting of long-term bank debentures up to the mid-1950s, and supported the activities of government financial institutions all through the post-war period. Through these latter institutions, much of the risk of long-term financing has ultimately been borne by the government, just as it was under the wartime system.

3.2. Rigidity in interest rates

A system evolved during the war years, as I have mentioned, to hold down interest rates. As demand for recovery funds began to grow after the war, all interest rates, led by lending rates, rose to high levels through to the end of 1946. It therefore became extremely difficult for recovery bonds and government bonds, whose interest rates were regulated, to be absorbed. To resolve the situation, the Bank of Japan and the Federation of Bankers' Associations agreed to fix an upper limit on lending rates. There were difficulties in implementing this strategy because it conflicted with anti-trust legislation, but this problem was solved with the passage of the Temporary Interest Rates Adjustment Law (*Rinji Kinri Chōsei Hō*) in December 1947.

Moves to tighten other interest rates began at the same time. In June 1947, a Bond Flotation Adjustment Council (*Kisai Chōsei Kyōgikai*) was set up within the Bank of Japan with the object of standardizing terms for the flotation of various types of bonds. Such organizations as the Federation of Bankers' Associations and the Regional Banks Association began to bring interest rates into line through agreements on deposit rates. These interest rate agreements are said to have 'strongly reflected the wishes of the authorities'.[29]

It has frequently been pointed out that interest rates were lower than the levels needed to match demand and supply of funds.[30] For instance, yields on bank debentures were on many occasions lower than yields on negotiable bonds. This was to hold down the long-term prime rate. However, it meant that deposit rates in institutions absorbing bank debentures also had to be kept low. Some incentive was therefore needed to encourage institutions to hold bank debentures, such as making them acceptable collateral for Bank of Japan financing. In these respects, too, the post-war system closely resembles its wartime predecessor.[31]

Should interest rates fall below the level required to maintain equilibrium, some sort of artificial allocation of credit takes place. In this, asserting the necessity for low interest rates endorses the necessity of funds allocation by government.[32] This appears in concrete form in funds allocation arranged by government financial institutions and the close relations between the government and the long-term credit banks.

Thus, as we have seen, many of the characteristics of the post-war financial system are arguably the legacy of Japan's experience since the inter-war period. And a policy style that shows a preference for discretionary measures over hard-and-fast rules undoubtedly persists as a principle guiding the actions of Japan's policy-makers.

4. Conclusion

In this chapter I have shown that the roots of Japan's post-war financial system can be traced to the inter-war and Second World War periods. In conclusion, I would like to add two further points for consideration.

First, how could a wartime system be adapted so smoothly for use in peacetime? I would like to offer a tentative explanation. Figure 2.8 shows surpluses and deficits of funds by sector through the pre-war and post-war periods. It is characterized from the second half of the 1920s onwards by the flow of household savings to the government sector. This obviously corresponds to the wartime economic system. As I have said, to achieve the non-economic objectives of managing a war, a mechanism for the planned and controlled allocation of resources was needed, rather than a decentralized allocation mechanism.

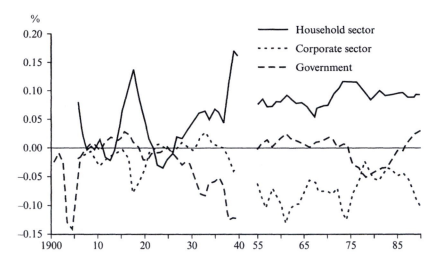

Figure 2.8. Excess savings/GNP, by sector
Sources: Bank of Japan (1966); National Income Accounts Statistics.

The characteristic feature of the post-war era is the flow of funds from household savings to corporate investment. It is difficult to claim that this could not have been achieved through a decentralized mechanism, but perhaps it is fair to say that for recovery from the immediate post-war chaos and for the early stages of high-speed growth, the use of decentralized financial markets would not necessarily have been advantageous. Due to the sudden drop in asset balances and the all-round lowering of incomes and assets, both the household sector and the financial institutions lacked the capacity to supply the rather more long-term funds needed for recovery and growth, and to shoulder risk. Long-term capital was therefore generated in two stages, through city banks and long-term credit banks, and was supplemented by government financial institutions, and because this whole system was backed by government credit, the intermediary costs of capital were reduced. This was precisely the sort of arrangement that had been learned from the wartime system.

This experience suggests that policies that require financial institutions in developing countries to increase their net worth could end up merely increasing agency costs and thereby obstruct growth. The Japanese-type long-term capital-allocation mechanism, however, relies on the credit-analysis capability of institutions such as industrial banks, as well as the existence of postal savings and so on, and therefore it cannot be readily implanted in countries lacking these features.

The second consideration is that a great number of the financial regulations that were kept in force after the war are only now being dismantled (a recent example being the regulation of deposit interest), and some still remain in force. What distinguishes these from regulations that have been abolished? Of particular interest is the fact that still in force are many of the regulations and instructions given as administrative guidance in connection with the Banking Act, which were introduced at a very early stage before the war. They remain because, as I have said, they are related to the government intervention that may be necessary even in advanced countries to maintain the stability of the financial system.[33]

Meanwhile, the systems adopted before 1945 largely for the war effort, and then later for economic recovery and high-speed growth, have now lost these imperatives. Since the war some have been abolished as an environment has been created in which market mechanisms operate, and others are gradually losing their relevance. Thus, even though the origins of the post-war financial system can be traced back to before 1945, the effects of these two categories of regulations and systems have been very different, and it is essential not to confuse them.

Finally, the government stance favouring discretionary measures over hard-and-fast rules is a Japanese feature that again has existed since the pre-war period. However, this surely cannot be directly related either to war circumstances, or to high-speed growth, or even to maintaining a stable financial system. This discussion, however, must be left for another occasion.

Notes

1. See e.g. Quick Research Institute (1993).
2. However, similar provisions already existed in the Banking Ordinance of 1890.
3. See 'A Hundred-Year History of the Bank of Japan', vol. 3: 283.
4. Ibid. vol. 4: 89.
5. Ibid. vol. 4: 266.
6. See Ministry of Finance, Daijin Kanbō Chōsa Kikakuka (1978).
7. Ibid.
8. 'A Hundred-Year History of the Bank of Japan', vol. 4.
9. Ibid. vol. 4: 300.
10. Under this designation system, however, large commercial banks also took on munitions funding as special banks, in the form of joint lending with the IBJ. Furthermore, in 1945, under the Special Measures for Munitions Financing Act, each firm was forced to deal with only one bank, effectively forcing all the large banks to play the same role in munitions financing as the IBJ. See Chapter Three for more on the significance of syndicated loans.
11. Industrial Bank of Japan (1982: 83). The proportion of munitions funding in other major banks was around 30% (p. 84).
12. The Deposits Bureau of the Ministry of Finance was set up to run postal savings, which effectively started in 1875. Subsequently, in the Deposits Regulations of 1885, the Deposits Bureau was institutionalized as a government financial institu-

tion, but the rules relating to its operations were unclear, and by the end of the Taisho period problems of large-scale, delinquent loans had arisen. This prompted massive reform of the bureau in 1925, with a view to making its operations more transparent. Later, at the time of the Shōwa Crisis, the Deposits Bureau took on the job of directing capital to the regions and rural areas, largely through investment in local government bonds, to deal with the crisis in agriculture (see Table 2.2). As explained in the text, with the onset of the wartime system, the bureau abruptly changed its role to investment in government bonds. (For more on this, see Chapter Six, Nakajima (1982), and Yoshino and Furukawa (1991).) It became the present Trust Fund Bureau after the war in 1953.

Under the wartime financial system, the Deposits Bureau handled not only postal savings, but the combined operation of postal insurance and post office pensions funds. This had been strongly opposed by the Ministry of Posts and Telecommunications, but in January 1943 the Ministries of Finance and Posts and Telecommunications came to an agreement, and the Deposits Bureau started to manage most of the reserves of postal insurance and post office pensions. This arrangement lasted until after the war in 1952.

13. Figure 2.2 indicates that during the 1980s postal savings accounted for the same high proportion of savings as during the Pacific War, and this was somewhat abnormal historically. Analysis of this phenomenon falls beyond the scope of this chapter, however.

14. As above, see Mukai (1991).

15. See Nakajima (1982: 282).

16. See Bond Underwriters Association (1980).

17. However, Deposits Bureau underwriting of IBJ debentures and Bank of Japan lending to IBJ was common even before the introduction of the wartime system. A total of 36.4% of IBJ debentures issued between 1914 and 1930 were underwritten by the Deposits Bureau. The funds raised by IBJ in this way were used for emergency lending at the time of the Shōwa Crisis and for national policy financing such as investment in the colonial areas, including the so-called Nishihara Loan.

18. 'Borrowed funds' includes those from capital combined banks (calculation based on data from Imuta (1991*b*) and Ministry of Finance (1962)).

19. After the war, the loss generated at the close in 1948 by the assets held by IBJ reached 46.1% of the book price of all assets under the so-called old accounting rules. Because of this fixed burden of loss, it was decided to transfer IBJ debentures held by financial institutions to old accounting rules (meaning no interest would be paid), so that ordinary banks shouldered *ex post facto* a share of wartime financing risk (see IBJ (1982: 115)).

20. 'A Hundred-Year History of the Bank of Japan', vol. 4: 307.

21. There was a period during the 1920s in which the interest rate on government bonds fell below deposit rates. This can be put down to the fact that a system existed under which the Bank of Japan supplied loans to financial institutions using government bonds as collateral, and so government bond holdings became a type of reserve requirement on deposits, and in this situation their interest rates were irrelevant.

22. 'A Hundred-Year History of the Bank of Japan', vol. 4: 352. There was, however, some resistance to this, as shown, for instance, in the fact that the Wartime Finance Bank was created separately from the IBJ.

23. Osamu Itoh (1986) sees the temporary rise in the ratio of net worth during 1955 as

due to the collapse in investment rates. When investment subsequently boomed, the ratio decreased.

24. In the end, the policy board proposal got no further than the setting up of a Bank of Japan Policy Committee which had no real authority.
25. See O. Itoh (1986: 236).
26. The same point is made by Sakakibara and Noguchi (1977) and Cargill and Royama (1991), among others.
27. See IBJ (1982: 206–7). These key industries figured even more prominently in Japan Development Bank lending, accounting for 91.6% of its outstanding loans at the close of FY1955.
28. Put a different way, the arrangement helped in turning short-term funds into long-term funds, which were in short supply (see e.g. Teranishi (1982: 413–17)).
29. 'A Hundred-Year History of the Bank of Japan', vol. 5: 157.
30. See e.g. Itoh and Ueda (1982). It has also been claimed that interest rates were not necessarily too low, however. A recent example is Horiuchi (1993).
31. Direct finance through corporate bonds was restricted, and through this measures were adopted to protect IBJ and other long-term financial institutions issuing bank debentures (see Iwata (1982)).
32. Capital allocation by means other than the price mechanism requires suspending arbitrage with overseas markets. To do this, a further Foreign Exchange Control Law was enacted in 1949. An example of intervention on the part of the authorities for direct capital allocation is the system often utilized until around 1950 of loan facilitation arranged by the Bank of Japan (see 'A Hundred-Year History of the Bank of Japan', vol. 6).
33. It is not my intention to suggest that current Japanese policy to maintain stability is ideal.

References

Bank of Japan, *Nihon Ginkō Hyakunen Shi* (A Hundred-Year History of the Bank of Japan).
——Statistics Bureau (1966), *Meiji Ikō: Honpō Shuyō Keizai Tōkei* (Main Economic Indicators of Japan since the Meiji Period).
Bond Underwriters Association (1980), *Nihon Kōshasai Shijō Shi* (The History of the Japanese Bond Market), University of Tokyo Press.
Cargill, T. F. and S. Royama (1991), 'The Evolution of Japanese Banking and Finance', in Kaufman (ed.), *Banking Structures in Major Countries*, Kluwer Academic Publishers, Boston.
Horiuchi, A. (1993), 'Government Control of Financial Mechanisms in Japan', unpublished manuscript, University of Tokyo.
Imuta, T. (1991*a*), 'Dainiji Taisenki no Kin'yū Kōzō (The Japanese Financial System during the Second World War)', in T. Imuta (ed.), *Senji Taiseika no Kin'yū Kōzō* (The Wartime Financial System), Nihon Hyōronsha.
——(1991*b*), 'Nihon Kōgyō Ginkō to Senji Kin'yū Kinko (The Industrial Bank of Japan and the Wartime Finance Bank)', in T. Imuta (ed.), *Senji Taiseika no Kin'yū Kōzō* (The Wartime Financial System), Nihon Hyōronsha.

Industrial Bank of Japan (1957), *Nihon Kōgyō Ginkō no 50-nen Shi* (Fifty-Year History of the Industrial Bank of Japan).

——(1982), *Nihon Kōgyō Ginkō no 75-nen Shi* (Seventy-Five-Year History of the Industrial Bank of Japan).

Itoh, M. (1989), *Nihon no Taigai Kin'yū to Kin'yū Seisaku* (Capital Flows and Japanese Monetary Policy), Nagoya University Press.

Itoh, O. (1983, 1984), 'Senji Kin'yū Saihensei: sono Sōten to Tenkai (Reconstruction of the Japanese Financial System during the War: Issues and Developments)', *Kin'yū Keizai*, 203, 204.

——(1986), 'Sengo Nihon Kin'yū Shisutemu no Keisei (Formation of the Japanese Financial System in the Post-war Period)', *Kanryōsei no Keisei to Tenkai*, Yamakawa Shuppansha.

Itoh, T. and K. Ueda (1982), 'Kashidashi Kinri no Kakaku Kinō ni tsuite (On the Flexibility of Bank Lending Rates)', *Kikan Riron Keizaigaku*, 33(1).

Iwata, K. (1982), 'Kisai Chōsei ni kansuru Shomondai (On the Rationing of the Issuance of Corporate Bonds)', *Jōchi Keizai Ronshū*, 29(2).

Ministry of Finance, Shōwa Zaiseishi Henshūshitsu (1962), *Shōwa Zaiseishi* (The History of Japanese Fiscal Policy in the Showa Period), vol. 12, Tōyō Keizai Shinpō-sha.

Ministry of Finance, Daijin Kanbō Chōsa Kikakuka (1978), *Bunshō Senji Zaisei Kin'yū Shi* (The History of Wartime Fiscal Policy), Ōkura Zaimu Kyōkai.

Mukai, M. (1991), 'Yokinbu Kan'i Seimeihoken Shikin no Dōin (On the Utilization of the Funds of the Trust Fund Bureau and Postal Insurance)', in T. Imuta (ed.), *Senji Taiseika no Kin'yū Kōzō* (The Wartime Financial System), Nihon Hyōronsha.

Nakajima, M. (1982), 'Kin'yū Shijō ni Okeru Yokinbu no Kinō Henka (The Changing Role of the Trust Fund Bureau in the Financial Markets)', in Nakamura, Cho, and Tamanoi (eds.), *Senkanki no Tsūka to Kin'yū*, Yuhikaku.

Quick Research Institute (1993), *Tōkyō Kin'yū Shihon Shijō Tōmeika Kokusaika Kaigi: Hōkokusho* (Report of the Committee on Making the Tokyo Money and Financial Markets More International and Transparent).

Sakakibara, H. and Y. Noguchi, (1977), 'Ōkurashō, Nichigin Ōchō no Bunseki—Sōryokusen Keizai Taisei no Shūen (Analysis of the Dynasty of the Ministry of Finance and Bank of Japan: An Economic System for Total War Draws to an End)', *Chūō Kōron*, August.

Shikano, Y. (1992), 'Wagakuni no Senkanki ni Okeru Ginkō Toritsuke no Makuro Keizai Bunseki (Macroeconomic Analysis of Bank Runs in Japan during the Inter-war Period)', unpublished manuscript, Bank of Japan Institute for Monetary and Economic Studies.

Shimura, Y. (1969), *Nihon Shihon Shijō Bunseki* (The Japanese Capital Market), University of Tokyo Press.

Takagi, S. (1989), 'Senkanki Nihon Keizai to Hendō Kawase Sōba (Flexible Exchange Rates and the Japanese Economy during the Inter-war Period)', *Kin'yū Kenkyū*.

Takasugi, R. (1986), *Shōsetsu Nihon Kōgyō Ginkō* (The Industrial Bank of Japan), Kadokawa Shoten.

Teranishi, J. (1982), *Nihon no Keizai Hatten to Kin'yū* (Finance and Japanese Economic Development), Iwanami Shoten.

Yoshino, N. and A. Furukawa (1991), *Kin'yū Jiyūka to Kōteki Kin'yū* (Financial Liberalization and Public Financial Institutions), Nihon Hyōronsha.

3

The Main Bank System

Juro Teranishi

1. Introduction

There is no single agreed definition of the term 'main bank', but in cases where a number of banks have made loans to a particular firm, it generally refers to the bank that has a particularly long and continuous record of business relations with the firm and has advanced the largest loans. In some cases a comprehensive range of business dealings, including shareholdings and directorships in the firm, and handling its pensions and financial settlements, are considered the characteristics of a main bank. Currently many firms in Japan have this sort of special relationship (though not always of the same type) with their 'main bank', and the arrangement is said to serve a variety of beneficial functions with regard to monitoring the firm, spreading associated risks, and so on. The link between Japan's post-war economic success and Japanese-style firms has long since been pointed out. The distinctive features of these firms are summed up in the long-term, harmonious relations that exist between the different levels within each firm, and between firms that do business together. The main bank system is regarded as a fundamental component of this so-called Japan-style capitalism.[1] The issue dealt with in this chapter is how and when the main bank system came about through the long process of Japan's economic development.

The significance of the main bank system to the economic development process is based on the assumption that capital circulation through the banks is relatively more important than other capital flows such as through the stock market, and that bank-sponsored monitoring and control of a firm's activities are relatively more important than those of the shareholders. Thus, to understand the process by which the main bank concept was born and developed, we must first note the changes to the relative roles of direct and indirect financing in capital circulation in the economy, and second, the changes that have occurred in the corporate monitoring system as a whole.

In relating the main bank system to the matter of direct and indirect financing, I see the financial system as being 'three-dimensional'. The first dimension measures the degree to which market mechanisms function or

government intervention exists, the second represents the practice of direct as
against indirect financing, and the third is the nature of the corporate monitoring system. In this chapter I will focus on the nature of the corporate
monitoring system within the changes to the financial system as a whole that
the interaction of these three 'dimensions' has brought about. The dimensions
are not independent of one another, and change in one impels change in the
others. They also complement one another in systemic complementary relationships. Thus, any consideration of changes to the corporate monitoring
system alone would not allow an adequate grasp of how the system came
about and developed.

Next, to understand the main bank system as part of the corporate monitoring system, the latter must be seen in terms of its multi-layered relationships:
relations between different levels within the firm, relations between the firm
and its banks, and relations between the banks and government agencies. This
is because corporate monitoring undertaken by banks within the main bank
system has an important distinctive feature. It functions not merely within the
usual lender–borrower type of relationship common wherever neo-classical-
type shareholder authority exists, but in an environment where shareholder
authority is not absolute, that is to say, where executives do not necessarily
always act to maximize shareholders' profits.

The approach to be used in this chapter can be alternatively summed up as
follows. The main bank system is regarded as one part of a broadly defined
corporate monitoring system that includes relations between government
agencies and banks as well as relations between different levels within the firm.
This broadly defined system has itself effected long-term changes within
the development of the financial system as a whole that have involved those
two other dimensions of the system, market versus government and direct
versus indirect financing. The birth and development of the main bank system
can thus be understood through relating it to changes in the corporate monitoring system that have occurred within the changes to the financial system
overall.

In the second section of this chapter, the role of the main bank system in
present-day Japan is briefly examined, and shown to be a consistent feature of
the wartime and post-war periods. The third section gives an outline of the
corporate monitoring system in the pre-war financial system, roughly up to
the mid-1930s. The fourth section examines the process by which the pre-war
financial system was completely transformed in adapting the economy for war,
and an embryonic main bank system was created in the form of loan syndicates, in response to the growing autonomy of corporate executives. The
process is examined by which, following corporate principles advocated under
the New Economic System by radical officials, the main bank system became
gradually more institutionalized, first in the form of emergency loan consortia,
and then as a system of designated financial institutions lending to munitions

industries. The fifth section deals with the struggle over corporate governance in the post-war period, showing how the level of government intervention increased and indirect financing took precedence, and it explains how the post-war main bank system became established within these developments in the financial system.

This analysis has two important implications. The first is that the main bank system is a product of the impact of history on economic realities at a particular stage of development. That is, in the process of adapting the financial system to meet the needs of rapid technological input and the changing industrial structure that came with the development of heavy industry, and through the effect of various external 'shocks' linked to wartime economic controls and post-war reforms, a main bank system was created which was both very Japanese and pro-growth. In explaining how this system came into being, recognition of the equal relevance of both the developmental stage and the external 'shocks' is vital for a well-balanced understanding. The legacy of the wartime controls certainly played a role in the formation of the system, but it forms only one part of the whole mechanism. The post-war financial system was moulded into shape by development-minded government agencies that regarded catching up with the West as their paramount mission, and the view that the main bank system formed part of this process is again incomplete. Even if we accept that bureaucratic aspirations for economic development were highly influential at a certain developmental stage, the process by which the post-war financial system came about cannot be discussed without including the major role played by external 'shocks'.

The second implication relates to the fact that the main bank system, a feature of Japanese-style corporate life, is in a tight, mutually dependent relationship with another characteristic of Japanese firms, their excessively competitive behaviour bent on maximizing their market share. The fully fledged post-war main bank system teams up with two other features of the economy, bank administration undertaken by government officials, and corporate governance undertaken by managements, to form the corporate monitoring system. The so-called convoy method used in bank administration stressed conformity, and the size of banks' deposits was used as a criterion in administrative guidance. Because of this, banks encouraged crossholdings of shares between the firms with which they had dealings and sought to build up a network of depositors. They also monitored firms in such a way as to maximize their sales turnover, which would boost deposits. For corporate managements, it was easier to comply with the banks' requirements because they were freed of the need to maximize shareholders' short-term profits through greater crossholdings of shares. Either way, this can be seen as one reason for the excessively competitive orientation of Japanese firms in the post-war period, and it should be remembered that Japanese-style corporate behaviour is closely tied to the workings of the financial system.

2. The role of main banks in the present-day Japanese system

The functions of the main bank system can be summarized in the following three points:[2]

1. *Reducing agency costs of external liabilities.* As shareholders' liability is limited, shareholders or executives may be tempted when borrowing to select a project with higher risks (and the potential for higher profits) than the contracted project. As long as such temptations exist, lenders will demand higher rates of interest to cover this possibility. Under the supervision of a main bank, however, contracts are honoured and so interest is kept low. This difference in interest means a reduction in agency costs for the shareholder/executive. For firms not exposed to moral hazard, main bank supervision prevents the occurrence of social costs in the form of distortions in resource allocation brought about by high interest rates.

2. *Risk sharing.* The main bank acts as a tacit insurer for the firm, taking actions such as lowering interest rates at times when performance is poor. If the firm should be threatened with bankruptcy, the main bank shoulders the costs by buying up defaulted loans and so on, and mediates in negotiations with other creditors.

3. *Syndicate loans.* For large loans, the main bank arranges a syndicate, and spreads the risk by involving a number of banks in lending to the firm.

Whether or not these functions are in reality all fulfilled has been the subject of much ongoing research. On agency costs, firms with main banks have easy access to external financing, which allows them to undertake long-term investment activities without suffering the restrictions of internal financing. The studies of Hoshi *et al.* (1990, 1991) provide analysis of the relationship between firms' investment activities and main banks from this viewpoint, and a largely affirmative conclusion has been reached. On risk sharing, research has been undertaken from the standpoint that if the main bank is providing insurance cover to the firm, a positive correlation should occur between operating profits and financial costs over a period of time. Horiuchi and Fukuda (1987) reached a negative conclusion on this, while Hirota (1989) reached an affirmative one. On syndicate loans, a recent study undertaken by Kato *et al.* (1992) suggested that a theoretical inconsistency exists between two virtually indisputable facts relating to main banks: the long-term nature of the main bank relationship, and the firm's behaviour in borrowing from multiple lenders. The long-term relationship is built on the premise that other banks do not benefit from a 'free ride' in gaining access to the main bank's privileged information. In reality, however, large numbers of banks participate in lending and do indeed appear to get a 'free ride'. The study suggested that to avoid this dilemma, this sort of lending can be regarded as a syndicated loan with the objective of spreading risk.

If these views on main bank functions are largely correct, then the existence of main banks in Japan could be an important factor explaining Japan's capital-investment-led growth through reduced risk premiums, etc. The reduction of agency costs has the potential to boost efficiency by correcting the distortions in resource allocation that they bring about. Furthermore, the long-term relationship between firm and bank that the main bank relationship promotes can have a multiplying effect in encouraging further long-term relationships in dealings with other firms and among the different levels within the firm, and thus may be closely involved in the good performance of so-called Japanese-style firms.

The importance of these main bank functions rests on the assumption that in Japan the flow of funds through banks, or so-called indirect financing, figures very significantly. In contrast to this, in what are known as Anglo-American-style economies, which are heavily reliant on direct financing, takeovers and shareholders' meetings are the major tools of corporate control. It has been pointed out, however, that corporate control through shareholders has serious shortcomings in a number of respects (Stiglitz 1985). The first is that shareholders' general meetings do not function adequately. Shareholders cannot be expected to vote intelligently at general meetings because the benefits to be gained from doing so may well fall far short of the costs of obtaining the information required to do so. This is particularly true in the case of small shareholders. Furthermore, shareholders' meetings tend to be strongly influenced by the intentions of the executive management, which has an absolute advantage in terms of information. Second, takeovers do not function effectively for the following reasons. First, since information is asymmetrical in nature, insiders are better informed and the takeover will only succeed if the purchaser pays a higher than necessary price to persuade insiders to release their shares. Similarly, due to the nature of information as a public good, takeovers cannot be accomplished easily except in cases where the takeover will lower the value of the firm. This is because, on the news of a takeover other shareholders will not release their shares in expectation of a rise in the value of the firm. Takeovers also signal certain information about the quality of the target firm, and this may attract other potential purchasers, which in turn will push up the share price and increase the cost of the takeover.

Of course, shareholders can function reasonably effectively in cases where a small number of large shareholders with sizeable stakes have the right of control (Schleifer and Vishny 1986). But the problem remains as to how to concentrate enough of the shares to fulfil this condition.

The expression 'main bank' is Japanese-manufactured English. The fact that a similar expression 'Hausbank' is used in Germany, another country that was a late-starter in development, offers a clue as to how main banks came about. In Germany, as in post-war Japan, banks have taken on the task of providing long-term investment funds, acting as industrial rather than commercial banks. This corresponds to the fact that main banks in Japan can be traced back as far as the 1930s but no further. Thus main banks appeared as industrialization was nearing a second import-substitution phase, during the period that spawned rapid development of heavy industry. As the lack of long-term capital and corporate information became more and more pronounced, firms turned increasingly to bank credit, while for the banks, the overall trend towards greater management autonomy generated a need to spread risk through loan syndication and to monitor managements. The system that these internal circumstances engineered turned out to be the main bank system. The concept appeared in embryonic form in the war period of the late 1930s, as the industrial structure was forcibly realigned towards priority industries, and the system became firmly established around 1950, when Japan was suffering the after-effects of defeat.

3. Corporate monitoring in the pre-war period

To show how the main bank system had its origins in the wartime economy of the late 1930s, I will give a brief outline of the corporate monitoring system from the Meiji period to the early years of Shōwa.[3]

3.1. The Meiji period

From the viewpoint of corporate monitoring, the Meiji period was basically a time of internal financing relying on shares and accumulated funds, and as large shareholders provided adequate leadership, agency costs did not pose many problems.

It is well known that the *zaibatsu* were backed by considerable internal funds as the result of having highly profitable sectors such as mining and overseas trade under their control, and they expanded through reinvestment of these internal savings. On the other hand, the various industries outside *zaibatsu* control, of which cotton spinning and railways are typical examples, were dependent on an internal-financing mechanism in which financing was provided using shareholders' stock as collateral. The usual behaviour of the merchants and landowners who formed the core of the wealthy at that time was to borrow from the banks using shareholdings as collateral, and reinvest the funds in further shares. To support this stock-secured financing from private-sector banks, the Bank of Japan financed the banks the same way, lending to them using the stock of firms such as Nippon Yūsen and the marine-insurance and leading railway companies as collateral. Looking at a breakdown by collateral of the state banks' lending in 1895, which was made mostly to the private-sector banks, we find government bonds accounting for 9.6 per cent, stock certificates 42.9 per cent, land and property 14.0 per cent, grain 3.8 per cent, miscellaneous goods 12.0 per cent, and credit 17.7 per cent, indicating that nearly half was stock-secured financing. A breakdown of lending by type of business for the same year gives farmers 5.2 per cent, industrialists 0.7 per cent, merchants 43.9 per cent, companies 4.8 per cent, and others 45.0 per cent, suggesting that firms hardly borrowed from banks and the bulk of bank lending was made to individuals, particularly merchants. Through borrowing, the merchants expanded their business and invested further in shares.

Most industries outside the *zaibatsu* depended largely on this internal financing from stock-secured lending, and this resulted in extremely low internal accumulation rates. This was because shareholders required firms to pay exceptionally high dividends to cover their interest payments to the banks. Thus, while they both were dependent on internal financing, there was a vast difference between *zaibatsu* and non-*zaibatsu* firms in terms of internal accumulation of funds.

In *zaibatsu* firms, the *zaibatsu* families imposed extremely tight control over management, but otherwise, shareholders' meetings and corporate takeovers are generally said to have fulfilled the function of effective management control. According to Kataoka (1988), large shareholders took the lead at shareholders' meetings, and they managed to get unanimous agreements from minority shareholders, even on contentious issues such as mergers, through their powers of persuasion. On this period of frequent corporate takeovers, Nagae's research on the cotton-spinning industry is most interesting (Nagae 1981).

3.2. The Taishō and Shōwa periods

From the end of the Meiji period, and particularly from the time of the First World War, Japan entered a period of burgeoning growth of heavy industry. Existing internal-financing mechanisms were unable to raise the required capital, and firms experienced a rapid increase in external capital provision. First, capital was mobilized from large numbers of external shareholders. For example, between 1915 and 1934 the number of shareholders in Tokyo Dentō (Tokyo Public Lighting) increased from 4,300 to 62,300, and the number of shares issued rose from 1,000,000 to 8,591,000. In Nippon Yūsen the number of shareholders rose from 4,200 to 23,700 and the number of shares from 880,000 to 2,125,000. Second, borrowing from banks became widespread, indicating a rise in firms' dependence on external liabilities. A notable feature of this period was the massive growth in firms opening up new banks and entrepreneurs doubling as bank executives or bank shareholders. The banks were called 'institution banks' and caused considerable instability in the financial system at that time.

In terms of market forces as against government intervention, my first dimension of the financial system, this period was characterized by the adequate functioning of market mechanisms. There was a tendency for groups of banks in different regions to conclude agreements on deposit and lending rates, but they were not always strictly adhered to, and because anyone could set up a bank provided they could raise the minimum capital, some twenty or thirty new banks were formed and an equal number collapsed each year. As for the second dimension, the financial system was characterized by a judicious balance between direct and indirect financing. Many firms increased their dependence on borrowing from institution banks, but at the same time the firms affiliated to the old *zaibatsu*, and the new Taishō *zaibatsu*, raised capital actively through share issues, and electric-power companies raised capital through issuing bonds in Japan and overseas. Because of its high credibility and profitability, the spinning industry was able to accumulate internal funds and also obtain short-term funds on the bills discount market at highly favourable terms.

As for the third dimension of the system, the corporate monitoring system, large shareholders maintained their hold over corporate control. But there was a tendency for the large shareholders of this period to join with firms' managements in actions that constituted considerable moral hazard for external capital providers, such as banks and small shareholders. First, false reports of company performance were issued, as a result of which dividends were paid despite the fact no profit had been made. Second, directors were granted large bonuses. In 1928, for instance, 25 out of 62 electric-power companies approved bonuses for directors of as much as 10 per cent of profits, and in 1919 and 1924, the average size of directors' bonuses in 42 companies across the industrial spectrum was 5 per cent of profits. The third problem was the unscrupulous behaviour of directors. There were many cases of directors forcing flourishing firms to merge with firms they themselves owned or to buy them up at inflated prices. They also used 'tunnel' companies to receive commissions for arranging procurement of goods, or manipulated share prices to make windfall profits from price rises (Takahashi 1977).

It was during this period that Kamekichi Takahashi published 'The Joint-Stock Company: A Cause for National Ruin' (1930), in which he decried corruption among managers, and at about the same time, Teijiro Ueda argued the need for 'morals befitting samurai' to match Marshall's 'economic chivalry'.[4]

The reasons for this frequent occurrence of moral hazard constitute an extremely interesting topic. Suffice it to say here that it was in the first instance due to bubble-type speculative trends that started with the boom of the First World War. The 'money game' tendencies that are associated with the early development stages of short-term financial markets were also involved. Second, the rapid introduction of external financing is implicated as increases in numbers of small shareholders and bank loans offered more opportunities for moral hazard. Third, there was the inadequacy of the government's so-called 'prudential regulations'. The Bank of Japan's easy-going provision of emergency financing during the crises of 1920 and 1922 may have aggravated this situation.

In passing, I should perhaps mention that the unreliable management of institution banks provoked a further agency issue at that time: the agency cost resulting from moral hazard in bank managers' and shareholders' treatment of depositors. However, this type of agency cost was all but eliminated in the 1930s through policies implemented under the Banking Act passed at the time of the 1927 financial crisis. These included increasing government supervision of banks by means of a new Bank Relations and Supervision Department (*Kōsa Kyoku*) in the Bank of Japan, and further amalgamations in the banking sector prompted by a substantial increase in the minimum capital requirement and forcefully applied administrative guidance.

4. The emergence of the main bank system during wartime

With the outbreak of the Sino-Japanese War in July 1937, the government began to intervene more actively in the financial system as the economy was adapted for war, and in the course of that process a main bank system was created in embryonic form. At the start of the period, from 1937 to 1940, government intervention targeted funds allocation and set upper limits on dividend rates to allow realignment of the industrial structure and boost production. This was a period that saw a rapid shift to heavy industry, the expansion of munitions-related industries, and sharp growth in the number of national policy enterprises. There was a rise in dependence on external capital brought about by public share offerings, and a decline in large shareholders' corporate control through crossholdings of shares, as well as a growing need for a wider spread of lending because of lending risks and lack of information. Under such circumstances individual banks moved spontaneously to form loan syndicates. The years 1941 and 1942 correspond to the period of peak production. Under the second Konoe Cabinet that took office in July 1940, a 'New Economic System' was advocated and 'co-operative lending groups', or loan consortia, were incorporated into a control mechanism operated by the National Finance Control Association. This became an instrument for the running of the planned economy under the New Economic System. At the end of the period, after 1943, production levels began a gradual decline, and so direct regulations on production were used to force an industrial realignment giving priority to industries directed towards weapons production. After the Munitions Corporations Law brought in direct corporate control, the National Finance Control Association's facilitation system for lending and bond flotation was converted into a government-authorized main bank system that took the form of designated lending for munitions funding.

4.1. Wartime control of the financial system

First, let us analyse the situation from the outbreak of the Sino-Japanese War to the end of 1940 or thereabouts. Financial controls largely took the form of regulating funds allocation.

1. *September 1937: Emergency Funds Adjustment Law (Rinji Shikin Chōsei Hō)*. Regulation of equipment funds above a fixed level for industries related to the Production Capacities Expansion Plan and weapons production (particularly aircraft), to boost munitions production; and regulation of subscription for stocks and bonds of those industries.

2. *September 1939: Corporate Profits, Dividends and Capital Accommodation Directive (Kaisha Rieki Haitō Oyobi Shikin Yūzū Rei)*. Upper limits were set on dividend rates of firms above a certain size, and a command financing system for the Industrial Bank of Japan (IBJ) was introduced.

3. *October 1940: Bank Funds Operating Directive (Ginkōtō Shisan Unyō Rei)*. The provisions of the Emergency Funds Adjustment Law were extended to cover operating capital, and the command financing system was widened to apply to all banks.

These regulations on the financial system and parallel regulations on the labour market and on foreign trade brought about major changes to the industrial structure, as shown in Table 3.1. While consumer-oriented light industries such as foodstuffs, textiles, and wood products all saw significant declines in their share of bank lending, employment, and production, the equivalent shares of heavy industries, particularly machinery, rose sharply. Production indices for mining and heavy industry, as well as GNP, peaked in 1942, and in overall terms the regulations of the period brought about rapid industrial realignment as production expanded.

In the period before and immediately after the outbreak of the Pacific War production expanded steadily, and methods to switch to a planned economy were adopted to realign the industrial base. In other words, a command system to enforce the planned economy (Okazaki 1991) was incorporated by radical officials on the Planning Board (*Kikakuin*), through an iterative method that used the control associations of the different industries to provide information. Financial institutions complied with controls on capital absorption and asset management in line with national policy.

1. *August 1941: Major Industrial Associations Directive (Jūyō Sangyō Dantai Rei)*. This legislation set up control associations for each of the industrial associations, to play a central role in collecting information and issuing

Table 3.1. Distribution of production resources and output in manufacturing sector (%)

	Proportion of labour force			Proportion of outstanding loans from financial institutions			Proportion of output by value (1934–6 prices)			
	1932	1937	1941	1940 (June)	1941 (Feb.)	1945 (Mar.)	1932	1937	1941	1945
Foodstuffs	14.2	10.5	8.0	4.0	3.8	1.5	19.9	15.1	12.2	17.8
Textiles	39.7	30.7	20.3	18.4	15.0	7.0	32.6	29.3	14.7	4.6
Timber and wood products	7.2	6.8	7.2	—	—	—	3.2	2.6	3.0	3.0
Chemicals	7.1	9.7	8.9	14.4	14.6	11.8	13.3	17.2	17.5	11.6
Ceramics	3.8	4.1	3.8	2.0	1.9	0.9	2.4	2.6	2.6	1.8
Iron and steel	6.0	8.6	9.0	16.4	17.6	13.9	8.4	9.4	12.6	12.4
Non-ferrous metals							3.8	3.1	2.9	5.5
Machinery	11.3	20.3	35.5	30.8	36.7	60.2	9.7	14.4	30.2	40.8
Printing	4.4	3.0	2.3	—	—	—	3.0	2.3	1.9	1.0
Gas and electricity	—	—	—	10.9	8.0	2.3	—	—	—	—
Others	5.8	5.7	5.2	2.3	2.4	2.4	3.5	3.4	1.0	1.5
Total	99.5	99.4	97.2	99.2	100.0	100.0	99.8	99.4	98.6	100.0

Sources: Labour-force data from *Chōki Keizai Tōkei* (Long-Term Economic Statistics), vol. 2: *Rōdōryoku* (Manpower), Table 19; outstanding loan data from Bank of Japan, *Senjichū Kin'yū Tōkei Yōran* (Wartime Financial Statistics), Table 28; output data from Ohkawa and Shinohara (1979), *Patterns of Japanese Economic Development*, Yale University Press, Table A–21.

instructions for the Planning Board-initiated switch to a planned economy. In November 1941 nine control associations were designated, including the Iron and Steel Control Association, and the policy was extended to cover a further range of businesses in August 1942.

2. *April 1942: Finance Control Association Directive (Kin'yū Tōsei Dantai Rei)*. Lending operations were put under the centralized supervision of the National Finance Control Association, and banks were encouraged to merge in order to strengthen their capacity to collect funds and lower their capital costs.

3. *February 1942: Revision of the Bank of Japan Act (Nippon Ginkō Hō)*. Following the example of Nazi Germany's Bundesbank, central bank independence was abolished, and the Bank of Japan's mission was made the fulfilment of state objectives. A system to control the currency was also introduced.

From the spring of 1943, however, losses in shipping tonnage caused a decline in imports of goods and raw materials, resulting in a downturn in production. These circumstances led to further realignment of production to give priority to munitions. The Planning Board was abolished in October 1943, and under the Munitions Corporations Law, a new Ministry of Munitions set up in November 1943 administered direct control over production to promote munitions production, particularly that of aircraft. Corresponding control of the financial system was instituted.

1. *October 1943: Munitions Corporations Law (Gunju Kaisha Hō)*. Under this legislation, direct control over production was imposed and specific private-sector firms were designated for munitions production. Initially 150 and ultimately around 600 firms were affected. Where ministerial approval had been granted, the agreement of shareholders was not needed, and in this and other respects, such as in their right to refuse access to information, shareholders' rights were drastically curtailed.

2. *January 1944: System to Designate Financial Institutions for Munitions Funding (Gunju Yūshi Shitei Kin'yū Kikan Seidō)*. For the smoother provision of funds, a single 'main bank' was designated for each munitions-related firm.

3. *March 1945: Special Measures for Munitions Funding Law (Gunju Kin'yūtō Tokubetsu Sochi Hō)*. This law introduced a system to designate a particular financing institution to firms other than munitions firms.

4.2. 1937 to July 1941: the birth of the main bank system in the form of loan consortia

The regulation of funds allocation and external capital brought about by the shift to a wartime economy also prompted major changes in the corporate monitoring system. We shall examine first the period up to July 1941, and then the subsequent period.

An interesting phenomenon that occurred in the period up to July 1941 was the spontaneous formation after 1939 of a number of 'co-operative lending groups', or loan consortia. A detailed Tokyo Banks Association survey entitled 'Current Situation in Joint Investment Financing' (published 5 April 1942)[5] indicates that the number of loan consortia at the end of June 1941 was 130, and 113 firms benefited. The lending involved totalled ¥1.724 billion, accounting for 14 per cent of the total lending of ¥15.695 billion by the member financial institutions. In a separate study (Teranishi 1992*a*) I looked at various breakdowns of these 113 firms and reached the following conclusions:

1. A breakdown of the firms by the lead bank revealed that the vast majority of consortia were led by the Industrial Bank of Japan, which headed consortia lending to 70 firms. Other banks led consortia for 16 firms, trust banks for 22 firms, and so on.

2. Classified by type of firm, the largest group, of 39, were national policy enterprises, and of the remainder, 14 were old *zaibatsu* firms, 12 were new *zaibatsu* firms. Eight of the 14 old *zaibatsu* firms were related to the Mitsui *zaibatsu*, such as centrally placed Mitsui Kōzan and Mitsui Bussan, and the large affiliated firms Kanegafuchi Bōseki and Toshiba.

3. A breakdown by size showed that 12 of the firms were ranked among the top 100 in the heavy-industrial sector, and 14 firms ranked among the top 50 public-utilities firms.[6]

4. By industrial sector, there were four firms in foodstuffs, nine in textiles, 18 in chemicals, including paper and pulp, 13 in metals, 14 in machinery, 13 in transport and communications, 17 in electric power, six in mining, and so on. Thus, not only heavy industry but many light-industrial firms benefited from syndicate loans.

5. The average number of financial institutions participating in a syndicate was 6.9. For the top 10 firms the average was 17.0 and for national policy enterprises it was 10.4, indicating that many institutions were co-operating in this lending. There were also a higher-than-average 8.7 institutions in syndicates headed by the Industrial Bank of Japan.

This data suggests some fundamental reasons for the spontaneous formation of large numbers of loan consortia during this period. The principal reason for setting up these loan consortia or, if you like, the establishment of an embryonic main bank system, can be considered to be the spread of risk.

The outbreak of full-scale war in Europe in 1939 and the Tripartite Pact signed the following year led to widespread nervousness during this period, and many banks became noticeably more cautious in their lending activities. This is clear from Table 3.2, which shows the growth in lending by ordinary banks. After rapid growth in 1938, 1939, and into 1940, there was a significant

Table 3.2. Ordinary banks' lending

	Increase in outstanding loans (¥m.)	Loans (¥m.) (1)	Number of loan accounts ('000) (2)	(1)/(2)
1935	259	5,313	992	5.4
1936	571	5,688	1,031	5.5
1937	1,029	6,533	967	6.8
1938	1,057	7,485	917	8.2
1939	2,502	9,531	847	11.3
1940	2,488	12,284	769	16.0
1941	1,640	—	—	—
1942	2,639	—	—	—
1943	4,588	—	—	—

Source: Goto, Shinichi (1973), *Nihon no Kin'yū Tōkei* (Japanese Financial Statistics), Toyo Keizai Shinpō-sha, Tables 30–2, 58–3.

contraction between 1940 and 1941. Moreover, rapid industrial realignment brought about a doubling in average lending to individual clients between 1938 and the end of 1940, from ¥8,200 to ¥16,000.

Under these circumstances, the banks were naturally reluctant to make single large loans. It was mentioned earlier that among the old *zaibatsu*, the formation of loan consortia was most noticeable in the Mitsui group, and this can be easily understood in view of the relative decline in Mitsui Bank's capacity to collect deposits, against growing demands for large loans. From the beginning of the 1930s, Mitsui Bank had seen a remarkable growth in deposits compared with other major banks, but this was now blunted. This is in part put down to the bank's small network of branches,[7] although Mitsubishi Bank, with roughly the same number of branches, was experiencing rapid growth in deposits. Most probably, the major reason was that the Mitsui Group was late in moving into the heavy-industrial sector, as shown by the fact that the group was not able to bring Toshiba directly into the *zaibatsu* group.[8] Thus, the bank could not benefit from the enormous network of deposits that this sector generated. Mitsui Bank announced total deposits of ¥1.589 billion at the end of 1940, against syndicate loans of the order of ¥180 million to Mitsui Kōzan (jointly financed by Mitsui Bank, Mitsui Trust Bank, and IBJ), ¥36 million to Tōyō Kōatsu (as above), and ¥100 million to Mitsui Bussan (Mitsui Bank, Sumitomo Bank and Daiichi Bank). The situation was such that 'absorbing government bonds, providing construction capital for Manchuria, and then meeting the funding demands of wartime industries, and covering the financing of affiliated firms is already beyond what any single bank is capable of achieving'.[9]

In addition, rapid industrial realignment meant that the banks had to deal with new borrowers with whom they had no previous business relations, and lack of information on these borrowers heightened the need to spread the associated risk.

This problem of lack of information was particularly serious with regard to the national policy enterprises. They grew quickly in number, from 27 in 1937 at the start of the war, to 154 at the end of June 1941. Many were involved in investment financing in the colonial areas, and only a few, such as the Manchurian Railways, were in profit and paying a dividend. Not only were many of them running deficits, but some also refused to disclose corporate information on the grounds of national defence, and so lending became an extremely risky venture. Even so, banks were obliged to lend to these firms as a gesture of co-operating in national policy. Moreover, the food and textile industries that benefited from syndicate loans, as I indicated earlier, included many marketing and exporting associations, and funding these low-priority industries (or 'sacrificed industries') also required a considerable spread of risk.

A second reason for the appearance of loan consortia at this point in time was the broad trend towards a weakening of shareholders' control and growing management autonomy. Loan consortia became necessary because they provided a means to monitor managements, and in this sense, the loan consortia of that period resembled the main bank system of the post-war period. The following evidence testifies to this.

First, in terms of the need for external funds, the *zaibatsu* internal-financing mechanisms were inadequate. From 1930 *zaibatsu* shares were increasingly made available on the open market as a measure to counter widespread criticism. It has been shown that in the course of that process, there was rapid growth in crossholdings of shares between firms within each group.[10] Second, as has often been noted before, the *zaibatsu* style of control within each group weakened, and the managements of the individual firms grew more independent. Third, new *zaibatsu* groups grew quickly, riding the wave of heavy industrialization in the 1930s, and many of them did not follow the pattern of the old family asset-based *zaibatsu* but diversified their business on the basis of managerial control. At almost all the new firms apart from Nihon Chisso, a mechanism to control management through the active introduction of external capital was adopted.

These circumstances suggest the possibility that with managements becoming increasingly independent, a need had been gradually developing for monitoring through banks even before July 1941. However, in the period after August 1941, managements became considerably more powerful as actions taken by the state reduced shareholders' rights and strengthened management control. An official joint-lending system was set up, but under it banks were not able to supervise firms' managements and could act only as pipes to channel in funds, subordinate to the requirements of the munitions-related firms.

4.3. August 1941 to the end of the war: from joint lending groups to a system of designated financial institutions for munitions funding

In August 1941 the loan consortia formed between 1939 and 1941 were 'formalized' within the private sector under a newly established Emergency Joint Lending Group, made up of the top ten ordinary banks and the IBJ (the five leading trust banks joined later). Then in May 1942 the National Finance Control Association (*Zenkoku Kin'yū Tōsei Kai*) was formed on the basis of the Finance Control Association Directive (*Kin'yū Tōsei Dantai Rei*) that had come into force the previous month. More and more of the lending and mediation of joint-lending groups came under the supervision of this highly active Control Association, so that in fact in 1942 most lending was routed through the association. For commercial banks, participating in joint lending was an important strategy to find new customers for loans, and they are said to have contested fiercely over lending shares. Some firms and banks had business relations that dated back to the pre-war period, but many more new relations were forged during this period. In view of the heated competition for lending shares, the Bank of Japan tried to ensure through its branches that banks participated properly in joint lending. They were discouraged from monopolizing business with their established client firms, and urged to allow other banks to join in lending.[11]

In the final period of the war, the Munitions Corporations Law of October 1943 marked the switch from a planned economy to one of greater direct state intervention in production. In line with this, a system of designating specific financial institutions for munitions funding was introduced within the joint-lending system, leading to major changes in the way joint lending was conducted. Formerly, funding was divided between the members of the group and each bank made the appropriate loan under its own name, but now funding was concentrated on the lead bank, in whose name the loan was made. Under the Munitions Corporations Law, managements were granted full authority, and provided they had ministerial approval, their decisions did not require their shareholders' agreement, nor were they obliged to disclose corporate information. So banks were in effect forced to lend at the bidding of managements and the bank-monitoring function was virtually paralysed (Hoshi *et al.* 1991). Under the Special Measures for Munitions Funding Law of March 1945 this system was extended to cover ordinary firms as well, and a new one-firm-one-bank arrangement was introduced, making the supervision system all the more functional.

In designating banks to fund individual munitions-related firms, consideration was given to 'previous lending performance, business links, investment relations, and the bank's ability to raise funds', according to a Bank of Japan document dated 17 January 1944. Existing joint-financing groups were in most cases absorbed just as they were into new 'munitions funding co-operative groups' with their lead bank becoming the designated bank.[12]

4.4. Changes to the financial system and
their effect on the corporate monitoring system

I would now like to examine in outline the wartime changes to the financial system as a whole, and consider their links to the development of the corporate monitoring system.

Needless to say, in terms of my first dimension of market forces as against government intervention, the wartime financial system was characterized by very heavy government intervention. This was initially directed, as I have shown, towards regulating the distribution of funds, and later tightened regulations restricting the power of shareholders over corporate managements. Restrictions on shareholders' powers accorded with the 'Outline to Establish a New Economic System' (*Keizai Shin Taisei Kakuritsu Yōkō*) of December 1940 and closely reflected the views on the corporate sector held by the radical officials active largely in the Planning Board (Okazaki 1991). That these views reached their zenith in the corporate system instigated under the Munitions Corporations Law needs no further repetition here.

In terms of indirect as against direct financing, there was a rapid rise in the proportion of indirect financing, and data on the procurement of corporate funds, shown in Table 3.3, attests to this. The proportion of borrowing from private-sector financial institutions grew rapidly in 1939 and 1944, and the corresponding proportion raised through shares (as well as internal reserves) dropped. The changes in 1939 can be put down to the introduction of limits on dividend rates resulting from the Corporate Profits, Dividends and Capital Accommodation Directive. The changes in 1944 reflect the restrictions on shareholders' powers imposed by the Munitions Corporations Law.

So how do these changes to the first and second dimensions of the financial system relate to changes to the corporate monitoring system, the third dimension? Regulations on dividends and shareholders' powers may be regarded as having expanded the role of indirect financing, and the increased proportion of indirect financing gave managements greater room for manœuvre free of shareholders. Moreover, we should not overlook the fact that, independently of direct policy measures imposed by radical bureaucrats, the long-term trend towards greater management autonomy had the long-lasting effect of diminishing the role of the stock market. During the war, the main bank system developed basically in the form of loan consortia, propelled by the need to spread the risk attendant on the rapid realignment of industry. The impact of the subsequent intervention of radical officials into corporate organization and the stock market transformed the system into something substantially different, a system of designated financial institutions. Corporate managements came under strict administrative supervision of their production, but securing independence from shareholders was a fundamental precondition for this. These developments were played out against a background of an overall long-term weakening of shareholders' rights, rooted in a swing against capital-

Table 3.3. Breakdown of funds procurement in private-sector firms (%)

	Stocks	Bonds	Borrowings from private financial institutions	Borrowings of government finance	BOJ advances in foreign bills	Internal reserves
1931	34.0	11.7	-3.2	11.3	0.0	46.2
1932	22.0	16.7	-54.3	-3.9	0.0	119.7
1933	31.1	-4.0	-40.4	8.0	0.0	105.2
1934	55.4	2.9	-11.4	-1.6	0.0	54.8
1935	32.9	1.1	14.9	-0.5	0.0	51.6
1936	33.5	-2.3	18.3	0.3	0.0	47.4
1937	35.5	-0.1	31.9	-2.1	0.0	33.3
1938	34.6	5.4	29.9	-0.3	0.0	30.5
1939	24.5	7.9	38.4	2.1	0.0	27.2
1940	26.7	5.5	38.3	1.0	0.0	30.4
1941	29.1	10.1	28.1	-0.9	0.0	33.6
1942	25.7	8.9	32.9	1.4	0.0	31.2
1943	22.6	7.8	35.8	3.4	0.0	30.3
1944	9.1	8.3	57.8	0.7	0.0	24.2
1945	6.1	0.7	90.9	2.3	0.0	0.0
1946	5.8	-1.6	71.9	-0.3	0.0	24.2
1947	5.1	0.0	45.4	25.0	0.0	24.4
1948	11.3	0.0	59.2	12.5	0.0	17.0
1949	16.6	2.3	55.4	1.1	0.0	24.6
1950	3.7	5.1	43.4	1.6	6.1	40.2
1951	5.1	2.3	47.2	5.3	3.1	36.6
1952	8.3	2.5	54.2	6.6	-2.1	30.4
1953	9.7	2.4	43.1	5.5	1.7	37.6
1954	11.6	1.5	31.3	9.6	-5.7	51.8
1955	14.2	3.9	68.9	14.3	-1.3	0.0

Source: Bank of Japan, *Keizai Tōkei Nenpō* (Economic Statistics Annuals).

ism that formed an ideological thread running all through the twentieth century. A further background tendency was for the various problems associated with the supply and demand of information and long-term funds for the development of heavy industry in later developing countries to lead to increased government intervention and a higher proportion of indirect funding.

5. The financial system and main banks during the high-growth period

The post-war corporate monitoring system has three constituent elements: government control over banks, the main bank system, and management autonomy. It took shape in circumstances of fierce contention for corporate control that resulted from the impact of the changes, such as the disbanding of the *zaibatsu* and labour reforms, that came in the wake of Japan's defeat. Its form was also influenced by other shock waves, such as the confusion generated by the introduction of a more democratic system of small shareholders, and the credit crunch that followed the termination of Reconstruction Finance Bank lending. At the same time, the financial system was undergoing a huge transformation in terms of its two other dimensions: government intervention versus market forces, and indirect versus direct funding. The government intervened in resource distribution out of its strong supply-side concerns, and also increased control over the micro-level activities of banks. The circulation of capital became centred on indirect funding through the regulation of corporate bonds and also because the attempt to create an American-style stock market was unsuccessful.

As I will show below, the various characteristics of the corporate monitoring system interacted with aspects of these other two dimensions: the nature of government intervention, and the established preference for indirect lending. Overall, a coherent financial system was created during the high-speed growth period. The post-war main bank system was formed not simply through such direct factors as weakened shareholders' authority through crossholdings of shares, or the development of lending within *keiretsu* groups. It was also linked to the financial structure's institutional response to changes to the actualities of the economy that took the form of government intervention in financial markets and the establishment of indirect lending.

5.1. Transformation of the corporate monitoring system

With the defeat and subsequent Occupation, a fierce struggle ensued over the form that corporate control should take. Three causes can be identified. First, the Allies' General Headquarters (GHQ) liberalized the labour movement and gave it active support. Second, as many as 1,535 high-level executives were purged from office because of their war records. Third, firms and banks incurred massive losses when payment of wartime compensation was effectively stopped (it was paid, but subject to 100 per cent taxation) under the Special Measures for Wartime Compensation Law (*Senji Hoshō Tokubetsu Sochi Hō*). They were then effectively placed under government control through the Corporate Reconstruction Law (*Kigyō Saiken Seibi Hō*) and the Financial Institutions Reconstruction Law (*Kin'yū Kikan Saiken Seibi Hō*) of October 1946.

5.1.1. The battle for corporate control

Immediately after the war, struggles broke out between workers and managements over workers' rights and the 'right to manage'. After the Labour Unions Law (*Rōdō Kumiai Hō*) was passed in March 1946, workers became extremely militant and labour unions mushroomed in number from 1,945 in December 1945 to 4,849 in December 1946. In most cases, 'management councils' were set up between labour unions and firms' managements, and in ten leading firms including Nippon Kōkan, Nihon Seitetsu, and Toshiba, employees took over control of production.[13] Managements, meanwhile, saw their hands very much tied as a result of the dismantling of the *zaibatsu*, the directive freezing assets, the purge of officials, the Anti-Monopoly Law, the Elimination of Excessive Concentration of Economic Power Law (*Kado Keizairyoku Shūchū Haijo Hō*), and other such events. However, in April 1946, a group of younger managers under 50 years old got together to set up the *Keizai Dōyūkai* (Japan Association of Corporate Executives), claiming the 'right to manage' within a theoretical framework of revisionist capitalist thinking. Furthermore the Federation of Employers (*Keieisha Dantai Rengōkai*) formed in May 1947 was revamped, becoming the present-day *Nikkeiren* (Japan Federation of Employers Associations), and its anti-labour stance was strengthened.

From the moment General MacArthur's order ended the general strike of February 1947, the militant labour movement lost ground, particularly the Communist-party-affiliated industry councils (*sanbetsu kaigi*) that followed a revolutionary line. The focus of labour activism shifted from workers' status and the 'right to manage' to wages. This can be put down to progress in corporate reconstruction, getting production restarted, and greater management confidence, as well as shifts in the policies of the Occupation authorities prompted by the Cold War. The Labour Law (*Rōdō Hō*), and Labour Relations Adjustment Law (*Rōdō Kankei Chōsei Hō*) of May 1949, and the subsequent 'red purge' and employment cuts during the Dodge Plan deflation period, put the reins firmly back in the hands of managements.

Another problem linked to corporate control arose from the confused state of share ownership after the Securities Co-ordinating Liquidation Committee (SCLC) put a total of ¥25.2 billion of government-owned stock on the market. This represented 47 per cent of the ¥44.1 billion of paid-up capital of all corporate organizations nation-wide at the end of 1945. Most of the SCLC-owned stock consisted of shares that the Holding Companies Liquidation Committee (*Mochikabu Gaisha Seiri Iinkai*) had bought up from *zaibatsu* families or holding companies (¥7.5 billion) and shares formerly held by *zaibatsu* families which had passed into government ownership in lieu of property taxes (¥7.2 billion). The aim was to promote greater democracy by selling off this stock, derived from large shareholders, to individual buyers at fixed prices. The sell-off began in July 1947, and was based on a set of guidelines under which (i) priority was given to employees, (ii) sales to *zaibatsu* holding companies were prohibited, and (iii) sales were prohibited to anyone already in possession of more than 1 per cent of the stock of the firm concerned. It had the effect of increasing the proportion of shares in the hands of individual shareholders from 51.9 per cent in 1947 to 69.1 per cent in 1949, while the proportion held by corporate organizations dropped from 24.6 per cent to 5.6 per cent. The number of individual shareholders rose more than two-and-a-half times, from 1,674,000 in 1945 to 4,191,000 in 1949. But this great offloading of shares coincided with the launch of new share issues to increase capital for corporate reconstruction, with the result that share prices began to fall in the summer of 1949 and the stock market suffered a serious decline. Many of the individual investors who had only just purchased their shares ended up putting them back on the market. By 1951 the proportion of individually owned shares had fallen back to 57 per cent. The confusion that this trend towards smaller shareholders introduced into corporate control encouraged the growth of crossholdings, as we will see, and was a major factor in the emergence of the main bank system after the war.

5.1.2. The post-war main bank system

The formation of the main bank system after the war can be regarded as the outcome of the following three developments.[14] First, after the closure of the Reconstruction Finance Bank, there was an increase in lending by banks to firms in other *keiretsu* groupings and firms with whom they had had little or no previous dealings. Thus the need was felt for loan consortia to spread risk and for monitoring that was delegated to a main bank. Second, managements sought to expand their crossholdings of shares with banks because widening share ownership had created uncertainties in management–ownership relations. As managements' autonomy grew, so the banks' control of firms was strengthened. Third, firms increased crossholdings of shares with other firms to obtain more stable, long-term shareholders, in readiness for capital liberalization during the 1960s. By arranging these crossholdings and supplying funds, the banks came to take on the role of leaders of the various *keiretsu* groupings.

1. *Increased borrowing from non-affiliated banks.* As the Dodge fiscal retrenchment began in April 1949, no new lending was made available from the

84 *Juro Teranishi*

Table 3.4. Financial institutions' outstanding lending (¥m.)

End of month	Wartime Finance Bank (1)	Industrial Bank of Japan (2)	Reconstruction Finance Bank (3)	Ordinary banks (4)	[(1)+(2)+(3)]/(4) (%)
Mar. 1942	2,559	—	15,662	—	16.3
Mar. 1943	9,766	306	19,034	—	52.9
Mar. 1944	6,002	999	25,054	—	27.9
Mar. 1945	12,106	2,903	40,354	—	37.2
Sept. 1945	14,649	3,074	56,429	—	31.4
Dec. 1947	—	—	135,711	44,210	32.6
Dec. 1948	—	—	332,006	111,159	33.5
Mar. 1949	17,970	—	131,965	357,096	42.0
Dec. 1949	40,997	—	108,410	588,593	25.4
Dec. 1950	69,158	—	89,895	845,510	18.8
Dec. 1951	102,964	—	79,247	1,286,780	14.2

Notes: 1945 figure for ordinary banks is for end-August; 1949–51 figures for IBJ are for end-March of the following year.

Sources: Ministry of Finance, *Shōwa Zaisei Shi*, vol. 11: 323; Bank of Japan, *Senjichū Kin'yū Tōkei Yōran* (Wartime Financial Statistics), Oct. 1947; Bank of Japan, *Honpō Keizai Tōkei* (Economic Statistics); Industrial Bank of Japan, *Nihon Kōgyō Ginkō Gojūnen Shi* (Fifty-Year History of the Industrial Bank of Japan).

Reconstruction Finance Bank, which was gradually wound up. Commercial banks and firms had long been used to the supplementary provision of equipment capital and long-term operating capital in the form of lending from the Industrial Bank of Japan (IBJ) and the Wartime Finance Bank even before the Reconstruction Finance Bank existed. Thus, its closure had a far-reaching effect. Table 3.4 shows how these supplementary funds had accounted for roughly 30 per cent of commercial banks' lending from 1943 until the proportion dropped significantly after 1949. The result was that firms were all forced to seek other sources of funds, and banks were forced to lend to borrowers with whom they had had few, if any, previous dealings. Under the lending criteria introduced in March 1947, individual banks were required to supply capital in the form of 'loans' to firms in industries for which a certain allocation of funds had been designated. The regional banks, which had had no previous dealings with large corporations in these designated industries, found themselves in a particularly difficult situation. The Bank of Japan had started to offer loan-mediation services in January 1947, and under these circumstances became very busy. The numbers of cases and the sums involved, calculated quarterly, reached their peaks in July–September 1947 and October–December 1947 respectively. The Bank of Japan's loan-mediation system resembled that under wartime financial control, assisting in forming loan consortia in response to requests from the leading correspondent bank.[15] Its major function was to shift funds held by regional banks to industries designated by the central government. For this the Bank of Japan set up new loan-mediation departments at its six main branches in the different regions. The growth in arrangements with new customers is illustrated in Table 3.5 on page 86. Between March 1948 and September 1949, matching the fall in the proportion of lending from former designated financial institutions (i.e. banks in the same *keiretsu* group) and from government institutions (i.e. the Reconstruction Finance Bank), there is a corresponding rise in the share of the other financial institutions, and this applies across the industrial spectrum. The fall in the former designated financial institutions' share of lending is related to the decline in deposits from the large corporate customers of the war period, and the drop in the ability of the leading city banks to collect deposits because of restrictions on their branch networks. The fall in the proportion of borrowing from banks in the same *keiretsu* group persisted through the first half of the 1950s. In the second half of the decade the proportion stabilized at around 20 per cent, according to data in Kitsukawa (1992).

2. *Development of crossholdings between financial institutions and firms.* The trend towards small shareholdings prompted by moves to democratize the stock market stimulated takeover activity, which unsettled corporate managements. The main examples include moves to buy up Yōwa Fudōsan of the Mitsubishi *keiretsu*, and Taishō Kaijō Kasai of the Mitsui *keiretsu*. Managements regarded the loss of stability in the composition of ownership as a crisis and began to pursue active stabilization strategies through crossholdings of shares. To break up the *zaibatsu*, it had been expressly forbidden for *zaibatsu* firms or family members to hold shares in their own *zaibatsu*, but this measure was abandoned after the Peace Treaty, and crossholdings between *zaibatsu* firms grew. In the Sumitomo *keiretsu*, there was rapid growth in crossholdings between business firms, while in the Mitsubishi *keiretsu*, crossholdings were largely concentrated between firms and banks. Crossholdings did not develop quickly in the Mitsui *keiretsu*, and were limited to minor holdings between financial institutions.

The Anti-Monopoly Law (*Dokusen Kinshi Hō*) of April 1947 strictly prohibited firms from holding other firms' shares, and financial institutions were subject to a special restriction of an upper limit of 5 per cent of total stock on their holdings of firms' shares. Managements were just then regaining their confidence and drive, and launched a strong campaign through such organizations as the *Keidanren* (Federation of Economic Organizations) for this legislation to be revised. The revision of June 1949 relaxed the provisions and prohibited only firms' owning shares of competitors in the same business. In a second revision of September 1953, the special restriction on financial institutions was raised from 5 per cent to 10 per cent. This opened up the

Table 3.5. Borrowings of leading firms in major industrial sectors (¥m.)

		Mar. 1948	Sept. 1949	Sept. 1951
Metals (5 firms)	(a) former designated financial institutions	757 (42.7)	724 (37.5)	3,132 (26.4)
	(b) government financial institutions	718 (40.5)	370 (19.2)	2,393 (20.2)
	(c) other institutions	296 (16.7)	836 (43.3)	6,343 (53.4)
Machinery (10 firms)	(a) former designated financial institutions	3,120 (75.8)	4,946 (49.9)	10,933 (43.9)
	(b) government financial institutions	528 (12.8)	1,315 (13.3)	2,985 (12.0)
	(c) other institutions	467 (11.3)	3,655 (36.9)	10,989 (44.1)
Chemicals (5 firms)	(a) former designated financial institutions	912 (35.9)	2,879 (28.0)	3,987 (28.1)
	(b) government financial institutions	1,254 (49.4)	2,476 (24.1)	4,968 (35.1)
	(c) other institutions	374 (14.7)	4,930 (47.9)	5,218 (36.8)
Shipping/mining (4 firms)	(a) former designated financial institutions	1,375 (65.2)	1,127 (17.7)	2,792 (18.1)
	(b) government financial institutions	731 (34.7)	3,001 (47.2)	8,573 (55.5)
	(c) other institutions	2 (0.1)	2,224 (35.0)	4,080 (26.4)
Total (24 firms)	(a) former designated financial institutions	6,124 (58.5)	9,676 (34.0)	20,845 (31.4)
	(b) government financial institutions	3,230 (30.7)	7,162 (25.1)	18,918 (28.5)
	(c) other institutions	1,139 (10.8)	11,645 (40.9)	26,630 (40.1)

Notes: (*a*) borrowing from former designated financial institutions; (*b*) borrowing from Reconstruction Finance Bank (includes Hokkaido Colonial Bank, counterpart funds, Bank of Japan, etc.); (*c*) borrowing from other financial institutions. Figures in parentheses are percentages of all borrowing.

Source: Miyajima (1992), Table 5.5.

opportunity for growing crossholdings between banks and firms that were not part of the former *zaibatsu*. Fuji Bank increased crossholding relations with firms in the former Yasuda group, the former Asada group, and the former Nissan group. Daiichi Bank did likewise with firms of the former Shibusawa group, Furukawa group, and Kawasaki group, and Sanwa Bank with the former Nissan group and also with companies it had dealt with since the war. However, these crossholdings were largely between banks and firms, and there were only a few cases of crossholdings between different firms, mostly in the Furukawa group.

3. *Crossholdings between business firms.* Capital liberalization began in 1967 and encouraged further crossholdings between different firms and between firms and financial institutions, as a way of stabilizing share ownership. A device by which brokers were able to sell new stock issues preferentially to long-term shareholders, which became widespread from the 1970s, also spurred on this tendency. However, progress in crossholdings brought about the risk of monopoly control, and in a 1977 revision of the Anti-Monopoly Law, the proportion of shares that could be held by financial institutions was brought back down to 5 per cent.

The expansion of share ownership in the so-called *zaiteku* (money-game) boom of the 1980s encouraged the ownership of shares purely as assets, and was entirely unrelated to moves to stabilize shareholders. However, this also increased the proportion of crossholdings.

5.1.3. The post-war monitoring system

Corporate monitoring by a main bank is in theory a way of dealing with agency problems arising in neo-classical firms where shareholders and managements co-operate closely. In reality, however, there are many cases where the main bank is also one of the firm's principal shareholders, or else the firm and bank are related through crossholdings of shares. Monitoring often has to function in circumstances where managements have considerable independence from shareholders and moral hazard thus becomes an important issue. The job of main banks in Japan can therefore be expressed thus: the bank that is lending monitors the management of the firm that is borrowing. Put another way, the main bank system works on the precondition that corporate managements have considerable autonomy as a result of mutual crossholdings.

In such a case, how the actions of the main bank itself are controlled becomes a crucial issue. As the main bank is a bank, it has no direct interest in the firm's maximizing its profits or boosting its share price. The bank's concern is always directed towards the probability distribution of returns of the firm—particularly the lower tail and the possibility of insolvency. In a situation where shareholders are thus ignored, the possibility exists that firms monitored by banks might indulge in extremely negative, short-term behaviour.

Government control of banks is one way to eliminate this possibility and maximize the long-term interests of firms and banks. As I will explain, in the process of rebuilding financial institutions after the war, banks were placed under government control based on interest rate regulation and credit rationing aimed at strategic funds allocation, and this situation was maintained at least through the high-growth period. Government control of the banks changed from an initial policy basing criteria on ratios of income to outgoings, to one basing criteria on volume of deposits. Therefore during the high-growth period the number-one principle governing banks' behaviour was the maximization of deposits. This had three effects. First, with price and non-price competition restricted, the most effective means of collecting household deposits was to expand one's network of branches, and so a principal means of government control over banks was through approving new branches. Undeniably, because of the shortage of corporate information, approval was granted on the basis of their potential effectiveness (Teranishi 1993). However, this in no way contradicts the fact that bureaucratic hold over the banking structure (and probably the economic rent associated with it) lay in control over opening branch networks. The second outcome was that, given the government restrictions on branch networks, the banks made the securing of corporate deposits their major target of activity. Thus in their approach to firms, the banks encouraged behaviour that would maximize sales turnover, provided that there was little risk of bankruptcy, because this would lead to greater deposits. The third outcome was that the banks directed efforts to creating corporate deposit networks through the formation of *keiretsu*. This is seen as one reason why banks so often played a central role in promoting mutual crossholdings of shares between business firms.

To maximize firms' sales turnover or (slightly differently) to maximize growth, the popular view is that promotion opportunities need to be secured for employees under a system of life-long employment. Our hypothesis above does not entirely refute this; however, a comparison of these two hypotheses must remain a future issue. Furthermore, it also should be pointed out that banks' behaviour to maximize deposits under various given circumstances was not contradictory to maximization of profit. Interest on deposits was constant regardless of volume, and as is known, average costs gradually diminish measured against volume of deposits or other business variables (economies of scale). For the city banks, which had as their customers the large firms that were growth enterprises, it may be safely supposed that lending brought an unchanging rate of return. Now, if bank profit is shown as [return on lending – interest on deposits × amount of deposit – costs], and maximized under a balance sheet constraint of [deposits = lending], then as the first-order condition, we have [marginal return on lending = interest on deposits + marginal costs]. In this equation the left side is constant in relation to the deposit amount, while the right side gradually declines. The consequence is that with a small volume of deposits, if the marginal return exceeds the sum of the interest on deposits and marginal costs, then even if the volume of deposits should grow the first-order condition will not be fulfilled and so the more the volume of deposits is expanded the more bank profit will increase. Thus, firms' behaviour during the high-growth period of maximizing sales turnover and market share did not conflict with the banks' behaviour of maximizing profit.

5.2. The three dimensions of the financial system

In the post-war main bank system, as I have explained, a system of corporate control was formed which brought together management autonomy and government control of banks. A further important consideration is that in the post-war financial system overall, the corporate control system is in close systemic and mutually complementary relationships with the two other dimensions of the system: the extent of government intervention, and the well-known preference for indirect financing. This is illustrated in diagrammatic form in Figure 3.1.

I have already pursued this line of thinking in detail elsewhere (Teranishi 1992*b*), so here I will give only a brief explanation.

First, in contrast to pre-war financial markets, which functioned basically in accordance with market mechanisms, government intervention became markedly stronger in the post-war period. And whereas wartime intervention was directed to the supply side of the economy to realign industry, post-war intervention involved both supply-side intervention and management of the banks. Intervention was initiated in bank management when banks were taken into official protection under the Financial Institutions Reconstruction Law,

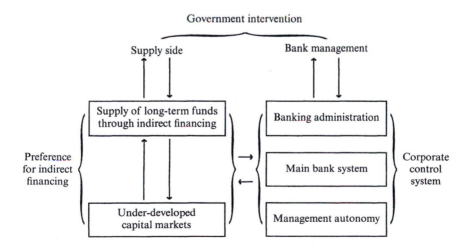

Figure 3.1. Financial system of the post-war period (high-growth period)

because of the massive losses they incurred through the effective cutting off of wartime compensation. Ninety per cent of bank stock was written off to cover the losses, and in this and the effects of measures designed to disband the *zaibatsu*, the rights of banks' shareholders were virtually ignored. From the second half of FY1949, when data first became available, dividend rates for the city banks were all standardized. For the regional banks, too, upper limits on dividends were strictly observed, except for some commemorative dividends. Government control was also imposed on wages paid by banks and their property purchases. The justification made for this sort of intervention was of course to maintain sound management in the banks, but at the same time it undoubtedly had the objective of tightening the hold on the banking sector.

The role played by finance (through lending criteria based on the Emergency Measures for Finance Directive (*Kin'yū Kinkyū Sochi Rei*)) in the priority production system during the inflationary period immediately after the war also indicates clearly that government intervention was strongly supply-side-oriented. Once inflation had been brought under control, there was certainly something of a desire to 'catch up' in the background. However, it is of interest that maintaining the health of financial institutions was always given as a major reason for increasing government intervention directed to supply-side issues in the financial sector.

First, when an allocation mechanism for corporate bonds was set up, the reason given was to rescue banks from their liquidity crunch. In advance of the May 1949 re-opening of the stock exchange, GHQ consulted with the Bank of Japan in April on the wisdom of floating public and corporate bonds. The Bank of Japan discouraged any such flotation on the grounds that the drop in market prices that the flotation would cause would generate large losses for the banks (Shimura 1978). But then in June of that year a 'national bond tie-up operation' was launched by the Bank of Japan, and at the same time a system of preferential lending on corporate bond collateral was established (*Nichigin Tekkaku Tanpō Shasai Jizen Shinsa Seido*).

In a second case, the launch of the Japan Development Bank and enactment of the Long-Term Credit Bank Law (*Chōki Shin'yō Ginkō Hō*) were the direct outcome of banks' over-lending. With the growth in demand for equipment capital generated by the Dodge Plan deflation and the outbreak of the Korean War, the commercial banks, particularly the city banks, became highly dependent on borrowing from the Bank of Japan (over-lending), the city banks were dependent on borrowing on the call market, and firms also demonstrated a high degree of dependence on borrowing (over-borrowing). These phenomena started to appear from about 1950, and were recognized as indications of the banks' liquidity crisis, symbolized in the provision of equipment capital by means of short-term lending from the city banks. The result was that a development bank was proposed as a re-financing institution for long-term lending, so that banking business could revert to its proper role of commercial banking. It appears that Dodge was initially negative about Finance Minister Ikeda's plan to set up the Japan Development Public Corporation (*Nippon Kaihatsu Kōsha*) because of the risk of re-igniting the sort of inflation that the Reconstruction Finance Bank had prompted. However, he apparently gave the project the go-ahead essentially because it was to be a re-financing institution. (From what has been confirmed, at least until the negotiations between the Finance Ministry and GHQ on 9 March 1951, the purpose of setting up the development bank was re-financing.) But in the final draft of the proposal submitted to the Cabinet on 22 March, the stated purpose was 'to supplement private-sector institutions and provide long-term funds for rebuilding the economy and industrial development', and this has remained the *raison d'être* of the Japan Development Bank right up to this day. Because raising long-term funds was basically regarded as the task of private-sector institutions, and the role of the Development Bank was only to provide supplementary funds, the Japan Long-Term Credit Bank Law (*Nihon Chōki Shin'yō Ginkō Hō*) was introduced the following year.

Thus, to summarize briefly, government intervention in the post-war financial system was based on two general tendencies, towards a strong supply-side orientation and intervention in banking activities. At least in the system reforms immediately after the war, the latter presented opportunities to boost the former.

The long-term credit bank system operates on the basis of government lending drawn from postal savings and made largely through the Japan Development Bank, and preference measures of financing bonds through the Bank of Japan. It is thus purely and simply a system to raise long-term funds through indirect financing. Together with the introduction of regulations on the public and private bond markets, it brought about the pre-eminent position of indirect financing in the post-war financial system. The failure of the American-style securities market that GHQ tried to introduce can be cited as a further decisive cause for the predominance of indirect financing.

I have already shown how moves to make securities holdings more democratic reduced incentives for shareholders to monitor, while motivating managements to use crossholdings of shares to stabilize shareholders. A further reason that hampered the successful introduction of the American system right from the start was that it totally ignored the pre-war dealing system. Before re-opening the stock market, GHQ announced the so-called 'three principles'. Dealing in futures would not be permitted and all dealing in listed stocks had to take place within the stock exchange—requirements that conflicted with the established division of the business between price determination at the stock exchange through brokers, and spot dealing. The 'price-discovery' and 'market-making' functions of the pre-war system would effectively be eliminated, but the specialist market-maker functions of the American system were not introduced to take their place. It was an extremely inadequate reform. It forced securities firms into market-making through dealing on their own accounts, and the resulting formation of short positions through the introduction of excessive liabilities led to the securities slump in the early 1960s.

Now, having prepared the way, we can identify the strong, mutually dependent relationships that exist between the characteristics of the first and second dimensions of the financial system and the third, the corporate monitoring system. First, the two aspects of government intervention—its supply-side orientation and control over the running of the banks—had considerable effect on the other two dimensions, the former through bringing influence to bear on long-term capital provision through indirect financing, and the latter by influencing the corporate control system through banking administration. Second, in the corporate control system the autonomy of managements and monitoring through the main bank were ways of substituting for the functions of the stock market, and only became effective as indirect financing came to predominate in capital circulation. From the opposite viewpoint, we can show that the establishment of this corporate monitoring system had the effect of further strengthening the dominant position of indirect financing, while ignoring the function of direct financing. Finally, while this combination of predominantly indirect financing and corporate monitoring through a main bank continues to produce investment-driven high growth, government intervention in the financial system can be seen as vindicated.

The main bank system has functioned during the post-war period as one part of the financial system, as shown in Figure 3.1, and has remained stable due to the coherent structure of the financial system overall.

6. Conclusion

Let us compare the main banks of the wartime and post-war periods. First, in terms of functions the two are very similar, and we can conclude that they came about in order to fulfil those functions. In both cases they developed alongside growing management autonomy, the necessity for corporate monitoring through banks given the stock market's reduced status, and also the need for a system of loan consortia to respond to rapid change in the industrial structure, the associated changes in business relations between banks and firms, and the rapid growth in demand for external funds.

Second, whereas in the pre-war and wartime periods the need for loan consortia to cope with higher lending risk was the more powerful factor, the need for corporate monitoring was the more significant factor in the formation of main banks after the war.

Third, we need to remember that there were major differences in the economic climate and in the nature of the 'external shocks' that generated the need for main bank functions. In the wartime period, the attitude of radical-thinking officials towards corporate reform and the creation of the New Economic System formed the background and opportunity for increased management autonomy. In the post-war period, however, the financial losses suffered by firms and banks as a result of Japan's defeat, and the various reforms introduced by the Occupation authorities, such as dismantling the *zaibatsu*, together provided the opportunity for management predominance. Moves towards increasing democracy in the stock market further provoked managements to increase crossholdings of shares.

Fourth, looking more long term, the main bank systems of both periods can be seen as phenomena taking the same course in terms of their timing matched to the development of the Japanese economy. On the one hand, they have appeared against a long-term current of anti-capitalism and criticism of liberal capitalism that dates back to the beginning of the twentieth century. Several factors played a part in this, such as the existence of an ideological climate that encouraged the restriction of shareholders' powers and neglect of the functions of the stock market, and also the Great Depression and the apparent success of the Soviet regime. Furthermore, for the Japanese economy in a late-developing capitalist country, these were both periods of manifold difficulties as they were phases of heavy industrialization. We must remember that Japan was behind in terms of production of corporate information and provision of long-term capital, and under circumstances of technical uncertainty the government had an advantage in information acquisition and must have felt very strongly drawn to intervene in market mechanisms. There is a strong possibility that the main bank system was born out of a necessity for a unique institutional adaptation to this particular developmental stage of the Japanese economy. Needless to say, however, the fact that it emerged as something unique does not preclude the possibility that it may have universal applications.

Next, I would like to touch on the overly competitive nature of Japanese firms in the post-war period and their behaviour to maximize market share. On this subject Giichi Miyazaki has offered a *keiretsu wansetto (one-set) shugi* hypothesis, suggesting that competition intensifies between rival firms in different *keiretsu*, and more recently Yasusuke Murakami, in a more broad-based discussion, has expressed the view that strategies directed towards maximizing market share could be the most appropriate under conditions of diminishing returns (Murakami 1992). Furthermore, in his 1988 paper, Aoki has shown that in negotiating games between groups of shareholders and employees, under the hypothesis that average employees will gain positive benefits from the firm's growth, it is possible that firms will seek high rates of growth rather than short-term maximization of the share price. In an earlier paper (Teranishi 1992c) I suggested that given the experience of fierce international competition before the war, and with trade liberalization forecast for the near future, competition in the confined domestic market under trade restrictions was driven to excessive levels.

The discussion in Section 5 of this chapter suggests there is a need to approach this corporate behaviour of focusing on sales turnover or growth from the standpoint of the financial system as well. If we regard corporate monitoring in the post-war financial system as made up of the three elements of bank administration, the main bank system, and control of corporate management, then as long as banking administration uses the size of deposits as a criterion, there is a strong likelihood that under bank monitoring, firms will act to maximize their sales turnover.[16] If we take into consideration the fact that this sort of mechanism was brought about through a range of external shocks, it is very possible that behaviour to maximize turnover could be a feature peculiar to Japanese firms. How one regards the differences between our way of thinking and the standpoint, as in Murakami (1992), of fixing upon the special nature of modern industrial technology and recognizing its universality, and whether there is a possibility that, as Aoki (1988) claims, the Japanese and Anglo-American systems in fact converge, are forthcoming issues of undoubted interest.

Notes

1. A project to ascertain possible implications of Japan's main bank system for the economic development of developing countries or the former socialist states is currently under way at the World Bank Economic Development Institute, under the leadership of Professors Hugh Patrick of Columbia University and Masahiko Aoki of Stanford University. The writer is also participating in this project and this chapter is in part drawn from its results. For a survey of the major theoretical and empirical results of analyses of main banks, see Horiuchi and Sui (1992).
2. The following discussion is only a review and is not exhaustive. See Horiuchi and Sui (1992) for more details.
3. The discussion in this and the following sections is largely drawn from Teranishi (1992a). A form of financing called federated lending (*renmei yūshi*) involving the Industrial Bank of Japan, Mitsui Bank, and others existed as an extremely primitive type of main bank lending. It was employed for emergency lending during the Shōwa Crisis, but no information is available on its form or functions.
4. I am indebted here to comments from Mr Tamotsu Nishizawa.
5. Appears in *Nippon Kin'yūshi Shiryō*, Shōwa edition, vol. 31.
6. Data for the top 100 and top 50 firms in specific sectors come from *Wagakuni Dai Kigyō no Keisei Hatten Katei* (The Process of Formation of Japan's Large Corporations) published by Sangyō Seisakushi Kenkyūsho. The ranking refers to 1940.
7. *An Eighty-Year History of Mitsui Bank.*
8. See Sawai (1992) for more on this.
9. *An Eighty-Year History of Mitsui Bank*, p. 272.
10. From the research of Shoichi Asajima. For more details, see Teranishi (1992a).
11. *Hundred-Year History of the Bank of Japan*, vol. 4: 300–2.

12. Ibid. 302.
13. For more details, see e.g. Tsuda (1984).
14. I am indebted to Dr Tetsuji Okazaki for his comments in the following discussion.
15. *Nihon Kin'yūshi Shiryō*, Shōwa edition, vol. 9: 294–8.
16. All other conditions being equal, banks would give priority to lending to those firms planning to maximize sales turnover rather than profits, and among different projects in the same firm they would take a more positive lending stance on those projects linked to increasing turnover or enlarging the size of the firm.

References

Aoki, Masahiko (1988), *Information, Incentives and Bargaining in the Japanese Economy*, Cambridge University Press.

Hirota, Shinichi (1989), 'Nihon ni Okeru Mein Bank no Hoken Teikyōkinō ni tsuite: Jisshō Bunseki (The Main Bank as an Insurance System: Empirical Investigation)', *Keizaigaku Ronsō*, 41(3), Dōshisha University.

Horiuchi, Akiyoshi and Shinichi Fukuda (1987), 'Nihon no Mein Bank wa dono yōna Yakuwari o Hatashitaka (What Role Do the Main Banks Perform in Japan)?', *Kin'yū Kenkyū*, 6(3).

——and Quig-Yuan Sui (1992), 'Mein Bank Kankei no Keizai Bunseki: Tenbō (Survey on the Economic Analysis of the Main Bank System)', Tokyo Daigaku Keizaigakubu discussion paper, 92-J-1.

Hoshi, T., A. Kashyap, and D. Scharfstein (1990), 'The Role of Banks in Reducing the Costs of Financial Distress in Japan', *Journal of Financial Economics*, 27.

————(1991), 'Corporate Structure, Liquidity and Investment: Evidence from Japanese Industrial Groups', *Quarterly Journal of Economics*, 106.

Kataoka, Yutaka (1988), 'Meiji-ki ni Okeru Kabunushi to Kabunushi Sōkai (Shareholders and Shareholders Meetings in Meiji Japan)', in *Keieishigaku*, 23(2): 33–58.

Kato, Masaaki, Frank Packer, and Akiyoshi Horiuchi (1992), 'Meinbanku to Kyōchōteki Yūshi (Main Banks and Joint Financing)', in *Keizaigaku Ronshū*, 58(1) (April): 1–22.

Kitsukawa, Takeo (1992), 'Sengogata Kigyō Shūdan no Keisei (Formation of Business Groups in Post-war Japan)' in Toshiro Hashimoto and Haruto Takeda (Hōsei Daigaku Sangyō Jōhō Center) (eds.), *Nihon Keizai no Hatten to Kigyō Shūdan* (Economic Development and Business Groups in Japan), University of Tokyo Press.

Miyajima, Hideaki (1992), 'Zaibatsu Kaitai (Dissolution of the *Zaibatsu*)', in Toshiro Hashimoto and Haruto Takeda (Hōsei Daigaku Sangyō Jōhō Center) (eds.), *Nihon Keizai no Hatten to Kigyō Shūdan* (Economic Development and Business Groups in Japan), University of Tokyo Press.

Murakami, Yasusuke (1992), *Han Koten no Seiji Keizaigaku, Jō, Ge* (Anti-classical Political Economy), Chūō Kōronsha.

Nagae, Masao (1981), 'Nichiro Sengoki ni Okeru Bōseki Kigyō Shūchū (Concentration of Cotton-Spinning Firms after the Russo-Japanese War)', *Keizaigaku Kenkyu Nenpō*.

Okazaki, Tetsuji (1991), 'Senji Keikaku Keizai to Kigyō (The Wartime Planned

Economy and Business Firms)', in *Gendai Nihon Shakai* (Modern Japanese Society), 4, University of Tokyo Press.

Sawai, Minoru (1992), 'Senji Keizai to Zaibatsu (The Wartime Economy and the *Zaibatsu*)' in Toshiro Hashimoto and Haruto Takeda (Hōsei Daigaku Sangyō Jōhō Center) (eds.), *Nihon Keizai no Hatten to Kigyō Shūdan* (Economic Development and Business Groups in Japan), University of Tokyo Press.

Schleifer, Andrei and Robert W. Vishny (1986), 'Large Shareholders and Corporate Control', *Journal of Political Economy*, 94(31): 461–88.

Shimura, Kaichi (1978) (ed.), *Gendai Nihon Kōshasai Ron* (Bond Markets in Japan), University of Tokyo Press.

Stiglitz, Joseph E. (1985), 'Credit Markets and the Control of Capital', *Journal of Money, Capital and Banking*, 17(2).

Takahashi, Kamekichi (1977), *Nihon no Kigyō, Keieisha Hattatsu-shi* (History of Business Firms in Japan), Tōyō Keizai Shinpō-sha.

Teranishi, Juro (1992*a*), 'Emergence of Loan Syndication in Wartime Japan: An Investigation into the Historical Origin of the Main Bank System', a paper presented for the 28 July–1 August 1992 Workshop at Westfield for the project 'Japanese Main Bank System and Its Relevance for Developing Markets and Transferring Socialist Economies' (World Bank, Stanford University, and Columbia University).

——(1992*b*), 'Emergence and Establishment of Highly Regulated and Bank Dominated Financial System in Post-war Japan', a paper prepared for the project 'Strategies for Rapid Growth: Public Policy and the Asian Miracle' (Country Economics Department, World Bank).

——(1992*c*), 'Nihon Keizai ni okeru Yunyū Daitaiteki Seichō (Import Substitution-led Growth in the Japanese Economy)', *Keizai Kenkyū*, 43(2).

——(1993), 'Japan: Finance and Economic Development', in Yung-chul Park and Hugh Patrick (eds.), *Growth, Repression and Liberalization: The Financial Development of Japan, Korea and Taiwan* (1994).

Tsuda, Masumi (1984), 'Sengo Keiei to Rōshi Kankei: Sono Hottan no Rekishiteki Igi (Employer–Employee Relations in Post-war Japan: An Analysis of Historical Origins)', *Bijinesu Revyū*, 31(2): 15–28.

4

Corporate Governance

Tetsuji Okazaki

1. Introduction

Since the 1980s remarkable progress has been made in research into Japan's corporate system, both within Japan and overseas. Developments in theoretical economics have contributed to this. Tools have been developed for handling the basic elements of corporate organizations such as information and incentives, and a recognized framework for the economic analysis of private-sector firms has been created. Firms are seen as 'coalitional associations of various stakeholders, including management, employees, banks, shareholders and business affiliates', or as 'legal entities functioning as a focus of complex, long-term contractual relations between human resources, capital and business affiliates' (Aoki 1984). The way the different stakeholders in the 'coalitional association' participate in the firm's decision-making and benefit from its proceeds is what forms the firm's individual features. In recent years increasing interest has been shown in the similarities and differences in corporate governance structure between different countries, and this too may be put down to these developments in the theoretical framework for the study of firms. This approach allows a better understanding of characteristics of Japanese firms that previously were recognized only as cultural peculiarities, and also provides a basis for international comparisons, so I would like to use it in this chapter.

Second, I would like to introduce the concept of comparative institutional analysis. As explained in Chapter Nine, comparative institutional analysis focuses on the complementarity existing between institutions and the multiple points of equilibrium and path-dependence that this creates. It holds that among the various institutions that go to form an economic system, some are mutually supportive, or complementary. If some historical event should provoke simultaneous change in these institutions, the whole system will shift to a different stable state, or equilibrium, and will not revert to the former state (see Chapter Nine, and also Milgrom and Roberts (1992)). The view that certain events have brought about irreversible developments in history is widely accepted among scholars of history, and this is a theoretical extension of that idea.

These two approaches lead us to the view that firms depend on the complementary existence of various institutions such as capital markets, financial markets, the labour market, and so on, with which they are mutually related, and the characteristics of these institutions will affect the structure and activities of firms. Furthermore, should some historical event cause these institutions to change all at the same time, a different set or system of stable institutions will be established, and firms will accordingly develop different structures and behavioural characteristics.

This combined approach can provide a thorough understanding of the history of Japanese firms from the pre-war through to the post-war period. Though in the process of a very gradual change, pre-war firms in Japan were reliant on all sorts of institutions that helped to maintain a stable state of equilibrium. The Second World War and events of the post-war period caused these institutions to change all at once, and in doing so formed the features of Japanese firms that we see today in a new equilibrium. Changes to Japanese firms that occurred from the pre-war into the wartime periods have been discussed elsewhere (Okazaki 1992, 1993). Here, I would like to emphasize some points made in earlier papers and then examine in some detail the process by which the post-war corporate system took hold.

2. The pre-war corporate governance structure

To illustrate just how much Japanese firms changed between the pre-war and post-war periods, I would like to use the interesting observations of a businessman who was active throughout the whole period. Tatsunosuke Takasaki graduated from the Fisheries Training Institute (*Suisan Kōshūjo*) in 1906, and then spent some years gaining technical experience in America. He returned to Japan in 1916 and the following year was appointed manager of a canning concern, Tōyō Seikan K. K. During the Second World War he was in Manchuria as vice-president, and later president, of Manshū Jūkōgyō (Manchuria Heavy Industries). He returned to Japan in 1947, and from 1952 served as president of Dengen Kaihatsu (Electric Power Generation Development) (Takasaki 1957). In his writings of 1954 entitled 'Corporate Managers Past and Present' he describes his impressions of Japanese firms on the two occasions he returned to Japan after long periods overseas (Takasaki 1954). Of the first occasion, his return in 1916, he writes:

The first thing I found unacceptable was that large blocks of a firm's stock could be transferred from A to B without the knowledge of the employees. Whenever this happened the top management would change and so there was never any consistency in company policy. Second, instead of working to improve the corporate base, directors opted to pay high dividends to curry favour with shareholders. They also aimed to boost the stock price. The management thus appeared to be more concerned with the ups and downs of the stock price than the overall performance of the firm or, to put it another way, the shareholders had enormous power while the wishes of the employees went unheard.

This is a succinct description of the classical capitalist type of enterprise in which shareholders reign supreme: exactly the type of pre-war Japanese firm so fiercely criticized by Kamekichi Takahashi in his *Kabushiki Kaisha Bōkoku Ron* (The Joint-Stock Company—A Cause for National Ruin) (Takahashi 1930; Okazaki 1993: 178–80). But after getting such a forceful impression of the out-and-out authority of shareholders in the Japanese corporate world of 1916, Takasaki was to be shocked in quite the opposite sense on his return from overseas thirty years later:

When I think of it now, it was a scandalous situation. The interests of shareholders were dismissed entirely and business was run at the behest of the workers. It was the exact opposite of the situation I found in 1916 when I returned to Japan the first time. Shareholders' dividends, the stock price and the like were all given low priority, while workers' pay and conditions were of paramount concern, and not a single person thought about strengthening the corporate base or building up capital. This state of affairs subsequently improved to some degree when the need for capital was felt, but there has been no significant major change right up to the present.

Thus, over the course of thirty years Japanese firms had changed from being run by all-powerful shareholders to the exact opposite orientation, and were run by all-powerful employees. As Takasaki went to Manchuria in 1941, we can assume that the greatest changes must have taken place during the war years or shortly after. At the same time it is worth while noting his remark in 1954 that the need for capital had brought about some slight improvement in the situation. The relatively strong position of employees is seen as charac-teristic also of present-day Japanese firms, but needless to say, this is entirely different from the situation in firms immediately after the war, in which Takasaki claims 'not a single person thought about strengthening the corpor-ate base or building up capital'. But he then suggests that after the war the excessive powers of employees were moderated out of a need to raise capital. Following these leads, I would like now to examine the corporate system and the institutions that underpin it from a historical perspective.

The joint-stock corporation system was introduced to Japan with the enact-ment of the National Banking Acts (*Kokuritsu Ginkō Jōrei*) of 1872, and be-came established during the 1890s in the modernized, so-called 'transplanted' industries, which included railways, cotton spinning, and banking (Miyamoto 1990: 360–73). Joint-stock corporations then spread rapidly throughout the entire economy, and during the period up to the Second World War they consistently accounted for almost 90 per cent of the total paid-up capital of all corporate firms (Table 4.1). To determine the size of capital flows through the stock market we can compare increases to joint-stock corporations' paid-up capital with non-housing private-sector investment (investment in buildings

Table 4.1. Development of joint-stock corporations

	Number of firms			Paid-up capital (¥m.)				Increases to joint-stock corporations' paid-up capital/non-housing private-sector investment (%)
	Total	Joint-stock corporations	% of total	Total	Joint-stock corporations	% of total		
1905	8,994	4,214	46.9	976	858	88.0		—
1910	12,300	5,025	40.9	1,481	1,244	84.0		24.1
1915	17,149	7,200	42.0	2,185	1,859	85.1		29.7
1920	29,917	16,228	54.2	8,238	7,280	88.4		67.7
1925	34,345	17,603	51.3	11,157	9,534	85.5		34.8
1930	63,553	19,341	30.4	13,953	11,844	84.9		35.7
1935	94,592	23,264	24.6	16,664	14,197	85.2		40.5
1940	91,028	35,497	39.0	31,337	25,799	82.3		60.3
1942	92,951	38,377	41.3	34,646	31,510	90.9		—

Sources: Management and Co-ordination Agency, Statistics Bureau (1987); Ministry of Commerce and Industry, *Kaisha Tōkei Hyō* (Corporate Statistics), published annually.

and equipment). The ratio varies between 25 per cent and 60 per cent during the pre-war period, and the figures would be higher if we took into account capital reductions and companies going out of business. Thus, the joint-stock corporation system played a significant role, quantitatively speaking, in capital formation in pre-war Japan, or in the flow of capital to that end. This point has been confirmed with other data on the provision of industrial capital (Chapter One, Table 1.5). In the early 1930s, during the last few years of the period, about 40 per cent of all industrial capital was raised through stocks and shares, which had become an important means of raising external capital. It is well known that the ratio of self-capitalization in pre-war firms, particularly the ratio of paid-up capital, greatly exceeded that of the post-war period.

One factor that encouraged capital provision through the stock market to play such an important role before the war was a macroeconomic feature: the distribution of income and assets. In line with the characteristics of capital flows, securities accounted for between 40 per cent and 60 per cent of financial asset portfolios in the private non-financial sector (Table 4.2). Because the fixed dealing costs of securities were large, and because securities included a considerable proportion of shares, which were regarded as risky assets, the facts suggest the existence in the pre-war period of wealthy investors who were able to diversify their vast assets. In fact, much corroborative research has shown there was considerable inequality in the distribution of assets and income in pre-war Japan (H. Yazawa 1992).

A further important role of capital raised on the stock market, in microeconomic terms, concerned its relation to corporate governance structure. The

Table 4.2. Financial asset portfolios in the private non-financial sector (%)

	Cash and deposits	Insurance	Securities
1900	44.2	0.7	55.0 (59.5)
1910	36.1	1.1	62.9 (32.3)
1920	51.3	1.9	46.9 (60.0)
1930	50.9	3.7	45.5 (51.2)
1940	61.4	4.9	33.7 (37.5)
1944	77.2	5.2	17.6 (20.2)
1950	72.5	3.0	24.4 (31.8)
1960	73.8	6.9	19.3 (40.7)
1970	76.5	7.3	16.2 (28.7)

Note: Values in parentheses represent the ratio of stocks to total public and corporate bonds including those held by the financial sector.

Source: Emi *et al.* (1988).

New Commercial Code (*Shin Shō Hō*), enacted in 1899, was based on the
German legal system and was characterized by its emphasis on the status of
shareholders. The shareholders' meeting was seen as the 'highest and most
powerful institution'. It was not limited to particular legally prescribed matters
but had the authority to make wide-ranging decisions, and its resolutions on
business operations were binding on directors (Kitazawa 1966: 67). Moreover,
the conditions existed for pre-war shareholders to exercise this powerful authority that the law accorded them.

To examine the actual state of corporate governance, let us study a sample
of twenty firms in the mining and manufacturing sectors, made up of the top
ten firms in terms of overall assets (1935) in the *zaibatsu* (Mitsui, Mitsubishi,
Sumitomo), and non-*zaibatsu* groups (Table 4.3). It is important to note that
most of the largest firms in mining and manufacturing were non-*zaibatsu*
firms; in 1935, out of the top sixty firms ranked by total capital, only ten were
zaibatsu firms. If we look at the distribution of share ownership for that year,
we find that shares were heavily concentrated in the hands of large shareholders (the top ten shareholders), especially holding companies in both
groups. However, there were differences between *zaibatsu* and non-*zaibatsu*
holding companies. The holding companies among the *zaibatsu* group were of
course the 'headquarters' of the *zaibatsu* (Mitsui Gōmei, Mitsubishi Gōshi,
Sumitomo Gōshi), and even in 1935, when public share offerings had made
some headway, they remained the leading shareholder, holding 40–60 per cent
of the shares in most cases, and never less than 20 per cent. On the other hand,
except in the case of Nippon Sangyō, which held a majority of Nippon Mining
shares, holding companies among the non-*zaibatsu* firms existed to preserve
the assets of wealthy individuals, and their proportions of shares were not
necessarily of controlling size.

Reflecting the differences in their shareholders, there were differing mechanisms in the *zaibatsu* and non-*zaibatsu* firms for shareholders to monitor management, and this is mirrored in the composition of their managerial boards
(Table 4.4). In 1935, more than 20 per cent of the directors in the non-*zaibatsu*
firms were among the top ten largest shareholders. This is a high proportion
when one considers that there were other directors who were also large shareholders but were not among the top ten. Thus in the non-*zaibatsu* firms, large
shareholders monitored the firm's management directly, by actual participation. Thus, we might say that a fundamental characteristic of the boards of
directors in these cases was that they monitored the execution of company
business from the shareholders' viewpoint.

In the *zaibatsu* firms, on the other hand, there were few cases of large shareholders becoming directors. Even including directors dispatched from the
holding companies, the proportion representing large shareholders was still
lower than in non-*zaibatsu* firms. A high proportion of directors were instead
internally promoted. Thus we can say that monitoring through direct participation in management was awarded only a relatively small role in the *zaibatsu*

Table 4.3. Changes in distribution of shareholdings (%)

	1935	1942	1947	1949	1951	1955
Total						
No. of stocks issued ('000)	23,905	70,069	105,349	341,753	390,700	1,113,000
Proportions held by:						
Top ten shareholders	40.3	37.8	38.5	19.4	20.3	20.0
Government	0.1	0.6	24.4	5.6	0.6	0.0
Holding companies	24.7	15.3	5.7	0.5	0.0	0.0
Financial institutions	6.7	8.3	5.3	3.2	8.5	15.5
Banks	3.0	1.3	1.3	0.5	2.7	2.4
Trust banks	0.2	0.6	0.6	0.1	2.2	7.8
Insurance companies	3.5	6.4	3.4	2.6	3.6	5.2
Securities firms	0.5	0.4	0.3	6.4	5.8	1.9
Other corporations	4.4	11.8	2.2	3.3	5.0	2.3
Individuals	3.9	1.6	0.6	0.4	0.3	0.3
Zaibatsu firms						
No. of stocks issued ('000)	5,840	34,482	53,971	154,800	169,600	550,400
Proportions held by:						
Top ten shareholders	65.9	48.7	50.2	29.7	27.6	23.3
Government	0.0	0.2	33.2	9.6	0.0	0.0
Holding companies	43.1	20.0	8.9	1.1	0.0	0.0
Financial institutions	7.1	11.4	5.7	3.8	10.0	17.7
Banks	0.9	1.5	1.2	0.3	4.1	2.8
Trust banks	0.8	1.1	0.8	0.1	2.3	8.8
Insurance companies	5.4	8.8	3.8	3.5	3.6	6.1
Securities firms	0.3	0.0	0.0	8.1	7.9	1.8
Other corporations	13.5	15.6	2.2	6.9	9.6	3.6
Individuals	1.8	1.4	0.2	0.1	0.1	0.2
Non-zaibatsu firms						
No. of stocks issued ('000)	18,065	35,588	51,378	186,953	221,100	562,600
Proportions held by:						
Top ten shareholders	32.1	27.3	26.2	10.8	14.7	16.7
Government	0.2	0.9	15.2	2.3	1.1	0.0
Holding companies	18.8	10.7	2.4	0.0	0.0	0.0
Financial institutions	6.6	5.3	4.8	2.6	7.4	13.2
Banks	3.7	1.1	1.4	0.6	1.6	2.0
Trust banks	0.0	0.1	0.5	0.1	2.2	6.9
Insurance companies	2.9	4.1	2.9	1.9	3.6	4.3
Securities firms	0.6	0.7	0.6	5.0	4.2	2.1
Other corporations	1.4	8.0	2.3	0.3	1.6	1.0
Individuals	4.5	1.8	1.0	0.7	0.4	0.3

Note: See Table 4.4 for details of firms in sample.

Sources: *Kabushiki Gaisha Nenkan* (Joint-Stock Corporations Annual), Tōyō Keizai Shinpō-sha; *Jōjō Kaisha Sōran* (Survey of Listed Firms), Tokyo Stock Exchange.

Table 4.4. Composition of boards of directors (%)

Ranking	Name of firm		1935	1942	1945	1947	1951
	Grand total	A	34	51	49	82	95
		B	15	9	8	0	0
Zaibatsu firms							
	Total	A	36	48	49	89	94
		B	6	8	6	0	0
		C	15	13	10	0	0
4	Mitsui Mining	A	63	69	73	88	100
		B	25	15	7	0	0
		C	13	8	0	0	0
6	Mitsubishi Heavy Industries	A	54	50	53	83	83
		B	8	11	12	0	0
		C	23	11	6	0	0
7	Mitsubishi Mining	A	80	81	83	100	100
		B	10	13	17	0	0
		C	0	0	0	0	0
23	Sumitomo Metal Industries	A	25	44	82	100	100
		B	0	0	0	0	0
		C	38	22	18	0	0
38	Toyo Rayon	A	0	27	25	100	70
		B	0	0	0	0	0
		C	0	0	0	0	0
39	Nippon Flour Mills	A	43	50	50	100	100
		B	14	10	13	0	0
		C	0	0	0	0	0
51	Mitsubishi Electric	A	43	55	33	79	92
		B	0	18	13	0	0
		C	43	27	20	0	0
52	Sumitomo Chemicals	A	13	10	19	78	100
		B	0	0	0	0	0
		C	25	50	24	0	0

59	Sumitomo Electric Wire and Cable	A	22	44	55	100	90
		B	0	0	0	0	0
		C	11	22	9	0	0
60	Toyo Koatsu Industries	A	0	22	25	80	100
		B	0	0	0	0	0
		C	0	0	0	0	0
Non-zaibatsu firms							
	Total	A	32	54	49	74	95
		B	23	11	10	0	0
1	Oji Paper Manufacturing	A	31	60	57	83	100
		B	23	7	7	0	0
2	Nippon Mining	A	80	71	53	67	100
		B	10	0	0	0	0
3	Kanegafuchi Cotton Spinning	A	89	86	50	92	100
		B	0	0	0	0	0
5	Toyo Spinning	A	64	92	81	89	100
		B	9	0	6	0	0
8	Kawasaki Shipbuilding	A	0	33	57	75	88
		B	11	11	7	0	0
9	Nippon Oil	A	11	40	23	43	73
		B	44	13	15	0	0
10	Asano Cement	A	0	36	30	79	100
		B	50	27	30	0	0
11	Dai Nippon Brewery	A	30	36	25	29	100
		B	10	0	0	0	0
12	Dai Nippon Spinning	A	0	38	54	89	92
		B	40	23	23	0	0
13	Japan Woolen Textile	A	11	13	33	70	100
		B	33	38	33	0	0

Notes: Rankings are 1935 rankings based on total assets of firms in mining and manufacturing sectors. A = internally promoted directors; B = large shareholders (top ten shareholders and *zaibatsu* families; excludes internally promoted directors); C = directors of *zaibatsu* holding companies (excludes directors promoted from the company concerned). Denominators include directors who do not fall in A, B, or C categories.

firms. What substituted for this was the systematic monitoring by the holding company of all its subordinate firms, a feature that has been well researched in historical studies of the *zaibatsu* (Morikawa 1980; Asajima 1987).

Let me explain this in more detail using Kasuga's study of the Mitsui *zaibatsu* (Asajima 1987). The holding company, Mitsui Gōmei, dispatched directors to the boards of subordinate firms who reported back on the firm's affairs on a daily basis. Important business was reported in advance to obtain directives from the holding company's president. A system was used whereby any such proposal of a subordinate firm's board was submitted for the approval of the holding company board and its business steering committee, and only then was a formal decision taken on it by the directors of the subordinate company. As investment plans were included among proposals to be sanctioned by the holding company, and as the holding company was a major capital provider for its subordinates, we might say that the *zaibatsu* system functioned as an internal capital market. Mitsui Gōmei had an organizational structure that supported the functioning of an internal capital market in the *zaibatsu*. It had separate head office, business, and finance divisions, and the auditing section in the head office division was responsible for monitoring documentation submitted by subordinate firms. The business division's research section was responsible for investigating new areas for investment. What all this means is that the *zaibatsu* firms used a relatively decentralized structure, in which the formulation and execution of management policy was entrusted to management teams made up largely of internally promoted directors, and they were monitored in the way I have described by the holding company.

In contrast to this decentralized decision-making in the *zaibatsu*, it is worth noting the rather more centralized nature of personnel management. For example in 1933, Mitsui Gōmei decided that important staff movements above the section-chief/store-manager level should be submitted for the consideration of the holding company's board (Matsumoto 1979: 240; Sawai 1992: 192). In the Sumitomo *zaibatsu*, too, Sumitomo Gōshi took on staff *en masse* for all its subordinate firms, and made decisions on the top personnel for those firms (Hashimoto 1992: 120). Looking at the organization of the *zaibatsu* overall, one can recognize a symmetry between decentralization of decision-making and centralized supervision of personnel that has also been observed in contemporary Japanese firms (Aoki 1988: 53).

Thus, whether or not affiliated to the *zaibatsu*, pre-war Japanese firms had built-in systems for shareholders to monitor management. This was an important condition that allowed stocks and shares to be the main channel for capital provision. Incentive systems for directors, moreover, were designed to match shareholders' profits. Comparing the ratios of directors' bonuses to profits before and after the war shows that pre-war ratios were considerably higher, and marginal propensities to pay directors' bonuses indicate that before the war these bonuses were far more closely tied to profits (Table 4.5).

Table 4.5. Directors' incentive system (propensity to pay directors' bonuses)

Name of firm	Average			Marginal		
	1921–36	1937–43	1961–70	1921–36	1937–43	1961–70
Grand total	0.0385	0.0199	0.0078	0.0248 (15.280)	0.0035 (6.14)	0.0057 (10.46)
Zaibatsu firms						
Total	0.0454	0.0186	0.0059	0.0283 (15.370)	0.0033 (6.86)	0.0042 (3.82)
Mitsui Mining	0.0660	0.0244	0.0000	0.0275 (5.810)	0.0008 (0.20)	0.0000 (—)
Mitsubishi Heavy Industries	0.0457	0.0099	0.0049	0.0351 (11.540)	0.0017 (2.59)	0.0032 (20.44)
Mitsubishi Mining	0.0317	0.0193	–0.0046	0.0254 (18.830)	0.0074 (0.07)	0.0007 (0.96)
Sumitomo Metal Industries	0.0119	0.0105	0.0040	0.0193 (11.050)	0.0130 (11.53)	0.0087 (5.71)
Toyo Rayon	0.0415	0.0050	0.0046	0.0498 (8.590)	0.0193 (5.79)	0.0049 (7.74)
Nippon Flour Mills	0.0940	0.0626	0.0198	0.0420 (5.310)	0.0149 (4.66)	–0.015 (–2.47)
Mitsubishi Electric	0.0637	0.0365	0.0052	0.0540 (10.960)	0.0000 (7.63)	0.0045 (14.89)
Sumitomo Chemicals	0.0239	0.0245	0.0087	0.0219 (5.120)	0.0097 (5.11)	0.0062 (12.85)
Sumitomo Electric Wire and Cable	0.0248	0.0205	0.0094	0.0249 (7.080)	0.0000 (—)	0.0053 (11.86)
Toyo Koatsu Industries	0.0471	0.0364	0.0126	— (—)	0.0266 (1.74)	0.0078 (5.14)
Non-zaibatsu firms						
Total	0.0363	0.0209	0.0118	0.0184 (10.460)	0.0042 (3.82)	0.0075 (9.05)
Oji Paper Manufacturing	0.0497	0.0194	0.0191	0.0218 (10.780)	–0.0701 (–0.92)	0.0056 (1.91)
Nippon Mining	0.0308	0.0122	0.0111	0.0273 (12.490)	–0.0274 (–0.39)	0.0078 (13.25)
Kanegafuchi Cotton Spinning	0.0315	0.0182	0.0098	0.0324 (2.880)	–0.0015 (–1.80)	0.0107 (4.34)
Toyo Spinning	0.0508	0.0325	0.0124	0.1050 (2.700)	–0.0012 (–1.05)	0.0097 (10.96)
Kawasaki Shipbuilding	0.0315	0.0197	0.0011	0.0388 (17.810)	0.0078 (5.42)	0.0051 (10.64)
Nippon Oil	0.0492	0.0250	0.0099	0.0496 (53.520)	–0.0067 (–4.35)	0.0066 (5.87)
Asano Cement	0.0000	0.0157	0.0120	0.0000 (—)	0.0420 (10.24)	0.0052 (5.44)
Dai Nippon Brewery	0.0571	0.0363	0.0106	0.0475 (6.110)	0.0090 (3.49)	0.0060 (1.90)
Dai Nippon Spinning	0.0000	0.0126	0.0136	0.0000 (—)	0.0218 (9.36)	0.0063 (3.28)
Japan Woolen Textile	0.0421	0.0314	0.0148	0.0474 (9.770)	–0.0055 (–2.03)	0.0000 (—)

Notes: In order to avoid inconsistencies, totals for marginal propensities are calculated from data starting from 1926 and exclude Toyo Rayon, Toyo Koatsu, and Nippon Mining. Average figures = directors' bonus/profit; marginal figures = regression coefficient of bonus to profit; figures in parentheses are *t*-values.

Directors were thus much more strongly motivated to boost profits. A comparison of *zaibatsu* and non-*zaibatsu* firms indicates that the former showed a relatively higher propensity to pay. Because the *zaibatsu* used a more decentralized monitoring system, they relied more strongly on the incentive system, which acted as a substitute means of control.

Under this system of monitoring through shareholders, pre-war firms paid out a large portion of profits as dividends. The average dividend paid by the firms in the sample between 1921 and 1936 reached as high as 70 per cent. Dividends corresponded closely to profits, and in pre-war firms most of the profit gained was immediately distributed to shareholders (Okazaki 1993: 180). In terms of liquidity, large dividends became a condition for shareholders to comply with demands for capital increases. In the pre-war period, sizes of dividends greatly exceeded capital increases, both overall and in totals for the *zaibatsu* and non-*zaibatsu* groups (Table 4.6). Thus, capital increases in pre-war firms were a way of re-absorbing paid-out dividends.

There were some disparities between *zaibatsu* and non-*zaibatsu* firms in dividend policy. The high rates linked to profits that I have described were more evident in the latter, while the *zaibatsu* firms showed a relatively lower propensity to pay dividends, and were inclined to favour more stabilized rates. This is seen as relating to their more decentralized nature of control, and the relatively long time horizons of the *zaibatsu* holding companies. Relations between *zaibatsu* holding companies and their subordinate firms were long term in the literal sense, and the fact that the holding companies had the auditing sections I have mentioned was related to the long time horizons of their investment activities.

The prominent position of shareholders in corporate governance had an effect on labour policy. It is well known that in the inter-war period, large firms adopted policies that encouraged employees to stay with their firms (Hyodo 1971). This achieved nothing like the degree of labour stabilization that has been seen since the Second World War, however. This point is demonstrated in rates of employment adjustment. As we all know, in the large post-war corporations personnel cuts are avoided at all costs and employment adjustment is extremely slow by international standards (Kurosaka 1988). The rate of employment adjustment in the manufacturing sector between 1956 and 1970, on a per capita basis, never exceeded 0.38, whereas between 1921 and 1935 the equivalent figure was 0.98. Thus, before the war, employment was adjusted to reach a level close to the optimum within one year (Okazaki 1993: 182).

Labour unions received no legal protection before the war, and so even in 1936, the year the highest number of union members (420,000) was recorded, the proportion of organized labour still represented only about 3 per cent of the total. The system of factory committees that was used in place of labour unions to communicate the views of the workforce to management was limited to only a number of large firms mostly in the *zaibatsu* groups (Nishinarita 1988: 200–4). Bearing in mind the nature of shareholders' control in *zaibatsu*

Table 4.6. Capital flows between firms and shareholders (¥ '000)

Name of firm	1921–36			1937–43		
	Dividend	Capital increase	Balance	Dividend	Capital increase	Balance
Grand total	1,185,873	665,126	520,747	1,329,779	1,940,405	−610,626
Zaibatsu firms						
Total	248,767	137,126	111,641	529,324	1,063,262	−533,938
Mitsui Mining	78,136	11,000	67,136	108,658	126,500	−17,842
Mitsubishi Heavy Industries	37,125	5,000	32,125	88,725	300,000	−211,275
Mitsubishi Mining	73,325	12,500	60,825	113,144	128,700	−15,556
Sumitomo Metal Industries	13,046	13,750	−704	89,979	318,750	−228,771
Toyo Rayon	11,558	10,000	1,558	18,355	9,031	9,324
Nippon Flour Mills	7,001	17,126	−10,125	9,483	8,031	1,452
Mitsubishi Electric	4,823	18,750	−13,927	29,634	67,500	−37,866
Sumitomo Chemicals	5,727	17,500	−11,773	24,668	42,500	−17,832
Sumitomo Electric Wire and Cable	15,026	7,500	7,526	23,973	38,000	−14,027
Toyo Koatsu Industries	3,000	24,000	−21,000	22,705	24,250	−1,545
Non-zaibatsu firms						
Total	937,106	528,000	409,106	800,455	877,143	−76,688
Oji Paper Manufacturing	121,304	79,410	41,894	169,716	122,509	47,207
Nippon Mining	52,979	138,750	−85,771	147,407	303,056	−155,649
Kanegafuchi Cotton Spinning	130,870	23,277	107,593	99,663	52,136	47,527
Toyo Spinning	141,100	26,475	114,625	97,102	34,775	62,327
Kawasaki Shipbuilding	47,407	107,000	−59,593	61,705	220,000	−158,295
Nippon Oil	76,129	31,000	45,129	50,743	60,875	−10,132
Asano Cement	59,890	43,468	16,422	25,577	13,975	11,602
Dai Nippon Brewery	110,829	36,700	74,129	48,381	0	48,381
Dai Nippon Spinning	129,928	29,420	100,508	70,454	58,492	11,962
Japan Woolen Textile	66,670	12,500	54,170	29,707	11,325	18,382

Note: Capital increases through mergers are excluded.

Source: Eigyō Hōkoku Sho (Business Reports) of individual firms.

firms, it is significant that the *zaibatsu* firms took the lead in spreading the factory committee system. In the area of employment adjustment, too, the *zaibatsu* firms placed relatively more importance on long-term employment (Okazaki 1993: 182). These facts suggest that the status shareholders wielded in corporate governance was in an institutionally complementary relationship with the nature of firms' labour relations. Shareholders' powerful authority to dictate management policy lay behind the labour relations of the pre-war period, and at the same time the low level of employees' adherence to their firms meant that they did not see themselves as stakeholders, and less friction was generated by shareholders' power as a result.

3. Corporate governance under the wartime economy

3.1. Changes in corporate governance structure

With the outbreak of the Sino-Japanese War in 1937 resources needed to be directed to large-scale investment in munitions-related industries, and the pre-war corporate governance structure I have described had to be subjected to various restraints for the smooth running of the wartime economy. Corporate reform and the reform of related institutions thus came under discussion within the context of wartime institutional reforms. In the early stages of the war, the pre-war system of labour relations was seen as reducing the incentive to work and causing instability in the workplace. The government had been shocked by a sudden fourfold increase in 1937 in the number of workers participating in labour disputes, after a steady decline of such activity earlier in the decade. To resolve this problem a system of 'industrial patriotic societies' (*sangyō hōkoku kai*) was proposed. A separate society was set up in each workplace to act as a forum for discussion of labour-management issues and to provide welfare (Saguchi 1991: 168). Under instructions from the Ministries of Internal Affairs and Health and Welfare, which held joint responsibility for labour issues, industrial patriotic societies spread rapidly, covering 43 per cent of the workforce by the end of 1938 and 70 per cent by the end of 1940 (Sakurabayashi 1985: 1). The spread of these societies gave systematic recognition to the provision of opportunities for employees to voice their views to their managements.

These systems reforms took place against the emergence of a new corporate ideology. The industrial patriotic societies were proposed in 'Guidelines for Adjustment of Labour Relations' (*Rōshi Kankei Chōsei Hōsaku*), which were published by the Kyōchōkai Emergency Countermeasures Committee (*Kyōchōkai Jikyoku Taisaku Iinkai*) in March 1938. This document declared that 'industry is an organic structure linking proprietors and employees through their work contribution' and gave employees the status of legitimate members of firms (Okazaki 1993: 188). As there had been a wide gap in social status between blue-collar and white-collar workers before the war, the fact that the two were grouped together as 'employees' was an innovation in itself. The following is extracted from a paper published in April 1938, by an official of the Ministry of Health and Welfare (M. Suzuki 1938):

> Corporate shareholders sell their stock when the price rises to realize a profit, and also sell when the price falls to avoid a loss. This is the state of mind of many shareholders, who simply want to benefit from big dividends without making any contribution of their own. If corporate leadership is under the sway of such shareholders, if they are allowed to set management objectives and drain off the firm's profits, then there are obvious drawbacks to the joint-stock corporation system . . . What determines the success of the corporation is the quality of its products and its price levels, and this relies in no small measure on efforts of factory employees to improve product quality and reduce production costs. Where ups and downs in profits are concerned, it's not the shareholders, who never even visit the firm, but the factory employees who have a far greater interest and much more responsibility.

Clearly, government officials responsible for reforming labour relations were already critical of pre-war corporate governance and had some idea of how they wanted to replace it.

Reform was extended to cover other aspects of the pre-war corporate system besides labour relations. This began with a negative assessment of firms' high-dividend policy, seen from the standpoint of income distribution. The boom in munitions industries and the large dividends this produced were considered undesirable out of consideration for those involved in civilian industries that had been scaled down, and for the families of the war dead (Okazaki 1993: 189). Under the Corporate Profits, Dividends, and Capital Accommodation Directive (*Kaisha Rieki Haitō Oyobi Shikin Yūzū Rei*) of April 1939, dividends paid by firms capitalized at more than ¥200,000 became subject to regulation. The last dividend rate set between December 1937 and November 1938 was taken as a yardstick, and ministry-level approval was required to pay dividends at higher rates.[1] Results for the first half of FY1938 show that more than 60 per cent of the 212 leading firms in the mining and manufacturing sectors listed in Mitsubishi Economic Research Institute's 'Analysis of Business Performance in Japan' (*Honpō Jigyō Seiseki Bunseki*) paid dividends at rates over 10 per cent, suggesting that the system would be a fairly effective control of dividends. Between April 1939 and October 1940, 130 requests to raise dividends were submitted, but only 50 were approved (Shibata 1992: 14–15).

Dividend control had the effect of bolstering firms' internal reserves, but it was taken as bad news by the capital markets, for which dividends had long been of prime importance. The discussions surrounding its implementation caused stock prices to plummet, as shares began to look a less attractive investment (Figure 4.1). From the standpoint of liquidity, too, dividend control dampened stock market investment, because as stated above, capital increases

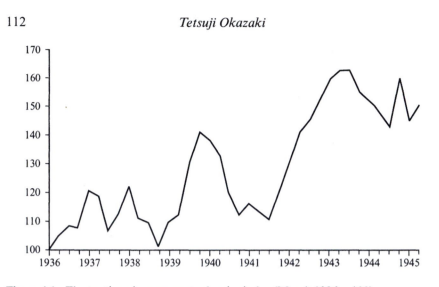

Figure 4.1. Fluctuations in average stock price index (March 1936 = 100)

Source: Bank of Japan, Statistics Department (1947), *Senjichū Kin'yū Tōkei Yōran* (Wartime Financial Statistics Summary).

before the war often represented a re-investment of dividend income. Dividend control thus had considerable impact on the micro-conditions affecting capital flows, which were centred on the stock market.

Furthermore, the macro-conditions that were created also worked to reduce the role of the stock market as a means of raising funds. The mobilization of resources for the war effort and munitions industries, in macro terms, meant the shrinking of consumption, and growth in individuals' savings. The wartime civilian savings rate (civilian savings/GNP) soared to 31.0 per cent in the 1936–40 period, and 54.8 per cent in 1941–4, due to a policy to boost savings directed at the general population (Okazaki 1993: 190–1). The mass of ordinary people with small per capita assets favoured deposits and savings over shares, which were both risky and costly. This had the effect of shifting the focus of the financial assets of the private non-financial sector as a whole from shares to deposits and savings (Table 4.2). The proportion of industrial capital provision raised through the stock market accordingly fell from 50 per cent in 1938 to 34 per cent in 1939 (Table 4.7).

Thus at both the micro and macro levels, the shift to the wartime economy led to a reduced role for the capital markets, which before the war had been the main channel of funds to the corporate sector.

Midway through the Sino-Japanese War, the pre-war corporate system and its governance structure had already been greatly modified. But the outbreak of the Second World War in Europe and an even greater concentration of resources to munitions industries in Japan aggravated friction between the system then existing and the requirements of the wartime economy, generating pressure for further corporate reform. This friction grew out of the contra-

Table 4.7. Industrial capital provision (¥m.)

	Total	Stocks	Corporate debentures	Loans and discounts	Private-sector financial institutions	Reconstruction Finance Bank
1936	1,562	996	−68	634	543	0
1937	3,733	1,986	−7	1,754	1,783	0
1938	4,598	2,286	357	1,955	1,975	0
1939	6,930	2,330	750	3,850	3,655	0
1940	7,653	2,940	609	4,104	4,213	0
1941	8,041	3,523	1,225	3,293	3,405	0
1942	10,518	3,930	1,362	5,226	5,019	0
1943	12,184	3,956	1,368	6,860	6,264	0
1944	19,225	2,303	2,098	14,824	14,655	0
1945	50,405	3,082	325	46,998	45,826	0
1946	59,153	4,516	−1,230	55,867	56,091	0
1947	133,403	9,030	10	124,363	80,181	44,210
1948	437,703	59,366	207	378,130	312,117	66,949
1949	491,837	108,529	14,963	368,345	363,139	−2,749
1950	512,898	31,919	43,476	437,503	372,555	−18,515

Source: Ministry of Finance, Financial History Section (1978).

dictory policies of holding down prices and boosting production, as explained in an earlier chapter. The government responded by introducing its New Economic System (*Keizai Shintaisei*), a core issue of which was comprehensive corporate reform (Okazaki 1993: 192–3). Price controls had removed profit incentives and production was stagnating. A bold attempt was made to deal with this situation, not by tinkering with the price controls, but by changing the very premise on which the corporate system worked: the profit motive.

The Planning Board (*Kikakuin*), which conceived of the New Economic System, recognized that firms made profits their objective because they were controlled by shareholders. So its original 'Outline to Establish a New Economic System' (*Keizai Shintaisei Kakuritsu Yōkō*) of 13 September 1940 stressed the need for 'separation from the control of capital, which makes enterprises' first duty the pursuit of profit'. In concrete terms, the Planning Board proposed revising the Commercial Code to separate ownership from management, making directors more like public servants, and bringing in a system to allow them to concentrate on increasing production without being obstructed by shareholders. The Commercial Code of 1899, mentioned earlier, had been revised in 1911 and again in 1938, but its basic thrust had not changed. The 1938 revisions removed the proviso that directors were required to be shareholders, but in other respects, such as in adding further matters for the decision of the shareholders' meeting, the revisions, if anything, had strengthened shareholders' authority (Kitazawa 1966: 72–6). It is unsurprising, then, that revising the Commercial Code was proposed as a means to bring about the New Economic System. It is also worth noting that a change was proposed to directors' incentive schemes. This involved introducing a system to reward managements for their 'patriotic contribution', thus contriving to link directors' bonuses to their degree of achievement of 'national objectives', or production plans, instead of to profits, as before the war.

There was strong opposition in financial circles to the Planning Board's proposals, and these reforms to the Commercial Code were never enacted. Significantly however, the 'Outline to Establish a New Economic System', agreed by the Cabinet, gave official recognition to the new corporate ideology of 'an organic unity of capital, management, and labour', and concrete revisions to various institutions within the corporate system did, in fact, proceed. First, in October 1940, in parallel with the formulation of the New Economic System, a Company Accounts Control Directive (*Kaisha Keiri Tōsei Rei*) was enacted to replace the earlier Corporate Profits, Dividends, and Capital Accommodation Directive (Shibata 1992). One of the focuses of the new directive was tightening control over dividends, so that for firms capitalized at more than ¥200,000, ministerial approval was required to pay a dividend that exceeded 8 per cent of capital or the rate of the previous year. The effects of this new, increasing control over dividends became evident from 1939. Both *zaibatsu* and non-*zaibatsu* firms reduced their dividend propensity during the war years, and dividend rates no longer reflected profit rates in any way (Okazaki 1993: 185).

Second, the Company Accounts Control Directive subjected directors' bonuses to regulation, and ministry approval was required to pay bonuses that exceeded either the statutory bonus or the previous bonus paid, whichever was the lower. Although the statutory bonus was linked to profits, the stipulation involving the previous bonus paid effectively limited the link between directors' bonuses and profits. Thus, directors' bonuses were not just lowered in proportion to profits, they were made virtually independent of profit rates (Table 4.5).

Change did not stop at directors' incentives but affected the very composition of company boards. In response to the New Economic System some companies replaced most of the directors on their boards. For instance at the annual general meeting of the Tokai Motor Company (*Tōkai Jidōsha*) in September 1940, the chairman advocated that 'the company needs to be freed from capitalists through the removal of current directors who represent such capitalists', and new directors were selected from the ranks of the employees (Hasegawa 1941: 52). In a government enterprise, too, the Japan Steel Corporation (*Nippon Seitetsu*), the directors resigned *en masse* in December 1940 and a new management team was appointed. Although not always quite so drastic, there was considerable change in the composition of the boards of the top twenty firms introduced earlier. Compared with 1935, boards in 1942 showed a sharp drop in the proportion of directors who were either large shareholders or externally appointed. They had been replaced by internally promoted directors (Table 4.4). It is particularly notable that internally promoted directors began to appear in firms which before the war had had no practice of promoting their staff to directorships.

Progress in corporate reform was also made in financial systems and labour relations. A clear relationship exists between the removal of shareholders' influence that I have described and the reform of labour relations. The 'Outline to Establish a New Labour System' (*Kinrō Shintaisei Kakuritsu Yōkō*) (Planning Board Third Division, October 1940), which formed part of the New Economic System, proposed 'the establishment of proper status for labour' and saw as a precondition for the reform of labour relations a switch from firms that 'awarded paramount status to capital' to firms that awarded priority to 'the actual managing body' of managers, technical staff, administrative staff, and workers. This reform was designed to boost the status of employees and managers to balance shareholders' loss of status. In concrete terms, it proposed setting up 'production co-operation groups' (*seisan kyōryoku kaigi*) as staff organizations at different levels within the firm, to discuss a wide range of issues including wages, working conditions, and welfare (Okazaki 1993: 195). Production co-operation groups were introduced from August 1941 by integrating the industrial patriotic societies into firms' administrative organization (Kanda 1981: 604–5).

3.2. Changes to the financial system

These changes to corporate governance structure were closely matched with changes to the financial system. The New Economic System concept included a plan to eliminate shareholders' control over managements by reducing firms' dependence on capital markets, and the Planning Board was studying a New Financial System to line up with the New Economic System and New Labour System. A government paper prepared during the process maintained that firms pursued profits largely due to their need to raise capital, and claimed that this problem would be resolved if capital could be provided in a methodical way through the establishment of a New Financial System (Okazaki 1993: 194). While this system was under study, attention was increasingly focused on the concept of loan consortia, which the private-sector financial institutions had themselves already initiated (Yamazaki 1991: 450–62). The 'Outline of the New Financial Policy' (*Zaisei Kin'yū Kihon Hōsaku Yōkō*) agreed by Cabinet in July 1941, set out policy objectives organizing the Bank of Japan (BOJ) and other financial institutions for this purpose and 'urging closer relations between industry and finance'.

But it can also be argued that changes to corporate governance in a sense forced reform on the financial system. One factor prompting reform was the slump in capital provision to munitions industries that occurred from around 1940. From April 1940 the stock market stagnated, averse to the New Economic Structure and the Company Accounts Control Directive. The system of control of corporate management through monitoring and incentives that had functioned before the war was now restricted, and the government was tightening control over prices (and therefore profits) and dividends. Naturally, investors were losing interest in the stock market, and the fall in share prices can be interpreted as a demonstration of their opposition to corporate reform and economic controls. Then when war broke out between Germany and the Soviet Union in June 1941, share prices plummeted (Tōyō Keizai Shinpō, 18 July 1941). All this prompted the government to begin comprehensive intervention in the stock market, and in April 1941, the Japan Joint Securities Corporation (*Nippon Kyōdō Shōken Kabushiki Gaisha*) was set up under the supervision of the Industrial Bank of Japan (IBJ) to support share prices. From June onwards the corporation embarked on unrestricted stock purchasing at government direction (Tōyō Keizai Shinpō, 30 August 1941, pp. 390–1) with funds provided as 'command funding' by the IBJ (Imuta 1991: 250). This mechanism, therefore, removed from the stock market the function of monitoring firms through their share price.

From the autumn of 1940, however, the banks that were intended to take over the task of funds provision became very cautious and the growth in bank lending slowed (Table 4.7). This prompted the government to shift swiftly to the New Financial System, in parallel with its intervention in the stock market. In a speech to bank representatives given at the Tokyo Banks Association (*Tōkyō Ginkō Kyōkai*) in August 1941, the Finance Minister, Masatsune Ogura, remarked that while in the past ordinary banks' lending had been largely for commercial financing, the focus of demand was now moving to industrial financing, due to the changing circumstances. He therefore advocated that past banking practices should be reformed, and lending instituted by the method best able to handle industrial financing. This proposal set out the need for a system of indirect financing to provide long-term capital, as the stock market slump meant that banks would have to replace the stock market in meeting long-term capital needs.

The Industrial Bank of Japan and eleven other banks accordingly set up an Emergency Joint Financing Group (*Jikyoku Kyōdō Yūshi Dan*) in August 1941. Co-operative funding was provided under a system in which the client firm's leading correspondent bank managed the loan and monitored the firm. The system therefore institutionalized delegated monitoring and created a main bank system (Chapter Three; Teranishi 1992).[2] It evolved into a system of facilitation for loan consortia provided by the National Finance Control Association (*Zenkoku Kin'yū Tōseikai*), set up in 1942, and grew in scale. The National Finance Control Association, or the BOJ through which it acted, facilitated loan consortia on the basis of screening and monitoring to be undertaken by the main bank (Bank of Japan 1984*a*: 299–302). The ability of the stock market or shareholders to monitor and provide funds had been reduced and a switch to indirect financing had become necessary. As firms' debt–equity ratios were increasing and lending risks were growing, the system that was introduced allowed banks to monitor firms and spread the lending risk. Many banks that had not previously had independent screening departments began to implement organizational reforms to set up such departments (Okazaki 1995).

As the banks had little experience of long-term financing and insufficient expertise in credit analysis, the mechanism of delegated monitoring was used to cut back on the need for credit analysis by making efficient use of the skills available. Furthermore, mediation by the National Finance Control Association and the BOJ backed up the monitoring capability of main banks and guaranteed their reliability. This new system of indirect finance restarted the stalled provision of industrial funds through financial institutions, and the role of the capital markets lost yet more ground (Table 4.7).

3.3. The Munitions Corporation Law

The series of institutional reforms that together comprised corporate reform, the New Economic System, the New Financial System, and the New Labour System, were closely interrelated in a complementary way. They brought about far-reaching change in a corporate governance structure where shareholders had wielded the greatest power, and which had remained largely unchanged before the war. Both the power and the role of shareholders were reduced, the status of managements and employees rose, and in their capacity as capital providers loan consortia, or the main bank, replaced the leading shareholders in monitoring corporate management.

But as explained in an earlier chapter, these reforms did not achieve their original purpose of eliminating profit as a corporate objective. Thus, at the beginning of 1943 price-control policy was changed to make greater allowance for profits and the corporate system once more became the subject of review (Okazaki 1993: 196–7). This brought about the enactment of the Munitions Corporation Law (*Gunju Gaisha Hō*) of October 1943, which together with the corporate reforms of the New Systems, represented a major step in the wartime changes to corporate governance structure.

Re-examination of the corporate system that led to the Munitions Corporations Law was also taking place among private-sector institutions. In February 1943, a complete reappraisal of the corporate system was initiated by the Wartime Corporate System Committee (*Senji Kigyō Taisei Iinkai*), set up by the Major Industries Council (*Jūyō Sangyō Kyōgikai*), an affiliation of leading firms organized by the control associations (*tōseikai*). Opposed to the arguments for state ownership or state control of corporations that were being put forward at that time, they aimed for a 'corporate system that exploited managers' vigorous entrepreneurial skills and sense of responsibility' within the framework of the joint-stock corporation system, and through wartime emergency regulations restricting the Commercial Code (Major Industries Council 'Reasons for Establishment of Wartime Corporate System Committee', 1943).[3]

During the course of these deliberations, the government decided to put the Munitions Corporations Law before the Diet. A document drawn up by the Major Industries Council, entitled 'Urgent Views on Establishment of a System of Wartime Production Enterprises—Request for Enactment and Enforcement of the Munitions Corporations Law' was quickly submitted to the government (October 1943).[4] It stressed that firms were 'united bodies of people', and sought to strengthen the status of presidents as 'persons responsible for production' by requiring that company presidents be enabled to run their business on the basis of approval from government or control association, irrespective of any decisions taken at shareholders' meetings. It further sought to establish the president's overall authority in connection with appointments of directors and the running of the board. It required that a procedure be used to appoint directors that would 'eliminate the use of connections to the firm's shareholders or government officials, and allow the selection of suitable competent candidates with management experience in the firm, especially those with technical skills and experience of production facilities'. Limiting shareholders' authority and appointing board members from among internally promoted candidates were measures that had already received agreement in business circles. With regard to employees' remuneration and welfare facilities, the document required that measures be taken to safeguard people's livelihood during wartime and increase production efficiency. On this point it is of interest that during deliberations, the view was expressed within the council that 'profit, as the term is generally understood, should no longer belong solely to shareholders . . . but should in principle belong to the enterprise as a whole. Thus profit should be allocated in fixed proportions to three groups: shareholders, directors and workers'.[5]

The Munitions Corporations Law was highly significant legislation in the sense that it pointedly restricted the rights of shareholders as set down in the Commercial Code. Under this law, in firms designated munitions corporations an 'officer responsible for production' was appointed who had exclusive authority to represent the firm. This officer was 'in principle to be selected from among existing directors, and should be the firm's president wherever possible' (Kitano 1944), but the government could approve or veto appointments and dismissals. Thus, in effect, the government guaranteed the president's status *vis-à-vis* the shareholders. Furthermore, the 'special resolution matters' of shareholders' meetings as specified under the Commercial Code were made 'ordinary resolution matters', and the officer responsible for production was also authorized to take action without referral to shareholders on matters that the Commercial Code had specified 'for shareholders' meetings'. The managers of the munitions firms were thus freed by legislation from the constraints of shareholders' meetings (Okazaki 1993: 197). In January 1944, the first group of 150 firms were designated munitions corporations, followed by a second group of 424 firms in April of the same year, and by March 1945, the number had grown to 678 firms (BOJ 1984*a*: 306).

It was not only release from the restrictions imposed by shareholders that increased the freedom of directors of munitions corporations. The Munitions Corporations Law also allowed some exemptions from various troublesome controls. At a meeting of munitions corporation representatives held in February 1944, an official of the Ministry of Munitions explained that under the Munitions Corporations Law, supervision would be unlike that carried out under the Directive for Supervision of Factories and Places of Business (*Kōjō Jigyōba Kanri Rei*), in that 'many bothersome control regulations would be either relaxed, or else abolished'.[6] As explained by the Vice-Minister of Commerce and Industry during Diet deliberations on the Munitions Corporations Law, the principle behind the law was to allow managers a free hand (Okazaki 1993: 198).

The system of munitions corporations led to changes in firms' relations with banks. On the basis of a Ministry of Finance memorandum 'Matters relating to Capital Accommodation for Munitions Corporations' (*Gunju Kaisha ni Kansuru Shikin Yūzū ni Kansuru Ken*), a system was introduced in January 1944 under which the Ministry of Finance designated in principle one financial institution to fund each munitions corporation, giving consideration to previous lending history, business relations, and so on. Funds were to be provided by the designated institution in a 'timely, straightforward, swift and appropriate' way. Other institutions that had previously participated in joint lending were able to lend to the designated institutions as members of Munitions Financing Co-operation Groups (*Gunju Yūshi Kyōryoku Dan*). To ensure smooth funds provision from the designated institutions, from July 1944 their lending was covered by bond guarantees of the Wartime Finance Bank (*Senji Kin'yū Kinko*) (BOJ 1984*a*: 308). This system of designating specific financial institutions to munitions corporations was also intended to encourage the efficient use of funds through monitoring on the part of that institution. However, bond guarantees and the safeguarding of profits through price controls weakened the incentive to monitor and thus had the effect of increasing managers' freedom *vis-à-vis* lending institutions as well.

Under these circumstances of increased freedom, munitions corporations' managers were authorized to run their firms to make profits. These profits were incentives not to shareholders, however, but to employees. A system introduced in 1943 awarded 'price compensation' to firms that had boosted productivity, and employees could also receive monetary awards. In effect this system redistributed profits to employees. Distribution of profits among employees was introduced in a more obvious form in the closing stages of the war. In March 1944, the Ministry of Munitions formulated an 'Outline of Measures to Clarify State Orientation of Enterprises (First Draft)' (*Kigyō no Kokkasei Meikakuka Sochi Yōkō (Shian Dai Ichigo)*). Shareholders were assured a 'reasonable' annual dividend of around 5 per cent, but their rights concerning the disposal of profits, appointment of directors and bond flotations were terminated. Once the 'reasonable' dividend had been paid, profits were distributed according to government guidelines to managers and employees as 'compensation'. The remainder could be used for company welfare facilities and anything left after that was to be paid into the national treasury. Under this system stocks and shares became in effect fixed interest-bearing securities, and profits remaining after the fixed dividend had been paid were distributed among managers and employees in a profit-sharing system. The system was agreed by Cabinet in February 1945 as 'Matters Relating to the Running of Munitions Corporations' (*Gunju Kaisha no Kessen Un'ei Taisei ni kansuru Ken*) (Okazaki 1993: 199).

This series of wartime reforms brought about drastic changes to the governance structure of firms that before the war had been characterized by the predominant authority of their shareholders. By the closing stages of the war they had been transformed into organizations with profit-sharing systems that closely resembled model 'labour-managed firms'. Thus by the end of the war firms had been granted freedom both from financial monitoring and from government controls. The Bank of Japan described these firms as 'a privileged sector . . . free from all controlling restraints' (BOJ 1953: 494). The firms' behaviour under these circumstances is eloquently summed up in reports of munitions corporations using funds from designated lending institutions to 'buy up concerns such as restaurants at exorbitant prices' (BOJ 1984a: 308). In other words, with weakened financial monitoring, firms reverted to the sort of behaviour typical under so-called 'soft budget constraint'.

4. The corporate system under post-war economic recovery

4.1. GHQ's occupation policies and the Japanese government's corporate reconstruction measures

After the war, various reforms imposed by the Occupation authorities (GHQ) served to amplify the wartime changes made to corporate governance structure. First, with the enactment of the Labour Unions Law (*Rōdō Kumiai Hō*) in December 1945, labour unions were legally recognized and thus employees' rights of expression were dramatically increased. Based on the industrial patriotic societies, new labour unions incorporating both blue- and white-collar workers were set up in individual firms. They formed national organizations to represent their particular industries, and were further amalgamated into federated bodies, of which the main two were *Nippon Rōdō Sōdōmei* (Japanese Federation of Labour) and *Zenkoku Sangyōbetsu Rōdō Kumiai Kaigi* (National Council of Sectoral Labour Unions). By the end of 1947, the proportion of organized labour had shot up from a mere 3 per cent or so before the war to close to 50 per cent. Just as production in macro terms was falling due to massive reductions in imported materials, and the real incomes of employers were shrinking, the newly formed labour unions received GHQ backing and grew into an active labour movement.

The shareholder class, meanwhile, was treated by GHQ with indifference. The November 1945 Memorandum on the Dismantling of Holding Companies (*Mochikabu Kaisha Kaitai ni kansuru Oboegaki*) marked the start of the disbanding of the *zaibatsu*, with stocks and shares held by holding companies and *zaibatsu* families transferred to a Holding Companies Liquidation Committee (*Mochikabu Kaisha Seiri Iinkai*), or HCLC. A series of measures that included winding up the holding companies and removing *zaibatsu* family members or their appointees from firms' boards, resulted in the total dismantling of the *zaibatsu* monitoring system that had functioned before the war (Ministry of Finance, Financial History Section 1982: ch. 3). As a measure to redistribute wealth, a property tax was levied on the wealthy which in 1946 yielded the equivalent of close to 10 per cent of GNP. The fact that 29 per cent of payments of this tax made in kind was in stocks and shares shows how hard this measure hit large shareholders. In addition, nominal asset values set for the purposes of emergency financing measures and land reform had the effect, under rampant inflation, of levying an inflation tax on the propertied class. The outcome of all this was that by the end of FY1947, shares of non-*zaibatsu* and *zaibatsu* firms alike were concentrated in the hands of government institutions such as the HCLC, the Non-operational Institutions Liquidation Committee (*Heisa Kikan Seiri Iinkai*) and the Ministry of Finance (Table 4.3).

So through actions that raised the status of employees and lowered the status of shareholders, GHQ's Occupation policies reinforced changes to the corporate 'balance of power' that had started during the war. The Japanese government formulated and implemented a corporate restructuring policy for economic recovery on the assumption that these trends would persist. One reason for corporate restructuring becoming a major policy issue immediately after the war was that GHQ sought to end the munitions corporations' right to claim wartime compensation. Should this happen, the munitions corporations would incur 'special' losses on a vast scale, and their financial difficulties might then disrupt the policy of restarting production by switching these firms' orientation from military to civilian production. Before the final decision was taken on ending wartime compensation, work had started on a corporate restructuring policy bill that would split off the equipment and personnel necessary for civilian production from firms with large claims for wartime compensation. These resources were to be transferred to newly established firms (Ministry of Finance, Financial History Section 1983: 704–12).

Of interest here is the concern addressed to governance structure in the government's corporate restructuring policy. In setting up new firms for civilian production, the Ministry of Commerce and Industry advocated 'new corporate principles'. In these, legal measures eliminated requirements for the approval of shareholders and mortgage creditors if the necessity arose, and an employees' shareholding system was introduced to encourage employees' involvement in restarting production. To finance the new firms, the formation of loan consortia through the Industrial Bank of Japan and the commercial banks was considered (Ministry of Finance, Financial History Section 1983: 711).

The Ministry of Commerce and Industry began studying policy objectives relating to corporate governance from the end of 1945. A document entitled Policy Proposals for the Democratization of the Industrial Economy (*Sangyō Keizai no Minshushugika Hōsaku An*) (Ministry of Commerce and Industry Planning Bureau, November 1945) raised as an objective the 'promotion of democratic corporate control' and to this end recognized employees' priority rights to hold shares, and proposed to devise ways of incorporating employees' views on major management issues. The draft 'Outline of New Industrial Policy to Overcome Economic Crisis' (*Keizai Kiki o Dakai Suru Tame no Shin Sangyō Seisaku Yōkō*) (Ministry of Commerce and Industry Planning Bureau, May 1946) offered more concrete ideas. They are included here in some detail because they clearly indicate the thinking in government at that time.

First, management councils were set up in individual firms to 'gain the participation and co-operation in the running of the firm of the workers who carry out production, and to boost production by preserving industrial peace'. These councils discussed a range of issues including production plans, and their decisions were binding on both management and labour. Thus the authority of both shareholders and boards as set out in the Commercial Code was restricted. Second, a 'co-operative work group' system was introduced to 'guarantee equal rights and opportunities to all parties comprising the firm, and to establish a democratic corporate system to eliminate the non-personified control of capital, through principles of co-operative labour based on each individual's skills'. Co-operative work groups were to offer four different types of competence: management, technical skills, administration, and labour. The four types of participants held equal voting rights, and profits were distributed as wages and salaries on the basis of skills, and as dividends according to investment. Thus restricting shareholders' rights and entrusting the running of firms to those offering management capability, that is managements and employees, was the Ministry of Commerce and Industry's basic design for post-war corporate reconstruction.

The 'Policy Outline to Increase Production to Deal with the Emergency Situation' (*Kinkyū Jitai ni taisho Suru Seisan Zōkyō Hōsaku Yōkō*) (February 1946)[7] based on the Ministry of Commerce and Industry's proposals and agreed by Cabinet, dealt with employees' involvement in management. Committees of managers and employees were set up to discuss rationed goods and welfare facilities, work planning, labour conditions, and so forth, 'to reflect workers' views on the proper, effective running of the firm'. We can see that in terms of restricting shareholders' rights and encouraging participation and co-operation from employees, and in looking to loan consortia made up of banks rather than to shareholders for capital provision, the corporate system proposed here closely resembled the corporate 'New System' introduced during the war.

These overall objectives were converted into various regulations and policy measures. The most fundamental pieces of legislation on corporate enterprises were the Emergency Measures on Corporate Accounting Law (*Kaisha Keiri Ōkyū Sochi Hō*) of August 1946, and the Corporate Reconstruction Law (*Kigyō Saiken Seibi Hō*) of October of the same year, which were both enacted in response to the decision to terminate wartime compensation liability. Under the former law, firms that on 11 August 1946 were capitalized at over ¥200,000 and had received wartime compensation or had the right to claim it, or had overseas assets, were designated special corporate account firms (*tokubetsu keiri gaisha*). The law also required these firms' financial affairs to be separated into two accounts: one dealing with current needs for remaining in business and resuming production (new account) and one dealing with other matters (old account). The number of firms designated as special corporate account firms reached a total of 8,373 (Ministry of Finance, Financial History Section 1983: 752).

Dividing up of assets and the management of old account assets were to be done under ministerial supervision by special supervisors, consisting of two of the firm's directors and two former creditors. Special corporate account firms were not in principle permitted to break up or merge, to change their organizational structure or to raise or lower their capital (Ministry of Finance, Financial History Section 1983: 735–6). The vast majority of special supervisors representing creditors were appointed from the firm's largest creditor, which in almost all cases was its former designated financial institution.

The second piece of legislation, the Corporate Reconstruction Law, set out a formula to calculate the 'special' losses incurred from the termination of wartime compensation and a way of writing off the loss. The special supervisors were required to draw up for ministerial approval a corporate reconstruction plan indicating the special loss incurred and how it would be written off. Shareholders and creditors were permitted to voice objections to the plan, but shareholders' consent was not required for its acceptance. These two laws in effect, then, placed firms hit by the ending of wartime compensation under bank supervision, and then planned for their reconstruction.[8] On the matter of employees' participation in corporate reconstruction there was some debate as to whether or not employees' representatives should be eligible to become special supervisors, but they were not, in the end, accepted. Instead, under a December 1947 revision to the Corporate Reconstruction Law labour unions were permitted to lodge objections to reconstruction plans (Ministry of Finance, Financial History Section 1983: 740–4).

The banks that provided special supervisors played a further significant role in furnishing the new money needed for reconstruction. The Reconstruction Finance Bank (*Fukko Kin'yū Kinko*) or RFB, set up to provide capital for economic recovery, provided 33 per cent of industrial capital in 1947, but that figure fell to a mere 15 per cent in 1948 due to increased lending from private-sector banks (Table 4.7). It was loan consortia based on Bank of Japan loan mediation that formed the organizational framework for bank lending. In December 1946 the Bank of Japan agreed a Nation-wide Capital Circulation Mediation Policy (*Chūō Chihō o Tsūzuru Shikin Kōryū Assen Hōshin*), and in January 1947 set up a Loan Mediation Committee and a Loan Mediation Section (*Yūshi Assen Ka*) in the head office. The committee was later abolished and a Loan Mediation Department (*Yūshi Assen Bu*) was set up in the Business Division in August of the same year. The Bank of Japan facilitated 'co-operative financing', the forming of loan consortia, based mainly on requests from the leading correspondent bank of the firm concerned, and in 1947–8 it is said to have 'supplied the necessary funds to almost all the leading corporations through facilitated loans' (BOJ 1959: 295).

As loan mediation expanded, in July 1948 a Loan Mediation Committee was established comprising the senior manager for lending from each of nineteen commercial banks, and the BOJ's Business Division Director, Funds Division Director, Auditing Division Director, General Affairs Division Director, and Business Division's Loan Mediation Manager. The committee reviewed basic mediation policy and major instances of lending, as well as past records of loan mediation. The committee's 'Outline on Handling Loan Mediation' suggested the following procedure. Selected firms had to be in industries highly ranked in the priority listing for industrial-funds lending (see Chapter One). They had to be experiencing difficulty in raising funds despite sound management and the existence of conditions beneficial to restarting production. Requests were in principle to be routed through the leading correspondent bank and 'the Bank of Japan will work to mediate appropriate lending jointly with the leading correspondent bank on the basis of discussion of the results of a thorough investigation undertaken by that bank'. Once the loan had been made 'the leading correspondent bank is to take responsibility for monitoring the firm's circumstances, providing reports to the Bank of Japan and other lending banks as required and discussing issues where necessary' (BOJ 1959: 297–8). So this was almost identical to the wartime system of mediation through the National Finance Control Association (which in practice was also implemented by the Bank of Japan), and it served to insti-tutionalize delegated monitoring—in other words, the main bank system. Considering the functions of the special supervisors and those of the managers of loan consortia, we can conclude that the leading correspondent banks of special corporate account firms took on the role of a main bank in rescuing firms experiencing difficulties.

Turning to employees' participation in management, a system of management councils was set up for this purpose. Acting on General MacArthur's declaration on the food-supply crisis in May 1946, the Japanese government issued a statement on preserving social order (June 1946), asserting that struggles over production control, which were then the labour unions' main tactic, were illegal. At the same time, however, the government published a document, 'Chief Cabinet Secretary's Talks on Management Councils', that called for management councils to be set up in individual firms to achieve democratic co-operation between management and labour. The management side was to report to the management council on overall planning and the financial situation of the firm, and discuss general policies affecting personnel, and 'reasonable requests from the workers' side should be incorporated in all aspects of the firm's management as far as possible' (Ministry of Labour 1969: 282–92). Management councils quickly spread and by the end of 1947 the number of labour union branches that incorporated management councils had reached 11,883, or more than half of the total (Ministry of Labour 1954: 187). Many of the councils covered management policy and financial accounts as well as wages and working conditions in their discussions (Nishinarita 1992: 209), and thus functioned quite literally as systems to involve employees in management.

Shareholders, however, continued to suffer the same restrictions as in wartime on their rights of expression on corporate management and also on their right to receive a share of profits. According to a Directive to Limit or Prohibit Corporate Dividends (*Kaisha Haitōtō Kinshi Seigen Rei*) of April 1946, dividends greater than 5 per cent or dividends paid for by borrowing were prohibited in firms subject to the Restricted Enterprise Directive (*Seigen Gaisha Rei*) and those later designated special corporate account firms (Hiraoka 1950: 270). The directive was abolished in December 1947 with the enactment of the Emergency Measures on Corporate Profits and Dividends Law (*Kaisha Rieki Haitōtō Ōkyū Sochi Hō*), but in this legislation, too, dividends remained prohibited in the special corporate account firms and firms stipulated in the Elimination of Excessive Concentration of Economic Power Law (*Kado Keizairyoku Shūchū Haijō Hō*) (Tōyō Keizai Shinpō, 3 January 1948).

Coincidental to these developments, two pieces of legislation brought about a purge among managers. A directive of January 1947 to purge public officials over their war involvement removed 1,987 officials, while the January 1948 Abolition of *Zaibatsu* Family Control Law displaced some 145 executives (Ministry of Finance, Financial History Section 1982: 309–38). As institutional and substantive changes to corporate governance structure proceeded, executives were replaced, and their positions were mostly taken by internally promoted staff (Table 4.4). In general, the replacement of executives did not in itself lead to changes in the composition of managements, which was far more an expression of the changes in governance structure. This can be seen in appointment procedures for new directors, and we can take as an example Mitsui Mining Co. Ltd. (*Mitsui Kōzan*), for which the actual process has been disclosed.

In response to the January 1947 directive on purging public officials, all Mitsui Mining's directors resigned. The company listened to the views of its board of division chiefs, board of section chiefs and labour union, and drew up a list of candidates for directors made up entirely of internal promotees. This was submitted to the HCLC, the largest shareholder. The HCLC checked the list against legislation on purged officials and executives, and then finding that it 'incorporated the wishes of the labour union, and the boards of division chiefs and section chiefs on the matter of the appointment of new directors, and the desire to appoint those with a long continuous record of employment with the company being considered entirely proper, the appointments were confirmed upon notification of the Occupation authorities, and the mandate issued' (HCLC 1951: 264). In short, the views of the firm's personnel were taken into account in appointing internally promoted candidates as directors, and both selection method and outcome were found acceptable to the HCLC, the leading shareholder. In a separate case, the newly appointed president of Japan Petroleum Co. (*Nippon Sekiyu*) died as the result of illness only months after the purge. His replacement was selected by the board of directors; however, 'approval was obtained from the executive staff and labour union' (Japan Petroleum Co. 1988: 466).

A report entitled 'Democratization of Corporate Management' (August 1947) from a study group on democratizing the economy within the *Keizai Dōyūkai* (Japan Association of Corporate Executives) indicates the thinking on firms with these newly appointed directors. Its basic assertion was that ownership and management should be separate (*Keizai Dōyūkai* 1951: 39–45). Managements should become teams of 'management technicians' representing the public interest. They should be given independent legal status, and should work to bring about harmonious industrial relations. The paper expressed the view that 'making managements independent would scale down the status of capital while raising the status of labour, thus putting the two on an equal footing' and 'firms should become communities comprising the three elements of management, capital, and labour'. For this, the firm's highest decision-making body was to be a general company meeting in which the three elements of management, capital, and labour all participated, and the three should also be involved in the distribution of profits and sharing of risk. Clearly, this is very similar to the thinking on corporate reform that came with the New Economic System, and also that of the Ministry of Commerce and Industry after the war. The chairman of the *Keizai Dōyūkai* Committee for Democratization of the Economy, Manjo Otsuka, said that their aim should be to 'replace the private benefits of capitalists with the interests of the community' (Otsuka 1947). This shows even more clearly how closely the ideas of the *Keizai Dōyūkai* on corporate democratization resembled those contained in the New Economic System. There is also a striking similarity between the concept of a neutral management mediating between labour and capital, and the view held in present-day Japanese firms on the role of directors as arbitrators between shareholders and employees (Aoki 1988).

Thus, a new style of corporate governance structure was formed immediately after the war, together with a broad-based consensus in support of it. This is symbolized by the setting up, on government instruction, of the Economic Recovery Council (*Keizai Fukkō Kaigi*) in February 1947. At its centre were the Japanese Federation of Labour, seeking to restore production through labour's greater co-operative involvement in management, and the *Keizai Dōyūkai*, working for corporate democratization (Hayakawa and Yoshida 1982). The Council's 'Prospectus' called for 'workers to heighten their productive zeal while overthrowing the evils of capital, managements to boost efficiency while putting through comprehensive democratic reforms, both groups together pushing ahead to rebuild production for the stability and improvement of people's lives'. It can be seen as a declaration of solidarity between managements freed from shareholders' control and employees with increased power.

4.2. Changes in corporate behaviour

The behaviour of firms immediately after the end of the war is characterized by the remarkable phenomenon of massive over-employment. As a measure of over-employment we can use the disparity between the ratio of sales turnover to personnel costs for the year concerned and the same ratio at an optimum level of employment. In this, the elasticity of demand for labour to real wages and to sales turnover are assumed to be minus one and plus one respectively (Yoshikawa 1988: 83). Using as the base year of optimum employment the year 1957, which was the peak year of the Jimmu Boom (the first major economic boom in the post-war period), calculations show that between 1946 and 1948 employment across the industrial spectrum was far in excess of optimal figures (Table 4.8).[9] Not only this, but real wages also rose rapidly. The result was that firms still in the midst of reconstruction could only achieve low profit rates, even in their new accounts (Table 4.9), and many firms showed a deficit (Daiyamondosha 1948).

What made it possible for managements to support over-employment while running losses was policy framework. Roughly half the RFB's lending for operating funds was deficit financing, meaning 'lending for a set period to cover a firm's losses and support its operations' (Ministry of Finance, Financial History Section 1976: 671). Official price ceilings, which had been set systematically for the first time after the war in March 1946, were revised in July 1947 and again in June 1948. On both occasions official producer prices were based

Table 4.8. Estimated rates of over-employment

	All manufacturing industry	Foodstuffs	Textiles	Timber	Publishing and printing	Chemicals	Metals	Machinery
1946	0.490	0.272	0.497	0.455	-0.216	0.466	0.573	0.495
1947	0.477	0.450	0.467	0.467	-0.027	0.447	0.525	0.494
1948	0.468	0.346	0.548	0.340	0.244	0.434	0.521	0.547
1949	0.438	0.412	0.323	0.431	0.117	0.414	0.513	0.557
1950	0.266	0.336	0.009	0.344	-0.040	0.249	0.355	0.471
1951	0.053	0.153	-0.179	0.185	-0.292	0.124	0.077	0.274
1952	0.090	0.007	-0.037	0.175	-0.291	0.140	0.133	0.268
1953	0.059	-0.027	-0.086	0.042	-0.260	0.077	0.152	0.224
1954	0.111	-0.023	0.031	0.070	-0.064	0.128	0.251	0.245
1955	0.094	-0.011	0.048	0.123	-0.063	0.091	0.164	0.264
1956	0.013	0.011	-0.038	0.050	-0.019	0.037	-0.020	0.107
1957	0.000	0.000	0.000	0.000	0.000	0.000	0.000	0.000
1958	0.076	0.035	0.099	0.027	0.050	0.029	0.229	0.007
1959	0.043	0.669	0.086	0.004	0.061	-0.065	0.132	-0.007
1960	0.014	0.104	0.138	-0.026	0.075	-0.169	0.410	-0.105

Note: Over-employment rate = (ratio of personnel costs to value of shipments for year in question – ratio of personnel costs to value of shipments in 1957)/ratio of personnel costs to value of shipments in 1957 (see Ministry of Labour (1987), *Rōdō Hakusho* (Labour White Paper), p. 102).

Source: Tōyō Keizai Shinpō-sha (1991).

Table 4.9. Ratio of earnings on total
capital employed in manufacturing
industry

Period		Ratio
1945	1st half	−3.6
1946	1st half	0.9
1948	1st half	0.8
	2nd half	2.5
1949	1st half	3.7
	2nd half	3.2
1950	1st half	5.6
	2nd half	12.2
1951	1st half	10.2
	2nd half	5.9

Sources: Industrial Bank of Japan, *Sangyō
Kin'yū Jihō* (Industrial Finance Review),
22, 50, 56; Industrial Bank of Japan, *Honpō Shuyō Kaisha Gyōseki Chōsa* (Survey of
Leading Corporations' Business Results),
1949 1st half.

on costs, and the disparity with consumer prices was covered by price-
adjustment subsidies (Ministry of Finance, Financial History Section 1980:
334–65, 427–51). So firms dealt with the losses they incurred due to rising costs
through short-term deficit financing, which they later recouped by means of
official price increases or larger subsidies. At a round-table meeting of the
Japan Managers' Federation (*Nihon Keieisha Renmei*) in early 1949, Kin'ichi
Aoki, president of a construction-materials firm, Shinagawa Shiro Renga, and
a member of the Reconstruction Finance Committee (*Fukkō Kin'yū Iinkai*), is
quoted as saying that 'with wages so high, nothing can be done about deficits.
We just wait for the government to raise producer prices to cover the shortfall.
We've been doing this for a long time, so from the management viewpoint it's
better to wait for prices to be jacked up rather than struggle to reduce costs.
We're on the wrong course but it's just too easy' (Keieisha, February 1949, p.
14). This describes a typical 'soft budget constraint' situation, and under these
conditions no bank monitoring system such as described above could have
succeeded in imposing discipline on the firms.

Furthermore, because of this situation labour unions could support over-
employment and also demand wage increases without any concerns about
possible bankruptcy. Managers, too, were able to accept their demands and
maintain industrial peace.[10] Thus, the behaviour of firms immediately after
the war was characterized by just the same 'soft budget constraint' of the final
years of the war period. Considering the similarities between the wartime

mechanisms of the controlled economy and this post-war corporate governance structure, this is not surprising. Strengthening employees' power if anything had made the situation more serious. This was the corporate management style described as 'scandalous' by Tatsunosuke Takasaki, mentioned at the beginning of this chapter. In macro terms it led to an enormous budget deficit, rampant inflation of around 200 per cent per annum, and low investment and savings rates. What ultimately accommodated firms' soft budget constraints was the soft budget constraint on government finance, and it was indifference to investors' rights that lay behind low macro investment and savings rates.

From 1947, the HCLC began selling off the shares it had amassed, but this made no immediate difference to corporate behaviour. From the viewpoint of economic democratization, GHQ encouraged selling shares to employees, and as I have mentioned, many in Japanese government circles believed in employee share-ownership. The Securities Holdings Restrictions Directive (*Shōken Hoyū Seigen Rei*) of December 1946 specified that employees should be given the highest priority in the disposal of shares (Ministry of Finance, Financial History Section 1979: 385). Of the total shares sold off, 43 per cent ended up in the hands of employees, giving them a significant proportion (Ministry of Finance, Financial History Section 1982: 373). It has also been said that in disposing of shares, 'the Japanese side made an effort to ensure the firm could be run by its former management', and 'when releasing and dividing up the stock of old *zaibatsu* firms, the chairman of the HCLC struggled to allocate blocks of 20 per cent to 30 per cent to the parties concerned' (Tokyo Association of Securities Companies 1971: 98–101). As the main body involved in the disposal of shares, the HCLC took care that disposal should not affect existing corporate governance structure. This was consistent with the above-mentioned behaviour of the HCLC in appointing directors. It is well known that firms made efforts to ensure they obtained stable shareholders (Okumura 1969*a*, *b*; Miyajima 1992; K. Suzuki 1992). They were obliged to do this because during the war and in the immediate post-war period managements disregarded the interests of shareholders, and it was possible to do it because a wide consensus, including government, supported the existing governance structure. By the end of 1949 about 70 per cent of the shares of firms listed on the Tokyo stock market were in the hands of individuals, so shareholding was certainly more widely spread (Ministry of Finance, Financial History Section 1979: 387). However, it is safe to assume that a considerable number of the shares held by individuals were in the hands of employees or other stable shareholders.

Of course, not all shares could be placed with employees or stable shareholders, and even stable shareholders could not possibly continue to approve of the over-employment and low profit margins described above. From that time it was made clear that without the restoration of shareholders' rights and the protection of their profits, it would be difficult to dispose of shares smoothly and subsequently raise funds from shareholders. For instance, an

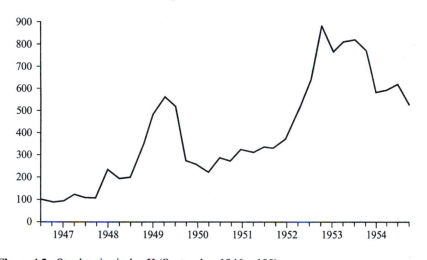

Figure 4.2. Stock price index II (September 1946 = 100)

Source: Bank of Japan, Statistics Department, *Honpō Keizai Tōkei* (Economic Statistics for Japan), published annually.

August 1947 editorial of Tōyō Keizai Shinpō entitled 'Lamenting Diminished Capital Accumulation' criticized the *Keizai Dōyūkai* report referred to above. What was most vital for economic recovery was capital. Large amounts of capital needed to be raised through shares, but with shareholders' rights restricted, 'shareholders will not be happy to provide capital without an equivalent degree of influence'.[11]

None the less, mocking all concerns, the disposal of shares proceeded steadily until the beginning of 1949, and through group dealings that sprang up with the closure of the stock market, share prices surged upward in something of a boom (Figure 4.2; Ministry of Finance, Financial History Section 1979: 351–7). This indicates how highly ordinary investors rated stocks and shares as assets. The justification for buying shares despite their low profit rates was that under rampant inflation, prices of corporate assets were expected to rise, and so shares were the preferred means of hedging against inflation. The fact that expansionist macroeconomic policy and the inflation it brought about alleviated shareholders' discontent somewhat by raising asset prices can be seen as a factor in the toleration of firms' soft budget constraint.

4.3. Changes brought about by the transition to a market economy

The Dodge Plan reforms that began in 1949 swept away all these conditions in a single stroke. Earlier, at the end of 1948, GHQ had introduced 'three corporate principles' which prohibited increases in subsidies and official prices, and wage rises paid for by deficit financing. This was an attempt to eliminate soft budgets by direct means. Next, under Dodge's guidance the budget for FY1949 was balanced and from April 1949 the RFB stopped new lending, thus eliminating the macro-conditions allowing soft budgets. At the same time progress was made on abolishing price controls and rationing, competition between firms revived in markets for manufactured goods, and the micro-conditions for soft budgets also disappeared.

Financial markets reacted sensitively to these changes. The first indication was the fall in share prices that started immediately after share dealing was re-opened in May 1949 (Figure 4.2). As inflation was reined in, capital that had been poured into the stock market as a hedge against inflation began to flow out again, averse to low corporate profit rates. GHQ had frozen new lending from the RFB, and now took measures to concentrate long-term and short-term financing on the capital markets and the banking institutions respectively. Approval of corporate reconstruction plans required that capital injections be increased until net worth matched fixed assets and regular current assets (Ministry of Finance, Financial History Section 1983: 876–7). The 'special' losses incurred through the termination of wartime compensation were written off by reducing paid-up capital by up to 90 per cent after subtracting the appraised value of current assets, and capital increases ballooned as a result. But the 1949 fall in stock prices made further capital increases difficult (Daiwa Securities Co. 1963: 270–1). The fall in inflation realized the fears of Tōyō Keizai Shinpō mentioned earlier. The situation can be seen as a protest on the part of the capital markets against the reconstruction of firms remaining in the control of management/employee groups who paid little heed to shareholders' profits. This sort of reaction was inevitable while firms lacked an effective monitoring system to protect shareholders' profits, and managements failed to boost profits and persisted in supporting over-employment.

Thus, capital market investors were moving out of the corporate sector, but the banks' response was different. They had increased their involvement in this sector during the war and now sought to maintain these closer relations, and exploit their rights of expression as creditors. Bank of Japan loan mediation continued to provide an institutional framework for bank lending. The expected provision of long-term financing through the capital markets to replace that of the RFB had not materialized, and so the Bank of Japan became more active in loan mediation (BOJ 1984*b*; Tōyō Keizai Shinpō, 11 June 1949, p. 1, and 29 October 1949, pp. 42–3). At a round table discussion published in the Tōyō Keizai Shinpō in June 1949, Toshio Inoue, a BOJ director, said of the provision of funds for rationalization (employment adjustment) through loan mediation, that he 'would like to see the commercial banks lending to firms with the prospect, as a result of rationalization, of getting back on their feet and reducing production costs'. He went on to say that 'if the banks are short of funds, the Bank of Japan will attend to it' (Tōyō Keizai Shinpō, 25 June 1949, p. 13).

At the same time, however, the elimination of economic controls and the terminating of loans from the RFB meant that providing funds to overstaffed firms performing poorly involved considerable risk. So the main banks of these firms, which had dispatched special supervisors to them, included employee adjustment in reconstruction plans. Their loan consortia, organized through BOJ mediation, also made the carrying through of employee adjustment a condition for continued and supplementary lending. As in the famous case of Toshiba, loan consortia even demanded that managements, where necessary, be replaced. With the transition from a controlled to a market economy, main banks made it clear that as corporate monitors, they would take corrective action over managements. Thus, whereas shareholders had lacked an effective monitoring system, the banks' monitoring system and its capabilities, developed since the war period, made it possible to provide funds to firms or industries under conditions of high risk during this transition period. The most significant difference with the capital market was that banks had the capability for interim monitoring, by which regular checks were made during the course of funded projects, allowing corrective measures to be taken if necessary (Aoki 1995).

A number of policies were implemented to stop the fall in share prices and restore the function of the capital markets. In August 1949 the Ministry of Finance revised regulations on lending by financial institutions, raising from third- to second-rank priority the lending of operating capital to securities brokers and stock-purchasing capital to investors. In December of that year this was again upgraded, to top-rank priority. In the same month the Bank of Japan asked banks and life insurance companies to start purchasing shares using funds supplied to them through BOJ market operations (Tokyo Stock Exchange 1963: 189–91). Through these policies, banks became more closely involved with the capital markets. GHQ envisioned separate roles for banks and capital markets and was therefore negative about banks' involvement in the capital markets, as shown by Clause 65 of the Securities and Exchange Act (*Shōken Torihiki Hō*). Yet without this involvement it would be difficult for the capital markets to recover. The BOJ Research Bureau said in a document dated February 1950,

over 90 per cent of corporate bonds issued are absorbed by financial institutions, and we need to encourage these institutions to buy shares and implement lending on securities collateral as stock recovery measures. This means that narrowly defined financial markets centred on the banks will be forced once again to take the capital markets under their wing . . . Substantive implementation of Clause 65 of the Securities and Exchange Law is facing difficulty. (BOJ 1950: 774)

Responding to the Bank of Japan's request, banks duly purchased shares and increased securities lending (ibid. 771–2). This lending enabled securities brokers to hold unsold publicly offered shares on their own accounts (Daiwa Securities Co. 1963: 271). Firms issuing shares were also allowed to hold their own shares under the name of a securities broker (BOJ 1954: 449; Okumura

1969*b*: 58; K. Suzuki 1992: 11). These circumstances may account for the prominence of securities companies in the distribution of share ownership at the end of FY1949 (BOJ 1954: 458). To complement these short-term measures to support share prices, long-term measures were used to build a framework of stable share ownership. With the revision of the Anti-Monopoly Law in June 1949, business firms were in principle free to own shares, something which had been prohibited under the 1947 law. This revision was designed to allow firms to hold newly issued shares as preparation for borrowing external capital and also in readiness for capital injections for their reconstruction (Ministry of Finance, Financial History Section 1982: 590; Daiwa Securities Co. 1963: 270). In addition to this revision, which had been drafted prior to the fall in share prices, there was some discussion over whether to set up securities holding institutions with 'counterpart funds' (*mikaeri shikin*) or to set up holding companies, as a measure to support share prices and promote capital increases. In fact, neither of these ideas was implemented, and investment trusts were launched as an alternative system in 1951 (Tokyo Stock Exchange 1963: 188–98).

The Ministry of Finance had first started looking at investment trusts in 1948 as a way of promoting more widespread investment in shares, but the idea had been shelved with the stock market boom. Now, however, in the face of difficulties in increasing investment, 'the idea of investment trusts was once again floated, not only to promote wider shareholding among the public, but also as a mechanism to absorb new share issues related to corporate reconstruction legislation, which were largely in the hands of stockbrokers' (BOJ 1954: 437). Investment trusts were a system in which trustees, the trust banks, bought, sold, and managed holdings of securities on the instructions of commissioning institutions, the securities brokers. Any stocks and shares involved were held in the name of the trust bank. Provided that trust banks did not wield voting rights, restrictions on financial institutions' ownership of shares under the Anti-Monopoly Law were waived (BOJ 1954: 439–40). The lifting in 1952 of the ban on crossholdings of shares for companies affiliated to the former *zaibatsu*, through abolition of the Restrictions on Holding Securities Directive (*Shōken Hoyū Seigen Rei*), and the easing of restrictions on share ownership by financial institutions through further revision of the Anti-Monopoly Law in 1953 (K. Suzuki 1992: 11–13), are both measures that can be seen as furthering the same general trend.

A series of measures implemented after 1949 brought about further major changes in the pattern of share ownership. There was a drop in the proportions of shares of listed companies held by individuals and securities companies, which in 1949 had been 68.5 per cent and 12.6 per cent respectively, and a corresponding advance in the positions of financial institutions and business firms (Ministry of Finance, Financial History Section 1983: 421). The growth of investment trusts was particularly fast, accounting for 5.2 per cent of share issues from listed firms by the end of FY1951, and reaching a peak of 9.4 per cent in FY1963. The importance of the role of investment trusts is shown more clearly in the composition of large shareholders in individual firms (Table 4.3). Over the period 1949 to 1955, government institutions and securities firms lost ground in favour of financial institutions, and particularly the trust banks, trustees for investment trusts. Trust banks went on to become the largest shareholding group until investment trusts suffered a major setback in the stock market slump of the 1960s. The second largest group was the life insurance companies (Yamanaka 1966: 340).

Asset management of investment trusts was based on Ministry of Finance guidelines. These guidelines required, for example, that the average stock price over the previous three months should be above par, dividends must be paid, or there must be definite prospects of paying a dividend, and the average stock price over the previous three months should give a yield of around 8 per cent (Tanaka 1953: 164). The life insurance companies became long-term shareholders in blue-chip firms and made it a principle to safeguard their investments and ensure high-dividend yields (Honma 1953: 149–50). The increase of institutional investors with these priorities indicates that from the shareholders' viewpoint corporate management during the early 1950s was returning to health. In fact from 1950 onwards, the massive over-employment that characterized the end of the 1940s was rapidly eliminated and corporate profit rates picked up (Table 4.9).[12] Over-employment was resolved partly as a result of the economic boom associated with the Korean War, and also through the implementation of employee adjustment plans. As I have said, the banks played a very significant role in the adjustment of excess personnel. The banks took the initiative in the reconstruction of corporate management, and on that understanding institutional investors built up their shareholdings.

Despite being large shareholders, institutional investors rarely dispatched directors to sit on firms' boards, and at the end of FY1951, as at the end of FY1947, most serving directors had been appointed through internal promotion (Table 4.4). Thus, instead of large shareholders monitoring either directly or indirectly, as was the case before the war, the system typically found in present-day Japanese firms took hold, in which monitoring by capital providers is wholly undertaken by the banks (Aoki 1988: 159–61). On this point it is of interest that capital increases from the end of the 1940s to the beginning of the 1950s were largely to repay debts (Ministry of Finance, Financial History Section 1979: 422–3). For the banks' part, in order to recover accumulated debts and avoid the risk inherent in high debt–equity ratios of the firms to which they were lending, they needed to maintain incentives to shareholders to promote smooth capital increases. This created a situation in which it was not unreasonable for long-term shareholders, as well as banks, to be prepared to delegate monitoring to the main bank.[13]

It is important to appreciate that the banks, life insurance companies, and securities companies or trust banks acting as investment trust managers, were anxious not only for returns from their investments. It was stressed in Chapter Three that banks aimed to establish long-term business relations with firms in order to collect deposits. In investing in securities, banks took account of their 'business policy objectives', of which the most important was 'whether acquisition of stocks and bonds would strengthen relations with the firm involved and lead to increased deposits' (Ono 1953: 138). The life insurance companies also developed a strong interest in maintaining corporate relations and in corporate growth. From 1948 these companies began doing business in group insurance, which had previously been a monopoly of Japan Group Life Insurance (*Nippon Dantai Seimei*), and this stimulated competition in securing firms' group insurance (Ministry of Finance, Financial History Section 1979: 210–11; Usami 1984: 272–4). For the securities companies there was much to be gained from becoming lead underwriting manager for share issues (Daiwa Securities Co. 1963: 307–11), and so securities companies, too, sought to maintain business relations with firms and promote their growth.

In resolving the problem of over-employment, confrontation surfaced between managements and their employees. Under the Dodge Plan reforms, corporate managements were forced to accept banks' demands and deal with over-employment, and this move naturally led to union protests and labour unrest. But the labour unions were at a disadvantage. First, GHQ changed its overall policy on labour and the government brought in a series of measures, including revision of the Labour Unions Law, to restrain the unions. More important was the removal of the policy framework that had tolerated over-employment. With changes in policy, banks changed their attitude to lending with the result that excessive demands from labour unions could drive firms to bankruptcy, which was not in their workers' interests.[14] Many of the struggles against employee adjustment ended in defeat for the union involved. The conditions of soft budget constraint that had persisted under economic controls for 10 years since the war period were steadily being eliminated, and the frequent labour struggles against 'corporate adjustments' during the late 1940s and early 1950s could be described as the friction generated until employees came to understand the significance of these adjustments. It has been pointed out that under the lifetime employment system, corporate growth brought about incentives such as promotion opportunities and increases in retirement allowances and employees therefore became very 'growth-minded' (Aoki 1988: 164–6; Iwai 1988). Taking this together with what has been said about banks and stable shareholders, we see that the interests of all the stakeholders in firms converged on corporate growth. Thus the corporate governance structure created out of changes during the war and the post-war recovery period was in essence very strongly growth-oriented.

5. Conclusion

It has been stressed in other papers that before the war Japanese enterprises were somewhat 'Anglo-Saxon' in terms of their corporate governance structure. This structure can be regarded as having developed out of several mutually complementary systems. First, in pre-war Japan there were many wealthy investors able to become influential shareholders. They devised a corporate monitoring system and became the leading capital providers for the corporate sector. In non-*zaibatsu* firms shareholders monitored management through a direct system in which large shareholders served on boards, and in *zaibatsu* firms holding companies monitored systematically. Second, banks did not play a significant role in corporate financing, especially long-term financing, and therefore individual banks had no system set up to monitor firms. Third, workers had no strong attachments to their firms, and there was very little development of procedures to guarantee workers' rights of expression *vis-à-vis* managements. The complementarity between the first two of these points is obvious. In pre-war corporate financing, shareholders took the lead and banks played only a supporting role. The prominent role of shareholders was complementary to the low commitment felt by employees to their firms. Strong shareholders' rights led to the adoption of management policies that made swift employment adjustments, and in fact workers' lack of commitment can be thought of as having reduced the friction that these sorts of management policies might have generated.

What occurred during the war and the post-war period of economic recovery were circumstances of concurrent and far-reaching change in these complementary institutions. As an incentive system to gain workers' cooperation for wartime production, the government encouraged participation in management across a broad spectrum of firms through industrial patriotic societies. Shareholders intervened in management from the standpoint of profits, and so measures were taken to limit the rights of shareholders in order to avoid any hampering of production. The restriction of shareholders' rights started with the control of dividends and progressed by the end of the war to bypassing the provisions of the Commercial Code by means of the Munitions Corporations Law. During this time large numbers of internally promoted directors joined the ranks of managements. As the monitoring system through shareholders no longer functioned effectively, capital provision from the stock market shrank and in response the government set up a system for funds provision through the banks. Scarce monitoring capability was used efficiently by means of delegated monitoring, and supplemented by the resources of the National Finance Control Association and the Bank of Japan. Thus, complementary changes took place during the war: as shareholders' rights were restricted, the status of workers rose and banks appeared as new monitors in response to the limitations on shareholders' rights. At the end of the war monitoring through the banks was eased, resulting in firms finding themselves under typical conditions of soft budget constraint.

Changes that took place during the post-war recovery period served to further the trends established during the war. Various reforms imposed by GHQ greatly enhanced workers' rights, while decimating the influential investor class made up of large shareholders. Given the wartime experience and the situation described above, the Japanese government took measures for corporate reconstruction and economic recovery that were based on the corporate governance structure formed during the war. Through the Corporate Accounts Special Measures Law and the Corporate Reconstruction Law enterprises were effectively placed under the supervision of the banks. A system was adopted to raise new money for reconstruction, with the Bank of Japan facilitating loan consortia, in each case under the leadership of the bank that had dispatched special supervisors to the firm concerned. The government took a favourable view of boards composed of internally promoted directors, and also encouraged workers' involvement in management through management councils. The role of shareholders was entirely overlooked as corporate reconstruction was planned around banks, managements, and employees. Economic recovery was based on this sort of corporate governance structure up to 1948, but it brought about the serious problem of soft budget constraint, which had also occurred during wartime. With economic controls still in place, the banks had little incentive for monitoring, and with workers wielding far stronger rights than during the war, there was massive over-employment.

Transition to a market economy through the Dodge Plan reforms removed these soft budget conditions. Banks acting as monitors imposed corrective measures on firms and rapidly eliminated over-employment, demanding where necessary that managements be replaced. The labour unrest that this brought about can be thought of as a manifestation of the friction generated by the shift from a controlled to a market economy. It was the banks that played the central role. It has been pointed out that a characteristic feature of governance structure in Japanese firms is the duality of interests it involves: employees' interests *vis-à-vis* financial interests (Aoki 1988). The series of post-war changes through which firms that were virtually under the control of their employees were forced through banks' intervention to adapt to the needs of a market economy can be said to provide the historical grounds for this view.

Through the process of correcting over-employment, employees learned that in a market economy, striving for corporate growth is very much in their own interests. Once over-employment had been eliminated, institutional investors who were in effect prepared to delegate monitoring to the main bank moved into the stock market. Banks, of course, and such institutional investors as life insurance companies and the trust banks and securities companies managing investment trusts, all had their own business dealings with firms, and thus had a strong interest in corporate growth. So by the early 1950s, a pro-growth corporate governance structure had been formed, its major players being growth-oriented lifetime employees and a similarly growth-oriented financing body of investors centred round a main bank.

Notes

1. Exceptions were made for raising the dividend rate to 6% in firms whose standard rate was set at below 6%, and raising the dividend by 1% provided that it remained below 10%.
2. For more on the concept and functioning of the main bank system, see Aoki (1995).
3. 'Major Industries Council/Corporate Adjustment, Wartime Corporate System Committee/Munitions Corporations Round Table Meeting', Ichiro Ishikawa Papers, University of Tokyo, Faculty of Economics.
4. 'Major Industries Council (1)', Ichiro Ishikawa Papers, as above.
5. 'Fourth Wartime Corporate System Committee Proceedings', in 'Major Industries Council/Corporate Adjustment, Wartime Corporate System Committee/Munitions Corporations Round Table Meeting'.
6. Preparatory Committee for the Munitions Corporations Round Table Meeting Report, as above.
7. Ministry of Finance, Financial History Section (1981: 622–3).
8. Tōyō Keizai Shinpō, 28 September 1946. It claims that from some points of view, it can be said that special supervisors played a leading role in the reconstruction of Japanese industry.
9. In a discussion featured in a Tōyō Keizai Shinpō-sha publication in January 1948, a BOJ director, Shozo Ezawa, is quoted as saying 'Firms are not profitable today because of their high personnel costs. These costs eat up almost all income, and if they still are not covered money has to be borrowed. There are 1.5 or 1.7 million extra people padding out employment in this way. Firms are doing the state's job of supporting the unemployed. There's no way firms can get back on their feet' (Tōyō Keizai Shinpō-sha, 10 January 1948, p. 11).
10. On this point, the Tōyō Keizai Shinpō on 24 April 1948 makes the harsh criticism that 'many of the new managers who have suddenly appeared since the war are extremely sloppy'. It goes on to say, 'by calling themselves management functionaries or management technicians they parry fierce attacks from the labour side, and their tactics are to give top priority to defending themselves' and 'they give way even at the very last line of defence, and as a result, there are countless cases of business collapse' (p. 4).
11. In a further editorial dated 17 January 1948, it was claimed that 'post-war trends stress only respect for labour, while capital is mistreated, and on occasions these distortions have been so extreme as to throw doubt on the new objectives of democratic management. Journalists of this publication have long maintained that correcting this bias and adopting policies that respect capital are essential conditions for the reconstruction of the Japanese economy (Tōyō Keizai Shinpō, 17 January 1948, p. 3). Similarly, the president of Nikko Securities Co. Ltd. stated that 'if clients are likely to make a loss, we cannot push them to buy stocks. With limits on dividends, high corporate taxation, and shareholders with no rights of expression on corporate management, capital is being very badly treated' (ibid. p. 13).
12. In a public address in 1952, the managing director of Daiichi Seimei Life Insurance Company, Yuichi Nishiyama, stated, 'currently, Daiichi Seimei holds 24 or 25 million shares, and their average return is about 17%. Lending brings a little over

10%, so if we invest in reliable shares the returns are extremely good. It is for this reason that I consider that we have to put considerable emphasis on investing in shares' (Yamanaka 1966: 340).

13. The 1950 revision to the Commercial Code had been intended to introduce a different type of monitoring system. GHQ ordered the revision with the objective of having the newly diversified shareholders maintain effective control over firms' managements, in recognition of the new situation of diversified shareholdings and separation of ownership and management (A. Yazawa 1967). The former system focused on the shareholders' meeting would be abolished, the authority of the board of directors strengthened, and the code brought in line with these circumstances, but it also planned for the right to appoint directors to be held by a small number of shareholders, and to protect shareholders from the abuse of directors' authority. In practice, for appointing more than one director, various new systems would be introduced, such as a cumulative voting system, and the right of shareholders to examine accounts would be increased. If a cumulative voting system were adopted, minority shareholders would be able to have a representative sit on the board, and 'under the 1950 revision, the wish of the legislators was that directors from outside the firm might also be selected to sit on firms' boards' (T. Suzuki 1967). But business circles did not favour this. As there were no restrictions placed on shareholders' rights to demand cumulative voting in the Justice Ministry's original bill 'Outline of Revisions to the Commercial Code', published in August 1949, it stirred up particularly strong reactions. The Federation of Economic Organization's 'Views on Revisions to the Commercial Code' (October 1949; *Keizai Rengō*, November 1949) demanded that the introduction of the cumulative voting system be put off, giving as a reason that 'the result of cumulative voting cannot produce a group of directors sharing the same sense of commitment to the running of the company'. Filling the board with internally promoted directors was favoured in the war years in business circles, as I have said, and was now put forward once again. In view of the criticism, the revised Commercial Code set out that cumulative voting could be restricted by article of incorporation except in cases where large shareholders with a holding of over 25% requested it.

14. The Tōyō Keizai Shinpō edition of 28 May 1949 reported that employee adjustment and wage reductions could be seen in the mechanical engineering and telecommunications machinery industries. It commented that 'when firms are driven to the brink, labour unions give up their former intransigence, accepting wage cuts and concluding that employee adjustment is inevitable under the circumstances' (p. 1).

References

Aoki, Masahiko (1988), *Information, Incentives and Bargaining in the Japanese Economy*, Cambridge University Press.

——(1995), 'Monitoring Characteristics of the Main Bank System', in Masakiho Aoki and Hugh Patrick (eds.), *The Japanese Main Bank System: Its Relevance for Developing and Transforming Economies*, Oxford University Press.

Asajima, Shoichi (1987) (ed.), *Zaibatsu Kin'yū Kōzō no Hikaku Kenkyū* (A Comparative Study on the Financing of the *Zaibatsu*), Ochanomizu Shobō.

Bank of Japan (1950), 'Saikin no Kabushiki Shijō (On the Recent Stock Market)', in Bank of Japan (ed.), *Nihon Kin'yū-shi Shiryō* (Materials on Japanese Financial History), Ministry of Finance Printing Bureau, vol. 8 of Shōwa Era later series.

——(1953), 'Kin Yushutsu Saikinshi yori Shūsen madeno Waga Kuni Keizai Tōsei no Suii (Economic Controls in Japan from the Abolition of the Gold Standard to the End of the War)', in Bank of Japan (ed.), *Nihon Kin'yū-shi Shiryō* (Materials on Japanese Financial History), Ministry of Finance Printing Bureau, vol. 27 of Shōwa Era series.

——(1954), 'Shōken Tōshi Shintaku no Kaisetsu to Mondaiten (Institutions and Controversial Points of Mutual Funds)', in Bank of Japan (ed.), *Nihon Kin'yū-shi Shiryō* (Materials on Japanese Financial History), Ministry of Finance Printing Bureau, vol. 11 of Showa Era later series.

——(1959), 'Yūshi Assen no Enkaku (History of the Loan Mediation System)', in Bank of Japan (ed.), *Nihon Kin'yū-shi Shiryō* (Materials on Japanese Financial History), Ministry of Finance Printing Bureau, vol. 9 of Shōwa Era later series.

——(1984a, b), *Nihon Ginkō 100nen-shi* (100-Year History of the Bank of Japan), vols. 4, 5, Bank of Japan.

Daiwa Securities Co. (1963), *Daiwa Shōken 60nen-shi* (60-Year History of Daiwa Securities), Daiwa Securities Co.

Daiyamondosha (1948), *Daiyamondo Kaisha Yōran* (Corporate Directory).

Emi, Koichi, Masakichi Ito, and Eiichi Eguchi (1988), *Chochiku to Tsūka* (Savings and Currency), Tōyō Keizai Shinpō-sha.

Hasegawa, Yasubei (1941), *Kabushiki Gaisha Dokuhon* (A Reader on the Joint-Stock Company System), Chikura Shobō.

Hashimoto, Juro (1992), 'Zaibatsu no "Konzern"-ka (Formation of Holding Companies by *Zaibatsu*)', in Juro Hashimoto and Haruhito Takeda (eds.), *Nihon no Keizai Hatten to Kigyō Shūdan* (Japanese Economic Development and Business Groups), University of Tokyo Press.

Hayakawa, Seiji and Kenji Yoshida (1982), 'Keizai Fukkō Kaigi no Soshiki to Undō (Organization and Movement of the Economic Reconstruction Congress)', Research Institute of Social and Labour Problems, Hosei University, and Ohara Institute of Social Problems, Hosei University (eds.), *Kenkyū Shiryō Geppō*, 283.

Hiraoka Research Institute of Political Economy (1950), *Kaisetsu Keizai Saihensei Hōrei Shū* (Commentary of Laws and Ordinances on Economic Reorganization), Mikasa Shobō.

Hirschman, Albert (1970), *Exit, Voice and Loyalty*, Cambridge University Press.

Holding Companies Liquidation Committee (1951), *Nihon Zaibatsu to sono Kaitai* (Japanese *Zaibatsu* and Their Dissolution), Holding Companies Liquidation Committee.

Honma, Kiichi (1953), 'Seiho Gaisha no Baibai Hō (Investment Policy of the Life Insurance Companies)', *Keiei Hyōron Rinji Zōkan: 100man Nin no Kabushiki no Tebiki*, (Special Issue of Keiei Hyōron: Investment Guide for Everybody), Okura Shuppan.

Hyodo, Tsutomu (1970), *Nihon ni okeru Rōshi Kankei no Tenkai* (Evolution of Industrial Relations in Japan), University of Tokyo Press.

——(1971), *Nihon niokeru Roshi Kankei no Tenkai* (Development of Labour Relations in Japan), University of Tokyo Press.

Imuta, Toshimitsu (1991), 'Nihon Kōgyō Ginkō to Senji Kin'yū Kinko (The Industrial Bank of Japan and the Wartime Finance Bank)', in Toshimitsu Imuta (ed.), *Senji Taisei kano Kin'yū Kōzō* (The Japanese Financial System in the War Economy), Nihon Hyōron-sha.

Iwai, Katsuhito (1988), 'Jūgyōin Kanri Kigyō toshiteno Nihon Kigyō (The Japanese Firm as a Labour-Managed Firm)', in Kikuo Iwata and Tsuneo Ishikawa (eds.), *Nihon Keizai Kenkyū* (Study on the Japanese Economy), University of Tokyo Press.

Japan Petroleum Co. (1988), *Nihon Sekiyu 100nen-shi* (100-Year History of Japan Petroleum Co.), Japan Petroleum Co.

Japan Steel Co. (1959), *Nippon Seitetsu Kabushiki Gaisha Shi* (A History of the Japan Steel Co.), Japan Steel Co.

Kanda, Fumito (1981), 'Explanatory Notes', in Fumito Kanda (ed.), *Shiryō Nihon Gendai Shi* (Materials on Modern History of Japan), Ōtsuki Shoten.

Keizai Doyukai (1951), *Keizai Dōyūkai Gonen-shi* (Five-Year History of Keizai Dōyūkai), Keizai Dōyūkai.

Kitano, Shigeo (1944), *Gunjushō oyobi Gunju Gaisha Hō* (The Ministry of Munitions and the Munitions Corporations Law), Takayama Shoin.

Kitazawa, Masahiro (1966), 'Kabushiki Gaisha no Shoyū Keiei Shihai (Ownership, Management, and Control of Joint-Stock Companies)', in Atsushi Yazawa (ed.), *Gendai Hō to Kigyō* (Modern Laws and Firms), Iwanami Shoten.

Kurosaka, Yoshio (1988), *Makuro Keizaigaku to Nihon no Rōdō Shijō* (Macro-economic Analysis of the Japanese Labour Market), Tōyō Keizai Shinpō-sha.

Matsumoto, Hiroshi (1979), *Mitsui Zaibatsu no Kenkyū* (A Study on Mitsui *Zaibatsu*), Yoshikawa Kobunkan.

Milgrom, Paul and John Roberts (1992), *Economics, Organizations and Management*, Prentice Hall.

Ministry of Finance, Financial History Section (1976, 1977, 1978, 1979, 1980, 1981, 1982, 1983), *Shōwa Zaisei Shi: Shūsen kara Kōwa made* (Financial History of the Showa Era: From the End of the War to the Peace), vols. 12, 7, 19, 14, 10, 17, 2, 13, Tōyō Keizai Shinpō-sha.

Ministry of Labour (1954), *Keiei Sanka Seidō* (The Management Participation System), Rōdō Gyōsei Kenkyūjo.

——(1969), *Rōdō Gyōsei Shi* (A History of Labour Policy), Rōdō Hōrei Kyōkai.

Miyajima, Hideaki (1992), 'Zaibatsu Kaitai (The Dissolution of the *Zaibatsu*)', in Juro Hashimoto and Haruhito Takeda (eds.), *Nihon no Keizai Hatten to Kigyō Shūdan* (Japanese Economic Development and Business Groups), University of Tokyo Press.

Miyamoto, Mataro (1990), 'Sangyōka to Kaisha Seidō no Hatten (Industrialization and the Evolution of the Corporate System)', in Shunsaku Nishikawa and Takeshi Abe (eds.), *Sangyōka no Jidai* (The Era of Industrialization), vol. 1, Iwanami Shoten.

Morikawa, Hidemasa (1980), *Zaibatsu no Keiesha teki Kenkyū* (Business History of the *Zaibatsu*), Tōyō Keizai Shinpō-sha.

Nishinarita, Yutaka (1988), *Kindai Nihon Rōshi Kankei Shi no Kenkyū* (A Historical Study on Industrial Relations in Modern Japan), University of Tokyo Press.

——(1992), 'Senryō Ki Nihon no Rōshi Kankei (Japanese Industrial Relations under the US Occupation)', in Masanori Nakamura (ed.), *Nihon no Kindai to Shihonshugi: Kokusaika to Chiiki* (Modern Japan and Capitalism: Internationalization and Regions), University of Tokyo Press.

Okazaki, Tetsuji (1992), 'Nihon no Kigyō Shisutemu wa dono yōni Keisei sareta ka (Evolutionary Process of the Japanese Corporate System)', *Keizai Seminaa*, December edition.

——(1993), 'The Japanese Firm under the Wartime Planned Economy', *Journal of the Japanese and International Economies*, 7.

——(1995), 'Dainiji Sekai Taisen Ki no Kin'yū Seidō Kaikaku to Kin'yū Shisutemu no Henka (Japanese Financial Reform and Evolution of the Financial System during the Second World War)', in Akira Hara (ed.), *Nihon no Senji Keizai* (The Japanese War Economy), University of Tokyo Press.

Okumura, Hiroshi (1969a), 'Sengo Nihon ni okeru Kabushiki Shoyū Kōzō (The Structure of Share Ownership in Post-war Japan)', in Osaka Shōken Keizai Kenkyūjo (ed.), *Sengo Shōken Keizai Ron* (A Study of the Securities Market in Post-war Japan), Tōyō Keizai Shinpō-sha.

——(1969b), 'Zaibatsu no Kaitai to Saihensei (The Dissolution and Reorganization of the *Zaibatsu*)', in Ichiro Kawai (ed.), *Kōza Nihon Shihonshugi Hattatsu Shi* (Lectures on the Development of Post-war Japanese Capitalism), vol. 4, Nihon Hyōron-sha.

Ono, Yoshimasa (1953), 'Ginkō no Shōken Tōshi (Banks' Investment in Securities)', *Keiei Hyōron Rinji Zōkan: 100man Nin no Kabushiki no Tebiki*, (Special Issue of Keiei Hyōron: Investment Guide for Everybody), Ōkura Shuppan.

Otsuka, Manjo (1947), 'Shūsei Shihonshugi no Kiso Kōzō (Basic Structure of Revised Capitalism)', *Tōyō Keizai Shinpō*, May 10.

Saguchi, Kazuro (1988), *Nihon ni okeru Sangyō Minshushugi no Zentei* (Preconditions for Industrial Democracy in Japan), University of Tokyo Press.

——(1991), *Nihon niokeru Sangyō Minshushugi no Zentei* (The Preconditions of Industrial Democracy in Japan), University of Tokyo Press.

Sakurabayashi, Makoto (1985), *Sangyō Hōkokukai no Soshiki to Kinō* (Organization and Function of the Industrial Patriotic Societies), Ochanomizu Shobō.

Sawai, Minoru (1992), 'Senji Keizai to Zaibatsu (*Zaibatsu* under the War Economy)', in Juro Hashimoto and Haruhito Takeda (eds.), *Nihon no Keizai Hatten to Kigyō Shūdan* (Japanese Economic Development and Business Groups), University of Tokyo Press.

Shibata, Yoshimasa (1992), 'Senji Kaisha Keiri Tōsei Taisei no Tenkai (Development of Wartime Control of Corporate Accounting)', *Shakai Keizai Shigaku*, 58(3).

Suzuki, Kunio (1992), 'Zaibatsu kara Kigyō Shūdan Kigyō Keiretsu e (From *Zaibatsu* to Corporate Groups and *Keiretsu*)', *Tochi Seido Shigaku*, 135.

Suzuki, Munemasa (1938), 'Kōjō no Rijun Bunpai Seido to Kōchingin Taisaku (The Profit-Sharing System and Countermeasures to High Wages)', *Shakai Seisaku Jihō*.

Suzuki, Takeo (1967), 'Sengo Hō Seido no 20-nen: Kabushiki Gaisha Seido (Twenty Years of the Post-war Legal System: The Joint-Stock Company System)', *Jūrisuto*, 361.

Takahashi, Kamekichi (1930), *Kabushiki Gaisha Bōkokuron* (The Joint-Stock Company: A Cause for National Ruin), Banrikaku Shobō.

Takasaki, Tatsunosuke (1954), 'Mukashi no Keieisha to Ima no Keieisha (Corporate Managers Past and Present)', *Keidanren Geppō*, March.

——(1957), 'Watashi no Rirekisho (My Personal History)', in Nihon Keizai Shinbunsha (ed.), *Watashi no Rirekisho*, vol. 2, Nihon Keizai Shinbunsha.

Tanaka, Tsutomu (1953), 'Tōshi Shintaku no Tōshi Hōshin (Investment Policy of Investment Trusts)', *Keiei Hyōron Rinji Zōkan: 100man Nin no Kabushiki no*

Tebiki, (Special Issue of Keiei Hyōron: Investment Guide for Everybody), Ōkura Shuppan.

Teranishi, Juro (1992), 'Shūsen Chokugo ni okeru Kin'yū Seido Kaikaku (Financial Reform Immediately after the War)', *Business Review*, 39(2).

Tokyo Association of Securities Companies (1971), *Shōken Gaishi* (Inside History of the Securities Market), Tokyo Association of Securities Companies.

——(1951), *Tōkyō Shōkengyō Kyōkai 10-nen-shi* (Ten-Year History of the Tokyo Association of Securities Companies), Tokyo Association of Securities Companies.

Tokyo Stock Exchange (1963), *Tōkyō Shōken Torihikijo 10-nen-shi* (Ten-Year History of the Tokyo Stock Exchange), Tokyo Stock Exchange.

Usami, Kenji (1984), *Seimei Hokengyō Hyakunen Shi Ron* (A Hundred-Year History of Life Insurance), Yuhikaku.

Yamanaka, Hiroshi (1966), *Seimei Hoken Kin'yū Hattatsu Shi* (Development of Finance by Life Insurance Companies), Yuhikaku.

Yamazaki, Shiro (1991), 'Kyōchō Kin'yū Taisei no Tenkai (Development of the Syndicate Loan System)', in Toshimitsu Imuta (ed.), *Senji Taisei kano Kin'yū Kōzō* (The Japanese Financial System in the War Economy), Nihon Hyōron-sha.

Yazawa, Atsushi (1967), 'Tōshi no Taishūka to Kabushikigaisha Hō no Kadai (Popularization of Stock Investment and the Role of Corporate Law)', *Hōritsu Jihō*, 33(2).

Yazawa, Hiroki (1992), 'Kōgaku Shotokusha no Bunpu ni kansuru Senzen Sengo Hikaku (A Comparative Study of Income Distribution in the Pre-war and Post-war Periods)', *Nihon Keizai Kenkyū*, 23.

Yoshikawa, Hiroshi (1988), 'Rōdō Shijō to Sangyō Kōzō Chōsei (The Labour Market and Adjustment to the Industrial Structure)', in Motoshige Ito, Kazuo Ueda, and Heizo Takenaka (eds.), *Pasupekutibu Nihon Keizai* (Perspectives on the Japanese Economy), Chikuma Shobō.

5

'Japanese-Style' Labour Relations

Konosuke Odaka

1. Present-day 'Japanese-style' labour relations

It has long been noted that labour relations in Japan have many features that differ from those in Europe and America. First, the Japanese labour market is said to be segregated into separate parts. An indication of this is the rate of voluntary retirement which, already low by international standards, gets lower as the enterprises involved get bigger. Male employees, and particularly the regular staff of large corporations, join their firms fresh from graduation, and after a few years they become very reluctant to leave. On the other hand, employees in small and medium-sized firms tend to change jobs frequently, slipping easily from one workplace to another. An exception to this is those people, such as professional baseball players, who can survive and prosper on their individual skills alone.

The explanation for this situation is that the labour market is not horizontally integrated, but is separated into two distinct parts: the large corporations first hire the type of staff they like in the numbers they need (the so-called 'skimming off the cream'), and then smaller firms can hire those left over. There is no free movement of labour between the large firms and the smaller ones; it is particularly difficult to move from a small or medium-sized firm to one of the large corporations. This means that the relatively favourable employment opportunities in large firms are limited, and not everyone can enjoy the chance. Some maintain that Japan's labour market, especially with respect to large firms, does not fulfil the textbook function of adjusting supply and demand but rather apportions employment opportunities according to the size of the demand.

The labour market has not displayed these features throughout the modern period, however. Able mechanics of the Meiji period are said to have moved about all over the country, reflecting the existence of a strong sellers' market for their skills. Although the market for labour in steel and machinery production in the early years of industrialization was thus horizontally integrated in the textbook sense, from the mid Taishō period, the large corporations that were then quickly proliferating began to hold on to their key skilled workers, who were increasingly recruited, trained and kept with the firm from boyhood (when they were called *kogai*). This spurred the split in the labour market, and in this case, the wheels of history turned not as advocates of modernization once predicted, from the specialized to the universal, but in the reverse direction (see Gordon (1985)).

Thinking of labour relations in the narrow sense of labour unions versus managements, the defining characteristic in Japan is more than anything else the fact that individual firms have separate labour unions. In terms of labour–management negotiations and in financial strength, the most important unit of union organization is the firm or place of business. This represents a significant difference in structure compared, say, with British trade unions organized to represent particular trades or industries over and above the level of individual firms. (We should not forget, however, that signs of change in labour relations began to appear in Britain after the oil crisis.)

Perhaps due to this organizational characteristic, relations between labour unions and managements in Japan from the mid-1960s have been relatively harmonious compared with those in some other countries. The main economic activity of Japanese labour unions is wage negotiations. In general the unions are extremely unwilling to accept staff cuts, but are not particularly active in pressing for training or the resolving of grievances. There have been periods of very grave disturbances, as immediately after the Second World War, and these were all the more fierce as conflicts because there was no great difference in social standing between the two sides. The Western European type of class conflict does not apply to Japan. Of course, high-speed growth was a boon for industrial peace, yet even at times of minus growth, after the oil shock for instance, Japanese labour unions took an extremely co-operative stance towards firms' policies of streamlining and wage restraint. However, partly due to the fall in the proportion of industrial labour, the level of union organization has been in steady decline since the 1970s, so much so that concern has been expressed that the power balance between labour and management in the workplace may gradually be lost.

These characteristics have had an important effect on the running of the economy. One obvious illustration is how very little labour–management conflict was aroused by the introduction of technical innovations in private-sector firms during Japan's high-growth period. Starting from this period Japanese labour unions have been prepared to concede a little in wage struggles in return for guarantees of employment during economic downturns, and in effect have co-operated in preventing cost inflation. The macroeconomic significance of this behaviour has been very great.

Finally, labour relations operate at the level of the day-to-day running of the workplace and methods of supervision. This means dealing with issues for negotiation and co-operation between labour and management that crop up daily, and is something separate from the functioning of the labour market or systems for labour–management relations. The relevant issues here are how to create an efficient workplace with a good working environment, or how to boost working morale and provide a fair and appropriate level of remuneration.

If we set out all the characteristics of Japanese-style labour relations at this level, the list becomes very long. It includes:

- importance placed on long-term employment relations, and the in-house training that goes with them;
- broad job classifications with indistinct divisions (*shokunō*);
- frequent exchanges of production information between supervisory and management staff and the shop floor (shop-floor-centred approach);
- employee involvement in the production process, as seen in suggestions systems, zero-defect campaigns, working in small teams within the enterprise, process supervision, co-operation in quality control, and so on;
- remuneration based mainly on *shokunō* as well as employees' attributes (educational background, number of dependants, number of years of continuous employment, and so on);
- providing employees with a sense of prestige, as well as remuneration, in return for their contribution to the firm, and using this in internal competitions and promotion systems to boost employees' motivation.

These Japanese characteristics of labour management are facts that leave little room for argument. Views are divided, however, over whether they are essentially different from principles of labour management in Europe and America, or whether the differences between the two are merely a matter of degree. If we maintain that Japanese-style labour relations are fundamentally different from those of the West, then the differences can be regarded as springing from cultural factors. However, the alternative view rejects the existence of unique Japanese characteristics and holds that everything can be interpreted through common economic principles.

Neither of these positions can be correct just as they stand. If contemporary business enterprises work within the restrictions imposed upon them to realize their corporate objectives by involving themselves in production based on rational criteria, whether in the East or in the West, they have to use the same type of production technology and the same sort of accounting principles. But just as people have individual characteristics and differing histories, the courses that individual firms take are influenced by environmental factors and so it is natural that individual characteristics related to time and place will appear. In practice, management methods suggest that the reality lies somewhere between the two.

The concern of this chapter is not, in fact, to debate the nature of the characteristics of 'Japanese-style' labour relations like this, but to search for the historical roots that have produced these characteristics in the period from the First World War, through the Second World War, and into the period of high-speed growth.

For this I would like to use two procedures. The first is to gain an overview of the origins of Japanese-style labour relations by examining as comprehensively as possible the existing research that deals with this period. The second is to secure a closer familiarity with the circumstances of those years by using statistics and data that have not yet been fully analysed. This chapter is an essential though small first step towards this objective.

2. Labour relations in the pre-war period

2.1. *Labour as a semi-fixed factor of production*

The inter-war period saw the emergence of large corporations. In terms of share of non-agricultural value-added production, mining industry began to lose its relatively dominant position, while manufacturing industry advanced. Within the manufacturing sector, the importance of non-textile industries (particularly machinery production) gradually increased, and at the same time groups of enterprises involved in large-scale production began to appear, though as yet small in overall numbers. The curtain had risen on the 'mass-production age', which was to become firmly entrenched in the high-growth period after the Second World War.

As the age of the large corporations began, there was an increase in administrative and supervisory work that had not been needed in small firms and factories, and a corresponding rise in the proportion of white-collar workers. Weber lived during this period and was the first to show that organizations became more bureaucratic, more and more well-educated staff were taken on, and specialized management techniques were introduced (Weber 1925: 650–78). Specialized departments were created for shop-floor management that handled employment, supervision of workers' performance, wages, and so on, and specialists were trained for these areas.

The labour provided by people working in large corporations can be classified into the following four types, seen from the two viewpoints of the degree to which this labour can be replaced by capital equipment, and the ease with which it can be procured from outside the firm.

		Extent capital can be substituted for labour:	
		Great (A)	Small (a)
Ease of procuring labour from outside firm:	High (B)	AB	aB
	Low (b)	Ab	ab

Labour that can be easily substituted with capital (A) is swallowed up, so to speak, by capital goods (production equipment) as technology advances. This corresponds to the phenomenon of de-skilling of labour. As industrialization proceeds former artisan skills are dispensed with or skilled workers are replaced by machines.

In contrast, labour that cannot be readily substituted with capital (i.e. labour that is highly complementary to capital) (a), is characterized by the fact that as technology becomes more complex, it is increasingly in demand. Technicians responsible for the maintenance and integrated operation of production systems, or highly educated technical research staff responsible for R&D fall into this category.[1]

On the other parameter, labour that is easily obtainable from outside (B) is clearly labelled and can perform standardized and visually discernible work. The quality of the work can readily be judged even by an unfamiliar eye. Labour of this type is suited to spot dealing on the labour market. It can be bought in at the times and in the quantities desired.

By contrast the (b) type of labour is closely involved with managing and running the organization. It is typified in the specialist services in which knowledge and experience in the development and maintenance of networks of human relations are most important, and which cannot be bought in from the labour market 'ready-made'. Inevitably, firms can only prepare people within the company to provide this sort of labour (see Arrow (1974)).

We have to consider category (b) because of specific circumstances in Japanese economic development. In the early stages of industrialization a great deal of production technology was imported, and this foreign-made technology was in many respects incompatible with existing domestic technology, despite some similarities. So the necessary training required something of a mental leap onto unfamiliar ground. To gain the know-how to install, modify and operate this 'borrowed' technology, however, measures often had to be taken that were unique to the particular plant. For this domestic resources were utilized and little by little the technology became 'Japanese'. There were, furthermore, small variations in the technology introduced in different plants for the same type of industrial process, as it had different overseas origins, and it was therefore not interchangeable. Very often, technology that was universal in its country of origin tended to remain firm-specific, at least for a while, after being imported into Japan.

For these reasons, labour of the (ab) type cannot be bought in from the market, but must be fostered through on-the-job training, and therefore kept for a relatively long time. As capital goods cannot easily be substituted for labour of this type, labour costs take on the nature of fixed costs and labour is 'artificially' allocated within the firm by those responsible for personnel management, through promotions and transfers. Because this is not labour that can be handled through spot dealing on the market, remuneration does not have to equal marginal productivity at the point in time when the labour is provided.

With the arrival of the large corporations, various phenomena appeared that suggested this semi-fixed nature of labour. From the time of the First World War the large corporations began increasingly to promote long-term, continuous employment, and adopt pay systems related to years of employment rather than type of work, as well as new systems of worker rankings and supervision in plants. From about 1925 separation rates fell dramatically in the large firms, in contrast with ongoing high rates for the country as a whole. If we exclude the Washington Arms Reduction Treaty, the Shōwa Crisis, and the other major period of mass lay-offs immediately after the war, annual average separation rates in manufacturing industry stayed at very low levels, and even for the period of post-war high-speed growth from 1965 to 1976, the rate fluctuated only within the range of 20–25 per cent, which was very much lower than in Britain or America.

Figure 5.1 shows separation rates after 1925 at four shipyards of Mitsubishi Heavy Industries. The data gives monthly figures, but the figure shows the total number of retirees for each year as a proportion of the average number in employment in that year. (The number of registered workers exceeds the number of workers receiving wages because of military service, but the difference is negligible except in the years 1943 and 1944, when the former exceeded the latter by around 5 per cent.) The reasons for separation covered lay-offs or

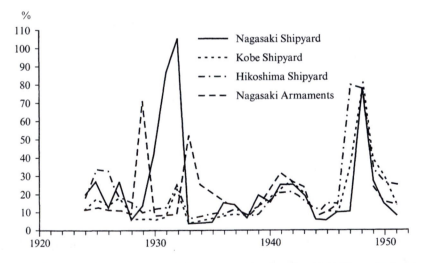

Figure 5.1. Separation rates of male factory workers in Mitsubishi Heavy Industries (yearly averages)

Notes: Serving and non-demobilized soldiers are not included as registered workers after 1944. If numbers of employees on payrolls are used instead of numbers of registered workers, on average figures for 1938–43 become 20% higher, while figures for 1944–6 become 25% lower.

Source: Odaka (1978: Table 4-5).

disciplinary dismissals initiated by the company, and also workers' voluntary retirement to change job, or because of illness or old age. We really need to distinguish between these two groups but unfortunately the data is not available.

Clearly, except for the period of the Shōwa Crisis and the time of mass lay-offs that followed the end of the Second World War, labour turnover was relatively low in the big firms. This could be observed long before the State Mobilization Law required that employees' names had to be registered and the freedom to change jobs was curtailed. Later, during the Second World War, the labour turnover rate actually increased, despite government restrictions, because of the scarcity of workers.

2.2. The disquiet caused by the labour movement

At the end of the Taishō and the beginning of the Shōwa period, a further reason besides production technology prompted managements of large firms to employ workers as far as possible on a long-term, continuous basis from their youth. It was the growing popularity of the labour movement. The influence of the movement could be seen directly in responses to the demands of newly appearing unions. But it also appeared indirectly (as Gordon (1985) also explains), either in the way the demands of the union, where one existed, were anticipated in an attempt to weed out seeds of potential conflict, or else in offering better working conditions to discourage workers from organizing. Either way, the views of the shop floor were incorporated with the aim of defusing employees' petty grievances.

Figure 5.2 shows two types of data on labour disputes. The participation rate (D) is the number of workers participating in strikes per year compared with the total number of employees in the non-agricultural and forestry sectors, and the propensity for labour disputes (d) is the number of workers participating in strikes per year, compared with the number of labour-union members (the data in the figure is given as natural logarithms). The inclination of labour unions to strike is more appropriately indicated by d rather than D, but as the two plots follow roughly parallel paths, there is little to choose between them.

The participation rate in strikes (D) indicates three peak periods in unions' inclination to strike: 1918–21, 1945–6, and 1959–73. What is particularly noticeable is that around the time of the First World War the participation rate suddenly rose sharply although it had never previously been very high. The full-scale industrialization and economic boom of that period created a seller's market for labour, and because of this and the influence of the Taishō Democracy, manufacturing industry was hit by a great wave of labour strife. Within firms, labour demands were quickly accepted whenever there was a dispute, bonuses were paid to factory hands (Shibaura Engineering Works

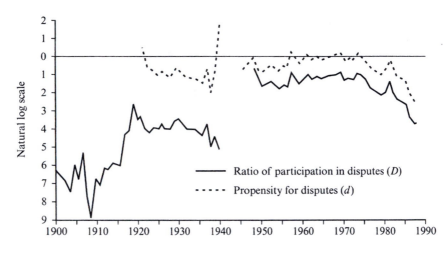

Figure 5.2. Frequency of labour disputes

Notes: D = number of participants in disputes/total number of employees in non-agricultural/ forestry sector; d = number of participants in disputes/size of union membership. After calculating percentages, data converted to natural logarithms.

Sources: Statistical data are mainly from Management and Co-ordination Agency Statistics Bureau, *Chōki Keizai Tōkei Sōran* (Historical Statistics of Japan), vols. 1, 4 (1987–8); *Rōdōryoku Nenpō* (Annual Report on Labour Force Survey), 1989; Umemura *et al.* (1988); Ministry of Labour, *Rōdō Tōkei Nenpō* (Yearbook of Labour Statistics), 1987–9.

1916; Nagasaki Shipyard 1917; Nippon Steel Hiroshima plant 1919) and a certain *zaibatsu* firm in 1917 set up a system of retirement allowances.

In the spring of 1919 workers campaigned outside parliament with four demands: the right to survive, the right to organize, the right to strike and the right to vote. In the second half of the year there were major strikes by the printers for 16 newspapers in Tokyo, at Tokyo Artillery Arsenal (*Tōkyō Hōhei Kōshō*) and at Ashio Copper Mine (*Ashio Dōzan*), and workers caused disruption at the Tokyo City Streetcar system (*Tōkyō Shiden*) and Kawasaki Shipyard (*Kawasaki Zōsen*). Labour unions sprung up in all areas. In 1921 the management side began to fight back, and so major strikes erupted in many places, demanding the right of organization and the right of collective bargaining. This activity reached a peak with strikes at Kawasaki Shipyard (*Kawasaki Zōsen*) and Mitsubishi's Kobe Shipyard (*Mitsubishi Kōbe Zōsen*) between June and August 1921. It was said that at the core of these two strikes, which involved more than 30,000 workers, were the most radical unions within the *Sōdōmei* (Japanese Federation of Labour). The Kawasaki strikers, whose demands were refused, tried to take over the running of the plant, but the management side moved to lock them out, claiming infringement of their property rights, and the police and army were brought in to guard the property. Ultimately all the strikes ended in crushing defeat for the unions.

The more and more frequent outbreak of disputes shocked managers.

Labour's aggressive stance, which was also apparent in Europe and America at that time, was enough to fill the managers with a sense of crisis, and they acknowledged, probably for the first time, the importance of labour management as a specialist job. Many of the large corporations set up some sort of labour-management department at this time.[2] The Mitsubishi Shipyard announced the adoption of a factory committee system, opening up a channel of communication with employees.[3] Furthermore, various systems for wage rises (not always at regular intervals) were introduced (Shibaura Engineering Works 1920; Kosaka Mine 1923; Hanshin Railway (*Hanshin Densha*) 1924), and some concerns researched American examples in an attempt to improve their welfare facilities (Okamoto 1960).

As their organizations grew to massive size, the large corporations suddenly became more circumspect in taking on workers. They no longer left new recruitment to factory foremen, as in the past, but began to investigate applicants' health, and their background, character and conduct. As the cost of selection and recruitment rose,[4] it was an obvious step to devise a remuneration system that would encourage continuous employment, in order to hold down turnover rates. If labour turnover could be reduced, then there would be increased investment in human resources to encourage more firm-specific skills, and as a result, labour would become that much more stabilized. It is interesting that these sorts of systemic changes of the 1910s and 1920s occurred in all the large corporations in the same way and at virtually the same time, as if by mutual agreement.

The increased activity of the labour movement also had a powerful impact on the government. Work was started on a Health Insurance Law (*Kenkō Hoken Hō*) and a revision of the Factory Law (*Kōjō Hō*), and a Social Affairs Bureau was established at the Ministry of Internal Affairs. According to an announcement at a 1919 meeting of top officials of the Ministry of Internal Affairs of the Hara Cabinet, 'harmonious relations between workers and management must be established at firms before class conflict occurs. For this the current issues are promoting mechanisms within firms for conciliation between management and labour, and setting up an institution to research and disseminate harmonious labour relations.' The announcement went on, 'Sector-wide unions will not be encouraged, but as no legislation exists to control unions, this has to be left to natural developments for the time being.'

A resemblance between Japan and America has been noted in trends in labour management after the First World War. Efforts to streamline management at machinery-production plants through rigorous control of base costs had been evident from around the turn of the century, but as firms later grew in size they became more bureaucratic. In both countries responsibility in factories for production management and personnel management was removed from the manager or foreman on the spot to become centrally controlled. The Taylor system, a typical American scientific management method, never took hold in Japan, but the fact that it drew considerable attention (Okuda 1985: ch.

2) was not simply because of a Japanese liking for all things new. In fact, advocacy of paternalistic managements as a means of stressing the harmonization of interests between labour and management, though not widespread, was nevertheless common to both countries (Jacoby 1985: ch. 2).

These sorts of development were less obvious in Britain (Littler 1982). In contrast to America and Japan, where the spread of labour unions was relatively new, in Britain union organizations had become firmly rooted in workplaces well before large corporations appeared (Jacoby 1985). And for the same reason, as unions began to extend their influence at the beginning of the century, in Japan and America the balance in labour relations tended more to favour management than was the case in Britain. Having to deal with the many disputes that occurred immediately after the First World War, Japan therefore opted to adopt a joint labour–management council system adapted from the American concept of factory committees, in preference to a British or German system. The system adopted 'does not reject the existence of labour unions out of hand', but 'it is certainly a measure to manage labour unions' and 'company intervention in the selection of committee members has become accepted practice' (Okamoto 1960: 84–5).

What made it easy to form factory-based organizations, and for them to function, was that the labour market basically had been broken up into units based on single firms. The labour unions of the Taishō and early Shōwa periods appeared from the outside to be more like industry-wide unions that extended beyond the confines of single firms, but 'in reality, they were only active at the level of individual factories or workplaces . . . and while on the outside they appeared to be industry-wide unions, in practice they can be seen as having prepared the ground for the individual company unions that have so predominated in the post-war period' (Komatsu 1971: 2, 5). In light of the circumstances described above, this is perfectly understandable. In fact, company-based unions are usually said to have emerged around 1921. They had existed in large plants from before this time, examples being Daishinkai at Hakubunkan Insatsusho (Hakubunkan Printing Company), Shibaura Giyūkai at Shibaura Engineering Works, Kōjōkai at Osaka Hōhei Kōshō (Osaka Artillery Arsenal), Shinshinkai at Sumitomo Shindōsho (Sumitomo Copper Plate), and Shokko Doshikai at Yawata Seitetsusho (Yawata Steelworks) (ibid. 5, 33–7). Between 1926 and 1930, 17 per cent of labour unions were company-based, and the proportion of members in company-based unions was 38 per cent (Sakurabayashi 1985: 72–3). Thus, there already existed a substantial bedrock from which the concept of enterprise-based unions grew to become a central feature of labour relations in the post-war period.

Of course, there were many differences between Japan and America in the field of labour relations. American unions in the twentieth century sought to spread the idea of industry-wide unions and established themselves in the large corporations. By contrast, the Japanese labour-union movement of the inter-war period received a cold reception from government, and spread more through the small and medium-sized firms than in the large corporations. After Japan started preparing for war, they were disbanded, some initially being absorbed into the industrial patriotic societies through the sponsorship of the Kyōchōkai (Society for the Promotion of Industrial Peace), and after 1938 into patriotic group organizations (units of patriotic societies) set up in every workplace through direct government intervention.

2.3. The origins of seniority pay

Using seniority, or the number of years of continuous employment, as one base on which to determine remuneration seems not to be a particularly new idea. Judging from statistical data, the salaries of full-time staff called 'regular employees' at famous-name firms have been tied to seniority from the Taishō period or even earlier. Many among these employees saw themselves as future managers, and the vast majority of them settled down permanently in the firm. A clear line was drawn between them and shop-floor workers, among whom turnover was particularly high until the end of the Taishō period.

We should not be too hasty, however, in concluding that the principle of seniority-related remuneration existed merely from the fact that remuneration rose together with the number of years of continuous employment. Even if firms were to base their pay rates on different types of work and ignore seniority, if employees hold positions of increasing responsibility or higher degrees of skill as time goes by, then a statistical correlation is likely to appear between remuneration levels and age or number of years of continuous employment.

But in the case of white-collar workers in Japan, starting in the inter-war period an individual's performance was evaluated from time to time, promotion considered and if promoted, his salary would increase. Promotion was based on the number of years' experience, as well as ability and performance. For example, at Mitsubishi Shipyard payment based on seniority was clearly systematized in 1919 for clerical staff.

Subsequently and at the latest by 1933, both factory hands and regular employees at Mitsubishi Shipyard received pay rises based on seniority. But as I have already pointed out, separation rates among production workers at large corporations (and labour turnover rates in general) fell dramatically from 1925 onwards, and so it is no surprise that finally, by the early years of Shōwa the seniority factor is evident in the wage curves of factory hands working for the large corporations. Data shows that average real wages for factory hands at Yawata Steelworks and Mitsubishi Heavy Industries increased together with the increase in the average number of years of continuous employment.[5]

However, wage increases were neither across the board nor automatic, either for regular staff or factory hands. This is clearly different from the post-war system of regular pay increases. In this sense the seniority wages of the pre-war period were not so much based on principle, as on an *ex post facto* or *de facto* basis. That is to say, as Okamoto points out, when the pre-war large corporations introduced in-house training in order to upgrade their senior technical workers, 'in the selection and promotion of workers for training, it was not seniority but general skills and ability that counted. Nevertheless the training period was standardized, and as promotions were made from among those qualified, rank and years of employment came to show a considerable degree of correlation' (Okamoto 1960: 67).

In mechanized production industries, including shipbuilding, wages of shop-floor workers were graded according to skill, and calculated on a daily basis. Then, to encourage productivity, a system was set up whereby a 'premium' calculated at a pre-decided rate was added to wages to reward a high level of productivity. Before the war hiring was not limited to taking on a batch of new school graduates all at one time; in a recession workers were laid off without hesitation, and even highly skilled workers were often fired. In other words, the way shop-floor workers were employed was far more like 'spot-dealing' than it was for other staff.

From the Taishō period, there was frequent debate on the issue that linking factory workers' wages directly to productivity was not in line with Japanese tradition and a method of setting wages should be devised that considered the protection of livelihood (Takeo Godo *et al.*, as quoted in Okamoto (1960: 73)).[6] This we can take as evidence that labour remuneration at that time (particularly shop-floor wages) was largely decided on levels of productivity.

Furthermore, even as the seniority factor was being introduced, people were expressing views in opposition. Influenced by the campaign to rationalize industry that began in 1929, the argument was gaining ground that shop-floor wages should be reformed not to a fixed wage (*kotei kyū*) but to something linked to the nature of the job and the level of skill of the worker (*shokumu kyū*). For example, the Production Management Committee of the Emergency Industrial Rationalization Bureau (*Rinji Sangyō Gōrikyoku Seisan Kanri Iinkai*) claimed in the 1932 publication *Chingin Seido* (Wage Systems) that:

1. 'Production efficiency is really the key to good wages, profits and appropriate prices'. Thus one should maintain production efficiency and pay wages that match it. However, minimum livelihood wage levels must of course be met.
2. For incentive pay, the Halsey premium system can be recommended, but once the premium rate has been set it should not be lowered except in circumstances such as improvements to facilities, changes in work methods, etc.
3. There is concern that fixed wages (a daily rate at that time) may bring about disparities between income and level of skill, and so *shokumu kyū* should be adopted.

Shokumu kyū can be defined as a basic wage proportional to the level of skill required for the job.

In a survey undertaken by the Labour Bureau of the Ministry of Health and Welfare in June 1940, a total of 1,521 different wage structures were examined at 784 factories. Of these, 53 per cent were fixed-wage systems (*teigaku sei*), 42 per cent were piece-rate systems (*dekidaka sei*), and the remainder were premium systems (*warimashi chingin sei*) (the Halsey and Rowan systems accounted for less than 2 per cent each).[7]

As time passed fewer and fewer people supported the concept of *shokumu kyū*, however. But it was nevertheless very much later before the remuneration of production workers was determined automatically on seniority (meaning a 'pure' seniority pay system was established). A 'wage for life' (*shōgai chingin*) came to be thought of as an appropriately Japanese wage system, linked to the wartime idea of labour as Imperial service, and so a theoretical basis had to be created before seniority pay, family allowances, etc. could be introduced (see Okamoto (1960: 100)).

3. Labour relations in the wartime economy

3.1. Procuring workers at a time of emergency

There is only fragmentary data available on the labour market during the Second World War, and it is very difficult to build up a consistent and comprehensive picture of that period. In this section I would like to use some statistical data to get a glimpse of the employment conditions of shop-floor workers (including the distribution of production workers across industries, average age, working hours, and so on) in the manufacturing sector, especially in mechanized production.

During the war, more and more factory workers were sent to the front. The scale of this is not entirely clear, but according to a hand-written document, Yearly Labour Survey Appendices (*Nenji Kinrō Chōsa Tsuika Oyobi Betten Shiryō*) submitted to GHQ, originating from the Labour section of the Cabinet Statistics Bureau and based on records that escaped destruction, in July, November, and December of 1944, and January 1945, between 0.9 per cent and 1.5 per cent of the employees (regular staff) working at government-designated 'major enterprises' in the mining, manufacturing, and transportation industries were sent off each month for military duties.[8] If this conscription rate was consistent, it means that the workforce was declining by between 10 per cent and 20 per cent per year.

However, according to government census results (*kokusei chōsa*), and population surveys (*jinkō chōsa*) from before, during, and after the Second World War, the total number of workers employed in manufacturing rose steadily all through the war period (Table 5.1). We are therefore forced to conclude that the shortage of labour must have been resolved in part by

Table 5.1. Gainfully occupied workers in manufacturing industries (from census returns)

	1940		1944		1955	
	Male	Female	Male	Female	Male	Female
Ceramics and stone-clay	233,517	57,017	163,353	61,662	259,651	87,287
Metals	632,115	56,869	707,768	115,119	682,654	82,114
Machinery	1,870,082	224,854	3,524,291	787,424	1,027,972	177,605
Chemicals	430,567	148,535	416,663	182,881	614,568	227,234
Spinning and weaving	582,684	1,043,625	239,225	569,527	553,421	989,304
Printing and bookbinding	113,596	21,533	73,907	32,820	269,043	61,888
Timber and wood products	445,757	35,195	303,593	62,713	647,902	108,211
Food	299,522	130,784	221,145	136,557	544,124	268,108
Other manufacturing industry	389,881	181,984	274,144	216,194	187,545	113,528
Total	4,997,721	1,900,396	5,924,089	2,164,897	4,786,880	2,115,279

Sources: Umemura *et al.* (1988: Table 22); *Shōwa 30-nen Kokusei Chōsa Hōkoku* (1955 Population Census of Japan), vol. 3: National Statistics no. 2, Table 2.

moving workers from other industries and by substituting female for male workers. There were also plans to put to work those not normally part of the labour force, such as schoolchildren and students. According to the data mentioned above, the number of schoolchildren and students working in the mining, manufacturing, and transportation sectors reached 860,000 in November 1944, accounting for about 13 per cent of the workforce of 6.56 million in that month. Groups of workers drafted from Korea and China, as well as prisoners of war, were also mobilized. The data gives a total of 230,000 workers from these backgrounds in this period.[9]

As Table 5.1 shows, in October 1940, the largest proportion of employees in manufacturing industry, 30 per cent, was working in machinery production (among male workers only, the figure rises to 37 per cent). This proportion increased rapidly during the war to reach 53 per cent, and 60 per cent for males only, in February 1944. The numbers fell back after the war, so that in 1955, the year in which the economy was considered to have returned to normal, the equivalent figures were 17 per cent, and 22 per cent for males only.[10] This testifies to the exceptional expansion of machinery production for the war effort.

By looking at machinery-production plants, we can thus get a good idea of the nature of labour relations in manufacturing industry during the war period. Machinery production accounted for a large part of the munitions industry. In fact, about 54.5 per cent of a national military expenditure of ¥6 billion in 1938 was for orders placed with machinery manufacturers in the private sector. The large private-sector firms were unable to meet this enormous demand, however, and unfulfilled orders in eight leading companies reached 2.7 times their production capacity in 1938. Other industries such as textiles were switched to military production, and this is one reason why small-scale machine-tools manufacturers appeared in large numbers at that time.

The importance of small plants in wartime industrial production is no doubt related to this situation. After the Great Depression small firms gradually disappeared from machinery production and the number of workers in small and medium-sized firms declined year on year as a proportion of the total number employed in manufacturing overall. However, from 1942 this trend was reversed (Umemura et al. 1988: Table 19). The situation can be assessed from employment trends in machinery production. The same Cabinet Statistics Bureau document mentioned previously indicates that in February 1938, the total number of workers in 'machinery plants employing five or more workers' was only 597,000. If we assume that this figure grew between 1940 and 1944 at the same rate as the number of workers in machinery production overall (annual growth rate of 19.8 per cent, from Table 5.1), then machinery plants with five or more workers would have accounted for about 1.75 million workers by 1944. In fact, a 1944 survey by the same bureau covering plants of all sizes gives the number of shop-floor workers in machinery production in that year as 4.22 million (not including temporary and day labourers). The difference between these two figures of about 2.47 million must therefore be the number employed in tiny shops with fewer than five workers. This is an astounding 59 per cent of the total number of production workers in machinery manufacturing in 1944.[11]

One reason why such a large number of workers was needed could be that productivity was declining. Machinery production at that time was highly labour-intensive and required manual skills, but the incoming manpower was largely unskilled. This tendency only worsened as the war progressed. Even in navy facilities, which should have been relatively fortunate in terms of both production technology and acquiring labour, there was an all-round shortage of technicians, skilled and unskilled workers, and as little training was provided there was a steady decline in the quality of labour as the years passed.

This decline in the quality of labour was also reflected in workers' performance. Figure 5.3(*a*) shows that even in the most prestigious plants absenteeism increased as the war proceeded. Under conditions in which negotiations with management were not permitted in any form, employees had no way to make the smallest protest except by working less efficiently or absenting themselves. Of course, we must also consider the overall decline in stamina resulting from war injuries, malnutrition and other privations. The resulting manpower shortages could only be covered, in part, by lengthening working hours (Figure 5.3(*b*)).

Though attendance rates fell, they never fell below 80 per cent, however (Figure 5.3(*a*)). According to a survey of all manufacturing industry by the Cabinet Statistics Bureau, between 1937 and 1943 the proportion of long-term absentees—those absent for more than three months—was only around

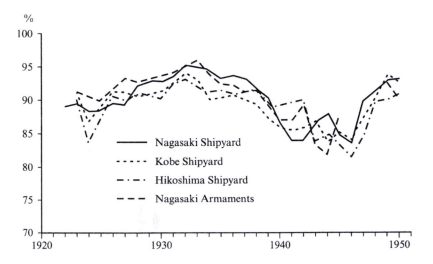

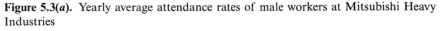

Figure 5.3(*a*). Yearly average attendance rates of male workers at Mitsubishi Heavy Industries

Source: Odaka (1978: Table 4-5).

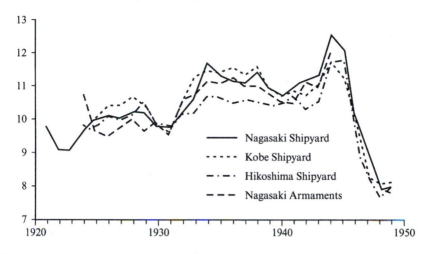

Figure 5.3(*b*). Daily working hours of male workers at Mitsubishi Heavy Industries (yearly averages)

Source: Odaka (1978: Table 4-5).

3 per cent of total employees, standing at 3.4 per cent in June 1944 (3.6 per cent for machinery production alone; all figures calculated from the Cabinet Statistics Bureau document mentioned earlier). In this sense, discipline on the shop floor did not break down entirely, even in the last phase of the war. But workers may have suffered greater pent-up frustrations instead.

It is interesting that when the war ended attendance rates suddenly increased rapidly. There were mass lay-offs after the war due to the temporary closure of some factories and a contraction in jobs. As students and other temporary workers were withdrawn from the labour force, those remaining in work were most likely core workers, and this probably contributed to lowering absentee rates.

3.2. Fixed-wage systems become established

One legacy of the labour policy promoted during the war years was that ideas on labour remuneration on the shop floor underwent a complete change. Wage systems based on *shokunō*, the broad job classification system, or productivity were abandoned, and in their place the concept of livelihood pay (*seikatsu kyū*), that had already appeared in embryonic form, became standard.

Starting from the period leading up to the war, the ideological environment had become increasingly right-wing, and a 'patriotic view of labour' was strongly advocated. Unlike the Western 'give-and-take' view, labour in Japan was regarded as service to the patriotic cause and conducted in an atmosphere of family-like trust and harmony. Negotiations and contracts were considered inappropriate for deciding working conditions and remuneration. The message repeatedly put over was that in the spirit of *messhihōkō*, or sacrificing one's personal interest for the public good, employees were expected to devote themselves to patriotic effort through their work, and managers were obliged to attend to the welfare of their staff with familial concern. Against this sort of thinking, it was argued that wages should not be coupled to a *shokunō*-type job classification or to productivity, but to the employee's age and number of years of continuous employment. The guiding principle for remuneration should be whether it was sufficient to support the worker and his family. The Navy Arsenal's abolition of its contract work system in 1937 (Okamoto 1960: 100) undoubtedly had much to do with arguments of this sort.

Some scholars maintain that paternalistic ideas of master and servants toiling in harmony were particularly strong in the steel-related industries such as metal-working and machinery, in contrast to light manufacturing where market forces prevailed. 'The idea that income should increase in accordance with years of employment is deeply entrenched in the minds of the Japanese people' and because these paternalistic ideas persist, 'workers are unlikely to co-operate fully with any contract work systems implemented in this sector that do not fit in with this idea' (Horigome 1942: 65).[12]

However, the June 1940 survey run by the Welfare Ministry's Labour Bureau, mentioned earlier, indicates that seniority, in the sense of fixed wages (*koteikyū*) was certainly not the only factor determining wages. The survey found that the adoption of piece-rate pay (*dekidaka kyū*) in machinery production (35 per cent) was lower than the average overall (42 per cent, in a survey covering 784 firms and 1,521 wage forms), and also lower than in the mining (54 per cent) and spinning (52 per cent) industries, but was high compared with printing (10 per cent), chemicals (30 per cent) and ceramics (30 per cent), and similar to the level in the metals and food industries (both 38 per cent). The most usual form of pay was a blend of fixed wages (*koteikyū*) and productivity pay (*nōritsukyū*), the only difference with the inter-war period being that the proportion of productivity pay was kept very low.

Calculating the ratio of annual bonuses to monthly income for shop-floor workers from the same data, we get median figures of 8.8 per cent for men and 7.5 per cent for women, which are extremely low compared with the post-war period. The opportunity for profit sharing, which is more likely to be included in bonuses than in regular wages, was thus limited.

Once into the war period, discussions began on whether the commonly used daily wage system should be abandoned in favour of monthly wages. Not only was it considered undesirable to use a system that encouraged instant satisfaction of material desires, but it was further argued that regular employees and shop-floor workers were all part of the same concern and so should come under the same remuneration system.

But it is hard to believe that entrepreneurs immediately made common cause with this sort of thinking. In August 1942 the *Nippon Keizai Renmei*

(Japan Economic Federation) criticized contract work pay (*ukeoi kyū*) and pressed for a monthly wage system, but firms were extremely slow to respond. The *Nippon Nōritsu Kyōkai* (Japan Management Association) held a congress on the theme of 'Factory Management and Working Efficiency' in order to encourage increased production. In an address, one director, Koichi Inoue, pointed out that 'although there was much discussion on the pros and cons of the monthly wage system' in the spring of 1943, in reality the number of firms who implemented the system was only 'about ten throughout the whole of Japan' (*Nippon Nōritsu*, 2(6) (June 1943): 39–40). In the machinery industry, too, not everyone was in favour of the monthly wage system. There was on the one hand the view that 'workers in general have a very low level of commitment . . . The monthly wage system is most Japanese in spirit, but the internal contracting system cannot be completely abandoned (Noguchi 1943: ch. 8).[13] Another view maintained that while the piece-rate and/or internal-contracting systems were not suited to precision work because they made workers hasty and careless, at the same time fixed wages would not promote working efficiency because they were not linked to the volume of work accomplished. One plant producing precision equipment used 'a system of fixed wages with a bonus based on piece-work pay as an incentive. The incentive pay element is tied to the worker's performance and so goes up and down' (Sugiyama 1943: 21).[14] Thus during the war period some combination of fixed wages and productivity pay was universal.

Nevertheless, in spite of these developments, a fixed-pay system that rejected wages linked to productivity, such as contract or piece-work pay, became established throughout the country due to wartime controls.

First, in March 1939 starting wages were set officially according to geographical area, age, and gender, in accordance with a Wage System Directive (*Chingin Tōsei Rei*), and from September of that year wages were frozen, meaning that wage rises were no longer formally recognized. However, the Labour Management in Major Enterprises Directive (*Jūyō Jigyōsho Rōmu Kanri Rei*) allowed that these ceilings on total wages could be abolished with the approval of the Minister of Welfare provided certain conditions were met.[15] These conditions required the adoption of wage guidelines by which 'wages must be raised once a year for all employees, and the maximum, standard and minimum increases should be stipulated' (Okuda 1985: 480). As a result, many firms, particularly the so-called major enterprises, established systems of regular wage increases by which all employees together received an increase once a year. As starting wages depended on the employee's age, wage rises also varied according to age group. In this way the typically Japanese wage-rise system took hold, although wage-rise curves remained far shallower than those of the post-war era (Okamoto 1960: 97–9).

Back in 1939, an Employee Recruitment Restriction Directive (*Jugyōsha Yatoiire Seigen Rei*) had come into force, followed by an Employee Transfer Prevention Order (*Jugyōsha Idō Soshi Rei*) in the following year. Changing jobs was no longer officially permitted. Labour thus lost mobility, but on the other hand the fixed-pay portion of remuneration grew dramatically, as I have said, and as the practice of raising base pay regularly and automatically became widespread, the well-known seniority-based wages appeared.

We should not conclude from this, however, that all labour remuneration was based on fixed pay. The document 'Views on the Rationalization of the Payment of Wages', published in May 1943 by the Central Prices Co-operation Council (*Chūō Bukka Kyōryoku Kaigi*), affirmed that base pay (the basic wage, job pay, supervisory rank pay, length of employment pay, and family allowance) should make up about 70–80 per cent of earned income, the remainder consisting of incentive pay, group bonuses and various other allowances. In June of the same year the Guidelines on Wage Forms and Composition (*Chingin Keitai ni Kansuru Shidō Hōshin*) agreed by the Central Wages Specialist Committee (*Chūō Chingin Senmon Iinkai*) were rather more concise but were essentially the same in content (as quoted in Okamoto (1960: 178–9)).

These views were substantially no different from those previously voiced by Inoue and Ueda (1939: 230–1), who asserted that 'workers are important members of the state and entrepreneurs rely upon them within the workplace and so should promote the stability of their livelihood and their welfare'. Therefore a 'wage system to guarantee livelihood based on Japan's family system should be devised and implemented, and entrepreneurs should undertake this on their own initiative'. The formula they advocated was:

Wages guaranteeing
livelihood   =   basic pay + supplementary pay

                      =   (age-related + seniority) + (job pay + qualification pay)
                                   50%   20%

                      +   (incentive pay)   +   bonus
                                   30%   10% of dividend

However, what is significant is that these writers were not necessarily in favour of setting up a remuneration system 'unrelated to productivity', and elsewhere in their book they predict that 'eventually the day will dawn in Japan, too, when the *shokumu kyū* system (of wages related to level of skill) will become more important than the daily wage (fixed-wage) system' (ibid. 78).

In any event, what was called 'fixed pay' none the less contained a productivity-pay element, and in important enterprises wage rises were in effect sanctioned. As the war proceeded the labour shortage became increasingly severe, with the result that towards the end remuneration for factory workers increased rapidly through additional allowances and other devices to boost income. At Mitsubishi Heavy Industries, for example, the disparity in monthly earnings between clerical and shop-floor employees shrank rapidly to the point where, at the end of the war, the shop-floor workers had the higher income (Figure 5.4). In this way the long-protested imbalance in the income of these two groups was eliminated.

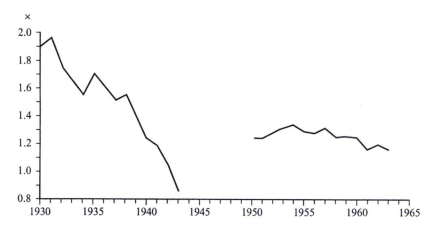

Figure 5.4. Disparities in monthly pay between clerical and shop-floor workers (Mitsubishi Heavy Industries)

Notes: Disparity = average monthly pay of clerical staff/average monthly pay of shop-floor workers. Bonuses are unlikely to be included. Missing figures for the pre-war period have been extrapolated from existing data.

Sources: Pre-war data from Odaka (1978: Tables 3–7) for Nagasaki and Hikoshima Shipyards and Nagasaki Armaments. Post-war data from Mitsubishi Heavy Industries (1967: 312) for Nagasaki and Shimonoseki (formerly Hikoshima) Shipyards, Nagasaki Precision Equipment (formerly Nagasaki Armaments), and Hiroshima Precision Equipment.

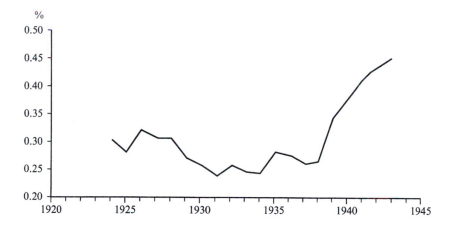

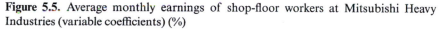

Figure 5.5. Average monthly earnings of shop-floor workers at Mitsubishi Heavy Industries (variable coefficients) (%)

Notes: Calculations based on eight different job categories at four plants: Nagasaki Shipyard, Kobe Shipyard, Hikoshima Shipyard, and Nagasaki Armaments. Average monthly earnings for the following eight job categories, weighted according to numbers in each category: division chief (*kōchō*), section chief (*kumichō*), foreman (*gochō*), ordinary worker (*nami shoku*), apprentice (*totei*), female worker (*jokō*), temporary worker (*rinjikō*), and others.

Source: Odaka (1978: Table 15).

However, we should also note that disparities in pay between different categories of workers within plants increased significantly during the war. This was because all sorts of workers had been taken on to cover the labour shortfall on the shop floor (Figure 5.5). So while a fairer distribution of wages was made between clerical and shop-floor workers, the greater diversity in the composition of shop-floor workers led to increasing wage inequality among them.

4. Labour relations in the post-war period

4.1. Four aspects of the labour movement

I would now like to give an outline of the organization of relations between labour and management, using statistics on labour disputes in Japan over the past 90 years to show how the nature of labour relations has changed. All currently available data has been used to give an estimation (Figure 5.6) of the rate of labour organization, calculated here as the total number of union members as a percentage of the total number of employees in non-agricultural sectors.

The labour movement in the 1920s and 1930s was widely regarded as dan-

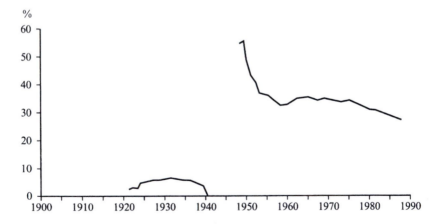

Figure 5.6. Rates of unionization (%)

Note: Rate of unionization = no. of union members/no. gainfully occupied in non-agricultural/forestry sectors.

Sources: Statistical data are mainly from Management and Co-ordination Agency Statistics Bureau, *Chōki Keizai Tōkei Sōran* (Historical Statistics of Japan), vols. 1, 4 (1987–8); *Rōdōryoku Nenpō* (Annual Report on Labour Force Survey), 1989; Umemura *et al.* (1988); Ministry of Labour, *Rōdō Tōkei Nenpō* (Yearbook of Labour Statistics), 1987–9.

gerous by government authorities such as the police, by managements, and also by fellow workers, and so joining a union took courage. As a result, the rate of unionization remained in single digits in the 1930s, but it then increased dramatically to more than 50 per cent by the end of the 1940s, underlining the dramatic changes taking place in social institutions. With a leap of such dimensions, it is not at all surprising to find evidence of no small change in behavioural norms in society and labour-management practices.

Some take the view that the post-war company-based labour unions were born out of the wartime Industrial Patriotic Movement (*Sangyō Hōkoku Undō*) (Okouchi 1972: 387), but this is a little difficult to accept. The reason is that

in general, in cases where the individual industrial patriotic society was the forbear of an enterprise union, its legacy is not so much seen in the activities or the organization of the union, but merely in its assets.[16] In terms of activities, labour–management round-table meetings had already died out, and even when resurrected after the war in the form of labour–management councils (*rōshi kyōgikai*) they did not persist.

The patriotic societies were 'different from enterprise unions. They imposed a system of rigorous social discrimination under which employees below the ranks of department managers and section chiefs were treated like outsiders or children' (Sakurabayashi 1985: 14). The individual patriotic societies were in effect 'subcontracted labour management for the firms' (ibid. 76).[17] There were some cases, such as *Tōkyō Kōtsū Rōsō* (Tokyo Transport Workers' Union) and *Mitsui Tankō Rōsō* (Mitsui Coal Mining Workers' Union), where the wartime organization and staff network continued into the post-war period, but this was certainly not true in all cases.

Moreover, the unions of the post-war period did not start out free of all links with the pre-war labour movement. A 1947 University of Tokyo Social Science Institute Survey reveals that in 113, or 27 per cent, of the total 412 labour unions covered, people with some pre-war experience in the labour movement were instrumental in setting up the post-war union. The proportion increases among the larger firms, to 36 per cent in firms with 1,000 or more employees, and among the various industrial categories it was high (34 per cent) in the machinery and metals industries (Yamamoto 1977: 269–70).

Of course, nothing was simply carried over from the pre-war to the post-war period. At the start of the war pre-war unions were all closed down or else converted into industrial patriotic societies. Leaders with experience in the pre-war labour movement did not necessarily oppose the industrial patriotic movement, and when the labour movement was re-launched after the war, some within it maintained the wartime mentality of seeking solidarity in support of the state (ibid. 295–307).

As I have shown in Section 2.2, there have been three peak periods of union militancy since the end of the Meiji Period: 1918–21, 1945–6, and 1959–73 (see Figure 5.2). These peaks are considered to represent three turning-points in the labour-union movement in Japan. Thus, Japan's labour movement has experienced four phases during the twentieth century:

1. The phase of industry unions, which flowered during the Taishō democratic period after the First World War, but soon disappeared as a result of the suppression that came with surging militarism after the Shōwa Crisis (the persecution phase).
2. A phase when unions prospered, reacting promptly to moves to democratize the economy after the Second World War. In a swing against earlier oppression, unions were distrustful of managements and tended towards political activism (the political phase).
3. The period of high-speed growth, when unions were forced to adapt to the overriding importance placed on economic growth (the economic growth phase).
4. A phase of difficulties as unions' power again began to wane after the oil shocks (the endurance phase).

The persecution phase was also the period that saw the weakening and disappearance of the friendship societies (*yūaikai*) of skilled workers, which had been formed in the early days of industrialization. The many disputes that occurred in the twenty-year period from 1910 to 1930 can be seen as a reflection of the structural changes that were going on, resulting not only from new technology and skills, but also from changes to organizational style and labour management.

For a number of years after 1945, a chorus of voices called for improvements to living standards, which had long been kept very low, and for the restoration of labour's basic freedoms. In the second half of the 1940s the labour stance was characterized by struggles in opposition to mass lay-offs and demands for wages that guaranteed a decent livelihood irrespective of productivity. This reflected circumstances in which production had yet to recover, shortages persisted, and workers were anxious to defend their livelihoods in the face of the threat of unemployment. A typical example of demands for wages that would guarantee a decent livelihood was the Densan strike[18] of October 1946, over demands for a wage structure that would be 'adequate to cover the cost of goods and services in the typical shopping basket'.

Managements suffered a temporary loss of confidence after the war and yielded to these demands, with the result that long-term continuous employment became in effect the norm for regular staff, and a system of fixed monthly wages became established, with automatic increases for all at regular intervals. This contained no element of productivity-based pay (which had been part of the official wages model during wartime). In the most extreme cases workers tried to take over the running of production, but ultimately failed.

However, when GHQ intervened to call off the general strike planned for February 1947, the labour–management power struggle had reached a turning-point. During the 1950s the labour unions' power and vitality quickly waned (Figure 5.6). This was to some extent the result of active manœuvring on the part of the conservative Cabinet.

Again in the period around 1960 many of the leading large corporations were faced with serious labour unrest. However, in this series of disputes hardly a single union achieved its initial objectives. By this time managers had taken back the reins and regained the confidence to confront labour head-on where necessary. *Nikkeiren*, the Japan Federation of Employers' Associations, stimulated discussion through its active support of such moves by individual corporate managements. The defeat of labour in a series of major strikes, especially the Oji Paper Co. strike of 1958–9 and the Miike coalminers' strike of 1959–60, is seen as giving the Japanese economy the chance to press on down the road of high-speed growth.

In the early stages of the high-growth period the labour unions were already losing their political bent, and a new style of labour relations emerged that gave priority to economic considerations. Two background factors encouraged this development. One was that Japan's labour organizations were highly dependent both in financial terms and in decision-making on individual company unions. The other was the start in 1955 of wage-rise negotiations for whole industries, known as the Spring Offensive, through the efforts of Kaoru Ota of the General Council of Trade Unions in Japan (*Nihon Rōdō Kumiai Sō Hyōgikai*, or *Sōhyō*). The outcome of this was that the annual wage-rise negotiations began directly to reflect firms' performance. In this sense the Spring Offensive is the Japanese version of 'business unionism'. One might say that unions that switched from political activism to supporting economic growth were rewarded by receiving a portion of the benefits of that growth.

The rate of unionization remained stable during the high-growth period, but towards the end of the 1970s it began to fall noticeably and the downward trend continued through the 1980s (Figure 5.6). The decline may well include factors such as a general drift from the unions, that cannot be accounted for by the decline in the proportion of employment in manufacturing, or the difficulty of organizing labour in the tertiary sector.[19]

Trends in labour–management disputes were also influenced by macroeconomic factors, however. Figure 5.7 is a comparison of the ratio of demand for labour to supply (v), which indicates the tightness of the labour market, and the propensity to strike (d).[20] According to this data, the four phases mentioned earlier have the following characteristics:

1. At the end of the persecution phase, the ratio of demand for labour to supply (v) was high, and the number of labour disputes remained low.
2. During the political activism phase, the ratio (v) was low and labour disputes occurred frequently.
3. During the economic growth phase, the ratio (v) was high and the propensity to strike was also rather high but stable.

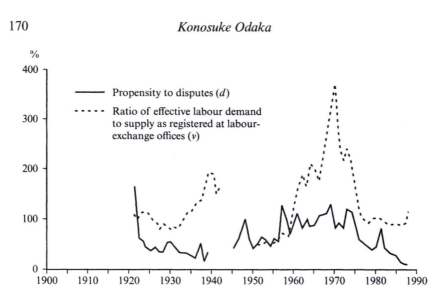

Figure 5.7. Supply and demand conditions of labour and propensity to strike (%)

Note: *v* includes new school-leavers.

Sources: Statistical data are mainly from Management and Co-ordination Agency Statistics Bureau, *Chōki Keizai Tōkei Sōran* (Historical Statistics of Japan), vols. 1, 4 (1987–8); *Rōdōryoku Nenpō* (Annual Report on Labour Force Survey), 1989; Umemura *et al.* (1988); Ministry of Labour, *Rōdō Tōkei Nenpō* (Yearbook of Labour Statistics), 1987–9.

4. During the endurance phase, the ratio (*v*) was low and the incidence of labour conflicts was also low.

In the first three phases there is on the whole an inverse relationship between the tightness of the labour market and the frequency of disputes, and only the last phase is an exception. Possibly the endurance phase is now seeing a shift in the power balance between labour and management.

4.2. From fixed pay to Japanese-style productivity pay

Around 1950, as the confusion following the end of the war abated, the Japan Productivity Center arranged for groups mostly from the large corporations to go to America for short periods to learn about American production technology. As a result, American personnel management techniques such as the job-ranking (*shokkai sei*) type of job classification, personnel evaluation, and training-within-industry (TWI) were enthusiastically adopted. Capital investment was booming, an awareness of the importance of price competitiveness was growing and naturally enough, ways were sought to trim back labour costs.

A few years before these practices were introduced, personnel managers in large corporations vigorously debated the need for wage-system reform in a series of articles published during 1948 and 1949 in the journal *Nippon Nōritsu* that I referred to earlier. A sample of the arguments is given here:

1. Keisaku Sato (Chief, Third Labour Section, Toshiba's Tsurumi plant; 1948: 21) argued that wages based solely on livelihood pay (*seikatsu kyū*) should be replaced by productivity pay (*nōritsu kyū*), and furthermore regional and family allowances should gradually be phased out. However, the preconditions he envisaged for this were that a system of (skill-based) *shokumu kyū* existed, set at fair levels through thorough analysis of job content, and that a minimum wage appropriate to socio-economic conditions was guaranteed.

2. According to Takeo Yoshioka (from Hitachi's Taga plant; 1948: 4), 'Wages should not fundamentally be related to livelihood pay, nor contain the elements of family allowances or seniority pay. . . . A system of pay for the type of work, in other words pay according to job-ranking (*shokkai kyū*) should be offered.' However, it would be impossible to transfer to a job-ranking system all at once so he suggested the proportion of job-ranked pay should be gradually increased as the efficiency of the plant increased.

3. Shinshichiro Kamiuma (a director of Kawasaki Heavy Industries; 1948: 4–5) maintained that for Japanese products once again to advance in world markets corporate reconstruction was needed, and to this end all costs, and particularly increases in the proportion of labour costs, had to be held down. However, he also expressed the desire to support and upgrade workers' living standards, and for this high efficiency and high wages would be needed. 'We have to plan for a rationalization of personnel in terms of quality and numbers. First, for quality, we should establish a job-ranking system (*shokkai sei*) to clarify workers' duties and responsibilities, and we must also set up an appropriate remuneration system to match it.' Next, under the job-ranking system, he advocated planning for the ideal composition of employees, cutting out unnecessary and wasteful allocation of personnel.

4. Matsutaro Fujii (of the Labour Section of Hitachi Shipbuilding's Muko-jima Shipyard; 1948: 25–6) alleged that the fixed-pay (*teigaku kyū*) system had deficiencies. People with limited ability were able to win rapid promotion, and there was plenty of scope for favouritism. The system was entirely unsuited to allocating 'the right man to the right job', and because ability and good service went unrewarded, the more competent and loyal the employee the greater his sense of grievance. Criteria could be established through a job-ranking system (*shokkai sei*) to rectify this, but it would not be possible to eliminate the livelihood type of remuneration very quickly.

5. According to Yota Omori (Advisor, Furukawa Electric Industries; 1949: March edition, p. 7; see also April edition), although the company had adopted a system of livelihood pay after the war 'this has in a sense perverted equality

and so is a problem'. A committee was eventually formed to study the adoption of a job-ranking system (*shokkai sei*).

6. Saburo Ewashi (Deputy Director, Labour Division, Nissan Chemical Industries; 1949: 6) alleged that the job-ranking system that would suit Japan at that time was the classification method (*bunruihō*) that was seen in the early days in America. Under this system, all types of work are evaluated from the same standpoint, a job-ranking table is drawn up and actual jobs are then matched to the ranking. He concluded this was very much the same system as the one then in use at his firm.

There were also those who argued the opposite viewpoint. One of them, Takeshi Fujimoto (of Labour Science Research Institute; 1949: 4) alleged that 'although one cannot deny that the job-related, efficiency-oriented (*shokkai kyū* or *shokumu kyū*) systems currently being introduced by various managements may correct the unfair aspects of existing wage rates for different types of work', 'they are also extremely dangerous' in that '*shokumu kyū* does not embrace the real argument for setting wage rates for different types of work, which is to ensure the regeneration of the workforce'. Fujimoto claimed he did not hold the view that 'equal wages should be paid' but argued that it was vital to 'arrive at a compromise between a minimum wage and an element linked to skills (*ginō*) through collective bargaining'. To decide wage levels purely on the basis of the cost of living, as the labour unions were demanding, was going too far, but on the other hand, the idea of productivity pay alone was also too simplistic, and he doused arguments for *shokunō* pay. Fujimoto's views were clearly exceptional among those expressed in the journal, but at the end of the day a *shokumu* job-classification system ultimately emerged in which it had become impossible to disregard the element of safeguarding livelihood.

By the first half of the 1950s corporate managers had acquired their own theoretical base on which to discuss wage issues, and in trying to substitute an automatic increase through a fixed-pay-rise system for the annual struggle with the unions over raising base pay, they moved little by little first towards a broad job-classified system and then a *shokumu kyū* system (see Okamoto (1960: 114–23)). As a result, the formula that many firms came to adopt was:

basic pay = job-classified pay + age and experience pay
(*shokkai kyū*)   (*nenrei keiken kyū*)[21]

Age and experience pay was a composite of age-based and experience-based pay. Age-based pay was an alternative name for livelihood pay, and experience-based pay was derived from livelihood pay and pay according to ability (*nōryoku kyū*). This formula was very similar to that used in the productivity wages (*nōritsu kyū*) that appeared during the inter-war period. Thus, attempts to create a *shokumu kyū* pay system that had once collapsed in the mid-1930s, were now revived thirty years later.

4.3. Contribution to a price-elastic economy

Nominal rates of wage increases ($G(W)$) are greater the tighter the demand in the labour market (v), suggesting that there is a direct correlation between them.[22] When the economy is booming, if the labour unions take a more aggressive stance, and/or if the negotiating power of the unions is stronger, the closer the correlation between v and ($G(W)$) will become.

To confirm this expectation, I have attempted the following linear regression analysis (the so-called Phillips curve), with v, d, and the rate of change in the consumer price index as independent variables, and $G(W)$ as the dependent variable. The following result is produced (data for 1921–88, except 1939–50 for which no data is available):

$$G(W) = -3.9242 + 4.2919 \text{ Dummy} + 0.3881 \text{ } G(p)$$
$$ (-3.9201) \qquad (1.4227) \qquad\quad (0.1137)$$
$$ + 0.03183(V/A) + 0.0356d, \qquad\qquad R^2 = 0.64$$
$$ (0.0093) \qquad\quad (0.0194)$$

Dummy is a variable with the value of 0 up to 1939, and 1 after 1950, R^2 is a coefficient of determination adjusted for degree of freedom (49), and the figures in brackets are standard errors. Wage fluctuation rates are most easily explained by the degree of tightening of demand and supply of labour. We also note that the effect of the index of union activity (d) is significantly positive, the Phillips curve shifted upwards between the pre-war and post-war periods, and that actual adjustment of wages through the labour market takes time since the coefficient of the rate of price changes is less than unity.

Of course, the influence of the unions extends beyond pay increases. Japan's labour unions have consistently resisted staff cuts, so much so that at times of severe economic retrenchment such as the oil shock of 1973, unions were prepared to agree to what amounted to wage cuts as long as staffing levels were maintained. Imbalances in the labour market were thus absorbed not by fluctuations in employment but by fluctuations in wages.

If we calculate fluctuation rates for wages and employment for the pre-war and post-war periods, we arrive at the figures shown in Table 5.2, which is based on data from the same source as Figure 5.2. From this we see that

1. while wage fluctuation rates are greater in the post-war period both in real and nominal terms, fluctuations in employment were greater in the pre-war period, and
2. the disparity in annual fluctuation rates (as measured by standard deviation) has shrunk considerably in the post-war period.

These facts are consistent with the interpretation that the unions' impact on determining wages and employment increased during the post-war period.

The combination of long-term, stable employment and flexibility in wages

Table 5.2. Fluctuations in wages and employment (%)

	Nominal wages	Real wages	Employment
(a) *Average annual*			
rate of change			
1900–37	4.98	2.20	5.36
1953–88	9.35	4.04	3.38
(b) *Standard deviation*			
of rate of change			
1900–37	10.67	7.15	4.13
1953–88	5.77	3.19	2.60

has undoubtedly contributed significantly to the ability of the Japanese economy to cope with change through flexible price adjustments. This feature highlights the different approaches used in Japan and in Europe or America to deal with the various economic shocks experienced since the war.[23]

5. Issues for the twenty-first century

Labour relations in Japan are likely to face a further turning-point within the next few years. Long-term continuous employment, also known as life-time employment, is a system that came to exist only because of high-speed growth. As the economy continued to grow, employment opportunities could be expected to expand further. Even though more and more freshmen were taken on, the number of management posts for them in the future would also continue to grow, so the role of the promotion system in generating motivation would not be hampered. (Of course, demand for labour does not increase to the same extent as growth in production because of technical innovation, but under full employment that poses no great problem.) Under these circumstances there is no fear of lay-offs, and therefore no labour unrest, when new technology is introduced, and managements have been able to invest freely in the latest production facilities to boost their competitive strength.

The Japanese-style employment system will face a crisis when the myths created in the high-growth period begin to crumble. The 1973 oil crisis was a fundamental test. Since that time there have been calls for cost-saving management and it appears that some corrections are being made in readiness for a period of 'stable' growth. The threshold to appointments at managerial level has become much higher and long-term guaranteed employment will probably be offered only to a nucleus of key staff (however, the pressure should be somewhat eased by the expected fall in the proportion of young staff, due to the overall ageing of the population).

Wage structure in Japan is inseparable from employment practices. Personnel management built around internal promotion as the major motivating factor is characteristic of Japanese-style labour management, and emphasis is placed on gaining shallow, wide-ranging skills. Therefore job content (*shokumu*) and wages have not been closely linked, and only loosely associated with a job-ranking (*shokkai sei*) system. But if the labour market becomes more and more fluid and less company-based, and if the number of workers in long-term continuous employment declines in relative terms and the proportion of foreign staff grows, then it is possible that the scale of internal labour markets will shrink, and in their place the proportion of people receiving productivity wages (through either a commission (*buai*) system or a group piecework (*shūdan dekidaka*) system) will increase. However, in so far as internal labour markets continue to be linked to the realities of production technology as well as to the needs of organizations, they are unlikely to disappear completely from Japanese corporate society and labour relations.

Since the 1970s, membership in labour unions has shown a clear decline in relative terms. Against a background of major socio-economic shifts, such as growing competitive pressure through privatization, the break-up of Sōhyō (General Council of Trade Unions of Japan), and weakening links between labour unions and the Japan Socialist Party, the influence of the labour unions will inevitably continue to wane. With the added possibility that the lifelong employment system will start to fade, employees with grievances about their workplace or employer will in the future be more inclined to 'exit' rather than voice their complaints.

There are areas that, despite their importance, have been largely ignored by both sides in Japanese labour relations. An example is the issue of working hours. A trend towards a long-term, gradual shortening of working hours at last began to appear in the final phase of the high-growth period, but it was not a straightforward development, and after the first oil shock average hours worked per week by male workers began to increase again. Clearly, company-based unions have done nothing about cutting working hours owing to a tendency to give precedence to maintaining the firm's domestic competitiveness.

No strong interest has been shown either in broader socio-economic issues, such as promoting women's participation in the workforce or greater job training. This is particularly true of the union side. However, it is no mistake to say that emphasizing merely the economic aspects of union activities will not attract the interest of the younger generation. Be that as it may, the labour unions have made a greater effort to publicize their views, particularly since the end of the high-growth era, by actively participating in government councils and so on. The movement is also in the midst of a reform process initiated internally (Kume 1988). It remains to be seen to what extent these efforts will bear fruit.

Notes

1. The research of Griliches (1969) examines the extent to which capital and labour in America are interchangeable or complementary. His results show that as capital accumulates, skilled labour tends to be replaced by semi-skilled; however, more and more better-educated and capital-complementary workers are needed. According to data on manufacturing industry in Japan between 1965 and 1985 (Suruga 1990), capital could be substituted for production workers, while non-production workers tended to be more complementary with capital.
2. There are cases where labour-management or personnel departments were set up well before this time, such as at Osaka Denki Fundo (Osaka Electric Metal Refining) in 1893, Kanebo Cotton Spinning Hyogo Plant in 1894, Kobe Steel in 1905, etc. Of interest is the fact that exactly the same occurrence was observed in the USA.
3. Of the 54 factory committees (49 in the private sector) in existence before 1922, 38 (all private-sector) were set up in 1921 (Ministry of Internal Affairs, Social Bureau, *Taishō Jūichinen Rōdō Undō Gaikyō* (A Survey of the Labour Movement in 1922), pp. 13–14).
4. The cost of recruiting female labour for the silk mills rose rapidly between 1915 and 1925.
5. For Yawata Steelworks, *Yawata Seitetsushō Kōjō Rōdō Tōkei* (Factory Labour Statistics), data for 1927–36. For Mitsubishi Heavy Industries, Odaka (1978: 118–19), data for 1921–3, 1940.
6. Takeo Godo was a technical officer at Kure Navy Arsenal, and later worked for Nippon Kōkan. He became Chairman of the Japan Management Association and was appointed Minister of Commerce and Industry.
7. At this time the use of incentive pay was lower than in 1934.
8. Regular staff here refers to workers who were not schoolchildren or students, or workers drafted in groups from colonial areas, or prisoners of war. The figures all refer to the end of each month. The document gives the overall numbers employed in the mining, manufacturing, and transportation industries as 6.2 million on average during these four months, with an average of over 60,000 per month drafted for military duties during the period. (For manufacturing alone, the figures were 5.16 million and 50,000 respectively.)
9. Based on reports from government-designated major enterprises in these three industrial sectors. Average figures for the four months July, November, and December 1944, and January 1945 were 660,000 schoolchildren and students, about 190,000 Korean draftees, and about 80,000 Chinese draftees and prisoners of war. The equivalent figures for manufacturing industry alone are 620,000, 50,000, and 20,000 respectively.
10. Census results for 1947 (as included in Umemura *et al.* (1988) and used in Table 5.1) give roughly the same figures: 20% and 23% for males only.
11. In February 1938 the total number of shop-floor workers employed in 'plants with five or more workers' excluding machinery plants was roughly 2.26 million. From 1940 to 1944 the number of employees in manufacturing industry excluding machinery production was declining at a rate of 5.8% per year. The number of plant workers, excluding machinery plants, in June 1944 was approximately 3.05 million.

Using these figures to estimate the number working in 1944 in non-machinery manufacturing industry at tiny shops with fewer than five workers, we arrive at an equally surprising 52% or 1.58 million.

However, Statistics Bureau data on numbers employed in 1944 give different figures according to different classifications. Moreover a comparison with 1944 census figures (Table 5.1) reveals many inconsistencies. For some industries the two sets of figures correspond and for others they do not. For example, the total number of workers in the Statistics Bureau data is roughly the same as the number employed in manufacturing industry according to the census. Thus, further analysis is needed. I suspect that reports submitted to the Statistics Bureau may have included numbers of workers temporarily transferred from other industries, and mobilized schoolchildren and students.

12. Horigome was at that time a department director in the Japan Management Association.
13. Noguchi was at that time Section Chief responsible for labour at the Kamata Plant of Niigata Steelworks.
14. Sugiyama was at that time President of Amagasaki Seiko K. K.
15. According to Okuda (1985: 479), 60% of enterprises in Tokyo applied for exemption from the wage freeze.
16. Few labour unions in reality inherited assets from industrial patriotic societies (Sakurabayashi 1985: 75).
17. Not all managements lent their support to the industrial patriotic societies. The firms had no objection to the advocacy of labour discipline, but tended to be against intervention in their right to manage and opposed the active promotion of workplace meetings (Okuda 1985: 488–503).
18. 'Densan' was the abbreviated name of the *Nippon Denki Sangyō Rōdō Kumiai Kyōgikai* (Japan Federation of Power Industry Unions).
19. The fall in the rate of labour organization in this period is something that can be seen in many industrialized countries, but is particularly striking in Japan and America (Freeman and Rebick 1989). Canada is an exception to this, partly accounted for by the high rate of organization among government-sector workers.
20. The ratio of demand for labour to supply (v) is the monthly number of effective job vacancies registered with official labour-exchange bureaux (V) (annual average figure) compared with the number of job enquiries (A) for the same month (V/A). Job vacancies described as 'effective' include those which are to be filled in the following month.

    The unemployment rate is often used as an indicator of the tightness of the labour market. The post-war unemployment rate has shown a clear inverse correlation with the ratio of labour demand to supply, except in the early 1950s. Unfortunately, there is no survey of time-series unemployment statistics before the Second World War.
21. This formula is based on Yoshioka (1948: 5).
22. The rate of change ($G(X)$) of the variable X is calculated as $100(X_{t+1} - X_t)/X_t$ (%).
23. The pre-war Japanese economy was also considerably price-elastic by international standards.

References

Note: For the English edition, some Japanese-language references have been omitted. Readers wishing to follow up points made in the text may refer to the equivalent passage and references in the Japanese edition.

Arrow, Kenneth J. (1974), *The Limits of Organization*, W. W. Norton, New York.

Ewatari, Saburo (1949), 'Shokkai Kyū to Haichi Tenkan (Job-Related Wages and Job Allocation)', *Nihon Nōritsu* (Work Efficiency in Japan), 8(5) (May).

Freeman, Richard B. and Marcus E. Rebick (1989), 'Crumbling Pillar? Declining Union Density in Japan', *Journal of the Japanese and International Economies*, 3(4) (December).

Fujii, Matsutaro (1948), 'Shokkai Seido no Kenkyū (Study of the Job-Related Wage System)', in *Nihon Nōritsu* (Work Efficiency in Japan), 7(7) (August).

Fujimoto, Takeshi (1949), 'Saitei Chingin Sei to Shokumu Kyū (The Minimum Wage System and the Job-Related Wage System)', in *Nihon Nōritsu* (Work Efficiency in Japan), 8(2) (February).

Gordon, Andrew (1985), *The Evolution of Labour Relations in Japan: Heavy Industry, 1853–1955*, Harvard University Press.

Griliches, Zvi (1969), 'Capital–Skill Complementarity', *Review of Economics and Statistics*, 51(4).

Horigome, Kenichi (1942), 'Sagyō Kenkyū to Ukeoi Seido (Motion Study and Internal Contracting System)', *Nihon Nōritsu* (Work Efficiency in Japan), 1(2) (July).

Inoue, Koichi and Taketo Ueda (1939), *Nōritsu Chingin Shiharai Hō* (Method of Paying Productivity Wages), Daiyamondo-sha.

Institute of Social Sciences, University of Tokyo (1950), *Sengo Rōdō Kumiai no Jittai* (A Survey of Labour Unions in Post-war Japan), Nihon Hyōron-sha.

Jacoby, Sanford M. (1985), *Employing Bureaucracy, Managers, Unions, and the Transformation of Work in American Industry, 1900–1945*, Columbia University Press.

Jinba, Shinshichiro (1948), 'Keiei Keiri ni okeru Jinkenhi no Mondai (The Problem of Personnel Costs in Managerial Cost Accounting)', *Nihon Nōritsu* (Work Efficiency in Japan), 7(7) (August).

Komatsu, Ryuji (1971), *Kigyōbetsu Kumiai no Seisei: Nihon Rōdō Kumiai Undō Shi no Hitokusari* (The Emergence of Enterprise Unionism in Japan: A Sketch of the Labour Movement), Ochanomizu Shobō.

Kume, Ikuo (1988), 'Changing Relations among the Government, Labour and Business in Japan after the Oil Crisis', *International Organization*, 42(4).

Littler, Craig R. (1982), *The Development of the Labour Process in Capitalist Societies: A Comparative Study of the Transformation of Work Organization in Britain, Japan and the USA*, Heinemann Educational Books, London.

Mitsubishi Heavy Industries (1967), *Mitsubishi Zōsen Kabushiki Gaisha Shi* (The History of Mitsubishi Shipbuilding Co.)

Noguchi, Hamajiro (1943), 'Nihonteki Chingin Seido no Kakuritsu (The Establishment of the Japanese Wage System)', *Nihon Nōritsu* (Work Efficiency in Japan), 2(3) (March).

Odaka, Konosuke (1978) (ed.), *Kyū Mitsubishi Jūkō no Rōdō Tōkei, Meiji 17-nen– Shōwa 38-nen: Kikai Kōgyō no Rōdō Tōkei Bassui* (Labour Statistics of Mitsubishi

Heavy Industries, 1884–1953, with Selected Labour Statistics for the Machinery Industry), Statistics Section, Institute of Economic Research, Hitotsubashi University.

[Okamoto, Hideaki] (1960), *Nihon no Keiei, sono Tenkai to Tokushitsu* (Japanese Management, Its Development and Characteristics), Nihon Management School.

Okouchi, Kazuo (1972), *Rōshi Kankei Ron no Hatten* (The Development of Labour Relations Studies), Yuhikaku.

Okuda, Kenji (1985), *Hito to Keiei: Nihon Keiei Kanri Shi Kenkyū* (Man and Management: A History of Corporate Management and Control in Japan), Managementsha.

Omori, Yota (1949), 'Shokkai Sei no Tebiki (A Handbook on Job-Related Wage Payment)', *Nihon Nōritsu* (Work Efficiency in Japan), 8(3) (March).

Sakurabayashi, Makoto (1985), *Sangyō Hōkokukai no Soshiki to Kinō* (The Organization and Function of the Industrial Patriotic Societies), Ochanomizu Shobō.

Sato, Keisaku (1948), 'Nōritsu Kyū Seido no Kakuritsu: Rōdō Nōritsu ni kansuru Shomondai II (The Establishment of the Efficiency-Related Wage System: The Problems of Work Efficiency II)', *Nihon Nōritsu* (Work Efficiency in Japan), 7(4) (June).

Sugiyama, Manabu (1943), 'Wagasha no Taryō Seisan Hōshiki to Setsubi no Nōritsu-teki Kaizen (2) (The Mass-Production System in our Firm, and Improvements to Production Equipment (2))', *Nihon Nōritsu* (Work Efficiency in Japan), 2(5) (May).

Suruga, Terukazu (1990), 'Substitution between Capital and Labour Inputs Differentiated by Educational Attainment in Japanese Manufacturing Industries', *Journal of the Japan Statistical Society*, 20(2).

Umemura, Mataji, *et al.* (1988), *Rōdōryoku* (Manpower), *Long-Term Economic Statistics of Japan*, 2, Tōyō Keizai Shinpō-sha.

Weber, Max (1925), *Wirtschaft und Gesellschaft*, vol. 2, 2nd edn., Tübingen: J. C. B. Mohr.

Yamamoto, Kiyoshi (1977), 'Sengo Rōdō Kumiai no Shuppatsuten (The Starting-Point of Labour Unions in Post-war Japan)', in Mikio Sumiya (ed.), *Nihon Rōshi Kankei Ron* (Industrial Relations in Japan), University of Tokyo Press.

Yoshioka, Takeo (1948), 'Shokumu Kakuzuke Hyōkago ni okeru Chinritsu Kettei Hōhō nami Chinritsu Kirikae Hōhō (Wage Rate Determination and Its Changes after Job Evaluation)', *Nihon Nōritsu* (Work Efficiency in Japan), 7(6) (July).

6

The Functions of Industrial Associations

Seiichiro Yonekura

1. Introduction

Ongoing research into Japanese industrial policy has led to some modification of the former so-called 'Japan Inc.' theories, in which this policy was interpreted as the 'fostering of industries under the guidance of the Ministry of International Trade and Industry (MITI)'. Now some of the more dynamic aspects of the policy have been highlighted, such as the way private-sector initiative and market mechanisms have coexisted with government planning. Particularly since the collapse of the centrally planned, command economies of the socialist countries, we need to clarify the major differences between planning in Japanese industrial policy and that in the socialist countries. More than ever, detailed, substantiating research into Japanese industrial policy is called for.

The object of this chapter is to examine how the role of Japanese industrial associations in implementing industrial policy has developed through the wartime and post-war periods, and show how the fundamental role of these associations in post-war industrial policy has been to use their position located midway between government and individual firms to relay information in both directions and thereby increase the policy's effectiveness. Their function thus has two aspects: on the one hand, passing information on corporate firms to the government for use in policy formulation, and on the other, acquainting firms with the policy and the various measures that it involves, as well as the technical and administrative information needed to put the policy into effect. In other words, the basic function of industrial associations in executing industrial policy in post-war Japan has been to boost its effectiveness by reducing the asymmetrical nature of information flows between government and the corporate sector.

Industrial associations are not exclusive to Japan. Known as trade associations, they have long existed in Europe and America. But just as industrial policy in Japan has charted its own unique course, so Japanese industrial associations are seen to fulfil a unique function. Lynn and McKeown show that trade associations in Japan and America have served broad and roughly comparable purposes, reflecting both the different economic environments and institutional structures of the two states and their differing philosophies of business-government relations (Lynn and McKeown 1988). Richard Samuels has pointed out that although it is well known that 'committees in the Diet and ruling Liberal Democratic Party (LDP), having limited expertise and staff, are dependent upon the bureaucracy for data and analysis, it is not as often recognized that the well-fabled Japanese bureaucracy is itself often dependent in the same way upon the industrial associations and firms with which it works so closely' (Samuels 1983). Daniel Okimoto also commends the function of industrial associations, from among the many policy-making networks in Japan, as agencies providing information. He suggests that they fulfil an important role as a means of liaison between MITI and the private-sector firms belonging to each industry, positioned as they are midway between the two (Okimoto 1991).

The usefulness of industrial associations in policy-making is not limited to Japan, however. In 1957 a policy research group in Britain applauded the role of trade associations, commenting that it was extremely beneficial from the government's viewpoint to have a single advisory body on each industry, and pointing out that trade associations are an important source of specialist knowledge and advisory skills for dealing with industrial problems (McRobie *et al.* 1957). In America, too, during the 1930s when the country was recovering from economic depression and later preparing for war, government and corporate enterprises co-operated through trade associations (Lynn and McKeown 1988). But the trade associations of Britain and America could never separate themselves from special interests, and their co-operative relationships with government did not last long. In fact, in America any trade associations that have encouraged co-operation between firms have tended to be seen as working counter to economic well-being, and have been subjected to the scrutiny of anti-monopoly legislation.

Post-war industrial associations in Japan have played an entirely different role from their counterparts in America and Europe, in their involvement in the planning and implementation of government policy to foster the development of particular industries, given a corporate structure based on freedom of intent. Japan's industrial associations have not acted simply as institutions to relay policy to individual firms, but have increased the effectiveness of policy by providing government with information from the shop floor, and also information on interim developments during policy implementation. Much more than merely passing on policy handed down from the government, they have acted as intermediaries in the passage of information in both directions, back and forth, between government and individual firms, creating a mechanism to generate information through the three parties of government, industrial associations and firms (Yonekura 1993).

Based on an awareness of these issues, I would like first in this chapter to set out the theoretical framework underlying all industrial associations, and then examine the essential functions of Japan's associations and their origins. For an analysis of their functions, I will refer to the Japan Iron and Steel Federation (*Tekkō Renmei*) and the Iron and Steel Control Association (*Tekkō Tōsei Kai*) for the pre-war and wartime periods, and as a post-war case study, I will focus on the Metal Mould Industry Association (*Kanagata Kōgyō Kai*) and the effects of the Temporary Measures for Machinery Promotion Law (*Kikai Kōgyō Shinkō Rinji Sochi Hō*).

2. Information-related functions of industrial associations

I would first like to examine the flow of information between government and firms in the functions of industrial associations, or trade associations, and study their theoretical structure.

The following nine functions and activities are considered common to all industrial associations:

1. product promotion
2. labour relations
3. standard setting
4. data collection
5. research and development
6. economic services, such as joint purchasing, member discounts, management guidance, insurance, etc.
7. educational services
8. conventions and general membership meetings
9. public relations   (Lynn and McKeown 1988: 3).

Considering these activities in terms of the flow of information between government, the associations, and individual firms, we can identify the following four basic functions of industrial associations:

1. pressure group function (upward flow of information)
2. policy implementation function (downward flow)
3. cartel function (lateral flow)
4. generation of information function (upward and downward flow)

In reality these four functions are, of course, interrelated and do not exist independently, but this classification is nevertheless meaningful to gain an understanding of what industrial associations are and what they do.

1. *The pressure group function.* Industrial associations are normally formed as organizations wielding collective power in order to represent the interests of individual firms in a particular industry. This is their so-called lobbying, or pressure group function. The association pressurizes the government for regu-

lations, standards, and protectionist policies that will benefit the industry, such as subsidies, import restrictions, and tariffs. Because the organization's mission is to guide government policy-making in a direction beneficial to the industry, its demands often work against the welfare of the economy and society as a whole. The main reason for this is that the upward flow of information to the government for these purposes is selective and does not disclose the full circumstances of the industry. In other words, the flow of information between government and firms is asymmetrical and the relationship between government and industrial association is not purely complementary. Furthermore, the existence of other industrial associations whose interests the lobbying may harm cannot be overlooked. In the pre-war steel industry, for example, tariffs on imports of pig iron worked to the benefit of pig-iron producers, but to the detriment of the steelmakers who used pig iron as a raw material.

2. *The policy implementation function.* The government sees the functions of industrial associations as supporting policy and simultaneously undertaking the process whereby policy is actually implemented. This may involve supervising the allocation of production and consumption quotas, distributing subsidies, and informing firms about new technology, industrial standards, and so on. Under regimes where the central government authority is extremely strong, such as in the socialist states or Japan's wartime controlled economy, the government can force industrial associations to implement policy, but in normal circumstances incentives such as subsidies or low-interest loans are provided in return for the associations' services. When incentives are granted as the result of association lobbying, this function can be seen as going hand in hand with the pressure group function.

Policies do not always work in the interests of the industry concerned, however, and industrial associations contracted to implement policy do not always implement it faithfully. The information flow between government, industrial association, and firms may thus be asymmetrical and agency costs likely to arise. In order to make industrial associations more effective in implementing policy, the government has to reduce the information gap with individual firms through the industrial associations.

3. *The cartel function.* One negative aspect of industrial associations is their cartel function. Basically, cartels are collaborative actions among companies to engage in price collusion, or adjust production levels or production content in order to support prices. As cartel activities hinder competition and therefore harm the interests of consumers, the relevant information is held only by the firms involved and is not publicly disclosed. Information flow in this case is therefore lateral or circular. However, because they increase prices by reducing plant operating rates, for example, cartel activities inevitably invite cartel busting within the industry, particularly by so-called outsider firms not part of the cartel. The job of the industrial association is to reduce the number of

outsiders and monitor members' adherence to cartel agreements, but without a means of enforcement, maintaining cartels is difficult. Particularly in industries with enormous fixed capital, such as the steel industry, there is a powerful incentive to recover that fixed capital by raising plant operating rates, and some sort of mechanism is needed to keep the cartel stable. In the steel industry in Japan and America before the war, cartels were maintained through the 'price leadership' of firms with the greatest share of the business, such as US Steel and Nippon Seitetsu (Japan Steel).

In post-war Japan, Nippon Seitetsu was broken up into Yawata and Fuji steel companies. When the pre-war furnace operators also began integrated iron and steelmaking the cartel could no longer be maintained under Yawata's price leadership. Through MITI intervention, price leadership and price-fixing cartels were disclosed. Fierce competition to expand facilities led to the open appearance of recession cartels, by which facilities and production are adjusted at times of recession. For the industrial association, in this case the Japan Iron and Steel Federation, implementing cartels involves collecting data, adjusting production levels and monitoring. In post-war cases of recession cartels in Japan, the industrial association involved has supplied information to firms and to the government, its function thus becoming that of generating new information on such matters as technology transfers and market conditions.

4. *The information function.* Industrial associations are positioned between the level of government and that of individual firms, and exchange information with both. The associations have often been involved in fostering the development of industries in post-war Japan, through formulating realistic policies and implementing those policies effectively. The industrial associations not only pass plant-level information from firms to government, but fulfil a range of complementary functions through their involvement in policy formulation and implementation. Government information concerning the fostering of the industry, and shop-floor information from individual firms is passed in opposite directions through the industrial association in a dynamic process of creating information that goes far beyond the static, so-called 'data processing' function. As organization theory has shown, Japan's middle managers are not simply relaying the wishes of top management to the lower ranks, or compiling information from the shop floor to edify those at higher levels. As the two types of information move among the three different levels, further new information is created. In the same way the industrial associations in their midway position produce new information on the fostering of the industry.[1] The information gap, or asymmetry of information, between government and firms has thus been greatly reduced through the intermediary function of industrial associations.

Bearing these functions in mind, I would now like to examine the historical development of industrial associations in Japan.

3. The history and functions of industrial associations: a case study of the steel industry

In the making of industrial policy in post-war Japan, industrial associations have become instrumental in generating information to be passed between government and private-sector firms. This is done through a wide range of activities, such as specifying policy targets, planning detailed policy content, organizing private-sector firms, running market surveys, and collecting and disseminating technical information. I would like first to examine the steel industry, and especially the Iron and Steel Control Association (*Tekkō Tōsei Kai*) and the Japan Iron and Steel Federation (*Nippon Tekkō Renmei*), to trace the historical origins of industrial associations performing such functions.

3.1. The Iron and Steel Control Association

Steel was a vital industry underpinning the war effort, and the government was therefore particularly concerned about establishing control. We cannot here examine pre-war control of the industry in detail, but a basic overview can be given in terms of the following four stages:

1. 1934—The founding of Nippon Seitetsu; a half-government-owned steel company
2. 1937—The Steelmaking Act (*Seitetsu Jigyō Hō*)
3. 1940—Regulations to control supply and demand for steel, and the founding of the Iron and Steel Control Association
4. 1942—The introduction of profit incentives and the transformation of the Control Association

The founding of Nippon Seitetsu was the most significant event in imposing indirect control over the steel industry before the war. By merging the state-owned Yawata Works with private iron- and steelmaking companies, the government and the industry planned to create an enormous, highly efficient integrated firm. Merging them was also an attempt to expand and control the production of steel. However, the major private steelmaking firms Nippon Kōkan, Kawasaki Heavy Industries (*Kawasaki Jūkō*), Kobe Steel (*Kōbe Seikōsho*) and Sumitomo Metal Industries (*Sumitomo Kinzoku*) backed out immediately prior to the merger, and so a dual structure persisted, of integrated steelmakers, such as Nippon Seitetsu, on the one hand and open-hearth-furnace steel producers on the other. The two groups each had an industrial association, the Pig Iron Joint Sales Corporation representing the integrated and blast-furnace iron producers, and the Joint Purchase Association representing the non-integrated steelmakers. The Joint Purchase Association aimed for more efficient production through joint purchasing of cheap, imported pig iron and scrap, while the Pig Iron Joint Sales Corporation wanted high tariffs levied on imported pig iron and scrap to help its member firms remain competitive. Thus these two pressure groups represented different, conflicting interests.[2]

Then, as the war with China intensified after the Marco Polo Bridge Incident of 1937, the government sought to expand the country's productive capacity in steel. At this point the Steelmaking Act was passed and control over steel entered its second stage. The Act basically covered the two aspects of control and promotion of the steel industry. It aimed to 'promote integrated steelmaking, and also set up a voluntary control organization to maintain stability in the market. If this is not effective, the state may take tougher measures' (MITI 1964: 244). In other words, in consideration of the deteriorating import situation, the Act basically sought to encourage the industry, and at the same time reconcile the interests of the integrated and non-integrated producers through controls.

As the steel industry was central to the Materials Mobilization Plan, under the Steelmaking Act an Iron and Steel Control Council (*Tekkō Tōsei Kyōgikai*) was set up in the Ministry of Commerce and Industry, to set quarterly production volumes for different types of steel, import and export volumes, and volumes for allocation to the various consumer sectors. Detailed plans for implementation were delegated to the autonomous control organizations representing the steelmakers, steel distributors, and consumers. However, after the Second World War broke out in 1939 the international environment became all the more difficult, and many of the Production Capacities Expansion Plans including that for steel, could not be met. Although production targets for ordinary steel, for instance, were lowered year by year, from 5.72 million tons in FY1939, 5.2 million tons in FY1940, to 4.71 million tons in FY1941, actual production volumes were consistently lower than the targets, at 4.66, 4.56, and 4.3 million tons respectively (MITI 1964: 373).

The Steelmaking Act was not as strict as some other wartime control legislation and assumed autonomous control in the industry. In the words of J. B. Cohen, the steel industry was 'half controlled and half free' (Cohen 1950: vol. 1: 39). The Act itself was merely information derived from the top levels of government, to be implemented by subordinate groups, the independent cartel organizations. There was thus no exchange of information between the two levels, and the independent control groups were not strong enough in terms of leadership to be able to implement everything that came from higher levels.

Because of this the second Konoe Cabinet, aiming at further expansion of production, decided to tighten economic control mechanisms in order to implement the government's so-called New Economic System (*Keizai Shin Taisei*). During this third stage of control the control associations were introduced. In 1940 the Ministry of Commerce and Industry and the Planning Board drew up proposals to submit to the Diet for an Industrial Association

Control Law (*Sangyō Dantai Tōsei Hō*) which would bring together all industrial organizations and allow integrated control. The proposed law met with strong resistance from industrial and political circles, however, and only a partial revision of the State General Mobilization Law (*Kokka Sōdōin Hō*) was passed. But for the iron and steel industry the need was most urgent, and in November an Outline for the Organization of the Iron and Steel Control Association (*Tekkō Tōseikai Soshiki Yōkō*) was submitted to introduce integrated control. Subsequently a network of control associations was gradually expanded to cover other industries through the Major Industrial Organizations Directive (*Jūyō Sangyō Dantai Rei*) issued in August 1941. It was the Iron and Steel Control Association that played the pioneering role in Japan's wartime system of control, however. Table 6.1 lists the various control associations set up around this time.

The Outline Agreement for the Iron and Steel Control Association (*Tekkō Tōseikai Kiyaku Yōkō*) sets out that 'in expectation of the setting up of an independent steel industry within the East Asia Co-prosperity Sphere, the purpose of this association is to plan the comprehensive control of the steel industry' and it handled first 'matters relating to formulating and carrying through raw materials plans, production plans and distribution plans for iron and steel', and 'other matters necessary to achieve the objectives of the control association' that covered prices, technology and standards (MITI 1964: 457). Compared with earlier autonomous control, the Iron and Steel Control Association was more thorough in its planning, and its chairman was granted considerable authority. Procedures took the form of the government drawing up aggregate plans based on information provided by the Control Association, which prepared non-aggregate and localized plans for government approval. As Okazaki has indicated, the system put in place under the New Economic System was a more highly perfected planned system incorporating the three levels of government, control association, and individual firm, and information from the lowest level, the firms, was utilized in the government's aggregate plans. It was also a command-type planned system with a mechanism to supervise and monitor the implementation of those plans (Okazaki 1988).

When Russia joined the war against Germany in 1941, Japanese forces started a southward advance and imports of iron ore from the region became less easy. Under these tense circumstances, the Control Association kept in close contact with the government in working to achieve the objectives of the Materials Mobilization and Production Capacities Expansion Plans, making priority allocations of production quotas and raw materials, and forcing the liquidation or merging of inefficient firms.

At this stage the control-association system provided the means for the government to gain access to fairly detailed information from private-sector firms, and to delegate the implementation of control to the associations' supervision and co-ordination. The Iron and Steel Control Association was a weighty organization with more than 300 full-time employees, made up largely of staff

Table 6.1. List of control associations (CA)

Name	Inauguration	Chairman	Chairman's previous occupation
First designated group			
Iron and Steel CA	21 Nov. 1941	Hachisaburo Hirao (later) Teijiro Toyoda	president of Nippon Seitetsu (Japan Steel) as above
Coal CA	26 Nov. 1941	Kenjiro Matsumoto	president of Nippon Coal
Mining CA	18 Dec. 1941	Bunkichi Ito	president of Nippon Mining
Cement CA	18 Dec. 1941	Soichiro Asano	president of Asano Cement
Electrical Machinery CA	12 Jan. 1942	Daigoro Yasukawa	president of Yasukawa Electric Manufacturing
Industrial Machinery CA	15 Jan. 1942	Masatoshi Okochi	president of Riken
Precision Machinery CA	10 Jan. 1942	Kiyoaki Hara	president of Osaka Kiko
Automobile CA	24 Dec. 1941	Shigeyasu Suzuki	president of Diesel Industries
Rolling Stock CA	22 Dec. 1941	Yasujiro Shima	president of Kisha Rolling Stock
Metal Manufacturing CA	15 Jan. 1942	Hajime Suzuki	managing director of Furukawa Electric
Foreign Trade CA	27 Jan. 1942	Gozaburo Minami	president of Nippon Menka
Shipbuilding CA	28 Jan. 1942	Koshiro Shiba	president of Mitsubishi Heavy Industries
Second designated group			
Cotton Textile CA	5 Oct. 1942	Kiyoshi Inoue	executive director of Kanegafuchi Cotton Spinning
Silk and Rayon CA	2 Oct. 1942	Asahiko Kojima	president of Toyo Rayon
Wool CA	19 Sept. 1942	Sakio Tsurumi	president of Daito Woollen Spinning and Weaving
Hemp CA	25 Sept. 1942	Kiyoshi Kano	president of Nippon Genma
Chemical Engineering CA	30 Oct. 1942	Ichiro Ishikawa	president of Nissan Chemical Industries
Light Metals CA	1 Sept. 1942	Atsushi Oya	president of Sumitomo Chemical
Oils and Fats CA	5 Oct. 1942	Masasuke Fujita	president of Nihon Yushi
Leather and Hides CA	21 Sept. 1942	Kumataro Suzuki	president of Nippon Gempi
Rubber CA	25 Jan. 1943	Zenji Hayashi	managing director of Nippon Tire
Rail Track CA	30 May 1942	Shogo Nakagawa	president of Tetsudo Doshikai

Source: Ando, Yoshio 1977, *Gendai Nihon Keizaishi Nyūmon* (Introduction to the Modern Economic History of Japan), University of Tokyo Press.

from member firms who were either temporarily transferred or who had retired. Such top-ranking Nippon Seitetsu directors as Hachisaburo Hirao and Yoshisuke Watanabe were appointed successively to the chairmanship of the Control Association after retiring from their posts. Clearly, the division of responsibilities seen after the war, of government formulating policy and industrial associations implementing it, was started in embryo form at this stage. The flow of information went in both directions, just as two-way communication had become the watchword of the New Economic System, which was the backdrop to the control associations (Hoashi 1943).

But at this stage under the control system, profit incentives were eliminated and firms were expected to boost production from a desire to 'give priority to the public good, and work devotedly for the state', as set out in the 'Outline to Establish the New Economic System' (*Keizai Shintaisei Kakuritsu Yōkō*). Furthermore, in spite of calling for 'independent business management based on entrepreneurial initiative and responsibility', admonitions to 'maintain production as a priority, and uphold the public nature of corporate management by giving private managers public status' dispensed with a basic tenet of private enterprise. Thus, through the system they sought to introduce under the New Economic System, the government tried to take hold even of the running of private-sector firms by utilizing the control associations (Nakamura 1974: 96). However, as the war situation worsened, so production became more difficult, and with prices frozen and producers' profits controlled, firms finally lost the will to co-operate. Even though increased steel production was vital and was given every sort of priority treatment, it could not meet the target set in the Materials Mobilization Plan for the first half of FY1942. The Control Association and the Ministry of Commerce and Industry pointed out to the Planning Board the unrealistic aspects of the control system, and subsidies were introduced to cover the shortfall between producer and consumer prices. Production revived as a result, and for the second half of FY1942 production expansion exceeded expectations, and control over the industry entered a new stage. This was the fourth stage, when the profit motive was restored and the nature of control changed. Okazaki's detailed research deals with the process by which this was accomplished (Okazaki 1988), so I will touch on it only briefly here. 'Major revisions' were required to the 'primitive command-type planned economic system' (Okazaki 1988: 109) at this stage, and a more realistic form of planning that could co-exist with the profit motive was sought.

This whole process is particularly important for an understanding of the role of post-war industrial associations. Through the New Economic System and the control associations, attempts were made to expand production for the war effort through a so-called 'top-down planned economy', where profit motivation was abandoned in preference for the state objective of 'giving priority to the public good', and the control associations imposed control. But the issue that confronted Ministry of Commerce and Industry officials was that firms were accumulating losses because selling prices were divorced from any sort of realistic price structure, and so there was no incentive to boost production. All economic indices were falling, the war situation was deteriorating, and to achieve increased industrial production in such a situation, the three parties of government, industrial association, and private firms would need to exchange more accurate and useful information, and work out more effective plans and the means to implement them. It seems that at this point the model of the post-war two-directional relationship between government and private firms via industrial associations, and the system of administrative guidance, first appeared. Ministry officials, members of the control association, and firms had all learned from the control-association system the potential of 'co-existence of economic planning with profit incentives in individual firms', or put another way, the 'coexistence of market mechanisms based on a private corporate system with a thorough-going planned economy'. And they had also learned from the collapse of the controlled economy the importance of withholding control. The war situation continued to deteriorate, however, and it is difficult to ascertain whether combining renewed planning with profit incentives would have worked effectively. But taking into account the extent to which policy-makers, officials of the control associations, and corporate managers continued to serve after the war, there was every possibility that this sort of thinking would be passed on into the post-war era. We will consider this in more detail in the following section.

3.2. Continuity into the post-war era

By examining the extent to which ministry officials, control associations officials, and corporate directors remained in their posts in the post-war era, and to which policies continued unchanged, we can determine whether the tendency to planning that had become essential during the war persisted in the years afterwards.

1. *Government officials' continuity in office.* It is clear that those officials in the Ministry of Commerce and Industry who in 1942 proposed wider use of the corporate profit motive within the command-type planned economy then under the control of the Planning Board continued to serve after the war. Table 6.2 compares the posts of prime minister, other senior ministers, and officials for the years 1942, 1945, 1949, 1956, and 1961. The degree of continuity that persisted from the pre-war period through the war and then for 20 years after the war is most surprising. For example, at the time of the ministry's introduction of price incentives in 1942, Nobusuke Kishi was serving as Minister of Commerce and Industry and Etsusaburo Shiina was Vice-Minister. Twenty years later we find that Kishi had resigned as Prime Minister in 1960, while Shiina had been appointed Minister of International

Table 6.2. Senior government officials in Ministry of Commerce and Industry and MITI

1942

Prime Minister	Hideki Tojo
Minister of Commerce and Industry	Nobusuke Kishi
Parliamentary Vice-Minister	
Administrative Vice-Minister	Etsusaburo Shiina

General Affairs Bureau

Bureau Chief	Akira Kanda
General Affairs Section Chief	Yoji Minobe
Production Expansion Section Chief	Takayuki Yamamoto
Materials Mobilization Section Chief	Tomisaburo Hirai

Iron and Steel Bureau

Bureau Chief	Kishi Sakai
Iron and Steel Section Chief	Yasuo Adachi

Enterprise Bureau

Bureau Chief	Masataka Toyoda

1945

Prime Minister	Kantaro Suzuki
Minister of Munitions	Chikuhei Nakajima
Parliamentary Vice-Minister	
Administrative Vice-Minister	Etsusaburo Shiina

General Mobilization Bureau

Bureau Chief	Meitatsu Takamine
General Affairs Section Chief	Takayuki Yamamoto
Mobilization Department Chief	Meitatsu Takamine
Executive Department Chief	Yoji Minobe

Iron and Steel Bureau

Bureau Chief	Takeyasu Minagawa
Iron and Steel Section Chief	Nagayuki Takahashi

Enterprise Bureau

Bureau Chief	Takeo Ishihara

1949

Prime Minister	Shigeru Yoshida
Minister of International Trade and Industry	Hayato Ikeda
Parliamentary Vice-Minister	Yasushi Miyahata
Administrative Vice-Minister	Takayuki Yamamoto

Minister's Secretariat

Secretariat Chief	Tokiko Nagayama
Secretarial Section Chief	Kenji Kawase
General Affairs Section Chief	Tsuneo Komuro
Accounts Section Chief	Shigeki Ito

(cont.)

Table 6.2. (*cont.*)

Bureau of International Trade, Iron and Steel
Bureau Chief   Ihei Shiseki
First Iron and Steel Section Chief   Yuji Koyama

Enterprise Bureau
Bureau Chief   Takeo Ishihara

1956
Prime Minister   Ichiro Hatoyama
                                                    (Nobusuke Kishi in 1960)
Minister of International Trade and Industry   Tanzan Ishibashi
Parliamentary Vice-Minister   Yoman Kawano
Administrative Vice-Minister   Takeo Ishihara

Minister's Secretariat
Secretariat Chief   Kinzo Matsuo
Secretarial Section Chief   Shigeru Sabashi
General Affairs Section Chief   Zen'ei Imai
Accounts Section Chief   Ryuta Kawasaki

Bureau of Heavy Industries
Bureau Chief   Yoshio Suzuki
Iron and Steel Production Section Chief   Shintaro Tabata

Enterprise Bureau
Bureau Chief   Kyuji Tokunaga

1961
Prime Minister   Hayato Ikeda
Minister of International Trade and Industry   Etsusaburo Shiina
Parliamentary Vice-Minister   Ihei Shiseki
Administrative Vice-Minister   Kaku Sunahara

Minister's Secretariat
Secretariat Chief   Nobuaki Hizume
Secretarial Section Chief   Teiji Kato
General Affairs Section Chief   Setsuo Takashima
Accounts Section Chief   Takeshi Inoue

Bureau of Heavy Industries
Bureau Chief   Shigeru Sabashi
Iron and Steel Production Section Chief   Takehiko Yasuhara

Enterprise Bureau
Bureau Chief   Kinzo Matsuo

Sources: Sangyō Seisakushi Kenkyūsho (1981); *Kanpō* (Official Gazette).

Trade and Industry in 1961, so both served in higher-ranking positions after the war. In 1942 Takayuki Yamamoto of the General Affairs Bureau (*Sōmu Kyoku*) of the Ministry of Commerce and Industry was responsible for production expansion. He remained in his post at the end of the war, and was later appointed Administrative Vice-Minister (*Jimu Jikan*) when the Ministry of International Trade and Industry (MITI) was established. His case is one of the most typical illustrating the continuity into post-war office of those who ran the wartime controlled economy.

To the same end we can look at those in leading positions in 1961, and examine what they were doing in 1942.[3] MITI's Parliamentary Vice-Minister Ihei Shiseki was Section Chief (*Kanri Kachō*) of the Enterprise Bureau (*Kigyō Kyoku*) in 1942. Section Chief of the Minister's Secretariat, Nobuaki Hizume, was drafted into the army in January 1938, and in March 1944 he returned to the General Mobilization Bureau in the Ministry of Munitions, where he was responsible for economic controls. Three other Section Chiefs in the Minister's Secretariat, Teiji Kato, Setsuo Takashima, and Takeshi Inoue all joined the ministry in 1940. They were, respectively, drafted into the army, the navy, and sent to the Mining Bureau of the Ministry of Commerce and Industry. The Chief of the Bureau of Heavy Industries, Shigeru Sabashi, had joined the ministry in 1937 and served in the Engineering Bureau from October 1941, the Metals Bureau from July 1943, and the Iron and Steel Bureau from November of that year. The Chief of the Enterprise Bureau, Kinzo Matsuo, had joined the ministry in 1934 and moved from the Enterprise Bureau to the Mobilization Bureau to work on implementing economic controls.

If we now look at the wartime posts of those who served as Administrative Vice-Ministers from 1960 onwards—Kyuji Tokunaga, Kinzo Matsuo, Zen'ei Imai, Shigeru Sabashi, Shigenobu Yamamoto, and Norifumi Kumagaya— we can see even more clearly how the influence of the controlled economy persisted into the post-war era. I have already mentioned Sabashi and Matsuo. Tokunaga joined the ministry in 1933. He worked in the General Affairs Bureau from March 1940, and in the Trade Bureau from June 1942. After promotion to Import Section Chief in the Trade Bureau in July, he was stationed in Shanghai during 1943, and in 1944 became a military adviser in Guangzhou. Imai joined the ministry in 1937, worked on the Planning Board from March 1941, the General Affairs Bureau from April 1943, and the Mobilization Bureau from November of that year. Kumagaya joined the ministry in 1940, started working in the Prices Bureau in April 1940, the Council Office in March 1941, and the Mobilization Bureau in November 1943. All these officials had thus belonged to units active in the war effort or responsible for implementing economic controls, representing, in the words of Chalmers Johnson, 'striking continuities' over the pre-war and post-war years (Johnson 1983: 308).

The bureaucrats who implemented post-war industrial policy were thus the very same people who had run the controlled economy and introduced its revisions during the war. Chalmers Johnson (1983) uses this continuity to stress that economic controls also persisted into the post-war era. However, what we should note is not so much the continuity of the officials themselves, but the course of their experience. There is no straight line connecting the controlled economy with post-war industrial policy, due to a major break around 1942 when the planned economy stalled. The bureaucrats thus understood the limits of economic controls from their own experience. They knew that dynamic economic development is not possible without an independent private sector and profit incentives, and they fully understood the limitations of one-directional 'instructions from above'.

It has also been shown that the post-war political climate would not easily accept the revival of bureaucratic control (Kono 1991). The very establishment of the Ministry of International Trade and Industry was at the instigation of Shigeru Yoshida's Democratic Liberal Party, which had checked the revival of the bureaucratic control of the Ministry of Commerce and Industry. The bureaucrats themselves did not favour controls. For example, after MITI was set up in 1949, the new ministry newsletter, *Tsūsan Jihō*, carried a discussion on corporate rationalization in its October edition in which Hiroshi Imai, Enterprise Section Chief of the Enterprise Bureau, comments:

One of the problems of controls is that they obstruct rationalization. In this sense we need to eliminate as many as we can. Even though a minimum level of controls will have to be maintained, we need to regard controls on goods and materials as far as possible from the standpoint of promoting efficient, intensive production and thereby facilitating rationalization.   (*Tsūsan Jihō*, October 1949)

Thus in contrast to wartime, economic controls were seen as something to be abolished to achieve the major target of rationalization. However, that does not mean that MITI bureaucrats were ready to countenance freedom of activity for the corporate sector. In the same discussion Imai goes on to say,

Next is the rationalization of the business environment. We do not at present have clearly formed ideas on how to provide information on the current situation or how to strengthen administrative guidance. During the war an efficiency division was set up to examine efficiency. Learning from this, we might set aside a certain budget to be used to commission experts to diagnose corporate efficiency.   (ibid.)

Here is a clear recommendation to follow on from the wartime experience with regard to providing external guidance for corporate rationalization.

It is therefore important to recognize that the continuity in experience from the wartime into the post-war periods of MITI bureaucrats does not follow a direct, unbroken course. There were two major interruptions: the failure of wartime controls, and post-war democratization. So it is safe to say that the wartime bureaucrats who continued to serve in MITI after the war had learned from the wartime economic controls the limitations of such controls and the meaning of 'withholding control'. Thus Etsusaburo Shiina, who once effectively played a leading role in imposing controls, was strongly opposed to government controls at the time of the 1973 oil shock. He had thoroughly understood both the importance and the limitations of controls.

2. *Continuity in the industrial associations.* Let us next look briefly at the degree of continuity evident in the control associations. In July 1945, as the end of the war approached, the Iron and Steel Control Association was in the process of merging with the Steel Sales Control Corporation (*Tekkō Hanbai Tōsei Kaisha*) in an attempt to strengthen control over production and sales. Iron and steel production was held in check, however, because all transportation for the import of materials had been stopped by the Allied powers. After Japan's surrender, the Occupation authorities (GHQ) indicated their intention to abolish all wartime systems and dismantle the controlled economy, and so the Control Association in effect suspended its activities and sought to set up a new self-governing control organization. In February 1946 the Steel Council (*Tekkō Kyōgikai*) was approved as an independent body. The Steel Council made a clear distinction between itself and the former Control Association, claiming that 'whereas the Control Association was an organization based on the leadership principle, in which the chairman had dictatorial powers, the Japan Steel Council is a democratic self-governing control institution which has as its highest decision-making body a standing committee made up of representatives of some ten of the leading steelmakers' (Japan Iron and Steel Federation 1959: 44). In the confusion directly following the war, the Steel Council acted as a subordinate agency of government to maintain control, and then through the Price Adjustment Public Corporation Law (*Kakaku Chōsei Kōdan Hō*) of April 1947 it was disbanded in accordance with the provision that 'control organizations that were engaged in providing subsidies in relation with managed prices shall be dismantled'. The Steel Federation (*Tekkō Rengōkai*) was formed instead, more as a friendly society. However, the Steel Federation was itself disbanded as further removal of all organizations associated with pre-war control was undertaken at the instigation of the Occupation authorities. This opened the way for the Japan Steel Association (*Nihon Tekkō Kai*), formed in December 1947 with the objectives of market research and social activities, and no hint of any sort of control functions.

Meanwhile, in order to deal with the increasingly active labour movement in the post-war years, managers in the steel industry set up the Japan Steel Industry Managers' Federation (*Nihon Tekkōgyō Keieisha Renmei*) in May 1946 with the aim of establishing the right to manage and boosting solidarity. In November 1948, the Japan Steel Association merged with this body to form the present-day Japan Iron and Steel Federation (*Nihon Tekkō Renmei*) (Japan Iron and Steel Federation 1959: 44–5). The fact that the Managers' Federation had been a managers' body launched to deal with the labour movement ensured that the Iron and Steel Federation was positioned squarely in the management camp. In fact, the position of Chairman of the Federation was reserved for the serving president of the leading steel firm: Nittetsu-Yawata Seitetsu until 1950, when it was split into Yawata and Fuji, and from 1970 Shin Nittetsu, the firm created when they merged again. The board of directors was filled with presidents or directors from member companies. So although the GHQ purge of top officials might suggest there was little continuity in the management of the steel industry between the wartime and post-war periods, this is in fact not so (Yonekura 1992). The chairman and the directors of the Iron and Steel Federation were all from the managements of the member companies, and were thus largely the same people who had implemented economic controls during the war.

The same sort of continuity can be identified among the administrative staff running the day-to-day business. Table 6.3 compares the administrative staff of the wartime Iron and Steel Control Association with that of the post-war Iron and Steel Federation. At the top, Yoshisuke Watanabe, the senior director (*Rijichō*) of the Control Association moved sideways to become the chairman of the Iron and Steel Federation. Then Toshisuke Suitsu, who as a director and Chief of the Investigation Department of the Control Association had been responsible for administering controls, became an executive director and Chief of the Labour Bureau in the post-war federation. Yuji Tejima, a former section chief in the pre-war General Affairs Department was appointed the General Secretary for Osaka in the post-war organization. From these and other examples we can conclude that there were no significant changes at all in leading personnel. Considerable continuity in personnel is thus evident even in the control organizations, which are widely believed to have been completely broken up by GHQ after the war.

3. *Continuity in policy implementation.* Let us now turn to continuity in policy. At the time of its launch in 1949, the Ministry of International Trade and Industry gave as one of its most important policies the rationalization of industry. Industry rationalization councils (*sangyō gōrika shingikai*) were organized as a major feature of a new style of executing industrial policy. The councils called on a wide range of personnel for the formulation of policy: not just bureaucrats but representatives of the business world and industrial associations, and experts from academic backgrounds. This method of using councils (*shingikai*) was a means of incorporating in policy meaningful information from the firms as well as other types of information from academic sources, and it made use of the wartime control experience. Rationalization plans for the various major industries were drawn up through the work of these councils, and post-war economic recovery began.

For the iron and steel industry there were three consecutive rationalization plans, starting in 1950. The plans had the look of a total package made up of separate plans put forward by individual firms, compiled by the federation and submitted to MITI for approval. However, in reality, it was a two-directional process. On the basis of an overall policy that MITI provided, such as the

Table 6.3. Senior staff in the Iron and Steel Control Association (CA) and the Japan Iron and Steel Federation

1942

CA Chairman	Teijiro Toyoda
Senior Director	Yoshisuke Watanabe

General Affairs Department

Chief	Yoshisuke Watanabe
Vice-Chief	Heigo Fujii
Section Chief	Yuji Tejima

Production Department

Chief	Kishi Sakai
Vice-Chief	Yoshihiro Inayama and others

Equipment Department

Chief	Shigeo Nagano
Vice-Chief	Ryujiro Funatsu and others

Labour Department

Chief	Choji Momoki
Vice-Chief	Rikio Katsuragi

Investigation Department

Chief	Toshisuke Suitsu
Vice-Chief	Dai Sengoku

Technology Department

Chief	Takeichi Imura
Vice-Chief	Shinji Satomura

1949

Chairman of Iron and Steel Federation	Yoshisuke Watanabe
Managing Director	Takeshi Okamura
Executive Director	Toshisuke Suitsu
Osaka Secretary General	Yuji Tejima

General Affairs Department

Chief	Takeshi Okamura
Vice-Chief	Hiroshi Sato

Investigation Bureau

Chief	——
Vice-Chief	Kyotaro Takaku

Labour Bureau

Chief	Toshisuke Suitsu
Vice-Chief	Tsutomu Tsuchiya

Note: Senior officials from member firms not included.

Sources: Jūyō Sangyō Kyōgikai (1944); Japan Iron and Steel Federation (1959).

'rationalization of the steel rolling process in strip mills', individual firms submitted data to the federation, the industrial association, which was put together by MITI into a draft proposal. In order to avoid the wartime control-like format, the process appears to be extremely democratic, but it was not simply a matter of integrating the individual plans of the private-sector firms. A case in point is Kawasaki Steel's plan for new blast furnaces, for example, which took no heed of MITI's rationalization strategy for steel-rolling, and was therefore effectively shelved for a number of years, classified as requiring 'separate consideration'. So formulation avoided the appearance of control imposed from above, and took on a style that stressed mutual interaction between government and the corporate sector. Formulation and implementation of rationalization plans, the greatest single industrial policy measure that MITI undertook, was thus perpetuated into the post-war period through a zigzag course of controls, the breakdown of controls, and then post-war democracy.

4. Post-war industrial associations: linking policy to the private sector

The process of formulating, implementing, and revising industrial policy at the three levels of government, industrial associations, and individual firms went on to become the fundamental model for MITI's industrial policy. To see how this model developed, I would like here to analyse the relationship between the Temporary Measures for Machinery Promotion Law (*Kikai Shinkō Rinji Sochi Hō*) and the metal-mould industry as a case study investigating the roles played by industrial policy and the industrial association.

4.1. The Temporary Measures for Machinery Promotion Law and the metal-mould industry

The government passed the Temporary Measures for Machinery Promotion Law in 1956 to raise standards throughout the machinery-production industry. It was designed to give concentrated support to the base-machine industry (machinery to make other machines, such as machine tools and metal moulds) and the machine-parts industry (springs, screws, etc.).

The metal moulds I refer to here are the shapes or primary moulds that are essential for mass production, and the metal-mould industry comprises the group of firms producing these moulds. Metal moulds are basic to mass-production methods in which identical parts are made using a mould rather than by cutting or shaving, and it is no exaggeration to say that the fundamental competitiveness of modern mass-production manufacturing rests on their precision and durability. Yet before the enactment of the law, few people knew of their existence, let alone their significance. With the enactment of the law, MITI prepared to actively promote the newly designated metal-moulding industry. The Japan Metal Mould Industry Association (*Nihon Kanagata Kōgyō Kai*) describes those times as follows:

In June 1956, prior to the enactment of the Temporary Measures for Machinery Promotion Law there were deliberations within the Ministry to decide on measures to promote machinery production. The main metal moulding firms in the Tokyo, Nagoya and Osaka regions were contacted, and in June 1956 (author's note: this was in fact March) the First Consultative Meeting for the Rationalization and Promotion of Precision Metal Moulding (*Seimitsu Kanagata Gōrika Sokushin Kondankai*) was held to study modernization and rationalization in the industry. (Japan Metal Mould Industry Association, Nijūnenshi Shi Hensan Iinkai 1977: 19)

Worthy of note here is that this preparatory work was not conducted in terms of instructions issued by MITI, top down, but was an all-encompassing process that included the government, the firms, and the mould-users. Starting in March 1956, MITI learned about the circumstances surrounding the industry from the leading metal-mould makers, and sought to set up an industrial association through which to apply the provisions of the Machinery Promotion Law. However, MITI seemed not to have a clear idea of how to organize the industry at this stage. As chairman of the Metal Mould Industry Association, Shoichi Kuroda, recalls, MITI's questioning was vague.

At that time ministry officials didn't know what a metal mould was. They didn't even know the correct reading of the Chinese characters. It all started when this company, which happened to be doing press moulding, got a telephone call from MITI. 'We understand that metal moulding is important and we'd like to hear more about it.' After a few ins and outs, they asked, 'can't this business be formally organized?' (Japan Metal Mould Industry Association, Sanjūshūnen Kinen Jigyō Iinkai 1987: 181–2)

As this indicates, MITI had no intention of trying to identify the metal-mould business sector straight off through 'top-down' control procedures. Instead they first made an enquiry about the industry and pressed for 'organization of the business'. From this evidence alone, however, it is hard to claim that MITI had no knowledge whatever about metal moulding.

For instance, the importance of metal moulds was recognized in a June 1956 publication of MITI's Bureau for Heavy Industry (*Jūkōgyō Kyoku*), 'Strategies to Promote the Machine Industry'. It commented that, given the technical shift in machine processing from cutting to plastic processing, 'the precision and tool-life of metal moulds directly affect product precision and costs, and therefore a high degree of precision and durability are urgently required' (MITI, Jūkōgyō Kyoku 1956: 157). Furthermore, from their experience of producing aircraft during the war, officials in the Ministry of Commerce and Industry and MITI must have been aware of the importance of metal moulds in the moulding of plastics.

So why was MITI initially so circumspect in its approach? From subsequent events we can suggest two possible explanations. The first is the possibility that although MITI understood the importance of metal moulding, they did not know how to go about identifying a sector that contained a wide range of different sorts of business. The MITI official responsible for castings and forgings at that time, Takeo Wakebe, commented that he 'wanted to assemble people involved in metal moulding, and made enquiries through senior colleagues and consulted a number of people, and around April 1956 the Metal Moulding Consultative Meeting was held. . . . People gave their views on what measures needed be taken to promote and modernize the metal mould industry'. This testifies to the fact that people involved in the industry participated in policy formulation.[4] It is possible that through being granted leeway for private-sector initiative, individual firms were prepared to disclose information to increase the effectiveness of policy.

The second possibility is that this rather vague request was designed to encourage the spontaneous involvement and organization of the private-sector firms. On the basis of MITI's request, the Precision Mould Rationalization and Promotion Consultative Meeting was held in March 1956 and the firms were advised to organize themselves into an industry. On this point Kuroda makes the following remarks:

We often hear these days that metal moulds are needed for powder metallurgy or are important in die-casting. The common factor in comments like these is 'metal moulds'. But moulds used in die casting and powder metallurgy, or in press or plastic moulding, are all different, and whether they should be treated as a single industry, or whether metal mould technology should be developed separately within each of these businesses was the point of the discussions on how to put the Machinery Promotion Law into effect. I think it highly significant that finally they could all be brought together in one metal moulding industry.   (Japan Metal Mould Industry Association, Sanjūshūnen Kinen Jigyō Iinkai 1987: 184)

As this shows, the identification of the industry was not something imposed by MITI in a one-way, top-down action, but was brought about through the spontaneous involvement of private-sector firms in their search for common ground. The result was that this group of small and assorted companies involved in metal moulding, an activity difficult to treat as a single entity, could for the first time be classified as an industry. The fact that the important decision-making involved in identifying the industry to which the provisions of the Machinery Promotion Law should be applied was not made one-way, but was accomplished through interaction with the private-sector firms, is significant for a proper understanding of industrial policy in Japan. MITI lacked hands-on information about the firms and the market, but through its unforced approach an industrial association was organized, and the interaction involved in that activity provided MITI with a grasp of the business that was to be fostered.

4.2. Assembling information on the market, technology, and private firms

When the Machinery Promotion Law came into force, MITI set up a Machinery Production Council (*Kikai Kōgyō Shingikai*) to draw up basic plans to promote modernization as well as implementation plans. Sub-groups were formed to act as advisory bodies for each of the individual businesses, and concrete objectives for each type of business as well as detailed guidelines to modernize facilities were agreed. Here, too, MITI incorporated the private-sector firms' initiative into policy-making. On the basis of the vague enquiry I mentioned earlier, MITI brought together the main metal-mould makers in Tokyo, Osaka, and Nagoya for the Consultative Meeting to study concrete measures to promote rationalization in the industry. Through the co-operation of this group MITI was able to get a better grasp of circumstances in the industry, and its overall objectives were established by its members. These were 'fostering independent metal mould firms which specialized in producing moulds for external sales' and 'introducing high-performance–high-precision machine tools, such as boring mills, milling machines, die mills and grinding machines'.

The Consultative Meeting, made up of manufacturers, users, and academics, formulated a 'Basic Plan for the Rationalization of Metal Mould Manufacture' to provide targets for rationalization. The plan set up precision targets in units of millimetres for each type of equipment, to be achieved by the end of FY1960, and selected for recommendation 16 models of machine tools and four types of heat-treatment equipment.

Besides setting these numerical precision targets, the plan examined the optimal size, sales turnover, and loan-repayment capability of the firms to be assisted under the Machinery Promotion Law. Moreover, the plan was based on a consideration of a better allocation of engineers and other staff who met certain qualification criteria. The model firm was seen as one placing priority on external sales of metal moulds, and having more than three employees who graduated from pre-war-system high schools and were specialists in mechanical engineering with five years' experience in metal-mould production, or equivalent qualifications. The firm was also expected to have an annual turnover of at least ¥50 million from external sales of metal moulds, once new facilities were in place. Illustrations of personnel allocation were given, such as 16 employees for materials processing, 15 for parts processing, 12 for milling, and so on. Because the recommended machine tools were expensive, arrangements were made to help with financing for all metal-processing machine manufacturers except the smallest specialist makers. But at the same time expected production volumes were set out in 'explanatory information' appended to the Basic Plan, because 'there is a possibility that firms involved also in other productive activities may use their metal mould manufacturing facilities for other purposes, and to prevent this firms are required to take responsibility for a certain production volume'.[5] In addition to numerical targets, the reasons that standards could be formulated for the number of technicians or the allocation of personnel was that the Basic Plan was not formulated only by Ministry officials and those in the industry, but also by users and academics—people who had no common interest except the target of rationalization, using information sources from different fields.

As we know from theory of the agency cost of regulations, when the government tries to foster or control industries or firms, a social cost is incurred and people's economic welfare is harmed if there is imbalance in the exchange of information among government, industry, and firms. Gaining market and technical information and internal information of individual firms has been suggested as an important way of resolving this. By this means the social cost generated by government intervention is reduced, preventing the occurrence of external diseconomies. Using councils and organizing industrial associations—methods that MITI has utilized widely in the post-war period—has not only made it possible to acquire this sort of diverse information on markets and technology from multiple sources, but has also been an important tool in getting firms to supply the sort of information on their business which is normally very difficult to obtain.

4.3. Integrated industrial policy

Industrial associations have promoted interaction between government and firms, and by providing the government with information on the market, on technology and on individual firms, they have not only helped to make industrial policy more effective, but have played the role of systematically integrating funding measures, the transfer of technology, market surveys, and export activities.

When the Machinery Promotion Law was first adopted, low-interest financing was secured from the Japan Development Bank as a means to implement rationalization. The interest rate was set at 6.5 per cent, which was low in comparison to the bank's standard interest rate of 9 per cent at that time. For the many small and medium-sized firms in the industry it was extremely beneficial. But on the other hand, a condition attached to loans from the Japan Development Bank was that half of the funds to be raised had to be found by the firm involved, and as a result the screening process was extremely strict, requiring the submission of detailed documentation. In the Metal Mould Industry Association's parent organization, the Machinery Manufacturing Promotion Association (*Kikai Kōgyō Shinkō Kyōkai*), a detailed handbook was made to assist small and medium-sized firms in particular to apply for Development Bank loans. The handbook contained specimens of the complex forms required by the Development Bank such as 'Company Profile', 'Comprehensive Long-term Facilities Plan', 'Table of Production Volumes Achieved

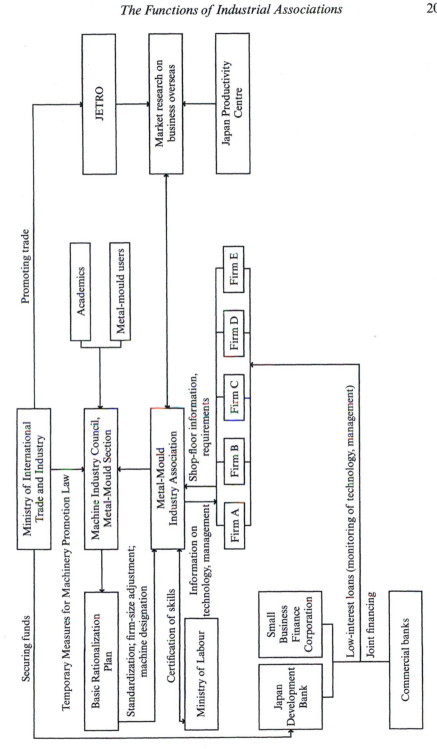

Figure 6.1. Flow of information and funds related to Temporary Measures for Machinery Promotion Law

and Planned', and 'Personnel Allocation Plan', as well as tables showing assets and liabilities, and profit and loss accounts. It also provided reference material for improving corporate management methods. Thus the industrial association also played a role in the modernization of management practices of small firms.

From 1951 the Metal Mould Industry Association began to co-operate with the Japan Productivity Center (*Nihon Seisansei Honbu*) in surveys of overseas markets, and pioneered the development of foreign markets for metal moulds. Of importance here is the fact that the Metal Mould Industry Association teamed up with separate government and private-sector organizations such as the Japan Productivity Center and JETRO (*Nihon Bōeki Shinkō Kyōkai*), to boost the effectiveness of industrial policy. In the same way, the testing of workers' skills organized jointly by the Metal Mould Industry Association and the Ministry of Labour has served to hone skills in metal moulding and has also made the important contribution of standardizing and disseminating technology. This process is dealt with in detail elsewhere (Yonekura 1993); however, Figure 6.1 shows a simplified outline of information flows involving the Industry Association. With the association in the middle, information passes back and forth between government and individual firms bringing together separate policies and different institutions in dynamic combinations to enhance policy effectiveness.

5. Conclusion

Through the experience of control associations in the wartime controlled economy, industrial associations in Japan, positioned midway between the government and individual firms, have learned the need to correct imbalances in information flows. They have worked to forge organic links between government planning at the macro level and corporate profit incentives at the micro level, by filling the gaps in information that occur between the two. This role was developed in embryonic form through wartime controls, which were imposed forcefully from above, but the limitations of this method were well understood when wartime controls broke down. Bureaucrats were forced to recognize that the productivity of the private sector could not basically be increased while firms' independent stance and profit incentives were ignored. The experience of the Iron and Steel Control Association bears this out.

But neither did this experience lead straight to a *laissez-faire* economy after the war. To achieve economic reconstruction and growth—targets as large as the prosecution of the war had been—the relationship between government and industry became as close as before, and many of the government officials, industrial association staff, and corporate managers earlier involved in this relationship continued to serve in important positions through the post-war period. It is therefore of no surprise to find the wartime controls, their limitations well understood, reappearing in the post-war economy built around the private sector. This was not, however, the sort of straight-line continuity described by Chalmers Johnson.

The new relationship between government, industrial associations, and private firms can be seen in the industrial policy relating to new post-war industries. The case of the Metal Mould Industry Association indicates how important the independent stance of the corporate sector has been considered in post-war industrial policy. In this, a vital role has been played by the industrial association, positioned as it is between the government and the individual firms and expediting the flow of information in both directions. Overall government objectives are conveyed to the firms, and information on the sector's firms and their needs is incorporated in policy initiatives directed upwards to the government. The association also takes on the task of implementing policy. The significant function of the industrial association in all of this is to reduce the asymmetry of information between government and the private sector.

Of course, not all industrial associations have carried out all these roles all the time. Among the new business sectors that appeared as mass production got on track after the war, those such as the metal-mould industry, where information was passed back and forth between government and firms, could perhaps be classed as exceptions. The functions of the industrial associations also changed according to the 'power balance' in the flow of information between government and firms. Thus, industrial associations can easily turn into nothing more than pressure groups or organizers of cartels because of government strategy or the problems facing their particular industry. But in implementing economic controls during the war, Japan's industrial associations bore the important function of promoting information flows in two directions, and in the post-war environment they have taken on roles not fully covered by government or firms, the wide-ranging tasks of formulation, implementation, and modification of policy, thereby eliminating the asymmetry in information between the two. All this needs to be acknowledged as the major complementary role that industrial associations have played in industrial policy throughout the post-war period.

Notes

1. On the model in which a centrally placed intermediary converts top-down and bottom-up information from simple data processing to information creation, see Nonaka (1985, 1988, 1990) in which the role of middle management in individual firms is explained. However, the theoretical concept of an intermediary function between top and lower management to formulate information and knowledge on the firm is largely applicable to industrial associations, which are positioned between

government and individual firms. For an analysis of industrial policy based on this information-generation function, see Yonekura (1993).

2. On the history of pressure groups in the iron and steel industry in Japan, see *Sentetsu Kyōhan Gyōseki Hensan Iinkai* (1941).

3. For the professional careers of Ministry officials in leading posts, I referred to Sangyō Seisakushi Kenkyūsho (1977) and *Kanpō*.

4. Takeo Wakebe, a division head of MITI, describes the situation at that time in Japan Metal Mould Industry Association, Nijūnenshi Hensan Iinkai (1977), and Kuroda, the chairman of the association, confirms this situation.

5. Projected volumes of production were presented in matrix form with the vertical axis representing production materials and the horizontal axis representing projected volumes broken down for separate years and firms. Detailed rules for administration and implementation were also given (MITI Notification No. 307, *Kanagata Seizō Gōrika Kihon Keikaku Setsumei Shiryō*). The point here is that it was difficult for MITI and individual firms to get an adequate grasp of detailed issues related to rationalization, on machinery, technology, degree of precision, capital, and number of employees, and so industrial associations acted as a central liaison in information collection, policy formulation, and policy dissemination.

References

Cohen, Jerome (1950) (in translation), *Senji Sengo no Nihon Keizai* (The Japanese Economy in the Wartime and Post-war Periods), Iwanami Shoten.

Hoashi, Kei (1943), *Tōseikai no Riron to Jissai* (Control Associations in Theory and Practice), Shin Keizai-sha.

Japan Iron and Steel Federation (1959) (ed.), *Sengo Tekkō Shi* (A History of the Post-war Iron and Steel Industry), Japan Iron and Steel Federation.

Japan Metal Mould Industry Association, Nijūnen Shi Hensan Iinkai (1977), *Sōritsu Nijūnen no Ayumi* (A Twenty-Year History of the Japan Metal Mould Industry Association), Japan Metal Mould Industry Association.

——Sanjūshūnen Kinen Jigyō Iinkai (1987), *Sōritsu Sanjūnen no Ayumi* (A Thirty-Year History of the Japan Metal Mould Industry Association), Japan Metal Mould Industry Association.

Johnson, Chalmers (1983) (in translation), *Tsūsanshō to Nihon no Kiseki* (MITI and the Japanese Miracle), TBS Britannica.

Jūyō Sangyō Kyōgikai (1944), *Tōseikai Hikkei* (A Handbook of the Control Associations), Tōhō-sha.

Kono, Yasuko (1991), 'Yoshida Gaikō to Kokunai Seiji: Tsūsanshō Setchi kara Denryoku Shakkan Dōnyū made (Yoshida's Foreign and Domestic Policies)', *Nihon Seiji Gakkai Nenpō*.

Lynn, Leonard and Timothy McKeown (1988), *Organizing Business: Trade Associations in America and Japan*, American Enterprise Institute, Washington, DC.

McRobie, George *et al.* (1957), *Industrial Trade Associations*, Political and Economic Planning, London.

Ministry of International Trade and Industry (1949), *Tsūsan Jihō* (Ministry newsletter), October.

——(1964), *Shōkō Seisaku Shi, 11, Sangyō Tōsei* (A History of Commercial and Industrial Policy, vol. 11, Industrial Control), Shōkō Seisakushi Kankō Iinkai.
——Notification no. 307, *Kanagata Seizō Gōrika Kihon Keikaku oyobi Kanagata Seizō Gōrika Kihon Keikaku Setsumei Shiryō* (A Basic Rationalization Plan for the Metal-Mould Industry), MITI.
——Jūkōgyō Kyoku(1956), *Kikai Kōgyō Shinkō no Hōto: Kikai Shinkō Rinji Sochihō no Kaisetsu oyobi Unyō* (A Prospectus for the Promotion of the Machine Industries), Tsūshō Sangyō Chōsakai.
Nakamura, Takafusa (1974), *Nihon no Keizai Tōsei* (Economic Controls in Japan), Nihon Keizai Shimbun-sha.
Nonaka, Ikujiro (1985), *Kigyō Shinka Ron* (A Theory of Organizational Evolution), Nihon Keizai Shinbun-sha.
——(1988), 'Toward Middle-Up-Down Management: Accelerating Information Creation', *Sloan Management Review*, 29(3).
——(1990), *Chishiki Sōzō no Keiei* (Managing the Creation of Knowledge), Nihon Keizai Shinbun-sha.
Okazaki, Tetsuji (1988), 'Dainiji Sekai Taisenki no Nihon ni okeru Senji Keikaku Keizai no Kōzō to Unkō: Tekkō Bumon o Chūshin to shite (The Structure and Working of the Wartime Planned Economy in Japan: The Steel Industry)', *Shakai Kagaku Kenkyū*.
Okimoto, Daniel (1991) (in translation), *Tsūsanshō to Haiteku Sangyō* (MITI and the Hi-Tech Industries), Simul Press.
Samuels, Richard (1983), 'The Industrial Destructuring of the Japanese Aluminium Industry', *Pacific Affairs*, 56(3) (autumn).
Sangyō Seisakushi Kenkyūsho (1981), *Shōkōshō Tsūsanshō Gyōsei Kikō oyobi Kanbu Shokuin no Hensan* (Changes to Administrative Structure and Officials in the Ministry of Commerce and Industry and MITI), Tsūshō Sangyō Chōsakai Toranomon Bunshitsu Sangyō Seisakushi Kenkyūsho.
Sentetsu Kyōhan Gyōseki Hensan Iinkai (1941), *Honpō Sentetsu Tōsei Hanbaishi* (A History of Pig Iron Control and Sales), Daiichi Shobō.
Yonekura, Seiichiro (1992), 'Keiei to Roshi Kankei niokeru Sengo Kakaku (The Post-War Reform in Management and Labour Relations)', *Business Review*, 39(2).
——(1993), 'Seifu to Kigyō no Dainamikusu: Sangyō Seisaku no Sofuto na Sokumen (Industrial Policy as a Dynamic Interaction between Government and Firms: A Case of the Temporary Measures Law for the Promotion of the Machinery Industry and Special Tool Industry)', *Hitotsubashi University Research Series: Commerce and Management*, 33.
——(1994), *Continuity and Discontinuity: The Japanese Iron and Steel Industry 1850–1990*, Macmillan.

7

The 'Japanese-Model' Fiscal System

Naohiko Jinno

1. Introduction

The eventful period heralded by the 1970s oil shocks has been characterized by calls for 'reform of the tax system' and 'administrative reform', and as a result the tax and public-finance system that underpinned Japan's post-war high-speed economic growth has come in for fundamental re-examination. This chapter represents a quest for the origins of Japan's modern fiscal system now so much in the spotlight, from among the many other aspects of the economic system being pressed to reform.

As we see from the fact that discussions on the tax system or administrative reform refer directly or indirectly to the Shoup Report, there is a shared belief that Japan's current fiscal system took shape through the reforms introduced after the Second World War. In this chapter, however, I intend to show that it was formed, like the other economic systems discussed in this book, during the war years as a 'full mobilization' system to support the war effort.

One thing I would like to point out at the outset is that although the current fiscal system was formed in the same period as other systems in the economy, it is not purely and simply an economic system. Certainly, it is the internal economic system of the economic entity known as the state. But whereas those economic entities known as enterprises procure goods and services for production objectives, and those economic entities known as households procure goods and services for consumption, the state procures goods and services for neither of these purposes, but for the political and administrative objectives of maintaining order throughout society.

If we thus accept that the fiscal system is a state economic system with a mission to maintain order in society, and as such straddles the economic and political systems, then to determine its specifically Japanese characteristics we must study it not only in the context of the economy, but as a constituent part of the social system, which encompasses both economic and political systems. Here, therefore, I would like to investigate the roots of Japan's present-day fiscal system using this sort of 'fiscal sociological' approach.

2. Features of the 'Japanese-model' fiscal system

2.1. The belief that income tax and corporate taxes should be the central taxes

In this chapter I will identify the special nature of the Japanese-model fiscal system as a centralized-deconcentrated system operated through the control of revenue sources.

The fiscal system differs from other systems in the economy not only in the sense that procured goods and services are used for the political objective of maintaining social order. The very activity of procuring those goods and services is also different. While their procurement is conducted in circumstances where market forces operate, the necessary funds for that procurement are collected forcibly from the economy, under circumstances of a monopoly of violence justified by its purpose of preserving social order.

It is common knowledge that in modern Japan this compulsory collection of funds takes the form of a tax system centred on direct taxation. As the key taxes are income tax and corporation tax, which are both highly elastic *vis-à-vis* income, the tax system has absorbed a considerable natural increase in revenue from an economy that has achieved remarkable growth. During the high-growth period, tax policy directed this revenue increase to tax reductions, and so increases in tax-burden ratios were held down. However, when income tax reduction could no longer be justified with the close of the high-growth period, differences in the degree of rigour with which taxes were collected heightened tax resistance. The business income earned by farmers and commercial proprietors is taxed through a self-assessment system while salary earners are taxed at source, and the growing discontent this caused turned into resistance to paying taxes on the part of the new middle class and the bulk of the labour force.

In respect of taxing wages and salaries at source, there is probably no other country in the world as thorough in tax collection as Japan. But this does not mean we should immediately stamp the hallmark 'Japanese model' on this sort of tax system centred on direct taxation through income and corporate taxes. Support for a direct-taxation-based tax system is more typical of America than Japan.

If we look at what sort of goods and services are procured with the funds collected and how they are used, the characteristically Japanese feature here is that the proportion of defence spending, the free service provided for the preservation of the state, is remarkably low. Moreover, during the period of high economic growth, social security expenses were also held down at levels that are low by international standards. So two highly expensive items, defence and social security, the cause of major headaches for many modern states, were held in check, and the plentiful natural revenue increase was used in part, as I have said, to fund tax reductions. During the high-growth period, the allocation of revenue to meet the costs of local government budgets and public works was also a priority, as shown in Figure 7.1.

Figure 7.1. Breakdown of general account expenditure

Sources: Ministry of Finance (1978), *Shōwa Zaisei Shi*, 19, Tōyō Keizai Shinpo-sha; Ministry of Finance, *Zaisei Tōkei* (published annually).

Local government budgets are financed through transfers from the central government. Public-works spending is heavily funded by such fiscal transfers, as is social security spending. Thus, the importance of fiscal transfers emerges as a characteristic of Japan's present-day fiscal system. In consideration of this, we have to analyse the system as one that involves multiple entities.

2.2. *A centralized-deconcentrated system*

The fiscal system is composed of multiple entities that include central government and large numbers of local administrations. These form a pyramid structure, rather as the social system is composed of national society and regional communities. If we look at the current system in terms of these multiple components, we see that fiscal transfers from central to local governments are noticeably larger than in other countries, as shown in Table 7.1. In other words, 'the redistribution to local authorities of more than half the monies collected as national taxes is an international feature seen in Japan but not in any other advanced country with the exception of the Netherlands.'[1]

Because of the relative importance of fiscal transfers, the provision of public services by local governments rather than central government has come to be seen as a characteristic feature of the Japanese system. Needless to say, these large-scale fiscal transfers are underpinned by a central tax system based on direct taxes, particularly income and corporate tax, as we have seen. As Table 7.1 shows, in terms of the degree of concentration of revenue sources, the figure for Japan is not particularly high for a unitary state, although it is remarkably concentrated compared with those for federal states. But if we look at expenditure, the part played by local government in Japan surpasses that of even the federal states.

In regarding the system as one of multiple components, the significance of fiscal transfers is not its only characteristic feature. We should perhaps highlight as its distinguishing feature the fact that all revenue sources procured by local governments, not only fiscal transfers, are subject to central government control. There are two channels for revenue-source control. One is through fiscal transfers, as I have mentioned, which means control of the transferred revenues through manipulation of local allocation tax and earmarked grants. The other is control of non-transferred revenue sources, which applies to local taxes and local government bonds.

Taxation control applied to local taxes includes tax denial, which is applied to the tax base, and restrictions on tax rates. Furthermore, some or all of certain national taxes can be allocated to local governments in so-called tax sharing, and this is a further form of taxation control. Local allocation tax falls into this category. Thus, the combination of taxation control and fiscal transfers in the form of local allocation tax, with their fiscal regulatory function, is something we can identify as a further characteristic of the 'Japan model' tax system.

With regard to tax denial, Japan implements a two-tier structure: the Local Tax Act stipulates those items that can be taxed locally, and taxation of any other items requires the approval of the Minister of Home Affairs. With regard to tax restrictions, rate limits are set for the major local taxes, and the highest-level tax rate is restricted, but in addition, through the setting of

Table 7.1. International comparisons of the fiscal weight of local government and fiscal transfers (%)

	Fiscal weight of local government			Fiscal transfers	
	Tax revenue	Final consumption expenditure	Gross fixed capital formation	Central government	Local governments
Federal states					
USA	43.3	55.9	81.4	21.9	17.8
West Germany	48.7	73.3	87.0	24.3	18.4
Unitary states					
UK	13.2	39.2	48.3	15.9	48.3
France	13.7	30.0	79.0	10.1	38.0
Japan	34.8	75.4	84.4	51.0	38.2

Notes: France's tax revenue is for 1988; all others are for 1989. Central government fiscal transfer = central government current transfer to other public sectors/central government current revenue. Local government fiscal transfer = local government current transfer from other public sectors/local government current revenue.

Sources: Data for tax revenues (excl. West Germany) are taken from Bank of Japan Statistics Dept. (1992), *Nihon Keizai o Chūshin to suru Kokusai Hikaku Tōkei*; data for West Germany's tax revenue, and all other items, are taken from OECD (1992), National Accounts.

standardized rates as 'widely applicable tax rates', local governments are in effect required to adopt uniform tax rates. In other words, through rigorous tax control local governments in Japan have been robbed of the right to make decisions on how the cost burden of public services should be borne, and the central government has forced local governments to adopt uniform local taxes. While it can be said that taxation control is seen to some extent in all unitary states, the Japanese system has earned the reputation of being particularly restrictive.[2]

With regard to bond flotations, too, control is imposed in the form of requiring authorization from the Minister of Home Affairs or the Prefectural Governor. Local government bond issues are drawn up and then in each instance have to be screened, in a very strict process. Japan appears to be the only country that not only regulates the overall volume of flotations, but also implements this sort of tight control over them.

Thus, if we focus on the relationship between the many constituent parts of the current fiscal system, we find that the central government implements large-scale transfers of funds, but also imposes rigorous controls on non-transferred sources of revenue. The point I would like to emphasize here, however, is that beyond imposing controls on every separate source of revenue, the central government even controls decision-making on how local governments run their administrations and how the goods and services necessary for this administration are procured. In other words, in holding the right to decide on the provision of public services and the associated cost burden by its control of revenue sources, the central government has total control over decision-making in the local government tax and expenditure systems.

This means that because of rigorous tax controls, local governments cannot procure revenue through tax efforts for the projects they themselves plan,[3] and they have also lost the freedom to fund such projects through bond issues. Local governments are therefore forced to rely on fiscal transfers to fund new projects. In the case of local allocation tax, local governments are free to decide how the tax is to be used, but not on the amount transferred. Therefore, they have no way to increase income to raise revenue for new projects. In this situation local governments are forced to use the tactic of securing earmarked grants, another form of fiscal transfer, as a method of increasing revenue. The use of this tactic, however, carries with it the implication that the local government has abandoned its right to set priorities on its policies, and accepts policy priorities dictated by the central government. Expressed from the opposite viewpoint, the central government can oblige local governments to execute those public services it judges to be of merit through the provision of earmarked grants.

The implementation of subsidized projects may also be induced by permitting bond issues for subsidized projects. But forcing uniform tax burdens through tax control can work against the central government's inducing local governments to implement subsidized projects. For a local government to implement a subsidized project, funds must be found to cover its own portion of the cost burden. In a situation of uniform tax burdens through tax control, however, less well-off local administrations may not be able to furnish these funds, and thus cannot implement the project planned by the central government.

This dilemma is resolved through local allocation tax grants for the correction of disparities in fiscal strength. In other words, local allocation tax ensures that even the less well-off local governments can implement centrally planned subsidized projects under centrally regulated taxation.

Thus, through revenue-source control within the framework of mutually complementary relations, local governments provide the public services planned by the central government with the burden of costs decided by the central government. By international standards, local governments in Japan certainly have much to do. Nevertheless, the central government's hold on decision-making through the medium of revenue-source control is a further characteristic feature of Japan's current fiscal system.

With reference to the implementation of public services, I will now use the terms 'concentrated' to mean that the process is heavily weighted towards central government, and 'deconcentrated' to mean that it is weighted towards local government. With reference to the provision and funding of public services, I will use the term 'centralized' to mean that the central government's decisions are paramount, and 'decentralized' to mean that the local government's autonomous decisions are paramount.[4] We can thus define Japan's fiscal system as a centralized-deconcentrated system operated through control of revenue sources.

3. The pre-war fiscal system

3.1. A centralized-concentrated system dependent on the traditional sector

Before giving a generalized assessment of the pre-war system, I will first show quantitatively that Japan's modern fiscal system was formulated during the war years and that the pre-war system was entirely different.

An examination of local government revenue from Figure 7.2 shows that the post-war composition of revenue sources, made up of local tax, earmarked grants, the local allocation tax, and local government bonds, took shape during the war years. In the pre-war period, fiscal transfers were of negligible significance and the local allocation tax did not even exist. Looking at changes in the composition of tax income in Figure 7.3, we see that the direct-tax-based tax system, in which income tax and corporation tax are the mainstays and which has underpinned fiscal transfers in the post-war period, was also formed during the war years. Thus we can infer that the centralized-deconcentrated

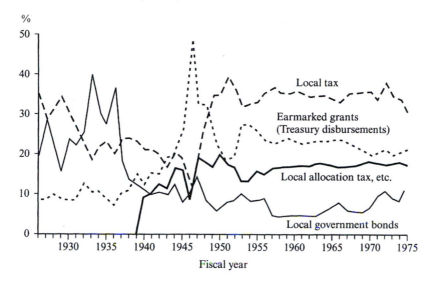

Figure 7.2. Composition of local government revenue

Notes: Local allocation tax includes local apportionment tax, local distribution tax, and local finance equalization grants. Earmarked grants (Treasury disbursements) include prefectural disbursements.

Source: Ministry of Finance (1978), *Shōwa Zaisei Shi*, 19, Tōyō Keizai Shinpō-sha.

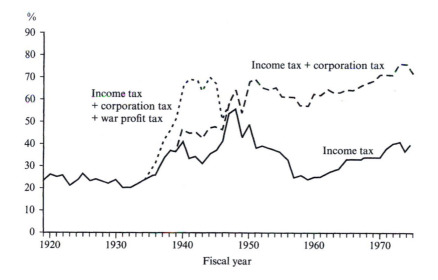

Figure 7.3. Share of income and corporation taxes

Sources: Ministry of Finance (1969), *Ōkura Shō Hyakunen Shi*, Ōkura Zaimu Kyōkai; Ministry of Finance (1978), *Shōwa Zaisei Shi*, 19, Tōyō Keizai Shinpō-sha.

system based on revenue-source control that became established after the war was formed during the wartime period, and in the pre-war period a totally different system was in existence.

But the fact that the post-war fiscal transfers that have maintained revenue-source control were of negligible significance before the war is not the only issue. The other mechanism of revenue-source control, the control of non-transferred revenue sources, was also considerably different in the pre-war period. With regard to tax control in pre-war times, collection of taxes by towns and villages was in principle not permitted, or else only a surcharge on national taxes could be collected. Thus tax denial was common, while restrictions on the setting of tax rates were relatively lenient. As for the control of bond issues, again in the pre-war period 'approval was easily granted, using local governments' solvency as the criterion'.[5]

The framework of the pre-war fiscal system took shape in the Meiji Period, and its form was determined under political conditions of perceived external threat and a socio-economic system that was backward and had certain unusual features. Under these conditions, the political system gave priority to strengthening the apparatus of violence to fulfil its function of preserving the state, and also provided guidance to modernize the economy. A fiscal system was designed to provide for the cost of this from the traditional sector of the economy. In the traditional sector, economic activities were undertaken by families as well as corporate enterprises, and no distinction was made between these different economic entities.[6] So it was difficult to make reasonable assessments of capital, and taxation had to be made on the basis of superficial external criteria. As a result, the tax system formed in the Meiji Period was centred on profits taxes levied on the basis of external criteria, such as land tax or business tax.

However, the same political system that was attempting to bring modernization to the economy utilized the backwardness and peculiarities of the social system to maintain order. It sought to maintain order by means of the 'autonomous order-maintenance function' of the traditional social system, in other words, through local community control.

To do this, local governments formed as functional groups bearing political and administrative responsibility for the maintenance of order were grafted onto traditional local communities (*Gemeinschaft*) that already fulfilled a broad range of functions. Thus it was possible for local governments to maintain order by relying on the traditional social control of local communities as well as their mutual-assistance function, and only a small degree of public services were required to supplement these community functions.

Under such circumstances there was little need for transfers of funds to local governments. They were able to raise sufficient funds with income from the community's assets or through a sort of taxation that took the form of a payment in proportion to one's assets. Therefore tax income from the traditional sector was concentrated in the hands of central government and financial resources could thus be directed towards preserving the state in the face of external threat. The central government, however, had misgivings that local government taxation would not stop at these community-based contributions, and might encroach on financial resources of potential use to the central government. As a result, pre-war tax control was centred on tax denial that limited local governments' utilization of potential revenue sources.

The system therefore concentrated financial resources and the provision of public services in the hands of central government. It was thus centralized, but not deconcentrated as in the post-war years.

3.2. *Decentralization and deconcentration of the fiscal system*

The pre-war system was forced to change drastically, however, with the coming of the First World War. The factors leading to this transformation lie in the growth of a modernized sector in the economy, which had been encouraged by the political leadership. Of even greater significance was the emergence in this sector of large-scale corporate organizations. The traditional sector, meanwhile, was in decline and a dual structure took hold.[7] As a result of these developments, the reform of a system dependent on the traditional sector for its revenue sources became a major policy issue.

This issue was not resolved, however, because the corporate organizations that had benefited from modernization brought about by the political system had at the same time increased their influence over that political system. Attempts by the Emergency Fiscal and Economic Commission (*Rinji Zaisei Keizai Chōsa Kai*) to set up a tax system centred on income tax supplemented by property tax, and thus shift dependence for financial resources on to the modernized sector, ended in failure because the 'bourgeoisie', in the words of Masao Kanbe, 'continued to oppose it fiercely'.[8]

Another factor came into play in this period. Because the external threat had diminished, fiscal demand for services for the preservation of the state had declined. Thus, there was no need to increase the tax burden, and the shifting of tax-revenue sources from the traditional to the modernized sector could be avoided.

But with the central government restricting public services to the function of preserving the state during this period, limits were reached in maintaining social order. Social order had been maintained through the 'autonomous order-maintenance function' of the local communities and so social consumer goods, grant services such as the redistribution of income in kind, or the provision of grant benefits, had been unnecessary. But with rapid advances in the modernization of the economy, the dual structure took a firmer hold, and the autonomous order-maintenance function in the local communities began to crack.

These cracks appeared as the result of two separate trends. First, the modernization of the economy introduced greater mobility among community members. Second, the old middle class of farmers and traditional tradespeople—merchants running their own businesses, who had supported traditional functions in the local communities—was in economic decline.

Generally speaking, communities cease to function so effectively when their members come and go more frequently. During this period, people left local communities and flowed into the cities in large numbers. Local communities supported by traditional tradespeople also existed in the cities, but their exclusive nature prevented the newcomers from being accepted. Consequently, increasing numbers of workers and other members of lower social classes were not absorbed into urban communities. When these people, cut off from community networks, could no longer maintain their livelihood, there were no communal means to support them and riots and other disturbances occurred. This meant that public services had to be provided to replace the mutual-assistance function of traditional communities.

We can say, however, that this demand for public services was relatively weak in Japan at that time. There was no lack of functional groups such as labour unions to organize such demands. But the corporate enterprises held misgivings about the organization of labour, and so tried to encourage a sense of belonging and to maintain morale among their workers, thus fulfilling their productive function by duplicating the communities' mutual-assistance function. In other words, the corporate enterprises that were functional groupings for the purposes of production extended their concerns to include wider aspects of their employees' lives, and thus Japanese-style management was formed, and *Gesellschaft* was turned into *Gemeinschaft*.[9] Under a situation where large numbers of disguised unemployed existed in the traditional sector, core workers saw themselves as privileged, and readily fell in with Japanese-style management. The demand for public services to substitute for the mutual-assistance function weakened and was limited to services such as the prevention of epidemics and so on, to defuse unrest in poor areas.

The second factor causing cracks in the order-maintenance function of local communities was economic decline in the traditional sector, which made both community-based control and community co-operative work difficult to maintain. Local governments had come to rely on local communities to maintain order and so their responsibility extended only to supplementing the co-operative work undertaken in these communities, as, for example, in supporting the maintenance and management of rural roads and irrigation facilities. As the economic decline of the traditional middle class became evident, local governments were forced to increase provision of public services to further supplement or substitute for communities' co-operative work, in order also to boost economic efficiency in this sector. Thus, they were obliged to organize public-works projects, such as the provision of rural roads and irrigation requested by farmers, and urban infrastructure requested by traditional tradespeople.

Family functions in the traditional sector remained intact, and so there was no strong demand for public services to replace them. Education was an exception, however. The central government enforced the provision of education not just for the sake of economic modernization and the expansion of the apparatus of violence, but also to boost economic independence among the old middle class.

Thus, after the First World War, the central government was forced to provide decentralized public services. It was not the intention, however, to change the overall policy of the political system, which included reliance on the local communities to maintain order. Decentralized provision was planned as a way of maintaining that system, both in rural communities and in the cities.

The modernization of the economic system led to increasing migration, and local governments sought to maintain order by fostering ascription, a sense of belonging, and a collective orientation in local communities. However, the more they did so, the greater the rivalry that developed between individual local governments. Attempts by the Ministry of Internal Affairs did not manage to alleviate these competitive pressures on local governments to increase the provision of public services, which grew larger and larger as a result.

However, in the pre-war fiscal system, as I have said, there was no budget allocated to support the provision of decentralized public services. The income of local governments was primarily property income, and taxation was controlled largely through tax denial. Thus, in order to meet increased provision of decentralized public services, the central government was forced to relax tax control.

First, the political system had to accept demands from the old middle class to revise tax denial (which permitted local taxes only in the form of a surtax on national tax), and recognize independent taxation. As I have said, taxes on profits comprising land tax and business tax, which fell on this class, had become the mainstays of national taxation in the pre-war system. The old middle class now demanded that these two profits taxes should be turned into independent local taxes that could fund public services replacing communal co-operative work. Although this demand was not carried through, in the tax reform of 1926 the household tax (*kosuwari*) was made an independent tax for cities, towns, and villages.

Turning to the surtax on national tax, restrictions on top rates of tax were relaxed in rapid succession, and if restrictions were not respected it was in effect overlooked, to the extent that taxation above permitted limits became the rule rather than the exception.

With regard to independent taxes, we can safely say that setting tax rates was left up to local governments. Household tax, the autonomous tax of cities, towns, and villages, was a form of quota taxation (*haibukazei*), and its equivalent in the prefectures and metropolitan regions, the house tax (*kaokuzei*), also contained many of the features of quota taxation. Quota taxation is the taxation method by which revenue shortfall is apportioned among taxpayers, so each local government determined its own tax rate to wipe out this short-fall. The existence of this quota taxation indicates that autonomous taxes took the form of reciprocal payments to the community in proportion to one's assets, and because of the nature of the tax, local-community-type local governments were able to decide on tax rates for themselves.

Thus, from the time of the First World War, not only was there greater decentralization and deconcentration in the fiscal system in the provision of public services, but decision-making on how the cost burden should be apportioned also became decentralized. As such, the pre-war system came very much more to resemble its Western counterparts during this period than was the case after the war.[10]

4. Plans to reform the fiscal system

4.1. Discord among local governments

As we have seen, the pre-war system relied on local communities to maintain social order, and when the emergence of a modernized sector in the economy, lacking political backing, threatened the stability of that system in the period after the First World War, attempts were made to shore it up through decentralization and deconcentration. However, while local governments tried to maintain order by fostering a greater sense of attachment in their local communities, increased decentralization and deconcentration of the fiscal system among multiple local government bodies led to growing rivalry and discord among them. Failure to moderate this discord would immediately make it much more difficult to maintain order throughout the nation, but competitiveness between local governments turned into outright animosity, and the final death-knell of the pre-war system was tolled by the onset of the Shōwa Crisis.

The Shōwa Crisis dealt a fatal blow to the traditional sector and significantly widened disparities in economic strength between the different regions. Because local taxes were inelastic *vis-à-vis* incomes, disparities in the tax burden of local taxes widened between the regions. On top of this, under a system where taxation is determined in a decentralized way, more local taxes had to be raised by local governments that suffered greater economic hardship. Table 7.2 compares figures for the local governments that paid the highest (Tokyo) and lowest (Okinawa) amounts of direct per capita national tax in 1935. It shows that the surtax rate on land tax was three times as high in Okinawa as in Tokyo, and for the house tax, which was an autonomous tax, the rate in Okinawa was fifteen times that in Tokyo.

Even though internal conflicts in local communities could be held in check through the order-maintenance function, as disparities in local tax burdens

Table 7.2. Tax rates of prefectural taxes, 1935

Prefecture	Surtax rate on land tax	Rate of house tax
Okinawa	1.695	9.75
Iwate	1.490	2.70
Aomori	1.467	4.15
Tokyo	0.560	0.65
Total	1.325	4.23

Notes: Surtax rate is the ratio of the surtax to the land tax. Rate of house tax is the ratio expressed in sen (1/100 yen) of the tax to the rental value in yen. Tokyo collects the largest per capita direct national taxes. The other three prefectures collect the smallest amounts per capita.

Source: Cabinet Survey Bureau (1936), *Chihō Zaisei ni Kansuru Naikaku Shingikai Chūkan Hōkoku*.

widened in this way, discord between different local communities increased and it became impossible to maintain order in the nation as a whole. Moreover, the old middle class that had been central in maintaining order was hit so hard that internal instability in local communities also sometimes occurred. Local governments, though, limited to the reciprocal taxation of local taxes, lacked the capacity to bring relief to this class by providing public services.

So it was to assist the old middle class of the traditional sector that the central government, which had previously only provided for the preservation of the state, started to provide social consumption goods to supplement or substitute for community co-operative work. As long as the intention was to maintain order through local community control, however, these public services had to be provided to each local government in a way that would reinforce the local community's maintenance of order. Even though the central government formulated the plan, it had to be left to the local governments to implement it. Thus the central government planned to use fiscal transfers in the form of special subsidies. The transfer of special subsidies to local governments as an economic measure prompted by the Shōwa Crisis was thus an attempt to force local governments to implement public services to substitute for community co-operative work.

This temporary assistance only served to heighten discord among local governments, however. Areas suffering greater economic hardship needed greater assistance, but local governments implementing civil engineering works for rural recovery using the special subsidies had to raise their own share of the cost. This meant that taxation was increased in areas of low economic capacity, which simply served to worsen the inequities in the tax burden between different areas.[11]

Table 7.3. Effects of the Baba Plan for Tax-System Reform (¥m.)

Type of tax	National tax		Local tax				Total	
			Surtax on national tax		Autonomous tax			
	Pre-reform	Post-reform	Pre-reform	Post-reform	Pre-reform	Post-reform	Pre-reform	Post-reform
Direct taxes								
Income tax	266	604 (98)	74	46			340	650
Land tax	59	45 (45)	113	59			172	104
Operating revenue tax	70	69 (69)	73	103			143	172
Capital interest tax	15	34 (34)					13	34
House tax (national tax)	—	34 (34)	—	45			—	79
Property tax	—	60					—	60
Other (national tax)	82	127 (8)					82	127
Household tax					148	—	148	—
Surtax on house tax					111	—	111	—
Surtax on miscellaneous local taxes					109	87	109	87
Other (local tax)					39	35	39	35
Total	492	973 (288)	260	235	407	122	1,159	1,348

Indirect taxes		
Liquor tax	218	224
Soft drinks tax	4	4
Sugar excise tax	91	113
Textiles excise tax	43	51
Government monopoly profits	202	252
Turnover tax	—	33
Customs duty	164	202
Other	73	116
Total	795	995
Grand total	1,289	1,967

Notes: Figures in parentheses show amounts appropriated for local finance grants. Figures in 'Pre-reform' columns show approximate revenues estimated for FY1937 without the plan in force. Figures in 'Post-reform' columns show expected tax revenues in an average fiscal year after the reform.

Source: Ministry of Finance, Tax Bureau (1937), *Dai Nanajukkai Teikoku Gikai Sōtei Mondō (Ippan no Bu)*.

At this point the Ministry of Internal Affairs tried to moderate the discord by introducing a public finance regulating system to transfer general subsidies from central to local governments to rectify imbalances of tax burdens in different areas. As they were intended to reduce tax burdens, these general subsidies would perhaps be better described as special subsidies. The system was the 'Subsidy System to Regulate Regional Public Finance Draft Proposal' (*Chihō Zaisei Chōsei Kofukin Seido Yōkō An*) which the Ministry of Internal Affairs announced in 1932.[12]

For the central government to implement fiscal transfers, however, financial resources had to be found, and as I have said, the national tax system that had to produce the funds was dependent on the traditional sector. It is true that profits taxes, which were a burden on the traditional sector, now figured less significantly while indirect consumption taxes, which applied broadly to both traditional and modernized sectors, had increased. But as Table 7.3 shows, not only were land tax and operating revenue tax, both profits taxes, considerable in volume, but surtaxes levied on them were 2.5 times the level of income tax.

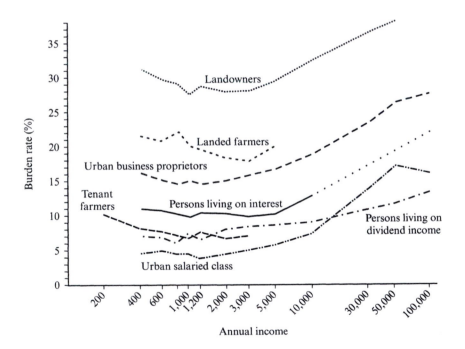

Figure 7.4. Tax burden rate curves by sector, 1936

Notes: Rates are burden rates of total national and local taxes and public imposts. The dotted segment of the 'Persons living on interest' line indicates lack of data.

Source: Ministry of Finance, Tax Bureau (1937), *Shōwa 11 Nenbun Sozei Kōka Futanritsu Kakei Shishutsu Jōkyō Shirabe.*

Additionally, the burden of autonomous taxes, such as the household and house taxes, was also borne by the traditional sector, as I have shown. So if we add up total tax burdens, as in Figure 7.4, we see that the system placed a remarkably heavy burden on the old middle class in the traditional sector.[13]

This meant that financial resources for fiscal transfers could only be raised by either creating new taxation or increasing existing taxes levied on the modernized sector, in other words, by tax sharing. The corporate organizations of the modernized sector, however, resisted greater taxation either through new or increased taxes. As a result, at the time of the Shōwa Crisis discord among different local governments and communities could not be controlled and social stability could thus not be maintained.

4.2. The Baba Plan for Tax-System Reform:
a prototype for the 'Japanese-model' fiscal system

The Shōwa Crisis was a period of both severe internal unrest and heightening tensions with the outside world. It saw the end of the 'retreat of external threat': the external conditions that had enabled order to be maintained through decentralization and deconcentration of the pre-war fiscal system. To deal with external tensions, the military authorities announced a strengthening of the service for the 'preservation of the state'. However, it was impossible for the central government to raise the extra financial resources that this would require under a decentralized-deconcentrated system that relied on the traditional sector for tax revenues. The major source of tax revenues would have to be shifted to the modernized sector of the economy. The corporate organizations of the modernized sector resisted such a shift, however, and further took a conciliatory stance on international relations, putting them at odds with the military authorities.

Thus, during the Shōwa Crisis period, confrontation surrounding the reform of the fiscal system surfaced. One point of conflict revolved around the fact that the existing system placed the burden of taxation on the traditional sector, and another questioned perpetuating a system that depended on local communities to maintain order.

These issues were resolved by the assassin's bullets in the 'February 26th Incident'. The military gained unassailable political authority and pressed on with preparations for war, and in light of these developments, a comprehensive tax-system reform was proposed. This was the 'Baba Plan for Tax-System Reform' shown in Table 7.3.

First and foremost, the Baba Plan provided for large increases to the service for the preservation of the state, and attempted to move the focus of the tax burden from the traditional to the modernized sector. To do this, the plan aimed to make income tax the main form of taxation and property taxes supplementary. To create a tax system based on income tax, the plan sought to more than double the revenue from income tax, as shown in Table 7.3. Moreover, it attempted to shift the burden in the modernized sector to capital income. This meant increasing revenue from individual income tax by about 80 per cent and further, as part of individual income tax, full taxation of income from dividends and interest.

At the same time, the Baba Plan effectively eliminated from national taxation two forms of profits tax that had been very burdensome to the traditional sector, land tax and operating revenue tax. Under the plan, the profits taxes of land tax, operating revenue tax, capital interest tax, as well as house tax, which had become a national tax, continued to appear as national taxes, but the total revenue raised was transferred to local governments in the form of tax sharing. These profits taxes therefore became in effect local government taxes, so that even when national taxes were increased during the war, the traditional sector escaped any increased burden.

Second, the Baba Plan tried to uphold social order by shoring up the weakening maintenance-of-order function of the local communities. To achieve this goal, the plan sought to lighten the tax burden on the old middle class in the traditional sector, the social group central in maintaining order in local communities. Land tax and operating revenue tax, the taxes that had fallen very heavily on this class, as well as house tax and the various surtaxes levied as local government taxes, were all reduced, and the household tax was abolished altogether.[14] As a Ministry of Finance document of the time pointed out, 'the middle class is the core of the state, and the decline of this class would threaten the very base of the state. Therefore to reduce the burden on this class is a most pressing need'.[15]

More importantly, however, the Baba Plan sought to introduce a mechanism to control the discord among local governments using the local communities' function to maintain order. In other words, the plan sought to create a mechanism to rectify the disparities in local tax burdens. For this purpose it sought to centralize and concentrate the decentralized-deconcentrated fiscal system, and secure the central government's right to control both national and local taxation.

First, some part of income tax, capital interest tax, and operating revenue tax, which were all in the hands of central government, was distributed to local governments in a way adjusted to their assets, that is to say, inversely proportional to the taxation strength of the local government, and directly proportional to asset demand and the amount needed to reduce taxes. As a source of revenue, it rectified the disparities in tax rates in local government taxes, and on this basis, restriction on tax rates was strengthened.

Furthermore, in spite of the fact that land tax and house tax were transferred complete to the local governments representing the areas from which they had been collected, they were not made autonomous local taxes but were retained as national taxes. So the power to decide taxation levels and tax rates was kept very firmly in the hands of the central government.

Thus the Baba Plan for Tax-System Reform robbed local governments of their decision-making rights over decentralized local government taxes through the implementation of large-scale tax sharing, but tried to even out local government tax rates by strengthening the system of control of public finance and taxation limits. In this way the Baba Plan sought to ameliorate the discord among local communities that surfaced during the Shōwa Crisis.

We can recognize by examining the Baba Plan in this way that it set out concepts that were to become the framework of the present fiscal system. First, it aimed to create a system centred on income tax, in which tax collection would be concentrated in the hands of central government. Second, through integrating the tax system and transferring revenues collected by the central government, it sought to create a system by which local governments could be controlled.

This sort of system was designed initially because a massive increase in the demand for funds was expected during the war period. A tax system centred on income tax including corporate income tax was formulated to get a secure hold on tax revenues from the modernized sector. The second reason was to perpetuate the traditional social system, to maintain stability and order during wartime. To do this a system was formulated that would be able to deal with the threatened ruptures in the traditional social system.

A comparison of the Baba Plan with Japan's present-day fiscal system throws up some important points of difference, however. Although the plan visualized central government control over local government, that control was focused very much on the cost burden of public services, while control over the provision of public services received scant attention. Formulation of a structure that gave central government control over the provision of public services had to wait until the tax reform of 1940.[16]

5. The 1940 reform of the fiscal system

5.1. Shifting of revenue sources from the traditional to the modernized sector

The Baba Plan met with strong opposition and was not carried through. Fierce resistance was put up in financial quarters representing the interests of corporate organizations. They opposed the abrupt shift to an income-tax-based tax system, the concept of consolidated income tax, and the creation of a property tax. In other words, they were against a sudden shift of the tax burden onto the modernized sector, particularly one that targeted capital income.

But the year the Baba Plan was aborted, 1937, saw the outbreak of the

Sino-Japanese War, which before long took on the appearance of all-out war. This new situation made it imperative to carry through the basic thrusts of the Baba Plan, both to satisfy the wartime demand for funds and to maintain public order. This precipitated the tax reform of 1940.[17]

The 1940 tax reform utilized the basic framework of the Baba Plan, but having said that, there were many points of difference. The fundamental factors that led to these differences were that war had actually started, and economic controls, that is to say direct, political intervention in the economic system, had begun.[18]

In the 1940 tax reform, as in the Baba Plan, reliance on the modernized sector for the financial resources needed to meet the revenue demand generated by the war was inevitable. Moreover, quota allocation under a controlled economy allowed the corporate organizations of the modernized sector to generate enormous economic rent. To meet the vast wartime demand for funds, inevitably, a system had to be established that taxed the resources of corporate organizations.

Be that as it may, the 1940 tax reform did not subject the corporate organizations to the sort of harsh taxation that would have come with the Baba Plan, steeped as it had been in national socialist ideology. The creation of a property tax, which had aroused such fierce opposition to the Baba Plan in financial circles, was abandoned, and neither did the reform incorporate full taxation of income. The Emergency Taxation Measures Act (*Rinji Sozei Sochi Hō*) of 1937 was extended, and an incentive system to achieve production expansion plans was designed, which persisted after the war in the form of special tax measures. Thus, the shift of taxation onto the modernized sector planned in the 1940 tax reform was delicately balanced against the system of incentives.

However, if incentives are afforded such a degree of consideration, then the capability to achieve national treasury objectives, the securing of tax revenue, will be correspondingly weakened. So in this tax reform, the degree to which taxation of the modernized sector's corporate organizations was weakened by consideration of profit incentives, had to be made up by increasing taxation of earned incomes in the modernized sector. As a way of taxing earned incomes, the introduction of a general sales tax was considered. The existing individual consumption tax had already reached its maximum revenue potential, so raising the rate would not lead to increased revenue. Furthermore, it was judged that a tax on quantity rather than price could not keep abreast of inflation. At the time of the Baba Plan, a general sales tax linked to a property tax had been proposed. Since the creation of a property tax was dropped from the 1940 tax reform due to the earlier fierce resistance of commercial proprietors, a general sales tax could not be introduced either.

So the 1940 tax reform aimed to contribute to treasury objectives by netting earned income in the modernized sector through personal income tax. For this purpose, personal income tax was built on two planks, consolidated income tax levied with graduated tax rates, and classified income tax levied with proportional rates. Second, a system to collect classified income tax at source was introduced.

Taxing salaried income at source was adopted in America in 1943, and in Britain in 1944, so Japan preceded both of them by a few years. In fact, a system had been introduced even earlier than this, in 1911, in Japanese-occupied Manchuria, which was well beyond the experimental stage.[19] Also in Manchuria, a surtax on this labour income tax was transferred to the local government as a 'partial tax transfer to local government', so the basic concepts behind the 1940 tax reform had already been tested out. Thus, ideas that were not implemented in the Japanese home islands were tested in occupied Manchuria and later re-imported to Japan.

Collection of earned income tax at source was eulogized as co-operating with 'assistance to the whole nation' on the part of the corporate organizations, for whom the profit incentive had been approved. The eagerness of the corporate organizations to co-operate in tax collection at source was praised as 'something that bears comparison with the zeal of the Imperial forces assaulting strongholds with iron walls.[20]

Whatever the case, whereas the Baba Plan had proposed a tax system with income tax as the central tax and property tax as the supplementary tax, and which would introduce a general sales tax, the tax system planned in the 1940 reform made income tax and corporation tax the main taxes, separating corporation tax from income tax, the latter being comprised of consolidated income tax and classified income tax. Nevertheless, the later reform was modelled on the Baba Plan and effectively eliminated from national tax the profits taxes of land tax and operating revenue tax that had been disproportionately burdensome on the old middle class of the traditional sector.

5.2. Control of the provision of public services

Thus in the 1940 tax reform, too, the focus of revenue sources had to be shifted from the traditional to the modernized sector, and at the same time the reform, like the Baba Plan, aimed to uphold stability by reinforcing the capability of local communities to maintain order. To do this, first of all, it sought to lighten the tax burden on the old middle class of the traditional sector, and second, by combining fiscal transfers from the central government with a tax-control system, it aimed to contain the discord among local governments based on local communities and preserve order and stability in the social system.

In this sense it was not fundamentally different from the Baba Plan. The only difference was that in the Baba Plan, under tax sharing, land tax and house tax were to be transferred to local governments for the areas from which the taxes originated, whereas in this reform land tax, house tax, and operating revenue tax would be transferred in this way, and some part of the revenue from income tax, corporation tax, admission tax, and amusements and restaurant tax would also be distributed among local governments on the basis of fiscal regulatory criteria.

With regard to tax control, however, there were important points of difference, in that a standardized rate was introduced on tax limits. This reform, like the Baba Plan, gave autonomous taxes for local governments little scope. In other words, local taxes were hardly more than surtaxes on national taxes.

As regards surtax rates, the Baba Plan sought only to implement restrictions that would set maximum tax rates at previous levels. However, it attempted to tighten restrictions by not permitting taxation outside those limits. This tax reform, however, introduced standard rates for surtax and required the adoption of uniform tax rates across the board.

Needless to say, this setting of standard rates was the precursor of the standardized tax rates that are such a conspicuous feature of Japan's current fiscal system in any international comparison. The introduction of tax control in the form of setting standard rates suggests that this tax reform was aiming to create a system that would also control local government provision of public services.

Undoubtedly, this reform resembled the Baba Plan in seeking to maintain stability in the social system by strengthening the local communities' ability to maintain order. But the Baba Plan merely left this task with the local communities and then sought to control the discord generated among them. At the time of the 1940 reform, however, the Sino-Japanese War had developed into all-out war, and the political system had to take over the running of an economy that had been left to the whim of market forces, to allow a general mobilization of all material and human resources for the war effort, and to support people's livelihoods. The provision of public services required for economic controls and the war effort, that is to say, wartime administration, would have to be run at the behest of the central government. But if economic controls were to be introduced for the war effort, the political system needed all the more to gain co-operation and support throughout society. Thus the 1940 tax reform also tried to utilize community control and the communities' mutual-assistance function for the wartime administration.

Through the 1940 tax reform it was therefore planned to run wartime administration through local government channels in order to make use of the local communities for this task. And in order to maintain centralized control, the tax reform aimed to create a fiscal system that would control this local government provision of public services.

5.3. *Provision of public services through local communities*

From the viewpoint of a fiscal system to control local government provision of public services, we should note that in connection with the 1940 reform, certain reforms were implemented, such as rectifying the split of costs between national and local budgets, tightening control over bond issues, and the systematic organization of neighbourhood groups. Of these, the intention behind the latter was clearly to have local governments run the wartime administration utilizing local community functions. To use these functions effectively, organization was needed, and in 1940 neighbourhood groups were organized on instructions from the Ministry of Internal Affairs.

In this way wartime administrative activities that included calling up troops, requisitioning labour for munitions industries, boosting production and distributing essential goods and daily necessities, air-raid defence, and so on, were undertaken by local governments utilizing community control and neighbourhood support functions. Coupons and ration books for obtaining essential commodities were distributed through neighbourhood groups, which also encouraged savings to raise war funds. For calling up troops and requisitioning labour for munitions work, community reward and sanction systems were used effectively among neighbourhood groups, and air-raid defence was also based on these groups.

Of course, fiscal support was needed for all these activities, and local governments had to be guaranteed appropriate financial resources to run the wartime administration despite the fact that local community functions were used. In requiring forbearance from local governments, control by means of sanctions on personnel issues, used in the past, may have been adequate. However, when requiring local governments to take action, funds had to be guaranteed.

None the less, fiscal resources needed to be directed as far as possible to war expenses. So even though local governments were guaranteed the necessary funds to run the wartime administration, they were limited to what the central government judged necessary. Funds were transferred in the form of earmarked grants, and were for a limited range of purposes. As Figure 7.2 on page 215 shows, earmarked grants swelled dramatically after the 1940 tax reform. Systematization of the split of costs between national and local budgets that came with the 1940 tax reform can be seen as preparing the way to allow this dramatic growth in earmarked grants.

The reason for the systematization of the split of costs between national and local budgets for such expenditures as compulsory education and the police force, was that in principle it was accepted that the central government should bear the burden of costs for tasks delegated to local governments. However much the central government declared its intention of shouldering the burden of costs, transfers through earmarked grants still placed a burden on local governments, which thus had to raise funds either through taxation or bond flotation. But local governments could not be permitted to float bonds indiscriminately. Capital had to be directed in a controlled way towards national bonds to raise war funds and as capital to raise productive capacity.

While the floating of local government bonds was controlled, it nevertheless had to be permitted in certain cases to force local governments to undertake essential subsidized projects. On 29 July 1940, the Ministry of Internal Affairs published an 'order relating to plans for bond issues or petitions for the same' (*Kisai Keikaku Narabi ni Kisai Keikaku Rinseisho ni kansuru Ken Imei Tsū-tatsu*). According to this, local government bonds were approved on the basis of a local government bond-flotation plan 'to accord with the Funds Control Plan and Materials Mobilization Plan decided by the government'. This method of approving bond flotations persisted after the war as a form of bond-flotation control.

Even though bond issues for subsidized projects were permitted, ultimately local government's portion to match earmarked grants had to be raised through local taxation. But the 1940 tax reform strengthened tax control and removed local governments' right to take decisions on local taxation. With regard to refund taxes (*kanpuzei*), taxation standards and tax rates were decided by central government and for surtaxes, a standard rate was set and they were forced to tax at a uniform rate.

Under such circumstances the poorer local governments with weak taxation capability could not raise the necessary funds for the local government portion to match earmarked grants, as they were unable to increase tax rates. Thus, earmarked grants could not be used to make these local governments undertake wartime administration duties. To ensure that even the weakest local government fulfilled these duties, therefore, funds were transferred from central government in the form of a distribution tax (*haifuzei*).

As I have said, the 1940 tax reform introduced a type of tax sharing modelled on the Baba Plan and called the local apportionment tax (*chihō bun'yozei*). It was made up of refund tax, distributed to local governments on the basis of the areas from which it was derived, and distribution tax, which was based on fiscal regulatory criteria. While there was a difference in the way the tax was made up, its framework was the same as that of the Baba Plan. The policy objectives, however, were entirely different.

The objective of tax sharing based on fiscal regulatory criteria in the Baba Plan was largely to rectify discrepancies in local taxes between different regions, but that of the 1940 tax reform went much further. Local governments, even those with weak taxation capability, had to undertake important wartime administration duties with a uniform burden of tax control. To ensure that local governments had the necessary financial resources, their taxation capability had to be calculated, and as a base for these calculations, a standard tax rate was essential.

Tax control under the Baba Plan went no further than tightening compliance with tax-rate limits, because the main consideration was adjusting the unequal burden posed by local taxes. However, in this tax-system reform, the added objective of ensuring fiscal resources for the provision of vital public services gave rise to the need to calculate taxation capability, and standardized rates were set for tax control.

5.4. A centralized-deconcentrated system in embryonic form

As we have seen, it can be argued that Japan's present-day centralized-deconcentrated fiscal system was formed in embryo as a result of the 1940 tax reform. Local government taxation that took the form of a proportion of income was abolished, and taxation of income was concentrated in the hands of central government, creating a tax system in which the key taxes were income tax and corporation tax. With a hold over income taxation, the central government had local governments run centrally determined administrations through transferring fiscal resources as earmarked grants. The implementation of subsidized projects was also managed through the control of local government bond issues.

However, to avoid discrepancies arising in the tax burden of local taxes, the central government decided taxation standards and tax rates. To this end it strengthened tax control. Despite a tax-sharing system to return taxes in full to the area from which they were collected, they were retained as national taxes and standard rates were introduced for surtaxes based on them. Through this system the provision of fiscal resources was restricted, the central government required local governments to run local administrations by providing earmarked grants, and those too impoverished to be able to comply received transfers of distribution tax.

So through this tax reform, a centralized-deconcentrated system operated by means of fiscal-resource control was formed in embryo. The public services it provided were decided by central government, as was the cost burden. Such a system was formed purely due to the political control of the economy and the attempt to provide public services in a centralized way, in order to support the war effort and people's livelihoods in circumstances of economic shortages. Public services were not supplied directly to the people, however, but provided by means of returning resources to local communities, and as a result a deconcentrated system was formed.

6. A centralized-deconcentrated system becomes established

6.1. Post-war reforms

After the Second World War, ironically, the centralized-deconcentrated system created during wartime became entrenched, despite historically significant post-war reforms that were designed with the US system very much in mind. Of course, there were attempts at decentralization. Prefectural governors were elected through public ballot, and the Ministry of Internal Affairs was eventually abolished. But economic shortages persisted, and in a situation where the political system had to take control of the economy, centralized decisions on the provision of public services were essential.

On the other hand, there were also attempts to find a way to implement those services in a more concentrated way. As prefectural governors were now publicly elected, and prefectural offices were thus no longer mere representative offices of central government, the various ministries each sought a more 'concentrated' form of provision of services by setting up their own branches in the different regions. Moreover, the neighbourhood groups that had served as end suppliers of deconcentrated provision of public services were disbanded, despite a claim by the Ministry of Internal Affairs that they were indispensable to the implementation of economic controls.

Although the neighbourhood-group system was abolished, however, the function the groups performed, in essence, survived. Regional offices of the Ministry of Internal Affairs claimed that they could provide comprehensive public services, and devolution from central to local governments was institutionalized. Thus, in the end, a deconcentrated system through the medium of local government persisted.

Furthermore, it can be argued that fiscal control in the post-war period was, if anything, tightened. The Ministry of Internal Affairs lost its right to control personnel, which had provided some leverage in obliging local governments to provide public services, and as a result, fiscal control had to be utilized as the means to control local governments' provision of services. As shown in Figure 7.2 on page 215, subsidies soared in the immediate post-war period. This was because 'subsidies alone fulfilled the important role of securing the implementation of public works projects'.[21]

The tax system based on income and corporation taxes that underpinned the wartime centralized-deconcentrated system was also endorsed despite post-war reforms. The income tax system introduced during the war years was modelled on the French system, and consisted of classified income tax and general income tax. It was argued that this system was undemocratic, however, because it differed from the American system, and so it was reformed to consist solely of general income tax. Also, the refund taxes of land tax, house tax, and operating revenue tax, which were allocated according to the areas where they were collected, became autonomous taxes. But the system of central control of local taxation nevertheless persisted.

6.2. The impact and limitations of the Shoup Report

The Shoup Report also served merely to endorse the tax system formed during the war period. The structure of the tax system it recommended, in which property tax would supplement general income tax, was nothing more than a reworking of the Baba Plan. The only point of difference was that whereas the Baba Plan envisaged an income tax based on the concept of the corporation as an actuality, in the Shoup Report it was based on the concept of the corporation as a legal fiction.

Be that as it may, the Shoup recommendations challenged head-on the use of fiscal revenue control for the centralized-deconcentrated system, by proposing the abolition of earmarked grants, which were the pivotal means of controlling local government provision of public services. It must be said, however, that the survival of earmarked grants had already been decided, because any abolition of such grants would require a complete clarification of the division of responsibilities between central and local government for the provision of public services. (Through the decision-making process on post-war reforms, an informal, workable division of responsibilities had already come about.)

No clear division of responsibilities could be made, and so no progress was made on terminating earmarked grants. After the Occupation period, in fact, earmarked grants were more and more widely utilized, and in 1954 the equalization grants which had served to absorb earmarked grants were abolished, and local allocation taxes were introduced to take over from the wartime form of tax sharing.

The Shoup recommendations were also negative on tax control. But in order for the equalization grants, proposed under the Shoup Report, to function effectively, standardized tax rates had to be endorsed. Thus, tax control was also maintained and a centralized-deconcentrated system persisted.

7. Conclusion

One might claim that the centralized-deconcentrated system operated through control of tax-revenue sources was formed during the war as a result of two factors. First, the political system had to take control of the economy and planned that the fiscal system should not merely provide for the preservation of the state but also provide public services on the basis of centralized decisions. Second, it sought to provide those services in a deconcentrated way, utilizing some backward features of the social system.

That this centralized-deconcentrated system should have survived through the period of high-speed growth suggests that these two factors remained relevant. After the war the economic controls evident during wartime disappeared, but the need for the political system to run the economy continued.

The attempt to utilize the backwardness of the social system for the provision of public services is exemplified in the re-emergence of neighbourhood groups after the Occupation ended in 1952. But undoubtedly, democratization through post-war reforms also had an enormous impact and the community-control and mutual-assistance functions at work in local communities began to fragment. Conversely, the differing interests of various levels of society became more forcibly expressed and without some balancing of these interests social order and stability could not be guaranteed. But during the high-speed growth period, as before, the approach used was to contain these conflicts of interests within each local community to keep them under control.

Centrally positioned in undertaking this task was the old middle class that fulfilled the role, though not always rigorously, of maintaining order in local communities. The interests of this class were conveyed from local to central government as the interests of the communities as a whole. The regulation of these interests by central government was dignified with the title of 'planning' to control the economy. Under the centralized-deconcentrated system, local governments implement the outcome of this central government regulation of interests. The cost burden of the public services provided in this way is adjusted under this system so as not to create disparities among different communities, and this adjustment is made possible through fiscal transfers supported by a tax system formed during the war, and built around income tax and corporation tax that draw revenues from the capital income and earned income of the modernized sector. As the modernized sector benefited from high levels of profits and dividends deriving from high-speed economic growth, no discontent was voiced.

But the centralized-deconcentrated system that delivered social stability under circumstances of high-speed economic growth was seen once that period ended as a system that defended vested interests, and it became the target of a barrage of criticism. Advocating the 'age of the regions', there were calls for a change to a decentralized-deconcentrated system that would bring together decision-making and implementation.

Traditional local communities have been dismembered, however, and one wonders whether they will be replaced by modern communities that have an autonomous capability to maintain order. Without such capability in local communities, one fears that reckless moves towards a decentralized-deconcentrated system will merely bring to the surface disparities and fractures that only central government has the ability to resolve.

Notes

1. Takahashi (1978: 12).
2. Reed (1990: 54).
3. Tax efforts include increasing tax rates and creating new taxes. On the relationship between fiscal transfers and tax systems, see Iwasaki (1990).
4. On the concepts of centralization, decentralization, concentration, and deconcentration, see Nishio (1990: ch. 12).
5. Sato (1968: 15).

6. On the structural elements of the social system, see Tominaga (1986: ch. 3).
7. On these points, see Odaka (1989).
8. Kanbe (1923: 52).
9. Analysis of Japanese-style management given by Hideo Hougi, managing director, BMW (K. K.).
10. On deconcentration and decentralization in this period, see Sato (1968).
11. On this point, see Yoshida (1972).
12. For more detail on this, see Jinno (1987: 139–43).
13. For more detail on this, see Jinno (1979).
14. Because household tax competed with income tax, in order to create a tax system based on income tax, household tax had to be abolished and local governments' taxation of income disallowed.
15. Ministry of Finance, Tax Bureau (1937), *Dai Nanajukkai Teikoku Gikai Sotei Mondo (Ippan no Bu)*, p. 120.
16. On Baba tax-reform proposals, see Jinno (1988: 58–61).
17. On the 1940 tax reform, see Jinno (1988: 71–5).
18. On economic controls, see Okazaki (1987).
19. See Kataoka (1939: ch. 5).
20. Kobayashi *et al.* (1941: ch. 3).
21. Shibata (1973: 28).

References

Iwasaki, Mikiko (1990), 'Chihō Kōfuzei to Hojokin o meguru Seijigaku (Political Implications of Intergovernmental Transfer Payments)', *Leviathan*, 6.
Jinno, Naohiko (1979), 'Baba Zeisei Kaikaku An (Finance Minister Baba's Tax Reform Plan)', *Shōken Keizai*, 127.
——(1987), 'Gendai Nihon Zaisei no Keisei Katei (Birth of the Modern Tax System in Japan) (1)', *Keizaigaku Zasshi* (Journal of Economics), 88(2–3).
——(1988), 'Gendai Nihon Zaisei no Keisei Katei (Birth of the Modern Tax System in Japan) (2)', *Keizaigaku Zasshi* (Journal of Economics), 88(5–6).
Kanbe, Masao (1923), *Sozei Kenkyū* (Studies on Taxation), vol. 4, Kōbundō Shobō.
Kataoka, Masaichi (1939), *Gensen Kōjozei* (Withholding Tax), Daiichi Shobō.
Kobayashi, Haseo, Shigeki Yukioka, and Uichi Taguchi (1941), *Gensen Kazei* (Withholding Tax), Kenbundō.
Nishio, Masaru (1990), *Gyōseigaku no Kiso Gainen* (The Basic Concepts of Public Administration), University of Tokyo Press.
Odaka, Konosuke (1989), 'Nijū Kōzō (Japan's Dual Industrial Structure)', in Takafusa Nakamura and Konosuke Odaka (eds.), *Nihon Keizai Shi* (Economic History of Japan), vol. 6, Iwanami Shoten.
Okazaki, Tetsuji (1987), 'Senji Keikaku Keizai to Kakaku Tōsei (The Wartime Planned Economy and Price-Control System)', *Kindai Nihon Kenkyū* (Modern Japanese Studies), 9.
Reed, Steven R. (1990) (in translation), *Japanese Prefectures and Policymaking*, Bokutaku-sha.

Sato, Susumu (1968), 'Senzen no Chihō Zaisei to Sengo no Chihō Zaisei (Japan's Local Public Finance in the Pre-war and Post-war Periods)', in *Sengo Chihō Zaisei no Tenkai* (Local Public Finance in Post-war Japan), Nihon Hyōron-sha.

Shibata, Mamoru (1973), *Chihō Zaisei no Shikumi to Un'ei* (Structure and Management of Local Government in Japan), Ryōsho Fukyūkai.

Takahashi, Makoto (1978), *Gendai Igirisu Gyōzaisei Ron* (Contemporary Local Public Administration and Finance in the UK), Yuhikaku.

Tominaga, Kenichi (1986), *Shakaigaku Genri* (Principles of Sociology), Iwanami Shoten.

Yoshida, Shintaro (1972), 'Takahashi Zaiseika no Chihō Zaisei (Local Public Finance under Finance Minister Takahashi's Fiscal Policy)', in Koichiro Takahashi (ed.), *Nihon Kindaika no Kenkyū* (Studies on Japan's Modernization), University of Tokyo Press.

8

The Food-Control System and Nōkyō

Toshihiko Kawagoe

1. Introduction

In the shadows of Japan's striking post-war economic recovery is the agricultural sector, which has been left behind in a state of backwardness. A variety of regulations that date back to the war years remain in force, and structural adjustment has been slow to get off the ground, with the result that high levels of protection have allowed inefficient production to persist. Thus, there has been little objective discussion of the so-called Japanese system of agriculture, and in such discussion as has taken place, Japanese agriculture has inevitably been regarded in a negative light.

A range of problematic issues has been highlighted as the features that have marked out Japanese post-war agriculture, particularly in the period since the onset of high-speed economic growth. These include the small size of farms and the trend to part-time farming, the government's wide-ranging regulations and generous protection of agriculture, Japan's low level of self-sufficiency in food, and the powerful agricultural co-operative organization. Most of these features are by no means unique to Japan, however. Protection of the agricultural sector is common in the USA and many countries in Europe, as are agricultural organizations that lobby for it. Part-time farming is also widespread. Thus, many of the problems facing agriculture in Japan are common to all advanced industrialized nations.

Nevertheless, there are certain aspects of post-war agriculture in Japan which may perhaps be deemed unique. One is the food-control system, an outcome of wartime controls, which has been maintained right up to the present day. Another is the powerful and highly integrated organization of agricultural co-operatives (Sōgo Nōkyō), which reaches out from its central hub to all parts of the country, and has virtually all farm households as members. A further point is the influence that Nōkyō wields in the forming of agricultural policy.

Japan was economically under-developed before the war, and it's not really possible to make any straightforward comparisons with agriculture in former periods up to the end of the Meiji period. Suffice it to say that farms at that time, too, were very small-scale concerns, and farming was combined with

other income-generating activities. Agricultural organizations (known as industrial associations) were in existence but were not directly involved in policy
implementation. The marketing of produce and supplies for agricultural
production was left to individual entrepreneurs, such as dealers for cereals or
fertilizer, and the market was basically one of free competition. Thus, those
aspects of Japan's present-day agriculture I have just mentioned—the food-
control system and the agricultural co-operatives—cannot be regarded as
uniquely Japanese phenomena that have been inherited from Meiji agriculture.
They were in fact formed after the onset of the Taishō period, and particularly
under the wartime economic controls.

By focusing on the food-control system and Nōkyō, the organization of
agricultural co-operatives, and examining when and how they came to be
formed, I hope in this chapter to elucidate the problems of Japan's agriculture,
which will be a good way to present the Japanese agricultural system. There
follows a simple summary of the present state of agriculture in Japan, followed
by an examination of the rice market and the development of food policy from
the Meiji period onwards, combined with the development of the agricultural
associations.

2. The current state of Japanese agriculture

2.1. The food-control system

The food-control system was created under circumstances of wartime
food shortages and it exhibits all the features one associates with a planned
economy. It seems remarkable that such a system should have persisted for
more than half a century since the end of the war. A rationing system for the
distribution of rice to consumers remained on paper until 1972. In addition to
the food-control system, quantities of regulations covering all aspects of
agriculture have been kept in force, and have produced the well-known result
of sustaining levels of protection that are internationally high.

Even today, many types of agricultural produce are subject to government
price controls. The tight control on prices of rice, wheat, and barley under the
Food Control Law are obvious examples, and there are also price supports
for dairy products, sugar, and the like, with the domestic market for these
goods being controlled by monopolistic, semi-official organizations. The consequence of these protectionist policies is high domestic food prices; the price
of rice, for example, is four times the US price and seven times the export price
of Thai rice.[1]

Japan's protectionist agricultural policies have been severely criticized both
at home and overseas. Import quotas for oranges and beef have been held up
as symbols of this protectionism, and the opening of the rice market is being

Table 8.1. Comparison of major agricultural indicators

	Japan	France	Germany[a]	Italy	USA
Proportion of part-time farmers[b] (%)	86	38	67	—	65
Agricultural land per farm worker[c] (ha./person)	1.3	22.9	10.9	10.2	150.2
Self-sufficiency rate in staple cereals[d] (%)	30	203	95	83	172
Nominal rate of farm protection[e] (composite, %)	85	30	44	57	0

[a] Former West Germany.
[b] Figures for 1975, based on Korenaga (1984).
[c] FAO estimates for 1989.
[d] Figures for 1985 (1989 for Japan), Ministry of Agriculture, Forestry, and Fisheries (*a*).
[e] Figures for 1980, based on Hayami (1986: 169).

Note: Nominal composite rate of protection = (agricultural production in domestic prices − agricultural production in international prices)/agricultural production in international prices.

pursued through the Uruguay Round of GATT talks. The degree of protection of staple cereals, beef, and dairy products is certainly higher than in some EC countries, and the nominal rate of protection measured as a composite of all agricultural produce is considerably higher (Table 8.1). And besides direct market intervention, there are countless numbers of subsidies paid out in the agricultural sector.[2]

Japanese agriculture has not always been so heavily protected, however, and up to around 1955, levels were lower than those of Western European countries.[3] Protectionism in Japan therefore does not have a long history; it is a phenomenon that started during the high-growth period.

2.2. Nōkyō

For an agricultural association, Japan's Nōkyō is an enormous organization. It consists of Sōgo Nōkyō, whose diverse operations cover agriculture generally and include financial services, and Senmon Nōkyō, which deals only with specific areas such as livestock farming or horticulture. Sōgo Nōkyō has an organization based on local administrative divisions such as towns and villages. Reaching nearly every farming district throughout the country, and counting almost all farm households as its members, it represents the main thrust of the association's activities. Senmon Nōkyō, on the other hand, serves groups of producers of particular categories of produce, though not all producers belong, neither is there necessarily a branch in every production area. In many cases its projects are limited to particular objectives, such as reaping scale benefits for small-scale producers through having joint facilities for storage or processing. In the USA and European countries, most agricultural co-operatives are of this specialized type, dealing with one specific area of agricultural activity. The discussion in this chapter will be largely confined to Sōgo Nōkyō, referred to hereafter simply as Nōkyō.

It is Nōkyō's strong organizational capability that lies behind the formidable influence it has come to exert over agricultural policy. It has a pyramid structure reaching out nation-wide from a central base to cities, towns, and villages in every prefecture throughout the country. Nōkyō has lost some ground with the emasculation of agriculture in recent years, but it remains a vast organization, with 3,600 branches nation-wide, 8.6 million members and 300,000 staff.[4]

Its size can be appreciated from the vast deposits held by the Nōrin Chūkin (Central Bank of Agriculture and Forestry), Nōkyō's central financial institution. In FY1989 these totalled ¥21 trillion, a figure not far off average total deposits of any one of the city banks. The total amount of savings on deposit with Nōkyō institutions exceeded ¥51 trillion.[5] Nōkyō's economic projects saw a turnover for FY1989 that reached ¥6.3 trillion. Of significance in Nōkyō's remarkable growth have been government protectionist and promotional policies in place since the time of the Shōwa financial crisis, and the economic controls that followed it. In the post-war period Nōkyō has gone on to sustain and extend its organization, benefiting from the food-control system and various other preferential measures.

2.3 The Trend to Part-Time Farming

Next I would like to take a brief look at farm households. It is well known that farm size in Japan is generally small, and farms are run increasingly on a part-time basis. The present population employed in agriculture is 4 million, and the area of land under agricultural use is 5.28 million hectares, which gives an average of only 1.32 hectares of agricultural land per farm-worker (Table 8.1).[6] If we consider only cultivated land and exclude grazing land, the average area managed by each farm household is a mere 1.15 hectares.[7]

Small-scale farming of this sort is widespread in the peasant economies centred on rice production that exist throughout Asia. Compared with other advanced countries, however, average farm size in Japan is exceptionally small, even discounting the newer, land-rich countries such as the USA and Australia. The equivalent figures for the area of agricultural land per farm-worker in Europe is 22.9 hectares for France and 10.2 hectares for Italy (Table 8.1). Of the 33.8 million farm households in Japan, only about 10 per cent are engaged full-time in farming, defined as those whose livelihoods are entirely supported by agriculture, while more than 80 per cent combine farming with some other activity. Furthermore, for 60 per cent of these part-time farm households, farming is the secondary occupation, meaning that they have a higher income from their non-farming activity. It can, of course, be claimed that small-scale farming has been a consistent feature of agriculture since pre-war years, as the average farm size in Japan was only 1.09 hectares at the start of the Pacific War in 1941. As there has been no significant change in the size of farms over the last 50 years, and part-time farming has become extremely common, we should perhaps regard these as characteristic features of Japanese agriculture.

3. Pre-war agriculture and agricultural associations

3.1. Pre-war agriculture

Japanese agriculture has traditionally been undertaken by large numbers of small-scale farm households. Many of these were rice farmers who supplemented wet rice cultivation with cash crops such as silkworms and vegetables. This basic pattern first took shape during the Edo period, and developed further amid the growth process into a modern state that took place after the Meiji Restoration (1868).[8] To combat the limitations brought about by the scarcity of land, technical advances, such as improved seed and fertilizer, tended to make use of labour while saving land, leading to the development of a highly labour-intensive, irrigated agriculture based on wet paddy cultivation.

Agricultural productivity grew prodigiously during the Meiji period, and enabled domestic agriculture to fulfil the increased demand for food brought about by the rapid population growth of that period. However, during the first decade of the twentieth century it became increasingly difficult to meet the food demand, and soon rice was being regularly imported (Figure 8.1). The imports were mostly the indica rice variety from South-East Asia, which differed significantly in flavour and quality from the home-grown varieties and thus did not compete head-on with domestically grown rice.

At this time, rice was traded in a free, competitive market, and distributed through commercial dealers. The Meiji-period rice market initially consisted of large numbers of local markets, having grown out of the Edo-period marketing system of tax rice and local (merchant's) rice, but with the increase in urban demand due to population growth and the building of railway networks, it expanded into a distribution market that covered the whole country. During this process, the fortunes of different routes of distribution rose and fell, competition thrived among brands originating in different producing areas, and the government refrained from active interference in the market (Mochida 1970).

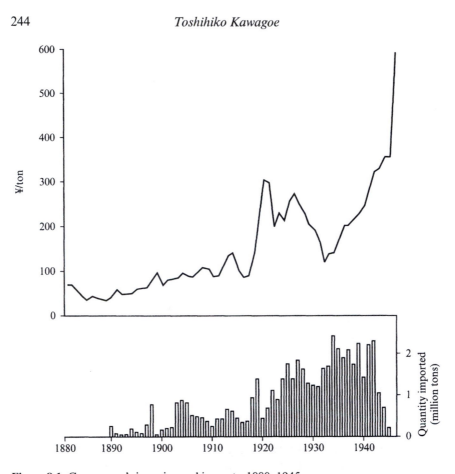

Figure 8.1. Consumers' rice price and imports, 1880–1945

Notes: Prices based on Tokyo standard rice price (unpolished rice) up to 1941; after 1941, the nation-wide consumers' price. Imported quantities include rice from Korea and Formosa.

Source: Ministry of Agriculture, Forestry, and Fisheries (*f*).

Government policy on rice began to change in the Taishō period (starting in 1912), and most changes came about during the inter-war period. Towards the end of the First World War, starting from about 1917, inflation led to big rises in the price of rice (Figure 8.1), sparking rice riots. The government sought to respond by increasing production, bringing the Reclamation Subsidy Act (*Kaikon Josei Hō*) into effect in 1919, and formulating a plan to increase rice cultivation in the Korean peninsula. The Rice Act (*Beikoku Hō*) of 1921 established a permanent system designed to regulate rice demand, and this enabled the government to buy up or sell off rice as circumstances required. It was backed up with a Special Accounting for Rice Supply and Demand Regulation Act (*Beikoku Jukyū Chōsetsu Tokubetsu Kaikei Hō*), and these together were the forerunners of the subsequent food-control system.

As regards international trade, after the revision of the Tariff Rate Act (*Kanzei Teiritsu Hō*) in 1910, import duty was levied on foreign rice in order to protect small farmers, but it was only after 1927 that it was enforced regularly in order to exert control over the market (Ouchi 1960: 226–7).

The Rice Act had been brought into being by soaring rice prices, but by the time it came into effect the economy was already in the throes of the world-wide recession that followed the First World War, and agricultural prices were falling. Furthermore, rice was more abundant as a result of the schemes to increase production in the Korean peninsula and Taiwan. Not only had these colonies' capability to ship out rice been strengthened, but the quality of the rice they produced had greatly improved. Rice from the colonies came more and more to rival domestically grown rice, adding further impetus to domestic price stagnation.

In view of these circumstances, the Rice Act was revised on several occasions, and the first revision of 1925 stipulated regulation of market prices. From 1930, effects of the world-wide Great Depression that began in 1929 began to be felt, and the prices of rice and other agricultural produce slumped, precipitating a grave crisis in agriculture. The crisis hit farming communities severely, plunging many farm households into debt, and sparking off frequent tenancy disputes. In 1931 the Rice Act was again revised. A licence system for rice imports and exports, and a system of floor and ceiling prices for government purchases and sales of rice were introduced. In the following year, a third revision set out a calculation method for floor and ceiling prices based on farm household expenses and production costs, and gave the government the right to purchase and sell rice from overseas. Then in 1933, the Rice Act was superseded by a Rice Control Act (*Beikoku Tōsei Hō*), which introduced a system permitting unlimited purchasing and selling of rice within floor and ceiling prices.

Thus, government intervention in the rice market slowly increased in scope during the inter-war period. Initially it was intended to bring about price stability, but later, due to the world-wide depression, and then through the tightening of the demand and supply situation with the approach of war, intervention gradually turned into rigid economic control. At the time all this was happening, agricultural associations were being put in place under a government policy of protecting and promoting agriculture. Let us look at this next.

3.2. The development and proliferation of agricultural associations

Starting in the Meiji period, agricultural associations developed as two different types of organization: agricultural societies (*nōkai*) and industrial associations (Table 8.2). The former handled technical aspects of agricultural production, mostly in the form of providing advice, while the latter were

Table 8.2. Development of agricultural associations and food policy

Agricultural associations and their policies		Food supply and demand situation; major agricultural policies
Agricultural societies (*Nōkai*)	Industrial associations (*Sangyō kumiai*)	
1880—*Nōdankai* (organized for exchange of information on agricultural techniques)		
1881—Japan Agricultural Association formed (nation-wide organization of *Nōdankai* groups)		
	1893—Organizations analogous to industrial associations formed	
1893—Moves to establish central, prefectural, district, and village-level organizations		
1895—*Zenkoku Nōjikai* breaks away from Japan Agricultural Association		
1899—Agricultural Societies Act (mostly regulations on subsidies)		
	1900—Industrial Associations Act	
	1905—Central Union for Japan Industrial Associations established	
	1910—Central Union of Industrial Unions founded	
1910—Agricultural Societies Act revised; Imperial Agricultural Society founded (systematic organization of agricultural associations)		
	1917—Agricultural Warehousing Act	
		1918—Rice riots
		1919—Reclamation Subsidy Act
		1920—1st Term Korean Rice Multiplication Plan devised
	1921—Rice Act (preferential purchase of rice from industrial associations)	
1922—(New) Agricultural Societies Act implemented (payment of association fees made compulsory, abolition of limits on subsidies, etc.)		

1929—Great Depression, agricultural crisis, and slump in rice price

1931—Rice Act revised (licence system introduced for imports and exports)

1932—Rice Act revised

1933—Rice Control Act (unlimited purchases and sales at official prices)

1938—Farmland Adjustment Law; allocation system for fertilizer

1939—Rice Distribution Control Act (licence system for rice dealers introduced, rice exchange abolished); Farm Rent Control Law; severe drought in western Japan and Korea

1940—Rice Control Rules (government control of rice, delivery quotas)

1942—Food Control Law

1946—Land reform

1946—Emergency Measures for Food (strong measures to assure rice deliveries instituted)

1931—National Federation of Rice Selling and Purchasing Associations founded (business expanded under rice control); Central Bank of Industrial Unions founded

1932—Anti-Association Movement; Rural Economy Revival Plan

1933—5-year Plan for Industrial Association Expansion

1940—Agricultural Societies Act revised (control of production and distribution vested in agricultural associations)

1941—Agricultural Production Adjustment Order (planting, organizing agricultural labour, abandoning farming, etc. are all controlled through agricultural associations)

1943—Agricultural Associations Act (various agricultural and industrial associations integrated to form Nōgyōkai)

1945—GHQ delivers 'Memorandum on Land Reform'

1947—Agricultural Co-operatives Act

1951—Agricultural Co-operatives Reconstruction and Adjustment Act

Sources: Ministry of Agriculture, Forestry, and Fisheries (*f*); also *Nōrinsuisan Shō Hyakunen Shi*; *Teikoku Nōkai Shikō*.

involved in the economic activities of marketing, purchasing, and credit arrangements.

The origins of the *nōkai* can be traced back to *nōdankai*, or farmers' meetings, which began around 1874 as spontaneous meetings of conscientious farmers and certain landowners. The *nōdankai* encouraged active exchange of information on better agricultural techniques and new plant varieties, against a background of growing interaction between the different regions of the country with the rapid development of the commercial economy. Then in the 1880s, as part of government policy to encourage agriculture, conventional agricultural methods were improved, and the *nōdankai* began to receive active support and were included in agricultural policy.[9] In 1881 the Greater Japan Agricultural Society (*Dai Nippon Nōkai*) was created to organize the individual *nōdankai* operating separately all over the country. As most of its officers were government officials from the Ministry of Agriculture and Commerce, it had the hallmarks of being a government creation, but it may be described as Japan's first agricultural association.

The Greater Japan Agricultural Society made its main concern the improvement of farming techniques through the exchange of knowledge and experience of agricultural affairs, and it avoided activities related to agricultural policy. But discontent among the land-owning class eventually led to a split, and the *Zenkoku Nōjikai* broke away in 1895 to become an independent organization for agricultural policy activities. From about this time, the *nōkai* began to agitate for legalization in order to strengthen their organizations, and in 1899 the Agricultural Societies Act (*Nōkai Hō*) was promulgated, coming into effect the following year.

During demands for legalization, the question of compulsory membership and the right to levy obligatory membership fees was raised. However, the Matsukata Cabinet was opposed to this from the standpoint of freedom, non-interference and non-intervention in private enterprise, and the Agricultural Societies Act was limited to regulations on subsidies. It was due to this that the *nōkai* started at such an early stage to become dependent on subsidies.[10] Subsequently demands were heard for *Zenkoku Nōjikai* to be made the central body of the agricultural associations, but this never came about due to government opposition. However, centralized organization was accomplished with a further revision of the Agricultural Societies Act in 1910, when the Imperial Agricultural Society (*Teikoku Nōkai*) was founded to be the central organ of the *nōkai*, and branch associations were set up at national, prefectural, district, and village levels, thus establishing an integrated system of *nōkai*.

The other type of agricultural organization was the industrial associations, which can also be traced back to the early Meiji years. Industrial association-type organizations first appeared at that time, but their numbers only began to grow significantly from about the turn of the century. They were largely credit and marketing associations. The credit associations had grown out of the *kō* and *mujin*, the mutual financing associations of the Edo period, and the marketing associations were set up by groups of entrepreneurs in the same business, mostly handling exported products such as tea and raw-silk thread, for the purposes of joint marketing and quality enhancement. From the middle of the Meiji period, purchasing groups began forming to purchase fertilizers. All these different groups were finally organized after the Industrial Associations Act (*Sangyō Kumiai Hō*) came into force in 1900. This Act recognized four types of industrial association: for credit, marketing, purchasing, and production. In the first year 21 organizations were approved by regional officials as industrial associations, and the numbers grew rapidly, to 2,000 five years later and more than 10,000 by the early years of the Taishō period. In 1909 the Industrial Associations Act was revised, approving the linkage of separate regional industrial associations in the Federation of Industrial Associations (*Sangyō Kumiai Rengokai*), with the Central Union (*Chūō Kai*) as its national organization. In this way industrial associations, like the *nōkai*, achieved a systematic integrated organization reaching from the centre to village level.

From the Taishō period and the pre-war years of the Shōwa period, industrial associations increased dramatically to about 15,000 in number, and by about 1940 more than 90 per cent of farm households were members (Table 8.3). It should be noted that this took place against a background of various government protectionist and promotional policies.

As an example of one such policy related to rice, the Agricultural Warehousing Act (*Nōgyō Sōkogyō Hō*) was established in 1917 to provide subsidies for the building of warehouses for farm produce. These were facilities for the assembly, joint storage, and joint shipping of farm produce such as rice, silk cocoons, sugar, etc., and they were almost all run by industrial associations. There were about 1,000 such warehouses in 1921, and by the late 1930s the number had reached between 5,000 and 6,000. As we saw previously, under the Rice Act of 1921 the government made preferential purchases of rice handled by the industrial associations, which also encouraged the rapid increase in

Table 8.3. Industrial associations and their membership, 1910–1939

	1910	1920	1930	1939
Number of industrial associations	7,308	13,442	14,082	15,101
Number of association members ('000)	534	2,290	4,743	7,709
of which farmers (1)	438	1,838	3,424	5,196
Total no. of farm households ('000) (2)	5,417	5,485	5,511	5,390
Proportion of farm-household members (= (1)/(2)) (%)	8	34	62	96

Sources: *Sangyō Kumiai Yōran* (Industrial Association Review); no. of farm households from Kayo (1977: Table C-a-1).

numbers of agricultural warehouses. In 1925, rice accounted for 18 per cent by value of the marketing business of industrial associations, and by 1935 this figure exceeded 40 per cent, and is estimated to have covered about 30 per cent of the distribution of rice nation-wide.[11]

From the early years of Shōwa, the growing use of the industrial associations for the implementation of a variety of agricultural policies was further impetus for their expansion. For instance, lending by the national treasury for fertilizer purchase, and the promotion of the Rural Economy Revival Plan (*Nōsangyoson Keizai Kōsei Keikaku*) after 1932, were both implemented by means of industrial associations and the *nōkai*. The Rural Economy Revival Plan was implemented to help the impoverished rural population at the time of the Shōwa Crisis, and was a comprehensive economic policy measure that included provision of low-interest loans, price support for agricultural produce, implementation of public-works projects, and so on. The nomination of industrial associations for the implementation of this plan encouraged farm households to become members and make use of these benefits. The industrial associations themselves took the opportunity to work at expanding their organizations by drawing up their own Five-Year Plan for Industrial Association Expansion (*Sangyō Kumiai Kakujū Gokanen Keikaku*). The result can be seen in their marketing and purchasing activities: in the five years between 1932 and 1937 their share of the rice market doubled and the wheat market grew fourfold, while sales turnover of chemical fertilizer grew from 19 per cent to 40 per cent of the total volume traded nation-wide.[12]

This series of preferential policies favouring the industrial associations, and the corresponding growth of these associations, of course met with strong resistance from established rice and fertilizer dealers. They formed a National Dealers' Rights Defence League (*Zen Nippon Shōken Yōgo Renmei*), and campaigned against the various tax-exemption mechanisms, low-interest financing, and provision of subsidies made to the industrial associations. Thus it was during this period that the so-called Anti-Association Movement (*Han San Undō*) gained strength. But as the economy shifted to a wartime system and economic controls got stronger, these opposition movements were to fizzle out.

4. The agricultural controls of the wartime economy

As we have seen in the preceding section, the rice market was formerly free and competitive but gradually more and more control was imposed, starting with the Rice Act of 1921, and then with the crash of the rice price due to world-wide depression. With the promulgation of the Rice Distribution Control Act (*Beikoku Haikyū Tōsei Hō*) in 1939, the rice exchange was abolished, and a licensing system for rice dealers introduced. Prior to this, legislation on emergency measures for rice (*Beikoku no Ōkyū Sochi ni kansuru Hōritsu*) was enacted, which was to enable the government to secure supplies of rice for the military. Thus, up to this point controls were largely involved with distribution procedures, and although a rationing system for fertilizer had been introduced, there were no direct controls affecting agricultural production.

Direct controls on agriculture began during the war years. They were precipitated by food shortages dating from 1939, when Korea and western Japan were afflicted by severe drought. The export of Korean rice halted, and the domestic demand and supply situation rapidly began to tighten. Domestic production peaked in the same year and subsequently declined. The decline was put down to the loss of farm labour and to shortages of fertilizers, agricultural chemicals and other materials. In 1940 supply quotas were imposed on producers and landowners, and in the following year controls on agricultural prices, the compulsory cultivation of abandoned land, and planting controls were implemented. Rationing was introduced to control consumption, and was gradually extended to cover more and more items. In 1942 the various controls affecting rice were consolidated and expanded into a Food Control Law (*Shokuryō Kanri Hō*). This finalized the imposition of direct government control on staple foodstuffs such as rice, and thus the production, distribution and consumption of agricultural products all came under strict government control.

As controls were gradually tightened, it was the agricultural associations that were used to implement them. The 1940 revision of the Agricultural Societies Act conferred control of production and shipping on the *nōkai*. Further tightening was imposed the following year and the *nōkai* had to take on the preparation and implementation of plans covering everything from planting to organization of farm labour, and allocation of production resources. As agricultural production was in the hands of large numbers of small-scale farm households, it was not easy for the government directly to implement such control measures as allocation for planned production. On the other hand, the agricultural associations such as the *nōkai* and industrial associations had integrated organizations reaching out from a central headquarters to the towns and villages, and almost all farm households were members, so it was logical to make use of them as a means of imposing controls. The agricultural associations had already been used to implement the Rural Economy Revival Plan at the time of the Shōwa Crisis and now came to be used again, this time to control the expansion of food production.

Regarding the implementation of controls, a highly significant role was played by the *nōjijikkōkumiai* and *nōkashōkumiai*, both small groups of farm households which formed the lowest level of agricultural association. These groups had grown out of village assemblies in rural communities defined and bound together by powerful blood and neighbourhood ties, and were basically separate from the *nōkai* system. But from the Taishō period onwards, the *nōkai* encouraged the establishment of these community organizations, and incorporated them at the lowest level of the organizational hierarchy. In the 1940 revision of the Agricultural Societies Act they were specified as coming under the town and village level *nōkai*, thus completing the pyramid of control: from government through *nōkai* and then through small village associations to farm households. From 1941 the town and village level *nōkai* were given the authority to draw up and implement agricultural production plans, but in reality they supervised the small village associations that had the production targets to meet, and achieving the target was the joint responsibility of these villages (Tanaka 1979).

In 1943 a new Agricultural Associations Act (*Nōgyō Dantai Hō*) came into force, and all agricultural groups, including the *nōkai* and industrial associations, were integrated into *nōgyōkai*. This brought together the two organizations that had often come into confrontation over their spheres of activity, namely the *nōkai* and the industrial associations, and sought to simplify control measures. The two central organizations, the Imperial Agricultural Society (*Teikoku Nōkai*) and the Central Union of Industrial Associations (*Sangyō Kumiai Chūōkai*) were combined to form the Central Union of Associations for Agricultural Affairs (*Chūō Nōjikai*), and at the prefectural, and town and village levels all the various associations and groups were turned into associations for agricultural affairs (*Nōjikai*).

5. Post-war food policy and Nōkyō

5.1. *Land reform and the launch of Nōkyō: the Federation of Agricultural Co-operative Associations*

After the war, land reform brought drastic change to rural communities. Before the war, half the agricultural land was tenant-farmed and one-third of all farm households were small-scale tenant farms. The purpose of land reform was to give these tenant farmers ownership rights over the land they cultivated. Under the supervision of the Occupation forces, a rigorous land-reform programme was implemented over five years from 1946. All agricultural land belonging to absentee landlords, and locally owned tenant farms exceeding 1 hectare in size, were forcibly purchased and sold to their current farmers. As a result, 90 per cent of the agricultural land became owner-farmed and tenant farmers virtually disappeared.[13]

Land reform evened out wealth and income disparities among farm households and is seen to have contributed significantly to the democratization and the political and social stability of rural communities in post-war Japan. Thus we can say that in terms of its political targets, land reform was a resounding success. However, it is not always evaluated so positively when considered from the standpoint of industrial policy (Kawagoe 1993*a*). This is first because land reform did not affect the structure of agricultural production. Ownership rights were simply transferred from the owner to the tenant cultivating the land, and tenant farmers thus became land-owning farmers, without any changes to the size of the units they farmed. The second reason was that the Agricultural Land Act (*Nōchi Hō*) brought about very tight control of the market for farmland.

The Agricultural Land Act was enacted in 1952 to perpetuate the results of land reform and prevent any reversion to the former land-ownership system. This was not entirely new legislation, but a single act designed to replace the wartime Farmland Adjustment Law (*Nōchi Chōsei Hō*), the Owner-Farmer Establishment Special Measures Act (*Jisakunō Sōsetsu Tokubetsu Sochi Hō*), the legal basis for the implementation of land reform, and Government Ordinance 307 (*Seirei 307-go*). Under the Agricultural Land Act, the purchase, sale, or rent of agricultural land was subject to strict regulations. For instance, rents were frozen at extremely low levels, landowners found it almost impossible to repossess tenanted land because cultivators' rights had become so strong, and land ownership was limited to three hectares (12 in Hokkaido). Furthermore, the renting, buying, or selling of farmland required the approval of the local agricultural committee. All this had the effect of freezing ownership and use of farmland in the state it had been in immediately after the completion of land reform (Dore 1959: 198).

During the land-reform period, the agricultural associations were reorganized. The GHQ memorandum of December 1945 which gave the order for land reform also made reference to the agricultural associations. It required that plans be drawn up to remove oppressive government control of agricultural associations which ignored the interests of farmers, and encourage instead an agricultural-union movement to promote economic and cultural progress for the rural population.[14] The government responded with an agricultural unions bill which GHQ initially rejected on the grounds that it did not entirely purge the new unions of the characteristics of a control organization, but later, after a period of negotiations, it was enacted in 1947 as the Agricultural Co-operatives Act (*Nōgyō Kyōdō Kumiai Hō*).

According to this legislation, the new Nōkyō was intended to become an entirely different organization from the earlier *nōkai* and industrial associations. The *nōkai* were government-created organizations dependent on subsidies and requiring compulsory membership, and the industrial associations, under government protection, had become little more than agencies for the implementation of various policy measures. By contrast, the new Nōkyō was to be by definition an independent farmers' organization which would not suffer government interference. In reality, however, the new Nōkyō did not always adhere to the principles set out in the Agricultural Co-operatives Act.

The Agricultural Co-operatives Act also affected the *nōgyōkai*, which had been the implementing agency for government controls in the wartime economy. Measures were taken to prevent disposal of their assets, and in August

1948 they were disbanded. Their assets, their business, and their staff were almost all passed on, just as they were, to the new Nōkyō. This was done to avoid unnecessary social upheaval at the time the *nōgyōkai* were disbanded, but a further consideration was the need felt for an implementing agency working at the local level to handle the many agricultural products and raw materials still under control at that time. So ultimately the newly launched Nōkyō inherited a great deal from its forbears, the pre-war *nōkai* and industrial associations, not least their characters as agencies of control (Kajinishi *et al.* 1965: 1376–82).

By 1948, some 15,000 Nōkyō associations had already been set up, most of them being Sōgo Nōkyō.[15] In addition, more than 900 federations had been set up at prefectural and district level. Many of the Nōkyō associations were poorly managed, tiny organizations, and some ran into operational difficulties, so that by 1949, 43 per cent of the Sōgo Nōkyō were running deficits, and some even stopped the repayment of savings (*Nōrinsuisan Shō Hyakunen Shi*, vol. 3: 106–9). So in 1951 the government enacted the Agricultural Co-operatives Reconstruction and Adjustment Act (*Nōringyōgyō Kumiai Saiken Seibi Hō*) and provided financial assistance in the form of incentive grants and interest subsidies on borrowed funds. As a result of this and other subsequent reconstruction measures, Nōkyō management improved from the second half of the 1950s. However, this was also the period when the food-control system switched to become a system for the protection of producers.

5.2. The food-control system and Nōkyō

Although the food situation improved somewhat in the 1950s, the possibility of shortages persisted. Both producers' and consumers' rice prices were fixed at levels below international prices (Figure 8.2). In 1951, for example, the government purchase price of a ton of unpolished rice was ¥47,000 and the consumers' price was ¥49,000, whereas the import price was ¥71,800. To keep the consumers' rice price low, the producers' price was held down at an artificially low level. In other words, the food-control system was functioning at that time as a system to protect consumers.

Controls on agricultural products were gradually lifted under the Dodge Plan, and between 1950 and 1952 controls were abolished on fertilizer, potatoes, sugar, and minor cereals. Controls on wheat and barley were dropped and replaced with a government purchase system at parity prices. In 1950 the Liberal Party, then in power, proposed abolishing controls on rice, a move that would benefit producers by raising the artificially low producers' rice price. The government, initially cautious about this, later planned for the abolition of rice controls, so that subsidies on imported foodstuffs could be reduced, thereby helping to balance the budget. But the plan was opposed by Dodge

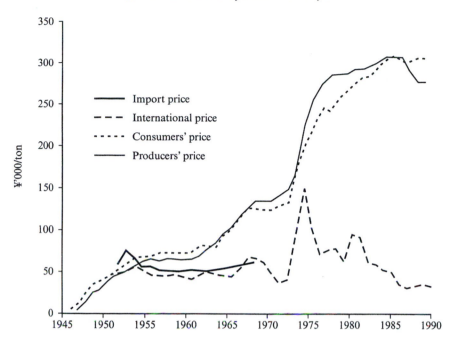

Figure 8.2. Producers', consumers', and international prices of rice in the post-war period, 1946–1990

Notes: To relate them to consumers' (government sale) prices, producers' (government purchase) prices are plotted against the year following that of production. Import price is the Food Agency price for rice imported from the Republic of Korea and Taiwan. International price is Bangkok f.o.b. price for polished 5% broken rice, converted to price for unpolished rice.

Sources: Ministry of Agriculture, Forestry, and Fisheries (*f*); IRRI (1988: Table 93).

and dropped. The reason is said to be that, with the Korean War situation deteriorating, there were fears that the resulting big increase in the consumers' rice price would re-ignite inflation, which was just then being brought under control (Ikeda 1952: 273–93; Mochida 1990: 141–4).

A fundamental food shortage continued. In 1953, storm and flood damage in western Japan combined with exceptionally low temperatures in eastern Japan to cause the rice crop to fail, and the following year's crop was also poor. The price of black-market rice remained high, and to ensure that producers supplied the government, the producers' price was raised 12.8 per cent in the first year and a further 9.5 per cent in the second. However, in a complete turnabout, the harvest in 1955 was excellent. At 12 million tons, rice production was 35 per cent higher than the average production of the previous five years, and the supply and demand situation greatly improved. It was from about this time that the domestic rice price began to exceed the import price.

Good rice harvests continued, but now were largely put down to improved techniques, such as the widespread introduction of protected rice nurseries. An annual production of 12 or 13 million tons became possible. Rice consumption per head, by contrast, peaked in 1962 and then began to decline, and overall demand for rice was shrinking.[16] Self-sufficiency in rice had been achieved, but the domestic market had quickly switched from shortage to surplus.

It should, by then, have been recognized that the food-control system had outlived its original purpose. But this was the period of high-speed growth, and the government tried to reduce the widening disparity in incomes between the industrial and agricultural sectors by increasing the income farmers gained from rice production. Under the food-control system, a transfer of income from the non-agricultural to the agricultural sector was implemented by means of agricultural protectionist policies centred on the high-rice-price policy. As a result, from the late 1950s onwards the domestic rice price rose sharply, and the disparity between that and the international price grew larger and larger. The food-control system which had previously functioned to protect consumers had been transformed into one that protected producers.

This trend became even more pronounced from 1960 onwards, when a production-cost and income-compensation formula (*Seisanhi Shotoku Hoshō*) was introduced to calculate the producers' rice price, which then increased by a large margin every year. This method established a rice price based on farmers' hours of labour, and calculated from average production costs over the previous three years and wage levels in non-agricultural sectors. This enabled the rice price to keep pace with the growth in wages in non-agricultural sectors. But on top of this, the obscure basis of calculation allowed the rice price to be manipulated for political reasons.

Under strong pressure from Nōkyō, the Liberal Democratic Party pressed for rice price increases through political negotiations with the government, and in exchange Nōkyō acted as a vote-gathering agency at election times. Through such an arrangement the food-control system became a means for both sides to protect their vested interests. As Figure 8.3 shows, between 1960, the year in which the production-cost and income-compensation formula was introduced, and 1969, when production regulation began, the rice price increased at a vastly higher rate than any other prices.

But of course, these rates of increase did not reflect market conditions and production efficiency, and made it possible for very small-scale, inefficient marginal farmers to continue with rice cultivation, thus becoming a major obstacle to the structural adjustment of Japanese agriculture. The rice price clearly acted in contradiction to basic agricultural policy of that time, which sought to increase farm size in order to modernize the structure of agriculture. Furthermore, attempting to achieve a social policy objective, income compensation, through an economic measure, price support, was both inefficient and unfair. The high-rice-price policy raised prices uniformly, regardless of scale or efficiency of production. Large-scale farmers' incomes soared because

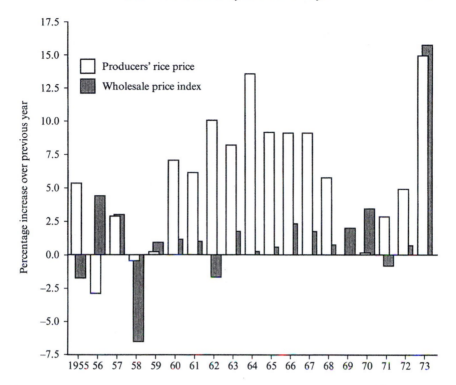

Figure 8.3. Increases in producers' rice price and wholesale prices, 1955–1973
Sources: Ministry of Agriculture, Forestry, and Fisheries (*f*); Kayo (1977: Table A-d-1).

of the large volumes they marketed, but small-scale farmers' incomes were very limited, despite the high prices, because they marketed only small quantities.[17]

Unsurprisingly, with increasing job opportunities outside agriculture, these small-scale farmers chose to take other jobs while continuing to grow rice. Because of the contradictions in policy, the government was not able to guide farmers in the direction it desired. It failed to promote independent, modern farming, and with almost all farmers becoming part-time farmers, the food-control system was further reduced to a meaningless shell.

The setting of a price for rice far higher than the market price naturally resulted in overproduction. The food-control system obliged the government to purchase rice, even in excess of needs, and this surplus rice accumulated, becoming 'old rice' (*komai*), to reach 7.2 million tons in 1970 (Figure 8.4). Moreover, the government's purchase price exceeded the selling price, and the loss this created, the so-called negative margin, caused the food-control account deficit to grow. On two occasions the government disposed of its stocks of *komai* by selling it for animal feed or industrial uses, but the selling

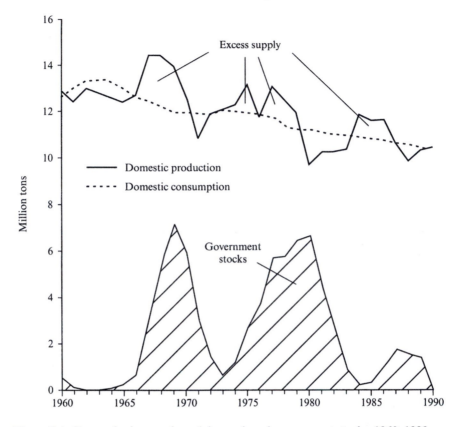

Figure 8.4. Domestic rice supply and demand, and government stocks, 1960–1990
Sources: Ministry of Agriculture, Forestry, and Fisheries (*a, f*).

price was extremely low, and the nation suffered a loss from this of ¥3 trillion (Management and Co-ordination Agency 1987).

To prevent surplus rice from building up and reduce the food-control account deficit, regulation of rice production began in 1969. The system offered subsidies to farmers who switched from rice to other crops, and this again created a large financial obligation. What is more, the measures were based on the continuing existence of the food-control system, and as attempts to resolve a failure of the market caused by excessive policy intervention with yet more regulations on switching crops, they were never likely to lead to a real solution of the problem.[18]

The beneficiaries of the food-control system were not only the rice farmers: Nōkyō also benefited considerably. Under the system, the government purchased rice through Nōkyō in its role as primary collecting agent, allowing Nōkyō to make a great deal of money from handling and storage charges.[19]

Table 8.4. Importance of agricultural co-operatives for farmers' savings and loans, 1960–1990 (¥'000, (%), averages for farm households nation-wide)

	1960	1970	1980	1990
Savings				
Agricultural co-operatives	101 (54)	820 (62)	3,766 (56)	7,879 (34)
Commercial banks, etc.[a]	87 (46)	495 (38)	2,957 (44)	15,000 (66)
Total	188 (100)	1,315 (100)	6,723 (100)	22,879 (100)
Loans				
Agricultural co-operatives	27 (46)	227 (59)	837 (51)	923 (43)
Treasury funds	10 (17)	70 (18)	270 (17)	381 (18)
Others	22 (37)	87 (23)	522 (32)	842 (39)
Total	59 (100)	384 (100)	1,629 (100)	2,146 (100)

[a] Includes postal savings.

Source: Ministry of Agriculture, Forestry, and Fisheries (*d*).

Furthermore, payment for rice was made through Nōkyō accounts, and these funds served to underpin Nōkyō's credit business. While other financial institutions had to compete aggressively to boost deposits, the food-control system enabled Nōkyō to build up deposits effortlessly. The proportion of farm households' savings held by Nōkyō (Table 8.4) is evidence of this.

Nōkyō was also used to implement a whole range of agricultural-policy measures quite apart from the food-control system, and through this was able to further its own business interests. For example, a system was launched in 1961 to provide low-interest loans through Nōkyō to farm households, under the Agricultural Basic Law Administration (*Kihon Hō Nōsei*), a strategy to modernize agriculture. Through the protectionist policies towards agriculture that began in the high-growth period a diverse range of subsidies flowed into rural communities. This stimulated the formation of a system within rural communities for support of the Liberal Democratic Party, in which Nōkyō has played no small role.

So with Nōkyō playing a number of different roles as the local-level agency in the administrative hierarchy, farmers had virtually no alternative but to join, even though membership was not obligatory. It was also deemed necessary to buy and sell one's produce and raw materials through Nōkyō to maintain good relations within the community. Thus Nōkyō's sales and purchasing business also expanded. At one time, rice accounted for as much as 60 per cent of Nōkyō's sales (Table 8.5), and even now, the food-control system gives Nōkyō a virtual monopoly in purchasing rice, while many other agricultural products are also marketed, and many raw materials purchased, through Nōkyō.

Of course, Nōkyō's economic activities are not in themselves anything to

Table 8.5. Agricultural co-operative sales and purchases by item, 1953–1989 (¥'00m., (%))

	1953	1970	1980	1989
Sales				
Rice	2,037 (59)	10,772 (51)	19,454 (35)	18,685 (30)
Vegetables	138 (4)	1,765 (8)	8,258 (15)	11,820 (19)
Fruit	0 (0)	1,989 (10)	5,659 (10)	7,123 (11)
Others	1,300 (37)	6,562 (31)	21,638 (40)	24,579 (40)
Total	3,475 (100)	21,088 (100)	55,009 (100)	62,207 (100)
Purchases				
Feed	126 (7)	2,840 (25)	7,874 (18)	5,524 (11)
Fertilizer	760 (43)	1,542 (13)	4,248 (10)	3,812 (8)
Agricultural machinery	99 (6)	1,224 (11)	2,047 (5)	3,410 (7)
Agricultural chemicals	66 (4)	672 (6)	2,528 (6)	2,977 (6)
Others	703 (40)	5,188 (45)	26,035 (61)	33,508 (68)
Total	1,754 (100)	11,466 (100)	42,732 (100)	49,231 (100)

Source: Ministry of Agriculture, Forestry, and Fisheries (*b*).

criticize. If a problem exists, it is that the heavily protected Nōkyō, beneficiary of preferential measures including various special tax privileges and exclusions from anti-monopoly laws, has moved into areas of business that compete with the private sector.[20]

Finally, I would like to refer to the policy of rice-acreage control as an example illustrating the mechanism through which Nōkyō has functioned as proxy for the administration, and as an agent to gather votes. To implement this policy, the government calculates the total area of paddy to be taken out of rice production every year on the basis of the demand for rice, and this is divided among the prefectures, and then among towns and villages. In each of the towns and villages an allocation has to be made to individual farm households, and this is the task Nōkyō, as 'farm management advisor', has performed, with the result that targets have always been met. One might say that this arrangement is in essence no different from the wartime agricultural associations organizing supply quotas to increase production.

Although Nōkyō's upper ranks have become heavily bureaucratic, at the local level it is based in village communities, and functions through the mutual regulation of parties in the community most typically seen in the deference shown to upholding good community relations (*tsukiai*). This has eased Nōkyō's task of imposing all manner of control measures in its role as implementing agency of government policy. The relationship of mutual dependence between Nōkyō and the government has been a continuing background feature from the war years all through the post-war era.

6. Conclusion

This chapter has focused on the food-control system and Nōkyō, the agricultural co-operatives organization, as characteristic features of present-day agriculture in Japan, or what might be called the Japanese system of agriculture. Before the First World War the market for farm produce was basically free and competitive, and agricultural associations, including industrial associations, were independent. This began to change from the time of the Shōwa Crisis, and during the war period the government increasingly intervened in agriculture and the market for farm produce in order to increase food production. The agricultural associations expanded through the role they acquired of implementing agency for government controls. A food-control system was perfected under the wartime economy to cope with food shortages, and a heavily planned economic system was created, with the agricultural associations used to implement the various controls.

After the war Japanese agriculture experienced a major upheaval in the form of land reform, and the agricultural associations were disbanded. The new Nōkyō set up after the war was launched as an independent organization operating under a new set of principles, but in reality it inherited many of the control-agency functions of the war years. The serious food shortages that continued for some years after the war necessitated a food-control system and the new Nōkyō was used to implement it, allocating supply quotas. Nōkyō itself was able to maintain and expand its own organization through its reliance on the food-control system. This arrangement, of the government using Nōkyō to implement policies and Nōkyō advancing its own interests through fulfilling that role, could be seen in many other instances of the carrying through of agricultural policy, not only the food-control system.

Looking at its functions slightly differently, Nōkyō could be described as the agricultural sector's industrial association, carrying through agricultural policy in the form of administrative guidance. An example illustrating this is the policy to switch from rice to other crops. The allocation of production cuts that this involved could be seen as a case of administrative guidance that required Nōkyō, the industrial association, to impose it. This is hardly different from the relationship between the supervisory ministries and industrial associations in other industrial sectors. If there is any difference, it is perhaps that any leverage in the agriculture sector, with its four to six million farm households, is politically extremely meaningful. Thus the system has been exploited for political purposes, as seen in the political 'bonus' added to the rice price.

The 'food-control system + Nōkyō' arrangement persisted through the high-growth period. A combination of the food-control system's high-rice-price policy, and the excessive controls on the agricultural land market imposed by the Agricultural Land Act, which took over wartime controls on farmland, held up structural adjustment in the agriculture sector, here meaning expansion of farm size, and hindered the modernization of agriculture.

Agriculture lost even more status during the high-growth period, and the disparity in incomes between the agricultural and industrial sectors widened. From about 1955 the supply and demand situation for rice improved and at that point the food-control system, having served out its purpose, should have been abolished. Instead, it was used as a means of transferring income to the agricultural sector, and so survived by changing into a system to protect agricultural producers. In other words, despite the changes to the economic environment after the war, the 'food-control system + Nōkyō' arrangement was maintained in the form it had taken during the war. It survived like this because of the existence of an extremely durable political and economic system which was based on mutual dependence between Nōkyō, acting as a political pressure group to protect profits in the agricultural sector and further its own interests, and the governing party, which relied on Nōkyō's vote-garnering strength.

With all the hallmarks of a planned economy, this system has persisted for more than half a century, and eliminated the concept of competition from post-war agriculture in Japan. The Agricultural Basic Law Administration, which was designed to modernize agriculture, was appropriate as a set of principles, but failed to direct the farming community in the way it intended because of the simultaneous implementation of conflicting policies of the Agricultural Land Act's strict controls on the land market and the high-rice-price policy. The problem of so-called incentive compatibility so often confronted in planned economies could not be avoided.

Farm households opted for part-time farming as the most logical choice in the circumstances they found themselves in, and as a result, income levels in farm households have overtaken those in the non-agricultural sector. But at the macro level, agriculture as a sector is in decline, and the food-control system has become an empty shell. Furthermore, the increase in part-time farmers has weakened Nōkyō's organizational capacity. As criticism of the protection afforded to agriculture intensifies, and pressure from overseas to open markets increases, the planned economy known as the Japanese agricultural system appears doomed to collapse, in just the same way that the planned economic systems of the Soviet Union and Eastern Europe collapsed.

Notes

1. Comparison based on the wholesalers' purchase price in the region of consumption of semi-controlled, medium-quality brand-name rice for Japanese rice, and millers' price of Californian Kokuho Rose rice for US rice (Forum for Policy Innovation

1990). The export price of Thai rice is the Bangkok f.o.b. price (Ministry of Agriculture, Forestry, and Fisheries (*c*)).
2. In the mid-1980s, agricultural subsidies accounted for as much as 80% of the total budget for agriculture (Hayami 1988: 57).
3. In 1955 the nominal protection rate for all agricultural produce was only 18% in Japan compared with 35% in Western Europe. For individual items, too, such as wheat, beef, milk, etc., levels of protection were lower in Japan than in Western Europe (Hayami 1988: 4–10).
4. Figures for 1990 (Ministry of Agriculture, Forestry, and Fisheries (*e*)). Of the total membership of 8.6 million, 5.5 million are farmers with full membership, and the remaining 3.1 million are associate members who are not farming.
5. Total deposits in the 13 city banks for FY1989 amounted to ¥340.35 trillion (Ministry of Finance, Banking Bureau 1990).
6. For the sake of international comparisons, the number of people employed in agriculture is here taken as FAO's estimate of the economically active population in agriculture (FAO 1987).
7. Total cultivated land according to agricultural census, divided by the total number of farm households (Ministry of Agriculture, Forestry, and Fisheries (*b*)).
8. For more on the agriculture of the Edo period and social structure in rural villages, see Smith (1959).
9. For example, in 1883, 545 *nōdankai* are reported to have been set up around the country (*Sangyō Kumiai Hattatsu Shi* (History of the Development of Industrial Associations), vol. 3: 452).
10. See Ministry of Agriculture, Forestry, and Fisheries, *Nōrinsuisan Shō Hyakunen Shi* (100-Year History of the Ministry of Agriculture, Forestry, and Fisheries), vol. 1: 241.
11. *Sangyō Kumiai Nenkan* (Industrial Associations Yearbook), 15 (1943): 142; *Sangyō Kumiai Hattatsu Shi* (History of the Development of Industrial Associations), 4: 6. Behind this increase in business was the establishment in 1931 of the Japan Federation of Industrial Associations for Rice Trading (*Zenkoku Beikoku Hanbai Kōbai Kumiai Rengōkai*) as the central organ for sales, and the formation of separate national federations for sales, purchasing, and utilization, made possible by the revision of the Industrial Associations Act in 1921.
12. See *Sangyō Kumiai Hattatsu Shi* (History of the Development of Industrial Associations), 4: 434.
13. In 1955, when land reform was completed, the remaining tenant-farmed land accounted for 9% of all cultivated land, and the proportion of tenant farmers who owned no agricultural land at all was 4% of all farm households (Kawagoe 1993*a*).
14. This was the SCAPIN-411 Rural Land Reform memorandum of 9 December. *Nōchi Kaikaku Shiryō Shusei*, 14: 114–16.
15. If non-paying associations are included, about 30,000 associations were set up (Kayo 1977: Tables P-b-1, 3).
16. Annual per capita consumption of rice reached a peak of 118 kg in 1962 and subsequently saw a steady decline. It was 70 kg in 1990.
17. The income of a rice farmer for a day's labour (1988) was ¥21,122 on farms greater than 3 ha., but on farms smaller than 0.3 ha. it was only ¥4,568. The rate for day labourers working in the cities was ¥13,824, so the income of large-scale rice farmers was more than 50% higher than that of urban labourers (Kawagoe 1993*b*).

18. The social costs created by the food-control system and the crop-switching policy have been estimated at 40% to 70% of total agricultural income in 1985, reaching between 1.7 and 2.1 trillion yen (Otsuka and Hayami 1985).
19. Only Ministry of Agriculture, Forestry, and Fisheries-authorized dealers could purchase rice from farmers, but in 1985, 70% were Nōkyō co-operatives and they handled 95% of the total shipped quantity of rice (Management and Co-ordination Agency 1987).
20. Nōkyō's economic activities benefiting from preferential measures are frequently criticized in financial quarters and elsewhere as pressurizing private-sector business. See Management and Co-ordination Agency (1987) for the results of a survey of Nōkyō.

References

Central Union of Agricultural Co-operatives (Zenkoku Nōgyō Kyōdō Kumiai Chūōkai), *Nōgyō Kyōdō Kumiai Nenkan* (Annual Report of Agricultural Co-operatives), various issues.

Dore, R. P. (1959), *Land Reform in Japan*, London: Oxford University Press.

FAO (1987), *Production Yearbook*, Rome: UN Food and Agriculture Organization.

Hayami, Yujiro (1986), *Nōgyō Keizai Ron* (Agricultural Economics), Iwanami Shoten.

——(1988), *Japanese Agriculture under Siege: The Political Economy of Agricultural Policies*, London: Macmillan.

Ikeda, Hayato (1952), *Kinkō Zaisei* (Balanced Financial Policy), Tokyo: Jitsugyō no Nihon-sha.

IRRI (1988), *World Rice Statistics 1987*, Los Baños, Philippines: International Rice Research Institute.

Kajinishi, Mitsuhaya, Toshihiko Kato, Kiyoshi Oshima, and Tsutomu Ouchi (1965), *Nihon Shihonshugi no Botsuraku V-sōsho: Nihon ni okeru Shihonshugi no Hattatsu 10* (Decline of Capitalism in Japan series, vol. 5: History of Japanese Capitalism, 10), Tokyo: University of Tokyo Press.

Kawagoe, Toshihiko (1993a), 'Land Reform in Post-war Japan', in Juro Teranishi and Yutaka Kosai (eds.), *The Japanese Experience of Economic Reforms*, London: St Martin's Press.

——(1993b), 'Deregulation and Protectionism in Japanese Agriculture', in Juro Teranishi and Yutaka Kosai (eds.), *The Japanese Experience of Economic Reforms*, London: St Martin's Press.

Kayo, Nobufumi (1977) (ed.), *Kaitei Nihon Nōgyō Kiso Tōkei* (Basic Statistics on Japanese Agriculture), rev. edn., Tokyo: Nōrin Tōkei Kyōkai.

Korenaga, Tohiko (1984), 'Kokusai Hikaku ni yoru Kengyō Nōgyō (International Comparisons of Part-Time Farmers)', in Toshiaki Matsuura and Tohiko Korenaga (eds.), *Senshinkoku Nōgyō no Kengyō Mondai* (Issues on Part-Time Farming in Developed Countries), Research Monograph 102, Tokyo: National Research Institute of Agricultural Economics.

Management and Co-ordination Agency, Administrative Inspection Bureau (1987), *Shokuryō Kanri no Genjō to Mondaiten* (Survey and Issues on the Food-Control System), Tokyo: Ministry of Finance Printing Office.

Ministry of Agriculture and Commerce (Nōshōmu-shō), *Sangyō Kumiai Yōran* (Report on Co-operatives), various issues.

Ministry of Agriculture, Forestry, and Fisheries, JMAFF (Nōrinsuisan-shō) (*a*), *Shokuryō Jukyū Hō* (Food Balance Sheets), various issues.

——(*b*), *Pocket Nōrin Suisan Tōkei* (Pocket Book Statistics on Agriculture, Forestry, and Fisheries), Tokyo: Nōrin Tōkei Kyōkai, various issues.

——(*c*), *Nōgyō Hakusho Fuzoku Tōkei Hyō* (Statistical Appendix to the Agricultural White Paper), Tokyo: Nōrin Tōkei Kyōkai, various issues.

——(*d*), *Nōka Keizai Chōsa Hōkoku* (Farm Household Survey), Tokyo: Nōrin Tōkei Kyōkai, various issues.

——(*e*), *Sōgō Nōkyō Tōkei Hyō* (Statistics of Farmers' Co-operatives), Tokyo: Nōrin Tōkei Kyōkai, various issues.

——(*f*), Shokuryō-chō (Food Agency), *Shokuryō Kanri Tōkei Nenpō* (Annual Statistics for Staple Food Control), Tokyo: Food Agency, various issues.

——Hyakunen-shi Hensan Iinkai (1979, 1980, 1981), *Nōrinsuisan-shō Hyakunen Shi* (A Century of the Ministry of Agriculture, Forestry, and Fisheries), Tokyo: Nōrin Tōkei Kyōkai.

Ministry of Finance, Banking Bureau, *Ginkō-kyoku Kin'yū Nenpō* (Banking Bureau Financial Annual), Tokyo: Kin'yū Zaisei Jigyō Kenkyūkai.

Mochida, Keizo (1970), *Beikoku Shijō no Tenkai Katei* (Development Process of the Rice Market), Tokyo: University of Tokyo Press.

——(1990), *Nihon no Kome* (Rice in Japan), Chikuma Library, vol. 45, Tokyo: Chikuma Shobo.

Nōchi Kaikaku Shiryō Hensan Iinkai (ed.), (1982), *Nōchi Kaikaku Shiryō Shūsei* (Collected Documents on Land Reform), vol. 14, GHQ/ESCAP documents, Tokyo: Nōsei Chōsa Kai, Ochanomizu Shobo.

Otsuka, Keijiro and Yujiro Hayami (1985), 'Goals and Consequences of Rice Policy in Japan, 1965–80', *American Journal of Agricultural Economics*, 67: 529–38.

Ouchi, Tsutomu (1960), *Nihon Nōgyō Shi* (Japanese Agricultural History), Tokyo: Tōyō Keizai Shinpō-sha.

Sangyō Kumiai Chūō Kai (1935, 1943), *Sangyō Kumiai Nenkan* (Co-operatives' Annual), vols. 8 and 15 (reprinted 1986, Tokyo: Kashiwa Shobō).

Sangyō Kumiai Shi Hensan Kai (1966), *Sangyō Kumiai Hattatsu Shi* (History of Co-operatives), vols. 1–5, Tokyo: Sangyō Kumiai-shi Kankō Kai.

Seisaku Kohsoh Forum (Forum for Policy Innovation) (1990), *Toward Tariffication for Opening the Rice Market in Japan: A Design to Promote International Harmony and Domestic Agricultural Development*, Tokyo: Seisaku Kohsoh Forum.

Smith, Thomas C. (1959), *The Agrarian Origins of Modern Japan*, Stanford: Stanford University Press.

Tanaka, Manabu (1979), 'Senji Nōgyō Tōsei (Wartime Regulations on Agriculture)', in Tokyo University, Institute of Social Science (ed.), *Fashizumu-ki no Kokka to Shakai, 2: Senji Nihon Keizai* (The State and Society Under Fascism, 2: Wartime Japanese Economy), Tokyo: University of Tokyo Press.

9

Japan's Present-Day Economic System: Its Structure and Potential for Reform

Masahiro Okuno-Fujiwara

1. Introduction

Japan's present-day economic system is often called the 'Japanese economic model'. This is because many people, whether they are aware of it or not, regard this system as very different from those of Europe and America, particularly the US system. The characteristic features of labour–management relations in Japan, such as long-term fixed employment, pay by seniority, and internal promotion; the features of the financial markets such as the preference for indirect funding and the main bank system; the characteristics of relations among firms, such as subcontracting and *keiretsu* alignments; the weakness of small shareholders, their power undermined by the practice of crossholdings of shares as well as boards comprised almost exclusively of internally promoted directors; government–enterprise relations, such as the liberal use of administrative guidance and the unique status of industrial associations run by ex-Ministry officials—these are frequently described as special characteristics of the Japanese economic model, and are rarely seen in other countries.

Views that stress the distinctness of Japan's economic system and its various differences from those of other countries are often referred to as theories of 'Japan's uniqueness' and are seen as deviating from orthodox economics. Mainstream Marxist economics holds that economic systems and structures make progress through history, and therefore many of the Japanese structures are seen as evidence of the backwardness of the Japanese economy. This standpoint would suggest that the elimination of such backward structures is the first necessary step for the modernization of the Japanese economy. Modern orthodox economics (neo-classical economics), on the other hand, has a theoretical framework that is defined in terms of Anglo-Saxon economic systems and structures, and the Japanese structures that differ from them are regarded as anomalous and misguided.

In contrast to these 'historically progressive' views that traditional economics takes as read, recent developments in the discipline are now coming up with numerous tests to analyse different economic systems and structures, tests that are free of preconceptions and use a pluralistic and non-hierarchical approach. This new area of research in economics is called *comparative institutional analysis*.[1] At this time of world-wide upheaval in economic systems as well as in political and diplomatic arenas, a time which requires an exploration of manifold possibilities for the future of the planet and the human race, the task of making an objective comparative analysis of Japan's economic system with the systems of other countries, especially those of Europe and America, is of undoubted significance.

My initial purpose in this chapter is to explain two points of fundamental importance to a study of the Japanese economic system using comparative institutional analysis. The first is that it is by no means inevitable that particular systems and structures will become established in a certain society. It is possible for totally different, yet stable, systems and structures to exist in two otherwise identical societies, because the systems that develop and become stable features in a society are usually the outcome of accidents of history. This is known as path-dependence. The second point is that the sort of economic structures that develop in a society will largely depend on what other structures are already in existence. The systems and structures to be found within one society do not exist in isolation but support one another in a complementary fashion, and it is precisely because of this that the whole persists as a stable economic system.

Other chapters have examined the historical chain of events that have brought about the present-day economic system. This can be summarized very simply by saying that most of the components of the present-day system were created at the time of the Sino-Japanese and Pacific Wars, through the *switch to a planned economy* that was needed to mobilize national resources for the wartime economy, and the *economic controls* that carried through the changes. Needless to say, superficially, the wartime economic system has been changed out of all recognition through the post-war democratization process imposed by the Occupation authorities, high-speed economic growth, and international integration of the economy. Nevertheless, as we have seen in other chapters, the essential nature of the present-day system was hammered out of a wartime system forcibly imposed by the authorities through the national mobilization programme.

The reasons underlying the current interest in these historical events derive from a realization of the need to address certain issues: how should the current economic system be reformed, and what are the crucial points that need to be considered if the Japanese system is to be transplanted to other countries as a development strategy? Growing economic friction with Europe and America and the rapid pace of international integration of the economy are fuelling demands for the reform of a system currently lacking transparency and international access. On the other hand, increasing interest is being shown in transplanting the Japanese system both to build market economies in the countries of the former Soviet Union and Eastern Europe, whose planned economies have collapsed, and as a development strategy for the developing countries that Japan and the newly industrialized economies (NIEs) have outpaced in the race for economic development.

My second purpose here is to draw attention to circumstances which form the background to the analysis made in this book. The various structural elements of the present-day Japanese economic system are characterized by the fact that each is strongly complementary to the others. If these elements had been introduced separately and independently, they would not have taken root or become stable practices, and the system may not have been created at all. In this sense, the birth of this system appears to be largely dependent on the fact that due to the wartime emergency, system-wide changes took place throughout the whole economy. In this chapter I would like to explore such possibilities, and use economic theory, in particular comparative institutional analysis, for an examination of the nature of the system's structural elements.

2. 'Co-operative games' and historical chance

This book has examined the *systemic features* of the Japanese economy, or more precisely its various *structures* and *practices*. What is clear from looking at Japanese labour relations is that the economic structures and practices existing in a free society such as Japan's are not necessarily created or maintained by force of law or authority. Despite the fact that no legal barriers prevent other structures or practices from being adopted, in most cases maintaining the existing ones has for some reason been considered advantageous by those involved, and they have taken hold and become the 'system'. The issue here is how incentives come about that drive the people involved to maintain structures and practices. I would like to examine this as an example of a *co-operative game*, a well-known technique from game theory.

Two people, one going up (A) and one going down (B), have to pass each other on a narrow staircase. Unlike driving on the roads, which side we pass others on a staircase is a matter of individual choice. Assuming that A and B have only two choices: to walk on the right (strategy $S = 0$) or to walk on the left (strategy $S = 1$), there are four possible situations that may arise on the staircase, as shown in the boxes of Figure 9.1. Of the four possibilities, the upper left box represents both A and B keeping to the left to pass each other. The numbers $(+1, +1)$ in the box indicate that A and B each gain merit $(+1)$ because they can pass each other smoothly without colliding. The lower left box, on the other hand, represents the case where A ascends on the right and B descends on the left. In this case, they may collide, they may even

A \ B	Walks on the left (S = 1)	Walks on the right (S = 0)
Walks on the left (S = 1)	+1 ⟍ +1	0 ⟍ 0
Walks on the right (S = 0)	0 ⟍ 0	+1 ⟍ +1

Figure 9.1

hurt themselves, and they will waste time. Thus, there is no merit (0) for either A or B in this case. The upper right box in Figure 9.1 represents an identical case.

If A and B have to pass each other a number of times, sooner or later they are likely to fall into a pattern of either both keeping to the left (upper left box), or both keeping to the right (lower right box). We should put this in slightly more specialist terms. Looking at the situation from A's point of view, whether A predicts that B will keep to the left or keep to the right will determine the more advantageous way for A to go, or A's strategy. If A predicts that B will choose to keep to the left, it will obviously be better for A to choose the left and gain the merit of +1, than to choose the right and gain no merit. This is expressed by saying that A's *best response* to B's choice of walking on the left is to walk on the left. In the same way, A's best response to B's selecting the right is to walk on the right. After a number of repetitions of the situation, prediction and reality will gradually converge to a steady state of both parties choosing the best response in respect of each other, or a state of *Nash equilibrium*. In our co-operative game, the upper left and lower right boxes represent cases of Nash equilibrium.

Co-operative games are not limited to two players. At major stations during the rush hour, there are some places where people tend to keep to the left on the stairs, and others where they keep to the right. This can be explained in the same way as with two people, as in Figure 9.1. Now let us consider that B choosing left or right in Figure 9.1 represents all the people at the station choosing either left or right to descend the stairs. Usually, of the people descending the stairs a certain proportion, p $(0 < p < 1)$, will choose to keep left, and the rest, $1 - p$, will choose to keep right. Now if a person ascending chooses to keep left, by the time he reaches the top, he will have collided with the proportion $(1 - p)$ of people descending, but will have had no collisions with the proportion p, so the merit he gains is $p \times (+1) + (1 - p) \times 0 = p$. On the other hand, the merit gained by a person ascending on the right will be $p \times 0 + (1 - p) \times (+1) = 1 - p$.

Clearly, if p is smaller than ½, then keeping to the right is the best response, but if it is larger, then keeping to the left is the best response. If we now say that the probability of choosing to walk on the left as the best strategic option is *s*, then the best response will become

$$s^*(p) = \begin{matrix} 0 & p < \frac{1}{2} \\ \text{a random value between 0 and 1} & p = \frac{1}{2} \\ 1 & p > \frac{1}{2} \end{matrix}$$

This can be expressed as a best-response curve, or lines in Figure 9.2, where *p* is plotted horizontally and *s* vertically. The game works the same way whether people are ascending or descending, so if *p* were to represent the proportion of people ascending on the left, the best response of those descending will be identical to that shown above.

If *p* is less than ½, $s^*(p) = 0$, so keeping to the right is the best response. The people who chose the left will gradually come round to choosing the right, and thus *p* will tend to decrease as indicated by the arrows in the figure. Finally, when $p = 0$, all the people will have chosen to walk on the more advantageous right side, and a stable, constant situation (Nash equilibrium *A*) will have been

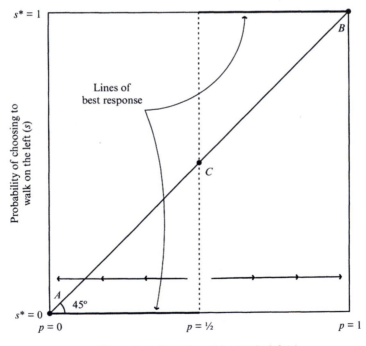

Proportion of people walking on the left (*p*)

Figure 9.2

reached. Conversely, if p is greater than ½, the more disadvantageous walking on the right will decrease until ultimately the Nash equilibrium B, where $p = 1$ (all the people walk on the left), will have been reached. The Nash equilibria are shown as the intersections of the best-response curves and the 45° line.[2] A stable Nash equilibrium occurs when the inclination of the best-response curve is smaller than the inclination of the 45° line. In co-operative games there are three Nash equilibria, two of which are stable, and this game has multiple equilibria.

What we see from this is that options left to the free choice of the individual are nevertheless dependent on what is advantageous to oneself and what options others in the community are taking. As a result, there are some stations where everyone tends to keep to the right on the stairs, and thus keeping to the right has become standard practice (or the equilibrium), and other stations where keeping to the left has become standard practice. In such cases, the way that is selected and will become the majority preference in a particular society (or station) is not determined by external factors such as the physical environment or legal restrictions, but by the internal factor of which way has already become the majority preference, or put another way, by historical chance or past policy intervention. Thus in two societies identical in physical terms, where there are rational reasons for differing structures to reach stable equilibrium, in one society one structure will take hold while in the other a different structure will become established. This in no way implies that one is more advanced than the other. The differences in the structures and systems is merely the result of historical chance or policy interventions in the past, and the fact that past historical events determine the present (path-dependence).[3]

3. Strategic complementarity and Japanese-type labour relations

With regard to Japan's actual economic system, one of the areas where its characteristics are particularly noticeable is that of labour relations. The Japanese system of labour relations lists life-long employment, pay by seniority, the bonus system, and internal promotion among its principal characteristics. Although it is said to be showing symptoms of change, it nevertheless remains the base on which Japanese-style management is conducted. As was explained with data in Chapter One, there is a strong tendency for workers in Japan, particularly full-time male employees, to be employed continuously and over the long term in one firm (so-called life-long employment), and accordingly the labour market lacks fluidity. Pinning wages to seniority occurs everywhere, but pay in Japan is far more heavily affected by the employee's number of years of continuous employment than in other countries. Bonus systems that redistribute a share of profits to all employees hardly exist at all in other countries. And in line with the practice of long-term employment, senior posts in firms are filled through the internal promotion of the firm's employees.

As discussed in Chapter One, in a situation where long-term, stable employment in the same firm is widespread, a mechanism has been generated by which ups and downs in the firm's business performance are transferred to employees as fluctuations in their earnings, largely through the bonus system. The internal-promotion system is a further method whereby benefit is redistributed to employees, by increasing the possibilities for promotion as the enterprise grows, its activities expand, and the number of senior posts increases.

This system of labour relations has contributed in various ways to the competitiveness, or efficient production, of Japanese firms. First, pay by seniority and the retirement allowance system are both forms of deferring payment for labour provided, and in this sense they are nothing short of incentives that virtually hold employees hostage in the company, since leaving would mean surrendering the opportunity to benefit from these payments. For the same reason, the incentive exists for employees to make the maximum possible contribution to the company's healthy growth, in terms of working conscientiously, making suggestions to improve quality standards, and so on, in order to reduce the possibility of being laid off. Second, employed long-term in one company where business success is redirected back to employees in the form of earnings and promotion, employees come to see their company as something in which they have made an investment, and this breeds the incentive to work hard at acquiring skills, particularly those firm-specific skills which can be of use only within the enterprise and would prove meaningless elsewhere. Third, through receiving direct benefits employees all come to the same way of thinking, seeing the success of their enterprise as their sole target, and this reduces conflicts of interests and promotes better communications and co-operation within the firm.

What we need to stress here is that these systems such as life-long employment, pay by seniority, and internal promotion (which we will call *Japanese-type labour-management practices*) share the feature of being strategically complementary. *Strategic complementarity* means that the more other firms come to utilize particular practices, the stronger the incentive becomes for each individual firm to adopt those practices.[4] This type of strategic complementarity, like the co-operative game discussed in Section 2 above, has multiple points of equilibrium, allowing the possibility of differing labour-management practices to develop in different countries. This is easier to understand from Figure 9.3, which shows the two extremes of Japanese-type labour-management practices and the opposite type of practices, such as fluid employment, pay based on skills, and promotion and higher pay achievable through external employment opportunities rather than internal promotion.

The horizontal axis of Figure 9.3 represents the average degree of 'Japanization' of labour-management practices (p) for all firms in a society. As p gets smaller towards the left, much of the society adopts non-Japanese labour-

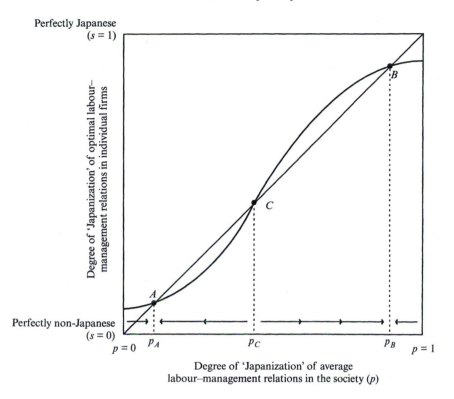

Figure 9.3

management practices, while further to the right, the degree of Japanization gets larger. The vertical axis represents the labour-management practices desired by each firm (or each employee), getting increasingly more Japanese in nature from perfectly non-Japanese at the bottom ($s = 0$) to perfectly Japanese ($s = 1$) at the top.[5] Here, the fact that the best-response curve $s^*(p)$ for each firm (each employee) rises towards the right must be due to the fact that Japanese labour-management practices have maximum strategic complementarity.[6] First, however, we must explain why the best-response curve extends from bottom left to top right.

Thinking about the life-long employment and pay by seniority systems, the more Japanese the average labour-management practices for the whole society (p is large), the less fluid the labour market, and the stronger the role of the retirement allowance and seniority pay systems in holding employees hostage. If someone loses his job, the possibility of finding work in another company is that much smaller, and even if he does find work, his earnings will be considerably lower because he will be starting from scratch in the new firm's seniority system. For the employee, life-long employment and pay by seniority mean that leaving one's present job for an employment opportunity outside one's firm (external option) can only be extremely disadvantageous in comparison with the internal option. So in this case, staying in a firm that observes Japanese practices (or selecting $s = 1$) is the employee's best response.

Conversely, if the society's labour-management practices are largely non-Japanese in nature (p approaching 0) it will be easy to find work in other firms, and because pay will not be dependent on years of service, income is not likely to be greatly affected. If the labour market is the fluid, non-Japanese type, there will be sufficient external options for employment. Moreover, if a worker chooses a firm with Japanese-type practices, because the firm may have less incentive to maintain those practices in such an environment, he may not in the end be paid enough in retirement benefits and so on to warrant submitting to being a hostage. Thus, if the labour market is the fluid, non-Japanese type ($p = 0$), selecting a non-Japanese-type firm ($s = 0$) will be the best response for the worker.

From the corporate side, too, the more life-long employment and pay by seniority become universal social norms, the more a firm's reputation will suffer if it is too ready to fire employees and cut the salaries of older staff at times of recession. Then the firm will not be able to recruit talented new graduates. This strengthens the incentive to keep on employees as far as is humanly possible. So the life-long employment system possesses strategic complementarity from the standpoint of incentives for employers, too. In other words, it is because life-long employment and pay by seniority are universally accepted throughout the society that they exist as stable practices. Conversely, if there are few enterprises using these practices, workers will dislike being held hostage, incentives will be created to move to other organizations, and there will be no need to worry about the company reputation in the eyes of new graduates. In other words, a situation where practices such as life-long employment and pay by seniority do not exist—meaning a situation of non-Japanese-type labour-management practices with a fluid employment market and pay according to skills—is also stable and rational.

Japanese-type labour relations that have strategic complementarity in this way generate two different stable points of equilibrium: when they are universal throughout the society (equilibrium B in Figure 9.3) and when they exist only as exceptional cases in the society (equilibrium A). If this interpretation is correct, the difference between present-day Japan's labour relations and those of other countries is not due to physical factors such as the preferences of the populace or the dearth or availability of land, but because these countries (and Japanese pre-war society) have settled around differing equilibria, due to historical and cultural factors or simply chance. Moreover, the Japanese-type labour relations that historical and cultural accidents have created have come to be maintained as stable social practices for the very reason that they exist universally throughout Japanese society.

4. Structural elements of Japan's economic system and their mutual complementarity

Strategic complementarity does not apply only to single systems or sets of practices. The strategic complementarity that exists between the various systems and sets of practices making up the economic system—what we might call mutual complementarity—is also essential to an understanding of the overall stability of an economic system.

For example, the Japanese-type labour relations examined in the previous section are not necessarily consistent with the interests of firms' shareholders. If the business climate takes a turn for the worse, shareholders looking for short-term profits may consider it desirable to fire workers and boost profits. Or if an affiliated company to which older staff members are regularly seconded is badly managed, shareholders may judge it better sold off or forced into liquidation, even though it is seen as essential for the maintenance of long-term stable employment through its acceptance of seconded personnel. Shareholders thinking like this are legally permitted to take action at annual shareholders' meetings by dismissing the present executive management or supporting hostile takeover bids. Thus, it is difficult to maintain Japanese-type labour-management relations without restrictions on the rights of shareholders. In reality, such practices as companies' crossholdings of shares and their having no external directors are the means by which shareholders' rights are restricted in Japan. Through crossholdings among former *zaibatsu* groups or other corporate groups, through shareholdings by funding institutions in the form of bank *keiretsu* groups, and through mutual shareholdings between companies with strong business connections, the proportion of 'stable shareholders' among listed companies is extremely high, and there have been hardly any hostile takeover bids since the onset of the high-growth period. In other words, the practices of crossholdings and boards composed exclusively of internal directors have helped to strengthen the stability of Japanese labour-management practices.

Let us first deal with the technical aspects of this, using the figures discussed in Sections 2 and 3. In Figure 9.4, as in Figure 9.3, the horizontal axis represents the proportion (p) of firms with Japanese-type labour-management practices, and the vertical axis represents the optimal labour-management practices for each firm. The best response for each firm is not dependent only on the proportion of firms with Japanese-type labour relations in the society. This is because, as I have explained, the more crossholdings there are in the society overall, the greater the advantage of Japanese-type labour-management practices with which this practice has a mutually complementary relationship. As a result, compared with the situation where there are no crossholdings, in a

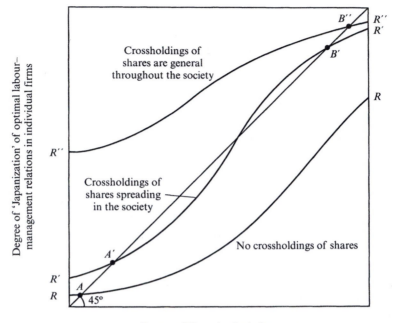

Degree of 'Japanization' of optimal labour–management relations in individual firms

Crossholdings of shares are general throughout the society

Crossholdings of shares spreading in the society

No crossholdings of shares

Degree of 'Japanization' of average
labour–management relations in the society

Figure 9.4

situation where crossholdings are universal throughout the society the best-response curve shifts higher up.[7]

Thus, in the case where there are no crossholdings and the best-response curve in Figure 9.4 takes the *RR* course, the only equilibrium to become established in the society may be at point *A*, where non-Japanese labour-management practices are prevalent. But if crossholdings become more common, the best-response curve shifts to *R'R'*, and in addition to the non-Japanese-type equilibrium at *A'*, Japanese-type labour-management practices may become established as another stable equilibrium at *B'*. Furthermore, should the mutual complementarity of the two become sufficiently great and crossholdings become universal throughout the whole business community, the best-response curve shifts to *R''R''*, the equilibrium based on non-Japanese labour-management practices disappears, and Japanese-type labour-management practices will form the sole base for a stable equilibrium at *B''*.[8]

The existence of strategic complementarity between the individual structures of the present Japanese economic system, such as labour relations and crossholdings, is not in itself necessarily sufficient to create stability. Only when mutually complementary structures each become universal throughout the society will the system as a whole become stable.

In point of fact, it is no longer all that easy to maintain crossholdings in Japan. With the advance of equity financing in the so-called bubble economy of the late 1980s, the proportion of stable shareholders declined. Now, generating capital through new share issues while maintaining crossholdings means partners having to buy up each other's new issues even if it requires plundering the firm's capital resources. One of the reasons that crossholdings are possible in Japan is that capital provision at the macro level has usually not taken the form of direct financing through shares or bonds, but of indirect financing through bank lending.

It was explained in Chapters One and Two that until the mid-1930s funds were raised through the issue of shares and bonds, and Japan's present financial system, the so-called indirect financing model in which bank lending forms the major channel for capital provision, was established during and after the war years. The widespread ownership of small numbers of shares that came with the disbanding of the old *zaibatsu* brought about a pattern of capital circulation in Japan in which indirect capital predominated, and the rapid growth in crossholdings that followed greatly curbed shareholders' rights, while the rights of stakeholders—employees and affiliated firms—who had made a long-term commitment to the firm were protected.

That said, there remained the possibility that allowing unlimited rights of expression to stakeholders might lead to moral hazard. In fact, the rise of the labour movement during the 1950s hampered production in many firms and investment declined. For firms to proceed efficiently with their activities, a means to suppress such moral hazard was necessary.

The most significant mechanism fulfilling this role in post-war Japan is the main bank system, dealt with by Dr Teranishi in Chapter Three. The system can be thought of as one in which the main bank in a group takes the lead and monitors the management of each of the firms borrowing from the group, thereby saving the other banks the costs of monitoring. For if the main bank does not monitor the firms rigorously, their performance may deteriorate, and should that happen the main bank (rather than the other banks) will need to rescue the firm concerned, thereby incurring considerable cost.[9] Thus the main bank has increased incentive to monitor the activities of firms it is funding, and the other funding institutions, knowing this, realize that they do not run any great risk by reducing their own monitoring activities. In other words, in Japan's indirect financing system the main bank system allows individual firms to be funded from a number of banks in order to avoid any financial handicap, and the risk of lending to a particular firm is spread among several banks, reducing the exposure of each one, while opening the way to rigorous monitoring at low social cost.

In this way, the discipline provided by main bank monitoring activities functions more effectively in dealing with moral-hazard situations within firms than the shareholders' rights and hostile takeovers featured in neo-classical economics. Furthermore, the 'reputation' of being a main bank implies a responsibility to rescue the firm in times of difficulty, committing the main bank to overseeing the firm's long-term stability and growth. In this sense, the post-war system of capital provision favouring indirect financing and the main bank system has a mutually complementary relationship with the life-long employment and pay by seniority practices that provide the incentive for the firm's employees also to make a long-term commitment.

Similar types of relationships can be seen in the manufacturing (or subcontracting) *keiretsu* between parts-makers and assembly firms, such as in the car industry and domestic-appliance manufacturing, and the distribution *keiretsu* between manufacturers and wholesale/retail distributors. In manufacturing *keiretsu*, for example, entrusting the supply of parts to a small number of parts-makers stimulates competition between those makers to reduce costs and boost quality, resulting in the assembly firm obtaining better parts at lower cost. For the parts-makers, an arrangement to supply parts until the next model change creates an environment that allows them to invest in equipment to produce those parts, and further incentive to reduce their costs is generated by returning to them some part of the profit deriving from lower costs. This type of manufacturing *keiretsu* also contributes to maintaining stable employment in assembly firms, because in times of recession they cut back on the supply of parts from parts-makers and switch to in-company production.

As I have explained, through its various structures between labour and management or individual firms, the present-day Japanese economic system creates incentives for all stakeholders—that is, employees, managers, main bank, affiliated companies, and so on—to make long-term commitments to the firm they are involved with. The long-term relationships of trust created in this way encourage co-operation and harmonious relations between the stakeholders and result in greater overall efficiency. But as typified in Japan's employment practices, this type of system goes hand in hand with business arrangements that are fixed and non-fluid in nature. Once such an arrangement breaks down, it is difficult to replace. If whole corporations and industries should collapse, large numbers of workers would lose their jobs, many groups of firms would go out of business, and the economic system as a whole would be plunged into crisis.

This systemic risk is covered through relations that exist between government and business. Each industry is supervised (or protected and nurtured) by a single administrative authority, and through this a long-term relationship develops between the supervising ministry and the industry's individual firms. The Japanese bureaucracy applies 'administrative guidance' widely through the medium of industrial associations and the like, to the extent that supervising ministries are said to stick their noses into firms' every move. It can be said that the concerns of the administrative side have been to maintain order and stability in the supervised industry by restraining excessive competition within it, and to prevent disruptive changes, particularly the collapse of major firms. This is plainly evident in industrial policy during the periods of post-war recovery and high-speed growth, and in the Ministry of Finance's 'convoy policy' for the administration of the banking sector. Here again, should one major enterprise meet with crisis, attempts are made to maintain stable employment and shore up business through arranging its takeover or merger with an affiliated company or else by direct administrative intervention.

That this sort of system has been able to function is essentially due to the give-and-take nature of the relationship between the two sides, which holds benefits for both. By complying with administrative guidance, private-sector firms can rely on the administration's assistance should it ever be needed, and the supervising ministry, while fulfilling its administrative responsibilities through administrative guidance, can find posts for its retiring bureaucrats in the firms and business groups under its supervision, a custom known as *ama-kudari* (descent from heaven). Again, relationships of this type are part of a system established after the war out of the wartime control associations, as discussed in Chapter One.

Thus the overall robustness and stability of the Japanese economic system have increased as a result of the mutual complementarity of its structural elements, such as life-long employment, pay by seniority, cross-shareholdings, relations between the government and private sector through the liberal use of administrative guidance, and so on. That the present-day system ever came about at all is most probably due in large part to the fact that the various structures making up the system were forcibly introduced together under exceptional wartime circumstances.

5. Conclusion: possibilities for reform and the system's inertia

In this chapter Japan's present-day economic system has been examined from a theoretical standpoint, around the concepts of strategic and mutual com-plementarity. A further implication of this theoretical approach is related to the fact that the roots of the present-day Japanese economic system, the sub-ject of this book, lie in the changes to the system that were imposed during the wartime period. To put this another way, if we understand the economic structures and systems established in a society to be in a state of stable equilibrium, then there is inertia built into the system that works to support it, and in order to bring about change a united and co-operative effort on the part of the whole society will be required.

To illustrate this let us go back to Figure 9.3. Let us assume that non-Japanese-type labour relations are prevalent in the society, these circumstances being represented by the point *A*. Accordingly, the extent of Japanization of average labour relations in the society, or the proportion of firms practising Japanese-style labour relations, is pA. As the arrows indicate, this point of equilibrium A is locally stable, and inertia in the society works to maintain it. Therefore, even though a number of firms may switch to Japanese-type labour relations, until that proportion has exceeded pC it will remain advantageous to practise non-Japanese labour relations. Over a period of time the practice of Japanese-type labour relations will decline and equilibrium A will be restored. In order to establish Japanese-type labour relations in the society, a proportion of firms greater than pC will all have to introduce Japanese labour relations at the same time. If this is done, Japanese-type labour relations will then become more advantageous for the firms that did not choose to adopt them, and over a period of time equilibrium B will be established. Moving from one point of equilibrium to another in this way thus requires the whole society to co-operate in implementing new systems and structures at the same time.

As we have seen in Figure 9.4, any attempt to change only one structural element of the system will frequently not of itself bring about change. If the various structural elements are mutually complementary, it will be impossible to overcome the inertia that works to maintain the original system, unless these elements are all changed together throughout the whole society. In the case of Japan's experience between 1930 and 1940, the unusual wartime circumstances caused an artificial system with a number of different features to be imposed forcibly on the whole society, an action that overcame this sort of inertia.

Thinking along these lines, clearly it will be no simple matter either to reform Japan's present-day corporate society, or to transplant the Japanese system overseas or change the economic systems of former socialist states. Ideally, the following tasks should precede any deliberate implementation of changes as a matter of policy. First, for one economic system to be changed to another, the new system under consideration must be examined to discover whether it has desirable characteristics as the system of the future. Second, if the new system is indeed considered desirable, its structures should be examined, the characteristics of its structural elements, such as their strategic complementarity and incentives, as well as the mutual complementarity between the structures should be studied, and whether or not the system as a whole is stable must be considered beforehand. Third, if the new system is found both desirable and stable, it must be made clear that efforts are indispensable on the part of the whole society to work together to overcome the inertia in the present system and put the new one in its place, as well as a commitment to creating the incentives that will bring all this about.

I am not entirely convinced that the enormous task taken on by Japan during the war period and examined in this book would have fulfilled these three requirements. However, compared with current discussions in Japan that focus only on separate structures and pay scant attention to the coherence and inertia existing in the system as a whole, what is at least certain is that the wartime circumstances were highly exceptional, and the task was based on systematic analysis and backed by adequate means for implementation.

Notes

1. See, for example, Aoki (1988). This should not be confused with 'comparative economic systems', a traditional area of research largely focusing on comparative studies of planned and market economic systems.
2. If $p = \frac{1}{2}$, keeping left and keeping right are equally good responses and p therefore has no incentive to move. In this case there is also a Nash equilibrium at C. However, should the value of p vary from $\frac{1}{2}$, however slightly, p will move in the direction shown by the arrows. Thus the Nash equilibrium at C is not stable.
3. See Cooper and John (1988) and Romer (1986) for more on multiple equilibria and path-dependence. For a study from the aspect of industrial policy, see Ito *et al.* (1988).
4. For more on strategic complementarity, see Bulow *et al.* (1985).
5. It may not be possible to define the degree of desired labour-management practices on a continuum from $s = 0$ to $s = 1$. However, the concept of strategic complementarity can easily be extended to discrete strategy spaces (see Milgrom *et al.* (1991)).
6. As is clear from the figure, the existence of strategic complementarity is a necessary but not sufficient condition for the existence of multiple equilibria. If, for instance, the slope of the response curve rising to the upper right were lower than that of the 45° line, there would only be one equilibrium.
7. Here for the understanding of readers I have differentiated between strategic complementarity and mutual complementarity, but they both derive from the same basic concept (see Bulow *et al.* 1985).
8. If crossholdings of shares and labour-management practices are mutually complementary, the reverse effect will of course hold true—that the more Japanese-type labour-management practices become universally established, the greater the advantage of crossholdings.
9. Why main banks should rescue poorly performing firms is also a point for discussion. Our opinion is that if the fall in the bank's reputation that would result from failing to rescue a firm is likely to exceed the cost of the rescue, the main bank will go ahead with the rescue.

References

Aoki, Masahiko (1988), *Information, Incentives and Bargaining in the Japanese Economy*, Cambridge University Press.
——(1994), 'The Japanese Firm as a System of Attributes', in Masahiko Aoki and R. Dore (eds.), *The Japanese Firm: Sources of Competitiveness*, Oxford University Press.

Bulow, J., J. Geanakoplos, and P. Klemperer (1985), 'Multimarket Oligopoly: Strategic Substitutes and Complements', *Journal of Political Economy*, 93: 488–511.

Cooper, R. and A. John (1988), 'Coordinating Coordination Failures in Keynesian Models', *Quarterly Journal of Economics*, 103: 441–64.

Gibbons, Robert (1992), *Game Theory for Applied Economists*, Princeton University Press.

Ito, Motoshige, Kazuharu Kiyono, Masahiro Okuno-Fujiwara, and Kotaro Suzumura (1988), 'Economic Analysis of Industrial Policy', *Economic Theory, Econometrics and Mathematical Economics*, Academic Press.

Milgrom, P., Y. Qian, and J. Roberts (1991), 'Complementarities, Momentum, and the Evolution of Modern Manufacturing', *American Economic Review*, 81: 85–8.

Romer, P. (1986), 'Increasing Returns and Long-Run Growth', *Journal of Political Economy*.

INDEX

Printed in the United Kingdom
by Lightning Source UK Ltd.
131778UK00001B/82-171/A